St. Paul the Traveller
and the Roman Citizen

Sir William M. Ramsay   1851-1939

St. Paul the Traveller and the Roman Citizen

New Edition

William M. Ramsay

With an Essay on the Author
by
W. Ward Gasque

Baker Book House
Grand Rapids, Michigan

Reprinted 1982 by
Baker Book House Company
from the fifteenth edition
published by Hodder and Stoughton, London,
in 1925

*Sir William M. Ramsay: Archaeologist
and New Testament Scholar*
by W. Ward Gasque
copyright 1966 by
Baker Book House Company

ISBN: 0-8010-7717-6 (cloth)
0-8010-7613-7 (paper)

Printed in the United States of America

PREFACE TO THE FOURTEENTH EDITION

TWENTY-FIVE years have elapsed since this book was written, and the time has come when its relation to the progress of study in the subject should be estimated. There is much to improve, but little to retract. It was founded on the firm conviction that Luke was, not merely trustworthy, but a historian of the highest order ; it followed his guidance unshrinkingly through regions and topics which were extremely obscure ; and in this respect I have nothing to withdraw, but would only emphasise anew what was said already "with stammering lips and insufficient tongue". It remains however unchanged except by the addition of a chapter, for its sole value is that it was written by one who was trying to reach a distant guiding light, viz., the personality of Luke.

Certain topics claim a note here. (1) The southern regions of the province Galatia, their condition in the first hundred years of the history of the province, and their relation to one another and to the province as a whole, were so obscure that nothing had ever been written on the subject. Marquardt, who had summed up all the little that was known about the province, has not a word to say on this point. Following unhesitatingly the footsteps of St. Paul as described by the historian of the Early Church, I sketched an outline of South Galatia in its geographical history about A.D. 45. The progress of discovery, and especially the incomplete excavation of Pisidian Antioch, reveal many confirmations and no contradiction of this sketch.

(2) Right chronology is the basis of sound history. New evidence has been discovered since 1895 and almost everything confirms the view taken then as to the succession of events. Some slight modifications and many corroborations are stated in *Pauline and Other Studies*, and a new chapter is added to the present book summing up this subject.

(3) I hold still that the "Macedonian" who appeared in the dream to the Apostle Paul at Troas was Luke, an Antiochian of Syria, of the tribe "Makedones"; but his praenomen Lucius (in the Greek familiar form Loukas)shows that he possessed the Roman citizenship.

(4) I missed the full import of *Acts* XVI, 2-7. The importance of the calling of Timothy was far greater than I conceived; and the first of three revelations (XVI, 6-9) prescribing the new work was given in Lystra at his consecration, a ceremony to which Paul often refers. Luke says little about it, and this is connected with his reticence about a group of his intimate friends (just as he refrains from mentioning himself). He says little about Timothy; the chief sources of our knowledge of Timothy are Thessalonians, Corinthians, and the two letters to him. He preserves absolute silence about Titus, evidently a great figure in the early history, probably a brother or cousin of Luke, as is hinted on p. 390. Timothy was connected with Luke only by association in work and not by birth, and therefore is not excluded so completely. Some other lesser figures of the group are not mentioned by the historian.

(5) The reason for the outburst of indignation which carried Paul to the front in the great scene before the proconsul at Paphos lies in the nature of the insults which Barjesus heaped upon the right ways of the Lord and the coming of the Saviour into the world.

Luke would not soil his pages by mentioning them, and Paul blazed into uncontrollable anger as he heard them. They played a great part in subsequent controversy for centuries, but it is characteristic both of Luke and of Paul that they take no notice of them in their writings.

These are all matters of psychological insight, and not of formal argument. The man who does not see the truth in these matters fails to appreciate the character of Luke and of Paul. It is the case everywhere throughout the New Testament that insight is more important than argument. To appreciate the value of this history one must begin by possessing or acquiring the power to distinguish a man from a clothes-pole, and to recognise a historian when one reads him. Applying these two qualifications to the understanding of Luke's work, one appreciates the man and the history, and sees the truth in numberless passages where intuition is required; but so long as a reader is troubled to determine whether and how far Luke's history is credible, he is debarred from understanding it.

W. M. RAMSAY

EDINBURGH, *February*, 1920

CONTENTS

x   *Contents*

Contents

THE LIFE OF ST. PAUL AS IT APPEARS IN
A.D. 1920

THE chronology of early Christian history 25-65 A.D., while complicated like ancient chronology generally, is far from being so difficult as it has been considered. The simple truth is that no period in ancient history is so assured and so well attested as this. The only period that can be compared with it in this respect is that covered by the letters of Cicero and his friends. A study of the history from the beginning of Christ's ministry to the death of the Apostle Paul, founded on a firm and confident grasp of the Lukan guiding thread, would solve every difficulty. There are few events which cannot be dated to the year, sometimes to the month, and even to the day. Needless difficulties have been introduced by prepossessions and prejudices, either of a religious and sectarian character, or by a false start from some presumed date. Much may, it is true, be learned from a book whose system as a whole is false: *e.g.*, Lewin's *Fasti Sacri* is an admirable résumé of the data as known in 1865.

The chronology of the following pages was founded on (1) a belief in the trustworthiness and minute accuracy of Luke, and (2) a certain view as to his method and literary art as a historian. Luke omits much; he passes over many events that might have been taken into his book. In doing so he was guided by a certain purpose and method of historical statement, and by a certain view of the comparative value of different incidents for his special purpose.   The interpreter who is to understand aright Luke's history must apprehend his method, thus getting a clue to guide him in every difficulty.

In surveying briefly my system I compare it with the recent work of a Dutch scholar, Dr. Plooij, who has written a book on the *Chronology of the Life of Paul* (known to me only through three articles by Rev. M. Jones in the *Expositor*, May, June, and August, 1919).   Either Dr. Plooij or Mr. Jones, or perhaps both, think the chronology of my own work is "based on such bold assumptions as to have little real value".   The assumptions on which I work are the two just stated.   It is therefore all the more interesting to find that the chronology which I reached through these "bold assumptions" approximates closely to Dr. Plooij's results, and that the crucial date—*viz.*, the year on which Paul travelled from Philippi to Jerusalem (*Acts* XX)—is fixed by both of us as 57.   So far as I am aware, no previous chronologist had proposed this date.   To me it seemed to stare out of Luke's narrative.   Roughly speaking Dr. Plooij's opinion (if I rightly gather it from Mr. Jones) is that my chronology is generally right, but the reasons which led me to this system are untrustworthy.   The reply is obvious : Dr. Plooij's confirmation of my dates is a strong argument that my reasons were correct.

Dr. Plooij is warmly commended by Mr. Jones for his wise caution in not using "such bold assumptions"; but as a matter of fact it is impossible to attain certainty with regard to any single pivotal point, and Dr. Plooij's cautious steps involve in every case a certain, or even a considerable, amount of assumption.[1]

[1] Mr. Jones takes no note of later books, *e.g.*, *Pauline and Other Studies in the History of Religion*, and much more recently *Pictures*

The distinction between bold assumption and sound reasoning is so difficult in the case of chronological arguments, owing to the number of uncertain factors which always play a part in the calculation, that the personal and subjective element determines largely the preference between the epithets. *E.g.*, the Armenian version of Eusebius errs in respect of the date when Festus came to Judea (which event it places in 54). Mr. Jones says (*Expositor*, June, 1919, p. 426): "The solution of the difficulty was first discovered by Erbes ('Die Todestage der Ap. Paulus u. Petrus,' *Texte u. Untersuchungen*, N.F. Bd. iv., Heft I., 1899), who suggested that Eusebius must have originally based his chronological scheme upon a Jewish source in which the dates of the Jewish kings were the most important factor." After expounding briefly the solution, he continues, "Ramsay also accepts Erbes' solution, and has some very interesting comments upon it in the *Expositor*, VII. vii., pp. 467-469, and Dr. Plooij looks upon it as the sheet anchor of his chronology". Now, while I accept Erbes' solution as probable, I am fully conscious of its extremely problematic character; and one of the best authorities on the chronology of this period rejected it absolutely as mere wild hypothesis. In accepting Erbes' solution I was and am guided largely by the fact that it agrees with Luke, or at least makes an agreement with Luke possible by explaining the divergence. That "bold as-

of the Apostolic Church (1910), in which I have stated new arguments confirming these " bold assumptions " about the year 57 and the day on which the journey from Philippi began ; and he ends his third article with a comparative Table showing the chronology of different scholars, ignoring some improvement of details in these later works ; these changes had on the whole approximated to Dr. Plooij's chronology. For brevity's sake I venture to refer to these published arguments instead of repeating them here.

sumption," which Dr. Plooij and Mr. Jones reject, is the sheet anchor in the stormy chronological sea, and I obtain some assurance by holding to it. Erbes' theory is a mere guess, until some confirmation for it is found; and the confirmation lies in Luke's wonderful accuracy, and in his marked and highly individual method of stating his historical facts. This historian is the prime authority and the touchstone of accuracy in respect of other accounts.

The following survey of the chief dates is cut so short as to appear dogmatic.

1. THE CRUCIAL DATE A.D. 57 (*Acts* XX). For this there are many arguments. The first, which Dr. Plooij and Mr. Jones regard as fundamental, has just been stated. I used it as a confirmation many years ago; but cannot regard it as strong, until it is proved by agreement with Luke.

(2) The second is that "bold assumption" which is stated in this book as the basis of my chronology.[1]

(3) Professor A. R. S. Kennedy pointed out that often there occurred a large emission of Roman coins in Palestine in the year when a new procurator entered on office. The bad economic condition of the country and the want of sufficient circulating medium of exchange were recognised by several procurators when they entered on their duty, and they proceeded to strike a more plentiful coinage. Thus in A.D. 5-6 (36th year of Augustus) there was struck a fair amount of coins. This may be connected reasonably with the energetic action of Quirinius as governor of Syria

---

[1] There is no sound argument in favour of any other year. Harnack rests his chronology on the Armenian translation of Eusebius, which places the coming of Festus in 54 (and the voyage of Paul from Philippi therefore in 52). This is a good authority; yet the dating must be rejected as impossible.

(shown in the great census). Again in 8-9 (39th year of Augustus) a considerable emission of coinage occurred, and was continued in the following two years 9-10 and 10-11 : this action might fairly be connected with the procurator-ship of Ambibulus, 9-12 A.D. Thereafter no Roman coinage in Palestine is known until 15-16 (2nd year of Tiberius) when an emission of coins lasting for three years was made while Valerius Gratus was procurator. Again in 24-25 (11th year of Tiberius), a considerable group of Roman coins was issued. Pontius Pilate is ordinarily said to have entered on office in A.D. 26, but this date is far from assured[1] and his coming may be connected with the coinage of the preceding year. At any rate Pilate struck another large group of coins in 29-30 (16th year of Tiberius) and the two following years.

There are in the British Museum Catalogue only two other groups of coins, dated respectively in the 14th year of Claudius, A.D. 54, and the 5th year of Nero, A.D. 58-59. Now 54 does not coincide with the first year of any procurator. Felix was already in office in 52 and administered Palestine for a number of years, as Paul remarked in the complimentary exordium of his speech reported by Luke in *Acts* XXVI. It is, however, certain that there were some difficulties connected with the beginning of Felix's term of office. Tacitus and Josephus differ pointedly in this matter, and the question is not satisfactorily settled by asserting that either is completely right and the other utterly wrong. It is not impossible that A.D. 54 marked the beginning of a fresh and energetic administration by Felix.

---

[1] The authority is the phrase δέκα ἔτεσιν in Josephus, *Ant.* 18, 4, 2. Pilate certainly left Judea late in 36, and reached Rome after Tiberius died (March, 37); but the statement by Josephus of the years that he governed may be taken fairly as a round number, and the accession of Pilate may have occurred 25-26.

The other group of coins in 59 is naturally connected with the coming of Festus. It is clear that Festus was disposed to be an active and energetic governor, and that he set to work immediately to clean up the mess left by the growing slackness of Felix. It would appear highly probable that the medium of exchange had become too scanty since the large emission in 54, and this was not sufficient for the convenience of trade. The activity in coinage of the Jewish insurgents, 66-69, was probably needed, and was not merely due to ostentation of their independence.

(4) Another argument is based on the death of Festus and the succession to the procuratorship of Palestine. This argument is somewhat elaborate and is partly numismatic, partly historical. The numismatic side of the argument is slighted by Dr. Plooij: numismatists will not agree with him. The argument based on the succession of Albinus he uses and reinforces.[1]

(5) Ananus during his brief high priesthood brought James the Just and some other Christians before the Sanhedrim and had them stoned to death. His violent and illegal action roused strong disapproval even among the Jews, some of whom sent secretly to King Agrippa asking him to prevent such conduct in future. Thereafter these Jews learned of the appointment of Albinus and sent messengers to meet him in Alexandria, denouncing the action of Ananus as contrary to Roman principles, inasmuch as it had been carried out without the approval of the procurator. Now Hegesippus says that the martyrdom occurred at the Passover, and the Martyrology of Hieronymus gave the day of the martyrdom as March 25. This points to the Passover of 61, which fell on March 24.

---

[1] It is stated at some length in *Pauline and Other Studies*.

During the actual celebration of the Passover, Jewish feeling and law forbade execution or murder. Even to put a criminal to death on the day after the Passover, while the feast cf unleavened bread still lasted, was repugnant to Jewish feeling. Now in 62 the Passover was on Apri 12 ; in 60 it was on April 4 ; and in 59 on April 15. So far as the Hieronymian Martyrology has any value the martyrdom of James and the others cannot have taken place i.1 any of these three years. Many scholars consider an argument like this as of small consequence ; to me it seems to be of the very highest value.

(6) The chronology of Eusebius as a whole confirms this date. This is too complicated a subject to discuss in detail here, but it is treated with some fullness in my *Pauline and Other Studies*, pp. 345-364, to which I may be permitted to refer.[1] Dr. Plooij also considers that Eusebian chronology confirms the date, and he treats this at considerable length in his noteworthy book.

These arguments in favour of the year 57 seem conclusive. The popular taste prefers A.D. 58 for no reason except that it was acquiesced in by Lightfoot, not because he saw any trustworthy argument in its favour, but simply as the least improbable in a period that was enveloped in obscurity. The consensus of so many arguments of totally different kinds is so rare in ancient chronology as to be almost unique. In truth ancient chronology is a system in which the various dates support one another, and give ground for confidence which is lacking in the case of any single date taken by itself. This is not peculiar to N.T. chronology; it is the character of all ancient chronology throughout the ages. A certain degree of bold assumption

[1] The Day of the Conversion is untrustworthy (Lightfoot *Clement* II 501.

and hypothesis is always necessary, and in spite of Dr. Plooij's objection to this character in chronology his own work exemplifies it from beginning to end. Not merely can the day be fixed. A reasonable approximation could be made to the hour of the day when the voyage began. Those who are familiar with Oriental and Greek habits of life, and who take into consideration the circumstances in respect of wind and weather at Neapolis with more intimate knowledge than I possess (for I have never visited the place), will come to a confident opinion as to the approximate hour when the journey began. Sailor's habits are very conservative; but those who know only steamer hours are apt to ignore this.

2. THE BEGINNING OF PAUL'S CHRISTIAN CAREER. As Dr. Plooij and I are agreed in respect of the critical later years 57-59, so too in regard to the beginning. He places the conversion of Paul in A.D. 31: I now agree.[1] There are several coincident arguments.

(1) The reckoning from Pentecost, A.D. 29, is vaguely stated in Acts; but the feeling grew in my mind, as I studied Luke's narrative, that a rapid series of events led up to Stephen's death. Then came a long interval with little development in method, during which occurred the scenes connected with Philip, Cornelius, etc. (learned by Luke from Philip, from his prophesying daughters, from Manaen, etc.). The case of Cornelius decided nothing, for it was treated as an individual and exceptional event, and the principle really involved in it was ignored by general consent (even by Peter himself, *Gal.* II 12).

---

[1] 31-32 is the date given in *Pauline and Other Studies*, p. 365, and in *Pictures of the Apostolic Church*, Ch. XIII : but A.D. 33 in *St. Paul the Traveller* (the date assigned to the second visit to Jerusalem bieng there 45 or 46, not 44 as is right).

(2) This year is confirmed by other arguments resulting from the considerations stated in § 3 and § 4.

It follows that the first and second visits to Jerusalem (*Acts* IX 26 and *Gal.* I 18, *Acts* XI 28 and *Gal.* II 1 ff.) must be dated in 33 and 44. Of this there are many confirmations in the sequel.

In respect of the marked arrangement in Luke's narrative XI 28—XII 25, I have maintained that this order means that Barnabas and Saul went to Jerusalem (XI 30) before the events of XII 1-24, and returned to Antioch (25) after those events had taken place. According to Mr. Jones's account of Dr. Plooij's views the arrangement only implies that the events in Ch. XII were contemporaneous with those in Ch. XI. The date of the visit to Jerusalem is not affected, whichever opinion is adopted.[1] Dr. Plooij accepts the general opinion that Herod died soon after the Passover in April or May, 44, and concludes that the return of Barnabas and Saul from Jerusalem to Antioch took place later than May, 44. In this we agree.

One of the many difficulties in chronological reckoning at this period lies in the varying incidence of the New Year. The exact reckoning of a certain lapse of years depends on the time of New Year according to the view of the writer who states the numbers. If Luke counted according to the Roman years, beginning on January 1, the interval from November to March extended over two years; but, if he reckoned according to a very frequent system in the Near East, beginning the New Year at the autumn equinox,

---

[1] It forms a part of my chronological system, that a long interval for the weekly collection of money in Antioch is implied in XI 29; and that Paul's journey to Jerusalem is mentioned proleptically, and really occurred only in August 44, after the harvest failed and scarcity was imminent. Then the visit lasted only a short time.

this interval would count only as one year. It has never been made out with certainty whether Luke counted according to the Roman reckoning or according to any of the numerous Greek or Oriental systems of New Year which were in vogue; but as he was writing to a Roman official, Theophilus, it is probable that he counted according to the ordinary Roman year, beginning January 1.[1] Paul, on the other hand, writing to Corinthians, Galatians, etc., was likely to count years on the general eastern system, with New Year in Autumn. The official Roman year in Asia was adapted to this system, with New Year on IX Kal Oct., the birthday of Augustus (September 23).

3. PAUL'S SECOND VISIT TO JERUSALEM. Dr. Plooij and I are agreed about the visit to Jerusalem in the 14th year, and we both consider that this second visit is the one described in *Gal.* II 1-12 and in *Acts* XI, XII; but whereas Dr. Plooij places it (as I formerly did in this book) in winter 45-46, I now carry it back a full year. Paul went up in 44 and returned at the end of that year or the beginning of 45. We are pinned down to this year by many considerations, affecting the entire career of Paul. This date is quite as fundamental a factor as the fixing of the events of 57-59. The early chronology of Paul's Christian life must be moved back a year. Dr. Plooij does so for the conversion, but not in its results generally.

This visit was connected with the famine in Jerusalem (*Acts* XI 28, *Gal.* II 10). Dr. Plooij clings to the usual opinion that "the great famine [2] over all the organised

---

[1] There is a slight error in Mr. Jones's exposition of Dr. Plooij's views. He speaks about "the new moon" of the month of April as being the date at which Claudius ordered that all Governors should depart for their provinces. Claudius fixed the middle of April.

[2] Agabus simply spoke of great scarcity over all the world.

world" (*i.e.*, the Roman Empire), which was prophesied by Agabus, implies one definite single famine raging at the same time in all parts of the Empire; and of course he finds no evidence of such a famine. That description, however, is not Luke's, nor is it contained in the prophecy of Agabus. The prophecy is fulfilled by the scarcity which occurred in various years under Claudius in various parts of the Empire, as mentioned by the authorities. The one thing that con-cerns Pauline chronology is : in what year did the famine rage in Palestine and Jerusalem?[1]   It does not, however, follow that Barnabas and Saul waited until the famine was at its height before they went to Jerusalem. They went up in accordance with prophecy (*Gal.* II 1 ; so *Acts* XI 28); the famine was at its worst in 45-46, but probably was so bad because two harvests, 44 and 45 had failed: it ended with harvest, summer 46.

4. THE GREAT REVELATION AND ITS IN-FLUENCE ON PAUL. The revelation which gave Paul such confidence in himself and his work, 2 *Cor.* XII 2-5, occurred in the 14th year before he was writing in 56, and must therefore be dated in 43-44, if he counted by eastern years beginning in autumn.[2] In that case this

[1] An untrustworthy chronological argument here is founded by Dr. Plooij (or Mr. Jones) upon the reading ἐπὶ τούτοις, which he prefers in Josephus, *Ant.* XX 5, 2. He understands this to mean "in the year when the two procurators just mentioned were in office successively," but this is impossible in Greek. The other reading ἐπὶ τούτου must be adopted, if the preposition is to be under-stood in a temporal sense, and it would imply that the famine con-tinued after Tiberius Alexander entered on office. The worst time of such a famine is the end, immediately before a new harvest brings relief: in this case before the harvest of 46 became available.

[2] I assume that 2 *Cor.* XII was written in late autumn or early winter 56. He was then intending to make a third visit to Corinth (XIII 1), where he stayed more than two months, called in ancient

The Life of St. Paul

great vision, which stood out in Paul's memory as pre-eminent in his Christian experience, must be identified with the vision mentioned in *Acts* XXII 17-21, and 43-44 must be its date. The year 43-44 was 14th before an event occurring after the year 56-57 began (IX Kal. Oct. 56).

This vision cut short Paul's desire to remain in Jerusalem administering personally to his own people the relief which he and Barnabas had brought. He was ordered now to go to the Gentiles, and some anticipation was opened to him of the glorious future that waited the Church and the world, and also himself as the minister of the Divine Will. It cannot reasonably be supposed that Paul in his bold, unhesitating and, so to say, revolutionary policy towards the Gentiles during the following years, was acting purely on his own individual judgment as a man (κατὰ ἄνθρωπον): he makes a marked distinction in I *Cor.* IX 8 between his own individual judgment, and what he gets from Divine inspiration or revelation. This revelation came after the eleven years which he spent in the province of Syria-Cilicia, where (as may be confidently declared) his attention was still mainly directed to the Jews and the synagogues. It was only in Syrian Antioch, after he was brought there by Barnabas, that a wider view began to open before him; yet even then his face still turned towards the Jews. He still felt that they must and would accept his testimony, and the Gentiles lay only in the distant view (in spite of older warnings). Then came that great revelation of the wider purpose and of the way in which this purpose should be attained (autumn 44). Soon after he "turned to the Gentiles" (*Acts* XIII 41 f., XIV 27, XV 3, 19 f., 24 f.),[1]

fashion three months (*Acts* XX 3): the plot there mentioned was concocted in March 57.

[1] Sergius Paullus heralded the movement of the Gentiles.

though always in every place making the first offer to the Jews.

Paul was methodical and accurate in stating the lapse of time (*Gal.* I 18, II 1, 2 *Cor.* XII 2, *Acts* XX 31, XXII 6, XXIV 11, XXVI 13; more vague XIII 18, 21, XXIV 10, 17),[1] yet little use has been made of his chronological statements. Controversy rages as to the purpose of the numbers in *Gal.* I, II. The opinion stated on p. 382 (justified in *Histor. Comm. on Epist. Gal.*, p. 271 f.) seems right : the numbers 3 and 14 are counted from the epoch of his Conversion, the beginning of his New Life. As regards 2 *Cor.* XII 2, hardly any attempt has been made to use the numerical statement as an aid to chronology : it did not suit any chronological system, and the inference is often drawn, not that systems are wrong, but that Paul's reckoning is vague. Yet he regards this number as important in his argument : it bears upon the purpose of the letter addressed to these Gentiles : fourteen years carry the readers back to the inauguration of the Gentile mission. Although the number has meant nothing to us, and although many scholars regard it as part of that loose emotional style of thinking which they attribute to Paul, whom they envisage as a mere mystic, careless of facts and practical system, yet those who see that Paul had an exact mind feel that the definiteness of the chronological statement is closely related to his purpose. He will not state exactly what occurred ; the words which he heard are not lawful for a man to utter ; but the vision constituted a supreme glory and honour, and made a new era in his career ; his life began anew from this event. Just as in

[1] *Acts* XX 31, "three years" means in ancient fashion over two here two years three months. Vagueness is due to want of knowledge, to deficient information, or to doubt as to facts.

Galatians, it is an essential part of his argument that the conversion and the superhuman means by which it was achieved form the era of his New Life, so here the second stage, the mission to the Gentiles, is counted from this greatest of all the visions and revelations that had been given to him. The truth and the reality of his life lay in these revelations : the rest was the imperfect attempt to carry into effect the message and the truth imparted to him. Further, the reckoning in both *Gal.* and *Cor.* from a great revelation is part of the proof that Paul was in no way inferior to the greatest of the Apostles, being charged with a Divine mission as great as theirs.

There is only one occasion on which this revelation, *Acts* XXII 18 f., with the change which it produced in Paul's aims, falls in its true place in his career [1]; and that is immediately before the first missionary journey, when the door was opened to the Gentiles. This vision with its compelling power is likely to have been quickly fulfilled, though certain steps were necessary. Paul convinced Barnabas, who previously had been his leader and guide, that the new era was beginning; and it would even appear that Barnabas was expressly mentioned in the revelation, as the words of XIII 2 definitely imply.[2]

A certain interval occurred at this point. It was necessary to communicate this Divine command to the leading Apostles (*Gal.* II 2 ff.).[3] There was no public meeting of

[1] It has been differently placed by others; but there results no illumination of Paul's career from any other date.

[2] " I have called *them.*"

[3] Peter had fled from Jerusalem ; doubtless he returned after Herod's death. The Apostles generally were not always in Jerusalem : Peter is described as often absent, *e.g.*, in Samaria, on the Phœnician coast, in Antioch : the evangelisation of the Holy Land was the great fact of the first period 29-44 (IX 31).

the Apostles and Elders (as took place in *Acts* XV). The matter was not ready for public statement; but Paul and Barnabas informed the three leaders that they were entrusted with the mission to the Gentiles, as the leaders were with the mission to the Jews. Read in this light and in this order the various parts of the narrative, *Gal.* II 1 ff., *Acts* XXII 17-21, *Acts* XIII 1 f., and 2 *Cor.* XII 2 ff., constitute a wonderful and perfect description of a marked development in the direction of Christian work, and of a great step in Paul's career. His confidence in the Divine guidance of his work was henceforth unshakable : from 44 onward he never hesitated. He was the Apostle to the Gentiles, with Barnabas as his coadjutor; and his face was always Romewards (except for visits to Jerusalem to perform his duties as a Jew, and to show his abiding memory of the poor in the original home of the Church, *Gal.* II 10).

Soon after Paul returned to Antioch the whole body of prophets and teachers there were warned that now the moment had come when Barnabas and Saul must begin the work to which God had called them. Both were already aware that they were chosen, and they knew the meaning of the order now issued to the governing body of the congregation.

The direction of the work was towards the West, and Paul's face was from this time steadily directed along one or other of the several roads that led to Rome. It is hardly possible to mistake the westward direction, and it ought not to be possible to doubt that in every apparent change the ultimate purpose was the same. Rome is not expressly mentioned by Luke until XIX 21, but it is implied in all the preceding narrative when properly read.

5. THE FIRST MISSIONARY JOURNEY. The Apostles sailed from Seleuceia in early spring, 45. With

regard to the time occupying this journey Dr. Plooij agrees
with Mr. C. H. Turner in confining it within a year and a
half. Two years and a half seems to me a more probable
period. The mere time spent in sailing and walking was
very considerable. Those who do not know the Cilician
sea look at the map and count the miles direct for a ship
between Seleuceia and Salamis ; but an ancient ship could
not make the run in that way and would require a good
many days. It was a difficult thing, which practically
ancient ships did not try, to run from the Syrian coast
along the south of Cyprus westward. Coming even from
Egypt, if they failed to clear the western point of Cyprus,
they had no other course than to round the eastern end of
the Island and then make their way slowly along the coast
of Asia Minor westward.[1]   The voyage from Paphos to
Perga would probably not be quick. On the other hand
thereturn voyage from Attalia to Seleuceia, though much
longer on the map, would be short and easy.

Add the time spent in preaching through the synagogues
from Salamis to Paphos ; then some time spent at Perga
for one reason or another ; the long walk across the Taurus
mountains to Antioch ; and the work in the double progress
through southern Galatia with its four cities. I cannot
believe that all this could be done in eighteen months, nor
does such hurry accord with Paul's subsequent work. It is
true that he conquered Pisidian Antioch in two Sabbaths,[2]

---

[1] " Roads and Travel in N.T.," in Hastings, *D.B.*, V. p. 380; also
in the present book, p. 319.

[2] I am now disposed to lay even more emphasis on the suddenness
of the success in Antioch and Lystra than in the present book, pp.
99, 116. Paul speaks of the instantaneousness of his conquest (*Gal.*
IV 14) ; but he was not content with a whirlwind conversion : he
organised and aimed at permanence.

say ten days, but XIII 49 points to a considerable period of work at Antioch, during which there was the opportunity of affecting the whole region, *i.e.*, the Phrygian region of the province Galatia. This process needed several months. People from the different cities of the region came to the capital Antioch for the various purposes of Graeco-Roman life and administration, and the whole Phrygian region was thus gradually affected: but this could not be achieved without the lapse of time. In Iconium there occurred at first marked and quick success, affecting the Jews and the circle of Greeks who were attracted to the synagogue. Then followed (XIV 2) dissension with the Jews, and through their action ill-feeling was caused among the Gentiles. This also occupied only a brief time; but thereafter the Apostles stayed "a long time," taking advantage of the division of feeling, and the freedom of action permitted in a Hellenic city,[1] until at last a riot arose and a determined attack was made on the Apostles, who fled into Lycaonia out of Phrygia.[2]

This was probably the longest residence in any Galatic city during the journey. The residence at Lystra seems to have been short, and the striking incidents which occurred there followed one another rapidly. Probably the incident of the lame man occurred at the Apostles' entrance into

---

[1] The transposition of verses XIV 2 and 3 which is favoured by some scholars, as *e.g.*, Dr. Moffatt, eliminates the variety and confuses the progress of the action : in the text as transmitted the development of events is perfectly natural and in accordance with many analogies.

[2] Riot was characteristic of Hellenic cities, Iconium, Ephesus, Thessalonica, action by magistrates of Roman towns (coloniae), Antioch, Philippi, Corinth : Lystra was an exception, but the rioters were Lycaonians and the colonial element was weak there. Athens stands apart and alone in the *Acts* and in reality.

Lystra, so that they were literally received as messengers
of God (*Gal.* IV 14 : *Bearing of Research on N.T.*, p. 45 f.).
On the other hand the residence at Derbe, which was
very much further away, seems to have been successful and
undisturbed.   Here Paul's method was matured.   The
Church was consolidated, presbyters were appointed to
manage the congregation.   A new year with new magistrates had begun in Lystra and the other cities ; and the
action of the magistrates who had ejected, or acquiesced in
the ejection of, Paul and Barnabas was not binding on or
heeded by their successors.[1]   The long walk occupying
several days to Lystra, the short walk to Iconium, the very
much longer walk to Antioch, and the still longer walk
across the mountain to Perga, required time.   The consoli-
dation of the congregations in the Galatic cities, the encouragement of all members to face cheerfully the dangers
and difficulties of the future which were inevitable, the
selection and appointment of presbyters (which was a process
that could not be accomplished in a day or even a week in
any one church), all imply a considerable lapse of time.
It is not necessary to suppose that the preaching in Pamphylia lasted long, and there is no allusion to any success ;
Paul never again set foot in Pamphylia (45—late 47).

6. THE RESIDENCE IN SYRIAN ANTIOCH
lasted a considerable time (οὐκ ὀλίγον, comp. XXI 39, οὐκ
ἀσήμου).[2]   During it the question of Gentile freedom
became acute, complicated by the visit of Peter (*Gal.* II

---

[1] The theory of eighteen months' journey violates this elementary
principle of city or colonial administration.   Paul could not return
to a city or colony while magistrates that had ejected him were still
in office.

[2] It is a common figure of ancient speech that the denial of anything is a strong assertion of the opposite : οὐκ ὀλίγον a long (time).

11-21), and the struggle demanded authoritative settlement by the Apostles. At this time arrived a letter or message from Galatia, mentioning among other serious facts that Paul's converts were observing the Sabbatic year 48 (*Gal.* IV 10). The struggle in Antioch for freedom was for the moment too pressing, and Paul wrote to the Galatians instead of visiting them.[1] At last, in the third visit to Jerusalem (*Acts* XV), the Council declared for freedom. Even then, some time was needed in Antioch to confirm the cause; thereafter Paul was free to revisit his new churches (XV 36). The contention with Barnabas caused some little delay; and thus it was the late winter of 49-50 before Paul and Silas started for Cilicia, and early spring 50, when they were free to cross Taurus and make the long walk to Derbe.

As to the date of the Epistle to the Galatians we have reached the same conclusion, that it was written before the Apostolic Council (*Acts* XV). In this point I have altered my opinion as stated in the present work (see *The Teaching of Paul*, Ch. LII). Mr. Jones maintains that "this date for the Epistle utterly destroys any faith we may have had in Luke's qualities as an accurate historian and demands that St. Paul was the most successful camouflageur of his day"; but I cannot understand his reasoning or his conclusion. The true chronology furnishes an even stronger proof than before that Luke is the most accurate of historians.

7. THE SECOND JOURNEY. Great part of 51 was spent in Galatia and Macedonia and Achaia. For different reasons the work in Philippi, Thessalonica, and Athens was cut short. Gallio's proconsulship in Achaia was dated

---

[1] It must have been a very urgent reason that made Paul content himself with writing instead of a visit. He does not even promise a visit. Jerusalem and Antioch demanded his presence.

by me in 52-3 on general evidence—the narrative of Luke, the theory which I have put forward with regard to the dating of Orosius, and other such arguments: "we must therefore conclude that he (Gallio) came to Achaia in the summer, 52, as governor. While he was in Achaia he took fever, and went a voyage for health."[1] Too late I learned of the important inscription discovered by M. Bourguet, published in 1905, but not known to me when I was preparing *Pauline and Other Studies* (published 1906).[2] This inscription leaves the year uncertain, either 51-2, or 52-3 (the governorship began shortly before July 1). Dr. Plooij recognises the uncertainty, but prefers 51-2 (and I accept his preference). Either year would suit the date 51-3 assigned here to Paul's residence in Corinth.

In accordance with the method of Luke's history, it may be asserted with some confidence that the attack by the Jews was made a few months after Paul came to Corinth. Their feelings were exasperated by Paul's action in fixing the Christian assembly next door to the Synagogue, and by his whole attitude (which they misconstrued). They were not likely to postpone legal attack; they were encouraged by the fact that his experience in Athens had not been brilliantly successful, and they hoped to drive him out of Corinth as he had been driven out of Thessalonica after a very brief stay there, and also out of Beroea and Philippi. Probably his whole history as a missionary was known to them, and it encouraged them to hope for a decision against

---

[1] *Pauline and Other Studies*, p. 361. The first illness was during his government of Achaia. After his consulship (which would be some years later) he went on a voyage, presumably from Italy to Egypt, on account of pthisis; below p. 261; but these two voyages must be distinguished from one another.

[2] I commented on it in *Expositor*, May, 1909, p. 467.

this disturber of the peace. The trial took place most probably in spring 52 (or even earlier) ; but, if Gallio came to Achaia only in May-June 52, then it occurred (as Dr. Plooij thinks) almost immediately after his arrival.

Dr. Plooij holds that Gallio came to Achaia May 51, after Paul had been there about seventeen months, and the trial occurred a month or so before Paul departed. Luke seems perhaps to imply, however, that Gallio was already in Corinth before Paul arrived there : this is the natural inference from XVIII 11.[1] Moreover, great stress should be laid on the "many days" of Paul's residence in Corinth after the trial. This phrase is comparative, and determined by the context. After this important decision, granting full freedom to preach, had been delivered by a provincial governor, Paul was not likely forthwith to leave Corinth. This decision, as I have argued on pp. 259 f., 304, constituted a precedent of the highest importance, and was likely to be referred to as determining the course of Roman procedure, until it was overturned by a higher Court. The higher Court did in the year 64-5 overturn the precedent, but until then Roman provincial procedure was largely determined by this legal decision. The whole character and action of Paul points to the inference that he used the opportunity and resided "a considerable time" in Corinth, taking advantage of the freedom now accorded to him. Gallio governed Corinth, 51-2. Paul was acquitted not later than early summer 52 : thereafter he spent a long time at Corinth, and finally departed with the intention of being at Jerusalem for the Feast, *viz.*, the Passover of A.D.

---

[1] ὄντος, " while Gallio was governing " : γενομένου would mean " after Gallio became governor ". Dr. Plooij and Mr. Jones reverse these translations. I lay no stress on this argument.

53.[1]   Dr. Plooij understands this Feast to be Tabernacles, 51. He tends to hurry unduly the work of the first two journeys and of the intervening time (46-51) and to protract unnecessarily the events of the third journey (51-spring 57): I make the periods 45-53 and 53-7.

It is in accordance with right method in interpreting Luke, that eighteen months (*Acts* XVIII 11) states the entire duration of Paul's residence in Corinth, and cannot be used as an argument about the date of the trial before Gallio.   In fact the government of Gallio should be placed early, for Seneca returned to power in 49, and no time would be lost in continuing Gallio's career of office, which had probably been interrupted during Seneca's exile.   Gallio could not in ordinary course attain the consulship, the goal of every Roman senator's ambition, until he had held some praetorian governorship, such as the proconsulship of Achaia.

8. DATE   OF   ST.   PAUL'S   DEATH   AS   A CHRONOLOGICAL   FACTOR.   High authority should be assigned to a statement ascribed (falsely) to Chrysostom, Vol. VIII, p. 621, Paris 1836, that Paul served God 35 years and died at the age of 68.   This represents an early tradition current in Asia Minor; and it affords a good chronological argument, if the year of Paul's death can be fixed.   In the tradition the years perhaps begin Jan. 1.

Some months after the great fire of Rome (Aug. 64) Paul was arrested (in winter 64-5, presumably at Nikopolis)[2]; and there ensued a formal trial in Rome.   These

---

[1] I regard the Western addition in XVIII 21 as true, but non-Lukan, an addition made in the second century resting on correct tradition.   See § 9 and footnote to § 10.

[2] *Titus* III 12.   I assume, as known to the reader, the obvious and necessary conditions attending arrest and a new trial of Paul the Roman citizen.   Formalities of the usual order must be complied with, and time was needed.

events (which are mentioned in 2 *Tim.*), have, of course, no connection with the former trial, alluded to as imminent in *Acts* XXVIII, which occurred in the spring of 62, and ended in the release (or acquittal) of Paul owing to the weakness of the case against him or the failure of the Jewish prosecution to appear (see *Teaching of Paul in Terms of the Present Day*, Ch. LI).

It is obvious from 2 *Tim.* IV 16 f. that the final trial of Paul was a far more serious matter, involving two stages with a long interval between them.   In the first stage Paul gained at least a partial victory ; he was not condemned ; he was saved out of the mouth of the lion ; but he was not completely acquitted.   Further proceedings were ordered to take place after the lapse of many months.   The explanation can hardly be other than that new evidence was called for.   Obviously Paul, who as a Roman citizen had a regular trial, was brought before the Supreme Court at Rome.   Ordinary provincials were not tried in this way. They had not Roman rights, and they could be treated very much at the Emperor's discretion in the great persecution. A mere wish or sign from the Emperor might consign provincial subjects to execution in any form, however rigorous.   Against the Roman Paullus however evidence had to be given, and in the first stage the evidence was insufficient : for Paul had been little in Italy and almost the whole time in confinement ; he obviously was not guilty in respect of the fire or any other action in the city ; but powerful enemies ("the lion") obtained a postponement until evidence from the Eastern provinces could be collected.[1]   Such was Nero's persecution, as Tacitus portrays

[1] Six months may be allowed for travelling to and fro, and for gathering evidence.

it : beginning in an attempt to throw on the Christians the guilt of incendiarism in the great fire (Aug. 64), it was extended to their action as enemies of social order in the Empire generally.   Paul was not deceived as to the probable result of the second hearing.   While his rights as a Roman citizen called for this show of fair trial, yet it is evident in his letter to Timothy that he anticipated condemnation.   During the long interval before the second hearing Timothy was invited to come from Asia to him. The whole circumstances carry with them a conviction of authenticity : all the separate details fit into one another and produce a remarkable picture of the final trial and the condemnation.

The chronological results are as follows.   The arrest took place in the winter of 64-5.   The first hearing was in spring 65 ; and after it Paul, looking forward to a long interval, wrote asking Timothy to come to him before winter (Nov. 65).   The trial, condemnation and execution would take little time ; and all was over before the end of 65.   Therefore the conversion must be dated in 31, the first visit to Jerusalem in 33, and the second in 44, *viz.*, in the 3rd and 14th year of Paul's New Life.

9.   THE   PAULINE   TRADITION   IN   ASIA MINOR.   It seems beyond doubt that a vivid recollection of the Apostle Paul was preserved in Anatolia, especially along the line of the great road from Ephesus to the Cilician Gates and Syrian Antioch.   There was no definite centre of tradition ; the tradition lived on the road, just as the life of Christianity lay in communication along the roads.   The personal appearance of Paul and the exact years of his life were remembered in the Anatolian tradition. That is not the case with any other Apostle.   The memory

of the Imperial road by which he travelled from Antioch towards Lystra, and of the situation of Iconium on a side branch of this road, was still retained in the latter part of the second century, although by that time the idea of a road from Antioch to Lystra had become obsolete, and the world thought only of a road from Antioch to Iconium.

Many of the Western interpolations in the *Acts* were due to this Anatolian tradition (see *The Church in the Roman Empire*, Ch. VIII). They are true, but they are not the work of Luke. As late as about A.D. 400 the memory of the true meaning and situation of the Galatian Churches was retained, although a stranger like Jerome was misled by the historical facts which came into existence in 295 (making an absolute severance between South Galatia and the Province Galatia, and transforming South Galatia into the Province Pisidia or the Province Lycaonia). The old tradition in Asia Minor with regard to the Galatia of the Pauline journeys is stated by Asterius, bishop of Amasia about A.D. 401, who explains *Acts* XVIII 23, " the Galatic region and Phrygia " as equivalent to " Lycaonia and the cities of Phrygia ". It is impossible to take this as a mere geographical blunder: it is the deliberate statement of the belief of Asterius. Now in his time Lycaonia had long ceased to be included in the province Galatia, and the only explanation of his opinion is that it was still the accepted tradition in the country. There was often a tendency to intrude later geographical facts into older history, and this intrusion gradually gave rise to the belief first of all among extra-Anatolian writers, and finally among writers who knew Anatolia, that the Galatic region must be part of Galatia in the accepted sense of their own time. From 295 onwards there was no connection, provincial or other-

wise, between Lycaonia and Galatia ; but the old tradition
and facts of Church history remained within the knowledge
of learned writers for a certain period, and so Asterius knew
that "the Galatic region" meant "Lycaonia".

The Western reading in XI 28 arose under the influence
of this Anatolian tradition, which remembered that Luke
was an Antiochian of Syria and desired to have some record
of this in his history by inserting ἡμῶν. Surely no one
could take the Western reading there as Lukan! Yet a few
have done so. Luke was a Macedonian, *i.e.*, of the
Antiochian tribe Makedones, whose name is preserved
fortunately by Josephus. His love for Philippi was due to
the long and successful evangelisation which he carried out
there. Titus was his brother, both *cives Romani* (which
meant a great deal in the first century): see p. 390.

10. There is a tendency in Dr. Plooij's work and elsewhere
to exaggerate the cessation of sailing during the winter in
the Aegean Sea. In early time, when ships were quite
small and navigation was still counted too dangerous, they
hugged the shore, and there was a much more complete
interruption than during the late Greek and the Roman
period, when ships ventured far out to sea making the run
across from the Lycian coast to Alexandria or from Sicily
to Alexandria, losing sight of land for several days. The
weather in the Aegean in the winter except in storms
(rarely lasting long) is not unsuited for navigation,[1] and it
is not open to doubt that ships plied in the forbidden winter
season with watchfulness on this sea. The very fact that so
many Jews went up to the Passover from various parts of

---

[1] Storms from the Black Sea sweeping down the Dardanelles
sometimes last for three or four weeks ; but they are exceptional
and local. A storm may occur in any part of the Aegean ; and ships
waited the end.

the Roman world is sufficient proof of this. Yet regardless of the fact that Paul actually was on the point of embarking on a ship from Corinth to go to the Passover of 57, Dr. Plooij seriously argues that he could not have intended to go to the Passover of 53, but that the Feast which he desired to attend was that of Tabernacles.[1]

11. That Lucius was the historian's name is proved by inscriptions found at Pisidian Antioch (see *The Bearing of Recent Research on N.T.*, Ch. XVIII). Lucius and Titus, the brothers (or cousins), may be compared with Lucius and Marcus, brothers, who inscribed a dedication at the Antiochian sanctuary, but who fortunately made a second dedication at a different time giving their full Roman names. It was common in those Græco-Asiatic cities that natives who had attained the Roman citizenship were in ordinary life called by the prænomen alone, although in more formal records they are designated by the full Roman title. Paul on the other hand, a Greek citizen of Tarsus and a Roman citizen and a Jew, was designated in Græco-Roman society by his cognomen alone; and the dedications at Pisidian Antioch show that this way of designation was even more common than the other. In Jewish surroundings he was the Hebrew Saul. Loukas was a Greek familiar form of Loukios (Lucius); it could hardly occur in Roman society, but is typical of Greek usage in respect of Roman names: cp. Tiberas, etc.

Dr. Plooij and I are entirely agreed that no chronological inferences for *Acts* can be drawn from the references either to Sergius Paullus at Cyprus or to Aretas at Damascus (2 *Cor.* XI 32 f.; *Acts* IX 23 ff.). The date of the incidents

---

[1] ἡ ἑορτή usually designates Tabernacles, but this Western interpolation was not made by a Jew and must not be interpreted according to strict Jewish usage.

must be fixed from the narrative. The authority at present is the *Acts.*

Every slight change that I have made in the chronology of the life of Paul since this book was written is in the direction of more perfect conformity with the narrative of Luke, and exemplifies the principles on which the book was written. The annexed table contains the chief dates of Paul's career (cp. p. 395): year I (to left) means the Asian-calendar-year 30-31 (during which the conversion occurred on some day not known).

NEW LIFE.		A.D.
I (30-31)	Conversion (age 33) . . . (before equinox Sept. 31)	31
3 (32-33)	First visit to Jerusalem . . (before equinox Sept. 33)	32-33
14 (43-44)	Second visit; the great revelation . (Aug.-Sept. 44)	44
15-17 or 18	First Mission . . . (Spring 45 to Sept. or Oct. 47)	45-47
18-19	Antioch; Struggle for Gentile rights; Galatian letter late in	48
19 (48-49)	Slow journey to Jerusalem (preaching); Apostolic Council	49
20-21	Separation from Barnabas; Cilicia; Galatia; Troas .	50
21 (50-51)	Troas; Macedonia; Athens (end of 50, Spring-Autumn)	51
22 (51-52)	Corinth (Oct. 51); (Gallio reaches Corinth, June 51 or 52)	51
22 (51-52)	Corinth; Trial before Gallio (Spring or Summer) . .	52
23 (52-53)	Corinth; Jerusalem? Syrian Antioch; Galatia . . .	53
24 (53-54)	Reaches Ephesus . . . . . (Jan.-Feb.)	54
26 (55-56)	Riot (Spring 56); Troas; Macedonia	56
27 (56-57)	Macedonia (2 Cor., written); Corinth (early 57); Philippi-Jerusalem; Pentecost . . . . . 56 and 57	
29 (58-59)	Coming of Festus . . . . . . (July?)	59
30 (59-60)	Melita (Winter 59); Rome . . . (early Spring)	60
32 (61-62)	Release (Spring 62); Crete	62
33-34	Asia; Macedonia; Nikopolis? Fire of Rome (Aug. 64) 63 and 64	
35 (64-65)	Arrest (end of 64); first hearing; six months' interval; second hearing; execution (before 23 Sept.) . .	65

CHAPTER I

THE ACTS OF THE APOSTLES

1. **TRUSTWORTHINESS.** The aim of our work is to treat its subject as a department of history and of literature. Christianity was not merely a religion, but also a system of life and action ; and its introduction by Paul amid the society of the Roman Empire produced changes of momentous consequence, which the historian must study. What does the student of Roman history find in the subject of our investigation ? How would an observant, educated, and unprejudiced citizen of the Roman Empire have regarded that new social force, that new philosophical system, if he had studied it with the eyes and the temper of a nineteenth century investigator?

As a preliminary the historian of Rome must make up his mind about the trustworthiness of the authorities. Those which we shall use are : (1) a work of history commonly entitled the *Acts of the Apostles* (the title does not originate from the author), (2) certain Epistles purporting to be written by Paul. Of the latter we make only slight and incidental use ; and probably even those who dispute their authenticity would admit that the facts we use are trustworthy, as being the settled belief of the Church at a very early period. It is, therefore, unnecessary to touch on the authenticity of the Epistles; but the question as to the date the composition, and the author of the *Acts* must be discussed. If the main position of this book is admitted, it will furnish a secure basis for the Epistles to rest on.

Works that profess to be historical are of various kinds and trustworthy in varying degrees. (1) There is the historical romance, which in a framework of history interweaves an invented tale. Some of the Apocryphal tales of the Apostles are of this class, springing apparently from a desire to provide Christian substitutes for the popular romances of the period. (2) There is the legend, in which popular fancy, working for generations, has surrounded a real person and real events with such a mass of extraneous matter that the historical kernel is hardly discernible. Certain of the Apocryphal tales of the Apostles may belong to this class, and many of the *Acta* of martyrs and saints certainly do. (3) There is the history of the second or third rate, in which the writer, either using good authorities carelessly and without judgment, or not possessing sufficiently detailed and correct authorities, gives a narrative of past events which is to a certain degree trustworthy, but contains errors in facts and in the grouping and proportions, and tinges the narrative of the past with the colour of his own time. In using works of this class the modern student has to exercise his historical tact, comparing the narrative with any other evidence that can be obtained from any source, and judging whether the action attributed to individuals is compatible with the possibilities of human nature. (4) There is, finally, the historical work of the highest order, in which a writer commands excellent means of knowledge either through personal acquaintance or through access to original authorities, and brings to the treatment of his subject genius, literary skill, and sympathetic historical insight into human character and the movement of events. Such an author seizes the critical events, concentrates the reader's attention on them by giving them fuller treatment, touches more lightly and briefly on the less important events, omits entirely a mass of unimportant details, and makes his work an artistic and idealised picture of the progressive tendency of the period.

Great historians are the rarest of writers. By general consent the typical example of the highest class of historians is Thucydides, and it is doubtful whether any other writer would be by general consent ranked along with him. But all historians, from Thucydides downwards, must be subjected to free criticism. The fire which consumes the second-rate historian only leaves the real master brighter and stronger and more evidently supreme. The keenest criticism will do him the best service in the long run. But the critic in his turn requires high qualities ; he must be able to distinguish the true from the false ; he must be candid and unbiassed and open-minded. There are many critics who have at great length stated their preference of the false before the true ; and it may safely be said that there is no class of literary productions in our century in which there is such an enormous preponderance of error and bad judgment as in that of historical criticism. To some of our critics Herodotus is the Father of History, to others he is an inaccurate reproducer of uneducated gossip : one writer at portentous length shows up the weakness of Thucydides, another can see no fault in him.

But, while recognising the risk, and the probable condemnation that awaits the rash attempt, I will venture to add one to the number of the critics, by stating in the following chapters reasons for placing the author of *Acts* among the historians of the first rank.

The first and the essential quality of the great historian is truth. What he says must be trustworthy. Now historical truth implies not merely truth in each detail, but also truth in the general effect, and that kind of truth cannot be attained without selection, grouping, and idealisation.

So far as one may judge from books, the opinion of scholars seems to have, on the whole, settled down to the conclusion that the author of *Acts* belongs either to the second- or the third-rate historians. Among those who assign him to the third rate we may rank all those who consider that the author clipped up older documents and patched together the fragments in a more or less intelligent way, making a certain number of errors in the process. Theories of this kind are quite compatible with assigning a high degree of trustworthiness to many statements in the book; but this trustworthiness belongs not to the author of the work, but to the older documents which he glued together. Such theories usually assign varying degrees of accuracy to the different older documents : all statements which suit the critic's own views on early Church history are taken from an original document of the highest character ; those which he likes less belong to a less trustworthy document ; and those which are absolutely inconsistent with his views are the work of the ignorant botcher who constructed the book. But this way of judging, common as it is, assumes the truth of the critic's own theory, and decides on the authenticity of ancient documents according to their agreement with that theory ; and the strangest part of this medley of uncritical method is that other writers, who dispute the first critic's theory of early Church history, yet attach some value to his opinion upon the spuriousness of documents which he has condemned solely on the ground that they disagree with his theory.

The most important group among those who assign the author to the second rank of historians, consists of them that accept his facts as true, although his selection of what he should say and what he should omit seems to them strangely capricious. They recognise many of the signs of extraordinary accuracy in his statements ; and these signs are so numerous that they feel bound to infer that the facts as a whole are stated with great accuracy by a personal friend of St. Paul. But when they compare the *Acts* with such documents as the Epistles of Paul, and when they study the history as a whole, they are strongly impressed with the inequalities of treatment, and the unexpected and puzzling gaps ; events of great importance seem to be dismissed in a brief and unsatisfactory way ; and, sometimes, when one of the actors (such as Paul) has left an account of an event described in *Acts*, they find difficulty in recognising the two accounts as descriptions of the same event. Bishop Lightfoot's comparison of *Gal.* II 1-10 with *Acts* XV may be quoted as a single specimen out of many : the elaborate process whereby he explains away the seeming discrepancies would alone be sufficient, if it were right, to prove that *Acts* was a second-rate work of history. We never feel on firm historical ground, when discrepancies are cleverly explained away : we need agreements to stand upon. Witnesses in a law court may give discrepant accounts of the same event ; but they are half-educated, confused, unable to rise to historical truth. But when a historian is compared with the reminiscences of an able and highly educated actor in the same scenes, and when the comparison consists chiefly in a laboured proof that the discrepancies do not amount to positive contradiction, the conclusion is very near, that, if the reminiscences are strictly honest, the historian's picture is not of the highest rank.

But there is a further difficulty. How does it come that a writer, who shows himself distinctly second-rate in his historical perception of the comparative importance of events, is able to attain such remarkable accuracy in describing many of them? The power of accurate description implies in itself a power of reconstructing the past, which involves the most delicate selection and grouping of details according to their truth and reality, *i.e.*, according to their comparative importance. *Acts*, as Lightfoot pictures it, is to me an inconceivable phenomenon ; such a mixture of strength and weakness, of historical insight and historical incapacity, would be unique and incredible. If the choice for an intelligible theory of *Acts* lay between Lightfoot's view and that which is presented in different forms by Clemen, Spitta, and other scholars, I could only adopt the same point of view as these critics. Lightfoot, with all his genius, has here led English scholarship into a *cul de sac :* we can make no progress, unless we retrace our steps and try a new path. But my belief is, that all the difficulties in which Lightfoot was involved spring from the attempt to identify the wrong events. In this attempt he naturally found discrepancies ; but by a liberal allowance of gaps in the narrative of *Acts*, and the supposition of different points of view and of deficient information on Luke's part, it was possible to show why the eye-witness saw one set of incidents, while *Acts* described quite a different set.

The historian who is to give a brief history of a great period need not reproduce on a reduced uniform scale all the facts which he would mention in a long history, like a picture reduced by a photographic process. If a brief history is to be a work of true art, it must omit a great deal, and concentrate the reader's attention on a certain number of critical points in the development of events, elaborating these sufficiently to present them in life-like and clearly intelligible form. True historical genius lies in selecting the great crises, the great agents, and the great movements, in making these clear to the reader in their real nature, in passing over with the lightest and slightest touch numerous events and many persons, but always keeping clear before the reader the plan of composition. The historian may dismiss years with a word, and devote considerable space to a single incident. In such a work, the omission of an event does not constitute a gap, but is merely a proof that the event had not sufficient importance to enter into the plan. A gap is some omission that offends our reason and our sense of harmony and propriety; and where something is omitted that bears on the author's plan, or where the plan as conceived by the author does not correspond to the march of events, but only to some fanciful and subjective view, there the work falls short of the level of history.

I may fairly claim to have entered on this investigation without any prejudice in favour of the conclusion which I shall now attempt to justify to the reader. On the contrary, I began with a mind unfavourable to it, for the ingenuity and apparent completeness of the Tübingen theory had at one time quite convinced me. It did not lie then in my line of life to investigate the subject minutely; but more recently I found myself often brought in contact with the book of *Acts* as an authority for the topography, antiquities, and society of Asia Minor. It was gradually borne in upon me that in various details the narrative showed marvellous truth. In fact, beginning with the fixed idea that the work was essentially a second-century composition, and never relying on its evidence as trust worthy for first-century conditions, I gradually came to find it a useful ally in some obscure and difficult investigations. But there remained still one serious objection to accepting it as entirely a first-century work. According to the almost universally accepted view, this history led Paul along a path and through surroundings which seemed to me historically and topographically self-contradictory. It was not possible to bring Paul's work in Asia Minor into accordance with the facts of history on the supposition that an important part of that work was devoted to a district in the northern part of the peninsula, called Galatia. It may appear at first sight a mere topographical subtlety whether Paul travelled through North Galatia or through Lycaonia ; but, when you consider that any details given of his journeys must be false to the one side just in proportion as they are true to the other, you will perceive that, if you try to apply the narrative to the wrong side of the country, it will not suit the scene, and if it does not suit, then it must appear to be written by a person ignorant of what he pretends to know. The case might be illustrated from our own experience. Suppose that an unknown person came to Auburn from New York, and you wished to find out whether he was an impostor or not. In our country we are exposed to frequent attempts at imposition, which can often be detected by a few questions; and you would probably ask him about his experiences on his journey from New York to Auburn. Now suppose you had been informed that he had come not along the direct road, but by a long detour through Boston, Montreal, and Toronto, and had thus arrived at Auburn; and suppose that you by questioning elicited from him various facts which suited only a route through Schenectady and Utica, you would condemn the man as an impostor, because he did not know the road which he pretended to have travelled. But suppose further that it was pointed out by some third party that this stranger had really travelled along the direct road, and that you had been misinformed when you supposed him to have come by the round-about way, your opinion as to the stranger's truthfulness would be instantly affected. Precisely similar is the case of *Acts* as a record of travel; generations and centuries have been attempting to apply it to the wrong countries. I must speak on this point confidently and uncompromisingly, for the facts stand out so clear and bold and simple that to affect to hesitate or to profess any doubt as to one's judgment would be a betrayal of truth.

I know the difficulties of this attempt to understand rightly a book so difficult, so familiar, and so much misunderstood as *Acts*. It is probable that I have missed the right turn or not grasped the full meaning in some cases. I am well aware that I leave some difficulties unexplained, sometimes from inability, sometimes from mere omission.

But I am sustained by the firm belief that I am on the right path, and by the hope that enough of difficulties have been cleared away to justify a dispassionate historical criticism in placing this great writer on the high pedestal that belongs to him.

2. DEVELOPMENT OF MODERN CRITICISM ON *ACTS*. With regard to the trustworthiness of *Acts* as a record of events, a change is perceptible in the tendency of recent criticism. Setting aside various exceptional cases, and also leaving out of sight the strictly "orthodox" view, which accepts *Acts* as truth without seeking to compare or to criticise (a view which in its simplicity and completeness needs neither defence nor examination), we may say that for a time the general drift of criticism was to conceive the book as a work composed in the second century with the intention of so representing (or rather misrepresenting) the facts as to suit the writer's opinion about the Church questions of his own time. All theories of this class imply that the atmosphere and surroundings of the work are of the second-century type; and such theories have to be founded on a proof that the details are represented in an inaccurate way and coloured by second-century ideas. The efforts of that earlier school of critics were directed to give the required proof; and in the attempt they displayed a misapprehension of the real character of ancient life and Roman history which is often astonishing, and which has been decisively disproved in the progress of Roman historical investigation. All such theories belong to the pre-Mommsenian epoch of Roman history : they are now impossible for a rational and educated critic; and they hardly survive except in popular magazines and novels for the semi-religious order.

But while one is occasionally tempted to judge harshly the assumption of knowledge made by the older critics where knowledge was at the time difficult or impossible, it is only fair also to emphatically acknᵣwledge the debt we owe them for practising in a fearless and independent spirit the right and much-needed task of investigating the nature and origin of the book.

Warned by the failure of the older theories, many recent critics take the line that *Acts* consists of various first-century scraps put together in the book as we have it by a second-century Redactor. The obvious signs of vivid accuracy in many of the details oblige these critics to assume that the Redactor incorporated the older scraps with no change except such as results from different surroundings and occasional wrong collocation. Some hold that the Redactor made considerable additions in order to make a proper setting for the older scraps. Others reduce the Redactor's action to a minimum ; Spitta is the most remarkable example of this class. In the latter form the Redaction-theory is the diametrical opposite of the old tendency theories ; the latter supposed that the second-century author coloured the whole narrative and put his own views into every paragraph, while, according to Spitta, the Redactor added nothing of consequence to his first-century materials except some blunders of arrangement. The older theories were founded on the proof of a uniformity of later style and purpose throughout the book ; the later theories depend on the proof of differences of style between the different parts. The old critics were impressed by the literary skill of the author, while the later critics can see no literary power or activity in him. Any argument in favour of the one class of theories tells against the other; and, if we admit (as I think we must admit), that each view is founded on a correct but one-sided perception of certain qualities in this remarkable book, we may fairly say that each disproves the other.

Certain theorists, and especially Clemen in his extra-ordinarily ingenious and bold work *Chronologie der Paulinischen Briefe*, see clearly that such a bald scissors-and-paste theory as Spitta's is quite inadequate to explain the many-sided character of this history. Dr. Clemen supposes that three older documents, a history of the Hellenistic Jews, a history of Peter, and a history of Paul, were worked into one work by a Judaist Redactor, who inserted many little touches and even passages of considerable length to give a tone favourable to the Judaising type of Christianity; and that this completed book was again worked over by an anti-Judaist Redactor II, who inserted other parts to give a tone unfavourable to the Judaising type of Christianity, but left the Judaistic insertions. Finally, a Redactor III of neutral tone incorporated a new document (VI 1-6), and gave the whole its present form by a number of small touches.

When a theory becomes so complicated as Clemen's, the humble scholar who has been trained only in philological and historical method finds himself unable to keep pace, and toils in vain behind this daring flight. We shall not at present stop to argue from examples in ancient and modern literature, that a dissection of this elaborate kind cannot be carried out. Style is seen in the whole rather than in single sentences, still less in parts of sentences; and a partition between six authors, clause by clause, sentence by sentence, paragraph by paragraph, of a work that seemed even to bold and revolutionary critics like Zeller and Baur in Germany and Renan in France to be a model of unity and individuality in style, is simply impossible. Moreover, the plan of this study is not to argue against other theories, but to set forth a plain and simple interpretation of the text, and appeal to the recognised principle of criticism that, where a simple theory of origin can be shown to hold together properly, complicated theories must give way to it.

One feature in Dr. Clemen's theory shows true insight. No simple theory of gluing together can exhaust the varied character of the *Acts* : a very complex system of junctures is needed to explain its many-sidedness. But Dr. Clemen has not gone far enough. There is only one kind of cause that is sufficiently complex to match the many-sided aspects of the book, and that cause is the many-sided character of a thoughtful and highly educated man.

Dr. Clemen seems to assume that every instance where Paul adopts an attitude of conciliation towards the Jews is added by a Judaistic Redactor, and every step in his growing estrangement from them is due to an anti-Judaistic Redactor. He does not, I venture to think, allow due scope to the possibility that an historian might record both classes of incidents in the interests of truth. It is admitted that a dislocation occurred in the early Church, and that the contention between the Judaising and the Universalising (to adopt a convenient designation) parties was keen for a time. It is natural that the estrangement should be gradual ; and the historian sets before us a gradual process. He shows us Paul acting on the principle that the Jews had the first claim (XIII 46), and always attempting to conciliate them ; but he also shows us that Paul did not struggle against the facts, but turned his back on the Jews when they rejected him (as their whole history proves, even without the evidence of *Acts*, that they were sure to do).

It is hard to find a sufficient foundation for Dr. Clemen's theory without the preliminary assumption that an early Christian must necessarily be incapable of taking a broad and unbiassed view of history as a whole. Grant that assumption, and his theory is built up with marvellous skill, patience and ingenuity.

3. WORKING HYPOTHESIS OF THE INVESTI-GATION. Our hypothesis is that *Acts* was written by a great historian, a writer who set himself to record the facts as they occurred, a strong partisan indeed, but raised above partiality by his perfect confidence that he had only to describe the facts as they occurred, in order to make the truth of Christianity and the honour of Paul apparent. To a Gentile Christian, as the author of *Acts* was, the refusal of the Jews to listen to Paul, and their natural hatred of him as untrue to their pride of birth, must appear due to pure malignity ; and the growing estrangement must seem to him the fault of the Jews alone. It is not my object to assume or to prove that there was no prejudice in the mind of Luke, no fault on the part of Paul ; but only to examine whether the facts stated are trustworthy, and leave them to speak for themselves (as the author does). I shall argue that the book was composed by a personal friend and disciple of Paul, and if this be once established there will be no hesitation in accepting the primitive tradition that Luke was the author.

We must face the facts boldly. If Luke wrote *Acts*, his narrative *must* agree in a striking and convincing way with Paul's : they *must* confirm, explain and com-plete one another. This is not a case of two commonplace, imperfectly educated, and not very observant witnesses who give divergent accounts of certain incidents which they saw without paying much attention to them. We have here two men of high education, one writing a formal history, the other speaking under every obligation of honour and conscience to be careful in his words: the subjects they speak of were of the most overpowering interest to both: their points of view must be very similar, for they were personal friends, and one was the teacher of the other, and naturally had moulded to some extent his mind during long companionship. If ever there was a case in which striking agreement was demanded by historical criticism between two classes of documents, it is between the writings of Paul and of Luke.

There is one subject in particular in which criticism demands absolute agreement. The difference of position and object between the two writers, one composing a formal history, the other writing letters or making speeches, may justifiably be invoked to account for some difference in the selection of details. But in regard to the influence of the Divine will on human affairs they ought to agree. Both firmly believed that God often guided the conduct of His Church by clear and open revelation of His will; and we should be slow to believe that one of them attributed to human volition what the other believed to be ordered by direct manifestation of God (p. 140). We shall try to prove that there is a remarkable agreement between them in regard to the actions which they attribute to direct revelation.

Further, we cannot admit readily that peculiarities of Luke's narrative are to be accounted for by want of information : in his case this explanation really amounts to an accusation of culpable neglect of a historian's first duty, for full information was within Luke's reach, if he had taken the trouble to seek it. We shall find no need of this supposition. Finally, it is hard to believe that Paul's letters were unknown to Luke ; he was in Paul's company when some of them were written ; he must have known about the rest, and could readily learn their contents in the intimate intercommunication that bound together the early Churches. We shall try to show that Luke had in mind the idea of explaining and elucidating the letters.

In maintaining our hypothesis it is not necessary either to show that the author made no mistake, or to solve every difficulty. From them that start with a different view more may be demanded ; but here we are making a historical and literary investigation. The greatest historians of other periods are not above error ; and we may admit the possibility that a first-century historian has made errors. We shall not make much use of this *proviso;* but still the conditions of the investigation must be clearly laid down.

Again, in almost every ancient writer of any value there remain unsolved problems by the score. Where would our philological scholars be, if every question were satisfactorily disposed of ? The plan and the date of Horace's longest work, the *Art of Poetry*, are unsolved and apparently insoluble ; every theory involves serious difficulties ; yet that does not make its authenticity doubtful. That there remain some difficulties not explained satisfactorily in *Acts* does not disprove its first-century origin.

Further, it is necessary to study every historian's method, and not to judge him according to whether or not he uses our methods. For example, Thucydides makes a practice of putting into the mouths of his characters speeches which they never delivered ; no modern historian would do this : the speeches of Thucydides, however, are the greatest and most instructive part of his history. They might be truly called unhistorical ; but the critic who summed up their character in that epithet would only show his incapacity for historical criticism. Similarly the critic must study Luke's method, and not judge him according to whether he writes exactly as the critic considers a history ought to be written.

Luke's style is compressed to the highest degree ; and he expects a great deal from the reader. He does not attempt to sketch the surroundings and set the whole scene like a picture before the reader ; he states the bare facts that seem to him important, and leaves the reader to imagine the situation. But there are many cases in which, to catch his meaning properly, you must imagine yourself standing with Paul on the deck of the ship, or before the Roman official ; and unless you reproduce the scene in imagination, you miss the sense. Hence, though his style is simple and clear, yet it often becomes obscure from its brevity; and the meaning is lost, because the reader has an incomplete, or a positively false idea of the situation. It is always hard to recreate the remote past ; knowledge, imagination, and, above all, sympathy and love are all needed. But Asia Minor, in which the scene is often laid, was not merely little known, but positively wrongly known.

I know of no person except Bishop Lightfoot who has seriously attempted to test or revise or improve the traditional statements (often, the traditional blunders) about Asian antiquities as bearing on *Acts ;* but the materials were not at his disposal for doing this successfully. But it is bad method to found theories of its composition on wrong interpretations of its meaning: the stock misconceptions should first be cleared away, and the book studied in relation to the localities and the antiquities.

Luke was deficient in the sense for time; and hence his chronology is bad. It would be quite impossible from *Acts* alone to get a true idea of the lapse of time. That is the fault of his age; Tacitus, writing the biography of Agricola (about 98 A.D.), makes no chronological statement, until in the last paragraph he gives a series of statistics. Luke had studied the sequence of events carefully, and observes it in his arrangement minutely, but he often has to carry forward one thread of his narrative, and then goes back in time to take up another thread; and these transitions are sometimes rather harsh. Yet, in respect of chronology, he was, perhaps, less careless than would appear: see p. 23.

His plan leads him to concentrate attention on the critical steps. Hence he often passes lightly over a long period of gradual development marked by no striking incident; and from his bad chronological sense he gives no measure of the lapse of time implied in a sentence, a clause, or even a word. He dismisses ten years in a breath, and devotes a chapter to a single incident. His character as an historian, therefore, depends on his selection of topics. Does he show the true historian's power of seizing the great facts, and marking clearly the stages in the development of his subject? Now, what impresses me is the sense of proportion in *Acts*, and the skill with which a complex and difficult subject is grouped to bring out the historical development from the primitive Church (Ch. I-V) through the successive steps associated with four great names, Stephen, Philip,

Peter, Paul. Where the author passes rapidly over a period or a journey, we shall find reason to believe that it was marked by no striking feature and no new foundation. The axiom from which we start must be that which is assumed in all literary investigations—preference is to be given to the interpretation which restores order, lucidity, and sanity to the work. All that we ask in this place is the admission of that axiom, and a patient hearing, and especially that the reader, before condemning our first steps as not in harmony with other incidents, will wait to see how we can interpret those incidents.

The dominant interpretation rests avowedly on the principle that *Acts* is full of gaps, and that "nothing is more striking than the want of proportion". Those unfortunate words of Bishop Lightfoot are worked out by some of his successors with that "illogical consistency" which often leads the weaker disciples of a great teacher to choose his errors for loving imitation and emphasis. With such a theory no historical absurdity is too gross to be imputed to Luke. But our hypothesis is that Luke's silence about an incident or person should always be investigated as a piece of evidence, on the principle that he had some reason for his silence; and in the course of this study we shall in several cases find that omission is a distinct element in the effect of his narrative.

There is a contrast between the early chapters of *Acts* and the later. In the later chapters there are few sentences that do not afford some test of their accuracy by mentioning external facts of life, history, and antiquities. But the earlier chapters contain comparatively few such details ; the subject in them is handled in a vaguer way, with a less vigorous and nervous grasp ; the facts are rarely given in their local and historical surroundings, and sometimes seem to float in air rather than to stand on solid ground.

This fundamental difference in handling must be acknowledged; but it can be fairly attributed to difference of information and of local knowledge. The writer shows himself in his later narrative to be a stranger to the Levant and familiar with the Ægean; he could not stand with the same confidence on the soil of Syria and Palestine, as on that of Asia Minor or Greece. Moreover, he was dealing with an earlier period; and he had not the advantage of formal historical narratives, such as he mentions for the period described in his First Book (the *Gospel*). Luke was dependent on various informants in the earlier chapters of *Acts* (among them Paul and Philip); and he put together their information, in many cases reproducing it almost *verbatim*. Sometimes the form of his record gives a clue to the circumstances in which he learned it. That line of investigation is liable to become subjective and fanciful; but modern historical investigation always tries to get behind the actual record and to investigate the ultimate sources of statements.

4. THE AUTHOR OF *ACTS* AND HIS HERO. It is rare to find a narrative so simple and so little forced as that of *Acts*. It is a mere uncoloured recital of the important facts in the briefest possible terms. The narrator's individuality and his personal feelings and preferences are almost wholly suppressed. He is entirely absorbed in his work; and he writes with the single aim to state the facts as he has learned them. It would be difficult in the whole range of literature to find a work where there is less attempt at pointing a moral or drawing

a lesson from the facts. The narrator is persuaded that the facts themselves in their barest form are a perfect lesson and a complete instruction, and he feels that it would be an impertinence and even an impiety to intrude his individual views into the narrative.

It is, however, impossible for an author to hide himself completely. Even in the selection of details, his personality shows itself. So in *Acts*, the author shows the true Greek feeling for the sea. He hardly ever omits to name the harbours which Paul sailed from or arrived at, even though little or nothing in the way of incident occurred in them. But on land journeys he confines himself to missionary facts, and gives no purely geographical information ; where any statements of a geographical character occur, they serve a distinct purpose in the narrative, and the reader who accepts them as mere geographical specifications has failed to catch the author's purpose (see p. 205 f.).

Under the surface of the narrative, there moves a current of strong personal affection and enthusiastic admiration for Paul. Paul is the author's hero ; his general aim is to describe the development of the Church ; but his affection and his interest turn to Paul ; and after a time his narrative groups itself round Paul. He is keenly concerned to show that Paul was in perfect accord with the leaders among the older Apostles, but so also was Paul himself in his letters. That is the point of view of a personal friend and disciple, full of affection, and jealous of Paul's honour and reputation.

The characterisation of Paul in *Acts* is so detailed and individualised as to prove the author's personal acquaintance. Moreover, the Paul of *Acts* is the Paul that appears to us in his own letters, in his ways and his thoughts, in his educated tone of polished courtesy, in his quick and vehement temper, in the extraordinary versatility and adaptability which made him at home in every society, moving at ease in all surroundings, and everywhere the centre of interest, whether he is the Socratic dialectician in the agora of Athens, or the rhetorician in its University, or conversing with kings and proconsuls, or advising in the council on shipboard, or cheering a broken-spirited crew to make one more effort for life.   Wherever Paul is, no one present has eyes for any but him.

Such a view could not have been taken by a second-century author.   The Church in the second century had passed into new circumstances and was interested in quite different questions.   The catastrophe of the persecution of Domitian, and the effect produced for the time on the attitude of the Church by the deliberate attempt to suppress and destroy it on the part of the imperial government, made a great gulf between the first century and the second century of Christian history.[1]   Though the policy of the great emperors of the second century came back to somewhat milder measures, the Church could not recover the same feeling that Paul had, so long as Christianity continued to be a proscribed religion, and a Christian was in theory at least an outlaw and a rebel.   Many questions that were evidently vital to the author of *Acts* were buried in oblivion during the persecution of Domitian, and could not have been present in the mind of a later author.   Our view classes *Acts* with I *Peter*, intermediate between the Pauline letters and the literature of the last decade of the century (such as *Revelation*).   Luke shows the same attitude as Paul, but he aims at proving what Paul feels.

[1] *Church in R. E.*, Ch. XIII.

The question must be fairly considered whether Luke
had completed his history.   There is one piece of evidence from his own hand that he had not completed it,
but contemplated a third book at least.   His work is
divided into two books, the *Gospel* and the *Acts*, but in the
opening line of the *Acts* he refers to the *Gospel* as the *First
Discourse* (πρῶτος λόγος).   Had he not contemplated a
third book, we expect the term *Former Discourse* (πρότερος).
In a marked position like the opening of a book, we must
take the word *first* strictly (*Note*, p. 27).

We shall argue that the plan of *Acts* has been obscured by the want of the proper climax and conclusion,
which would have made it clear, and also that the author
did not live to put the final touches to his second book.
Perhaps we may thus account for the failure of chronological data.   In Book I there are careful reckonings of
dates (in one case by several different eras) at the great
steps of the narrative.   In Book II there are no such
calculations (except the vague "under Claudius" in
XI 28, in itself a striking contrast to "the fifteenth
year of Tiberius," *Luke* III 1).   Tacitus, as we saw,
appends the dates to his *Agricola:* Luke incorporates
his dates, but they have all the appearance of being put
into an already finished narrative.   If other reasons prove
that *Acts* wants the finishing touches, we may reckon
among the touches that would have been added certain
calculations of synchronism, which would have furnished a
chronological skeleton for the narrative.

If the work was left incomplete, the reason, perhaps,
lay in the author's martyrdom under Domitian.

5. THE TEXT OF *ACTS*.   It was my wish to take
no notice here of differences of reading, but simply to

follow Westcott and Hort (except in two impossible cases, XI 20, XII 25). This, however, proved impracticable; for there are some cases in which over-estimate of the two great MSS. (the Sinaitic and the Vatican) has led to the adoption of a reading that obscures history. In several places I have been driven back on the Received Text and the Authorised Version, and in others the Bezan Text either contains or gives the clue to the original text; and wherever the Bezan Text is confirmed by old Versions and by certain Greek MSS., it seems to me to deserve very earnest consideration, as at least pointing in the direction of an original reading subjected to wide-spread corruption.

It is universally admitted that the text of *Acts* was exposed to very careless or free handling in the second century. This came about in various ways, for the most part unintentionally, but partly by deliberate action. At that time great interest was taken in gathering from trustworthy sources supplementary information, beyond what was contained in the *Gospels* and *Acts*. Eusebius, III 39, quotes a passage from Papias describing his eager inquiries after such information from those who had come into personal relations with the Apostles, and another, V 20, from Irenæus, describing how Polycarp used to tell of his intercourse with John and the rest that had seen the Lord. Now there was a natural tendency to note on the margin of a MS. additional information obtained on good authority about incidents mentioned in the text; and there is always a danger that such notes may be inserted in the text by a copyist, who takes them for parts accidentally omitted. There is also a certain probability that deliberate addi-

tions might be made to the text (as deliberate excisions
are said to have been made by Marcion). The balance
of evidence is, on the whole, that *Mark* XVI 9-20 is a
later composition, designed to complete a narrative that
had all the appearance of being defective. Again, explanatory notes on the margin of a MS. are often added
by a reader interested in the text; there is no doubt
that in some books such glosses have crept into the
text through the errors of the copyist; and there are on
our view three such cases at least in the generally
accepted text of *Acts.*

But, beyond this, when translations were made into
Syriac and Latin (the former certainly, the later probably,
as early as the middle of the second century), the attention
of scholars was necessarily directed to the difficulties in
interpretation of the text, with its occasional archaic expressions, obscure words, and harsh constructions; and
the practical usefulness of a simplified and modernised
text was thus suggested. Tatian's *Harmony of the Four
Gospels*, and Marcion's doctored editions, show how attempts were made from different points of view and in
different ways to adapt the sacred narrative for popular
use: Tatian changed the order, Marcion altered the text
by excision or worse. Thus the plan of a simplified
text was quite in keeping with the custom of the second
century; and the Bezan Text seems to be of that kind.
As a whole it is not Lukan: it has a fatal smoothness,
it loses the rather harsh but very individual style of Luke,
and it neglects some of the literary forms that Luke
observed. But it has a high value for several reasons:
(1) it preserves with corruptions a second-century witness
to the text, and often gives valuable, and sometimes

conclusive, evidence of readings; (2) it shows what view was held as to the meaning of various passages in the second century; (3) it adds several pieces of information which probably rest on good evidence, though they were not written by Luke. Thus we can often gather from the Bezan comment what was the original reading commented on; and it vindicates the great MSS. in XVI 12 against Dr. Hort's conjecture. It reveals to us the first beginnings of Pauline legend (p. 106); and in this respect it stands on much the same level as the original text of the *Acta of Paul and Thekla*, where also it is hard to distinguish where history ends and romance begins. With the help of these two authorities, combined with early Christian inscriptions (which begin only about 190, but give retrospective evidence), we can recover some faint idea of the intellectual life of the second-century Christians in Asia Minor and North Syria.

The Bezan Text will, indubitably, afford much study and some discoveries in the future. Its explanatory simplifications often show the influence of the translations which first suggested the idea of a simplified text. When the need for an explanation arose in connection with a rendering in Latin, or in Syriac, the simplification took a Latin or Syriac colour; but this was consciously adopted as a simplification, and not through mere blundering.

While the Bezan Text has gone furthest from the original Lukan Text, there is no MS. which has not suffered seriously from the various causes of depravation. Several of the errors that have affected the two great MSS. look like changes made intentionally in order to suit a mistaken idea of the meaning of other passages; but there is always a possibility that in these cases an editor was making a choice between varieties of reading that had been produced unintentionally. Only in the Bezan Text can we confidently say that deliberate alterations were made in the text.

I believe that the Bezan Reviser made many skilful changes in passages relating to Asia Minor and some foolish changes in European passages. In some of these cases, the view remains open that the Bezan reading is the original; but evidence is as yet not sufficient to give certainty. The home of the Revision is along the line of intercourse between Syrian Antioch and Ephesus, for the life of the early Church lay in intercommunication, but the Reviser was connected with Antioch, for he inserts "we" in XI 28.

Note. τὸν πρῶτον λόγον. The commentators universally regard this as an example of the misuse of πρῶτος; but they give no sufficient proof that Luke elsewhere misused that word. In Stephen's speech (VII 12) the adverb πρῶτον misused for πρότερον occurs, but a dispassionate consideration of the speeches in *Acts* must convince every reader that they are not composed by the author, but taken *verbatim* from other authorities (in this case from Philip at Cæsareia, XXI 8). Blass, p. 16, points out with his usual power, that the character and distinction of the comparative and superlative degrees was decaying in the Greek of the N.T., and that in many adjectives one of the two degrees played the part of both. But such changes do not affect all words simultaneously; and the distinction between πρότερος and πρῶτος might be expected to last longer than that between most other pairs. We observe that Paul uses both, and distinguishes them correctly (though he blurs the distinction in other words): τὸ πρότερον as the former of two visits *Gal.* IV 13, τὴν προτέραν ἀναστροφήν *Eph.* IV 22. Blass, with the grammarian's love for making absolute rules, conjectures the last example away, in order to lay down the law that the adjective πρότερος is not employed in N.T.; but we follow the MSS., and find in them the proof that the distinction was only in process of decay, and that the pair πρότερος-πρῶτος still survived among the more educated writers in N.T. So long as Paul could distinguish πρότερος and πρῶτος, there is a probability that Luke would not utterly confuse them; and the fact that John uses πρῶτος in the most glaring way for πρότερος has no bearing on Luke, who was a far better master of Greek. We find several instances where Luke uses πρῶτος correctly: in *Acts* XII 10 there were obviously three gates and three wards to pass (Peter was allowed to pass the first and the second, being taken presumably as a servant; but no servant would be expected to pass beyond the outermost ward at night, and a different course was needed there): in *Luke* II 2 a series of *census* are contemplated as having occurred, p. 386: in *Luke* XI 26 the man is described as passing through several stages: cp. XIII 30, XIV 18, XVI 5, XIX 16, XX 29. And, if there survived in Luke the slightest idea of any difference between comparative and superlative, the opening of a book is the place where we should expect to find the difference expressed. We conclude, then, that the use of πρῶτος there is more easily reconcilable with the plan of three books, than of two; but certainty is not attainable, as πρότερος does not actually occur in his writings.

CHAPTER II

THE ORIGIN OF ST. PAUL

1. PAUL'S NATIONALITY. In the growth of Christianity we observe that all the threads of development which had been formed in the life of the great races of older history are gathered together into one complex whole. Hence we have just the same assurance of the truth of Christianity that we have of the trustworthiness of earlier history: the earlier works into the later, the later grows out of the earlier, in such a way that all must be taken together. The correspondence is in itself a guarantee of truth. Each exists for the other: each derives its full comprehensibility from the other. We must accept the general outline of early history as a whole, or we must reject it as a whole on the plea of insufficient evidence. There is not a fact of early history, whether Christian or pre-Christian, which is not susceptible of being disputed with a fair show of rational and logical argument: the evidence is nowhere such as would convince a man whose mind is made up against the trustworthiness of ancient history. Let any one test the evidence for any point in regard to the battles of Salamis or of Marathon; and he will find that everywhere he is reduced to a balance of evidence, and frequently to a balance so delicate that no one can feel any assured confidence on the point. Yet

(29)

our confidence in the general facts regarding each battle and its results is not, as a rule, affected by our uncertainty as to the details. Doubtless there will always be some who argue that the trustworthiness of the whole must be proportionate to the trustworthiness of the parts, and conclude that, where all details are so uncertain, the whole is unworthy of study; and those who cannot see —or rather feel—for themselves the fallacy of the argument will not be convinced by any reasoning that can be adduced. But for those who do not adopt the extreme agnostic position, there is no other logical position except that of accepting the general scheme of ancient history, in which Christianity is the crowning factor that gives unity and rational plan to the whole.

The life of Paul partakes of the uncertainty that envelopes all ancient history. As regards every detail we shall find ourselves in the position of balancing evidence; as to almost every detail we shall find ourselves amid a bewildering variety of opposite opinion and assertion among modern scholars of every school and shade; and, strangest of all, in regard to two or three points where there exists the nearest approach to a general agreement between all the various schools, we shall find ourselves unable to agree. Owing to the peculiar character of the evidence, we shall find it best to begin in the middle of Paul's life and study the events of the years 44 to 61, and thereafter to sketch in outline the first half of his life.

At present, however, we must emphasise the complex influences amid which Paul grew up. According to the law of his country, he was first of all a Roman citizen. That character superseded all others before the law and in the general opinion of society ; and placed him amid the aristocracy of any provincial town. In the first century, when the citizenship was still jealously guarded, the *civitas* may be taken as a proof that his family was one of distinction and at least moderate wealth. It also implies that there was in the surroundings amid which he grew up, a certain attitude of friendliness to the Imperial government (for the new citizens in general, and the Jewish citizens in particular, were warm partisans of their protector, the new Imperial régime), and also of pride in a possession that ensured distinction and rank and general respect in Tarsus. As a Roman, Paul had a *nomen* and *prænomen*, probably taken from the Roman officer who gave his family *civitas ;* but Luke, a Greek, had no interest in Roman names. Paulus, his *cognomen*, was not determined by his *nomen :* there is no reason to think he was an Æmilius (as some suggest).

Paul was, in the second place, a " Tarsian, a citizen of a distinguished city " (XXI 39, IX 11). He was not merely a person born in Tarsus, owing to the accident of his family being there : he had a citizen's rights in Tarsus. We may confidently assume that Paul was careful to keep within demonstrable law and custom, when he claimed to be a Tarsian citizen in describing himself to the Tribune. According to the strict interpretation of the Roman law, the *civitas* superseded all other citizenship, but this theoretical exclusiveness was opposed to the Imperial spirit ; and it is clear that Roman *cives* in a provincial city commonly filled the position of high-class citizens, and even had magistracies pressed upon them by general consent. Now, if Paul's family had merely emigrated to Tarsus from Judæa some years before his birth, neither he nor his father would have been "Tarsians," but merely "residents" (*incolæ*). It is probable, but not certain, that the family had been planted in Tarsus with full rights as part of a colony settled there by one of the Seleucid kings in order to strengthen their hold on the city. Such a re-foundation took place at Tarsus, for the name Antiocheia was given it under Antiochus IV (175-164 B.C.). The Seleucid kings seem to have had a preference for Jewish colonists in their foundations in Asia Minor. Citizenship in Tarsus might also have been presented to Paul's father or grandfather for distinguished services to the State ; but that is much less probable.

In the third place, Paul was "a Hebrew *sprung* from Hebrews". The expression is a remarkable one. It is used not to a Jewish audience, but to a Greek Church (*Phil.* III 5), and it is similar to a familiar expression among the Greeks : "a priest *sprung* from priests " is a term commonly applied to members of the great sacerdotal families which play so important a part in the society of Asian cities. He was a Jew at least as much as he was a Tarsian and a Roman, as regards his early surroundings ; and it is obvious that the Jewish side of his nature and education proved infinitely the most important, as his character developed. But it is a too common error to ignore the other sides. Many interpreters seem to think only of his words, XXII 3, " I am a Jew born in Tarsus," and to forget that he said a few moments before, " I am a Jew, a Tarsian, a citizen of no mean city ". To the Hebrews he emphasises his Jewish character, and his birth in Tarsus is added as an accident : but to Claudius Lysias, a

Greek-Roman, he emphasises his Tarsian citizenship (after having told of his Roman citizenship). Now, there is no inconsistency between these descriptions of himself. Most of us have no difficulty in understanding that a Jew at the present day may be a thoroughly patriotic English citizen, and yet equally proud of his ancient and honourable origin. In the extraordinarily mixed society of the Eastern provinces, it was the usual rule in educated society that each man had at least two nationalities and two sides to his character. If we would clearly understand the society in which Paul worked, and the mission of Rome to make the idea of cosmopolitanism and universal citizenship a practical reality —an idea that had been first conceived by the Stoic philosophy in its attempt to fuse Greek and oriental thought into a unified system—we must constantly bear in mind that double or even triple character, which was so common.

To the Hebrew of that period it was specially easy to preserve the Hebraic side of his life along with his Greek citizenship; for the Jewish colony in a Seleucid city preserved as a body its double character. It was not merely a part of the city, whose members were citizens, but it was also recognised by the Seleucid Empire and afterwards by the Roman Empire as " the Nation of the Jews in that city ". Thus arose a strange and often puzzling complication of rights, which caused much heart-burning and jealousy among the non-Jewish citizens of the city, and which was at last terminated by the action of Vespasian in A.D. 70, when he put an end to the legal existence of a " Jewish nation," and resolved the Jews into the general population of the Empire.

From this wide and diversified training we may understand better Paul's suitability to develop the primitive Judaic Church into the Church of the Roman World (for beyond that he never went in practice, though in theory he recognised no limit short of universal humanity), his extraordinary versatility and adaptability (which evidently impressed Luke so much, p. 22), and his quickness to turn the resources of civilisation to his use. The Jew in his own land was rigidly conservative; but the Jew abroad has always been the most facile and ingenious of men. There are no stronger influences in education and in administration than rapidity and ease of travelling and the postal service; Paul both by precept and example impressed the importance of both on his Churches; and the subsequent development of the Church was determined greatly by the constant intercommunication of its parts and the stimulating influence thereby produced on the whole.

2. PAUL'S FAMILY. If Paul belonged to a family of wealth and position, how comes it that in great part of his career (but not in the whole, p. 312) he shows all the marks of poverty, maintaining himself by his own labour, and gratefully acknowledging his indebtedness to the contributions of his Philippian converts, in Rome, in Corinth, and twice in Thessalonica (*Phil.* IV 15, II *Cor.* XI 9; see p. 360)? It was not simply that he voluntarily worked with his hands in order to impress on his converts the dignity and duty of labour, for he conveys the impression, II *Cor.* XI 8 f., I *Thess.* II 9, that he had to choose between accepting help from his converts, and making his own living. But it often happens in our own experience that a member of a rich family is in a position

of poverty. It would be enough simply to accept the fact; but, as Paul in his later career is found in a different position, and as the same conjecture about his poverty must arise in every one's mind, we may glance for a moment at the relations in which Paul would stand to his own family after his conversion.

The relations between Paul and his family are never alluded to by himself, and only once by Luke, who tells how his sister's son saved his life in Jerusalem by giving private information of the secret conspiracy against him, XXIII 16. How could this young man get immediate information about a conspiracy, which was concocted by a band of zealots, and arranged in private with the high priests and elders? In absolute secrecy lay the sole hope of success; and the conspiracy must therefore have been imparted only to a few, and probably only the leaders of the extreme Jewish party were aware of it. We must, I think, infer that the nephew acquired his information in the house of some leading Jew (to which he had access as belonging to an influential family), and that he was himself not a Christian, for in the heated state of feeling it may be taken as practically certain that a Christian would not have had free and confidential entry to the house of one of the Jewish leaders. But, further, if Paul's nephew were trusted with such a secret, it must have been assumed that he was hostile to Paul.

Now, as Paul himself says, he had been brought up in strict Judaic feeling, not as a Sadducee, accepting the non-Jewish spirit, but as a Pharisee; and we must infer that the spirit of his family was strongly Pharisaic. The whole history of the Jews shows what was likely to be the feeling among his parents and brothers and sisters, when he not merely became a Christian, but went to the Gentiles. Their pride was outraged ; and we should naturally expect that such a family would regard Paul as an apostate, a foe to God and the chosen race, and a disgrace to the family ; his own relatives might be expected to be his most bitter enemies. Looking at these probabilities, we see a special force in Paul's words to the Philippians, III 8, that he had given up all for Christ, "for whom I suffered the loss of all things and do count them but refuse". These emphatic words suit the mouth of one who had been disowned by his family, and reduced from a position of wealth and influence in his nation to poverty and contempt.

Perhaps it is some terrible family scene that made Paul so keenly alive to the duty owed by a father to his children. Probably nothing in family life makes a more awful and lasting impression on a sensitive mind than a scene where a respected and beloved parent makes a demand beyond what love or duty permits, and tries to enforce that demand by authority and threats. If Paul had to face such a scene, we can appreciate the reason why he lays so much stress on the duty of parents to respect their children's just feelings : " ye fathers, provoke not your children to wrath ; but bring them up in the education and admonition of the Lord " (*Eph.* VI 4) : " fathers, provoke not your children, lest they lose heart " (*Col.* III 21). Not every person would think this one of the most important pieces of advice to give his young societies in Asia Minor. But, according to our conjecture, Paul had good cause to know the harm that parents may do by not reasonably considering their children's desires and beliefs. At the same time he strongly emphasises in the same passages the duty of children to obey their parents, and sets this before the duty of parents to their children. That also is characteristic of one who had been blameless as touching all the commandments (*Phil.* III 6), and who therefore must have gone to the fullest extreme in compliance with his father's orders before he announced that he could comply no further.

3. PERSONALITY. While Luke is very sparing of personal details, he gives us some few hints about Paul's physical characteristics as bearing on his moral influence. As an orator, he evidently used a good deal of gesture with his hands; for example, he enforced a point to the Ephesian Elders by showing them "these hands" (XX 34). When he addressed the audience at Pisidian Antioch, or the excited throng of Jews in Jerusalem, he beckoned with the hand; when he addressed Agrippa and the distinguished audience in the Roman governor's hall, he "stretched forth his hand". This was evidently a characteristic and hardly conscious feature of his more impassioned oratory; but, when more quiet and simple address was suitable (as in the opening of his speech to the Ephesian Elders, before the emotion was wrought up), or when a purely argumentative and restrained style was more likely to be effective (as in addressing the critical and cold Athenian audience, or the Roman procurator's court), no gesture is mentioned. On the other hand, in the extreme excitement at Lystra he "rent his garments"; and in the jailor's critical situation, XVI 28, Paul called

out with a loud voice. Wherever any little fact is mentioned by Luke, we can always observe some special force in it, and such details must have had real importance, when an author so brief and so impersonal as Luke mentions them ; and they are very rare in him. Alexander tried to obtain a hearing from the Ephesian mob by such a gesture ; and the din, as they howled like a lot of dervishes, is set before us strongly by the fact that speaking was impossible and gesture alone could be perceived. Peter, when he appeared to his astonished friends in Mary's house after his escape, beckoned to them to make no noise that might attract attention and betray his presence. Otherwise such gestures are mentioned only where the hand is stretched out to aid or to heal or to receive help.

Two of the most remarkable instances of Paul's power over others are prefaced by the statement that Paul "fixed his eyes on" the man (XIII 9, XIV 9, cp. XXIII 1); and this suggests that his fixed, steady gaze was a marked feature in his personality, and one source of his influence over them that were brought into relations with him. Luke frequently notes this trait. Peter tells that he fixed his gaze on the heavenly vision, XI 6 ; and he fixed his eyes on the lame man, III 4. Stephen turned his fixed gaze towards heaven, and saw it open to disclose the vision of glory to him. In these cases the power of the eye is strongly brought out. The same trait is alluded to where intense astonishment or admiration is involved, as when the bystanders gazed at Peter and John after they had healed the lame man, or Stephen's auditors stared on him as they saw his face suffused with glory, or the disciples gazed upwards as Jesus was taken away from them, or Cornelius stared at the Angel. In the Third Gospel, IV 20, the stare of the congregation in Nazareth at Jesus, when He first spoke in the synagogue after His baptism, suggests that a new glory and a new consciousness of power in Him were perceived by them. The power which looks from the eyes of an inspired person attracts and compels a corresponding fixed gaze on the part of them that are brought under his influence ; and this adds much probability to the Bezan reading in III 3, where the fixed gaze of the lame man on Peter seems to rouse the power that was latent in him. The Greek word (ἀτενίζειν) is almost peculiar to Luke, and occurs chiefly in *Acts*. Elsewhere in N.T. it is used only by Paul in II *Cor.* III 7, 13 ; and it has often seemed to me as if there were more of Lukan feeling and character in II *Cor.* than in any other of Paul's letters. A consideration of these passages must convince every one that the action implied by the word (ἀτενίζειν) is inconsistent with weakness of vision : in fact, Paul says that the Jews could not gaze fixedly on the glory of Moses' face, implying that their eyes were not strong enough. The theory which makes Paul a permanent sufferer in his eyes, unable to see distinctly persons quite near him, and repulsive to strangers on account of their hideous state (*Gal.* IV 13 f.), is hopelessly at variance with the evidence of Luke. In that word, as he uses it, the soul looks through the eyes.

The word twice occurs in the Third Gospel, once in a passage peculiar to Luke, and once when the servant-maid stared at Peter and recognised him, where her fixed gaze is not mentioned by Matthew or Mark.

CHAPTER III

THE CHURCH IN ANTIOCH

1. THE GENTILES IN THE CHURCH. (XI 19) THEY THEN THAT WERE SCATTERED THROUGH THE TRIBULATION THAT AROSE ON ACCOUNT OF STEPHEN TRAVELLED (*i.e., made missionary journeys*) AS FAR AS PHŒNICE AND CYPRUS AND ANTIOCH, SPEAKING THE WORD TO JEWS AND NONE SAVE JEWS. (20) BUT THERE WERE SOME OF THEM, MEN OF CYPRUS AND CYRENE, WHO WHEN THEY WERE COME TO ANTIOCH, USED TO SPEAK TO GREEKS ALSO, GIVING THE GOOD NEWS OF THE LORD JESUS. (21) AND THE HAND OF THE LORD WAS WITH THEM, AND A GREAT NUMBER THAT BELIEVED TURNED UNTO THE LORD.

When *Acts* was written, the Church of Antioch was only about fifty years old, but already its beginning seems to have been lost in obscurity. It had not been founded, it had grown by unrecorded and almost unobserved steps. In the dispersion of the primitive Church at Jerusalem, during the troubles ensuing on the bold action of Stephen, certain Cypriote and Cyrenaic Jews, who had been brought up in Greek lands and had wider outlook on the world than the Palestinian Jews, came to Antioch. There they made the innovation of addressing not merely Jews but also Greeks. We may understand here (1) that the words used imply successful preaching and the admission of Greeks to the Christian congregation, and (2) that such an innovation took place by slow degrees, and began in the synagogue, where Greek proselytes heard the word. The Cypriote and Cyrenaic Jews began pointedly to include these Greeks of the synagogue in their invitations, and thus a mixed body of Jews and Greeks constituted the primitive congregation of Antioch ; but the Greeks had entered through the door of the synagogue (see pp. 62, 85, 156).

In verses 19-21 the narrative for the moment goes back to a time earlier than X and XI 1-18, and starts a new thread of history from the death of Stephen (VII 60). That event was a critical one in the history of the Church. The primitive Church had clung to Jerusalem, and lived there in a state of simplicity and almost community of goods, which was an interesting phase of society, but was quite opposed to the spirit in which Jesus had said, " Go ye into all the world and preach the Gospel to the whole creation". For the time it seemed that the religion of Christ was stagnating into a sociological experiment. Stephen's vigour provoked a persecution, which dispersed itinerant missionaries over Judæa and Samaria (VIII 1-4), first among whom was Philip the colleague of Stephen. New congregations of Christians were formed in many towns (VIII 14, 25, 40, IX 31, 32, 35, 42, X 44) ; and it became necessary that, if these were to be kept in relation with the central body in Jerusalem, journeys of survey should be made by delegates from Jerusalem. The first of these journeys was made by Peter and John, who were sent to Samaria, when the news that a congregation had been formed there by Philip reached Jerusalem (VIII 14). This may be taken as a specimen of many similar journeys, one of which is recorded

(IX 32 f.) on account of the important development that took place in its course. It appears from *Acts* that Peter was the leading spirit in these journeys of organisation, which knit together the scattered congregations in Judæa and Samaria. Hence the first great question in the development of the Church was presented to him, *viz.*, whether Hebrew birth was a necessary condition for entrance into the kingdom of the Messiah and membership of the Christian Church. That question must necessarily be soon forced on the growing Church; for proselytes were not rare, and the Christian doctrine, which was preached in the synagogues, reached them. It was difficult to find any justification for making the door of the Church narrower than the door of the synagogue, and there is no record that any one explicitly advocated the view that Christianity should be confined to the chosen people, though the condition and regulations on which non-Jews should be admitted formed the subject of keen controversy in the following years.

According to *Acts*, this great question was first presented definitely to Peter in the case of a Roman centurion named Cornelius ; and a vision, which had appeared to him immediately before the question emerged, determined him to enter the house and the society of Cornelius, and set forth to him the good news, on the principle that " in every nation he that feareth God and worketh righteousness is acceptable to Him " (X 35). Peter's action was immediately confirmed by the communication of Divine grace to the audience in Cornelius's house ; and, though it was at first disputed in Jerusalem, yet Peter's defence was approved of by general consent.

But this step, though an important one, was only the first stage in a long advance that was still to be made.

Cornelius was a proselyte ; and Peter in his speech to the
assembly in his house laid it down as a condition of
reception into the Church that the non-Jew must approach
by way of the synagogue (X 35), and become "*one that
fears God*".

Without entering on the details of a matter which has
been and still is under discussion, we must here allude to
the regulations imposed on strangers who wished to enter
into relations with the Jews. Besides the proselytes who
came under the full Law and entered the community of
Moses, there was another class of persons who wished
only to enter into partial relations with the Jews. These
two classes were at a later time distinguished as "*Proselytes of
the Sanctuary*" and "*of the Gate*"; but in *Acts* the second
class is always described as "they that *fear God*".[1] *The
God-fearing proselytes* were bound to observe certain
ceremonial regulations of purity in order to be permitted
to come into any relations with the Jews; and it is
probable that these rules were the four prohibitions
enumerated in XV 28, to abstain from the flesh of animals
sacrificed to idols, and from blood, and from animals
strangled, and from marriage within the prohibited degrees
(many of which were not prohibited by Greek or Roman
law). These prohibitions stand in close relation to the
principles laid down in *Leviticus* XVII, XVIII, for the
conduct of strangers dwelling among the Israelites ; and
it would appear that they had become the recognised rule
for admission to the synagogue and for the first stage of
approximation to the Jewish communion. They stand on
a different plane from the moral law of the Ten Commandments, being rules of purity.

[1] φοβούμενοι or σεβόμενοι τὸν θεόν.

While no one, probably, urged that the Church should be confined to born Hebrews, there was a party in the Church which maintained that those non-Jews who were admitted should be required to conform to the entire " Law of God " : this was the party of " champions of the circumcision," [1] which played so great a part in the drama of subsequent years.   This party was silenced by Peter's explanation in the case of Cornelius, for the preliminary vision and the subsequent gift of grace could not be gainsaid.   But the main question was not yet definitely settled ; only an exceptional case was condoned and accepted.

The Church of Antioch then was in a somewhat anomalous condition.   It contained a number of Greeks, who were in the position of " God-fearing proselytes," but had not conformed to the entire law ; and the question was still unsettled what was their status in the Church.

2. THE COMING OF BARNABAS AND THE SUMMONING OF SAUL.   (XI 22) AND THE REPORT CONCERNING THEM CAME TO THE EARS OF THE CHURCH IN JERUSALEM ; AND THEY SENT FORTH BARNABAS AS FAR AS ANTIOCH : (23) WHO WHEN HE WAS COME, AND HAD SEEN THE GRACE OF GOD, WAS GLAD ; AND HE EXHORTED THEM ALL THAT WITH PURPOSE OF HEART THEY SHOULD CLEAVE UNTO THE LORD (24) (FOR HE WAS A GOOD MAN, AND FULL OF THE HOLY SPIRIT AND OF FAITH) ; AND MUCH PEOPLE WAS ADDED UNTO THE LORD.   (25) AND HE WENT FORTH TO TARSUS TO SEEK FOR SAUL ; (26) AND WHEN HE HAD FOUND HIM, HE BROUGHT HIM UNTO ANTIOCH.   AND IT CAME TO PASS THAT EVEN FOR A

---

[1] οἱ ἐκ περιτομῆς, XI 2, *Gal.* II 12 : "some of the sect of the Pharisees that believed," XV 5.

WHOLE YEAR THEY MET IN THE ASSEMBLY, AND TAUGHT
MUCH PEOPLE; AND THAT THE DISCIPLES WERE CALLED
"CHRISTIANS" FIRST IN ANTIOCH.

As in previous cases, an envoy was sent from the Church
in Jerusalem to survey this new congregation, and judge of
its worthiness; and Barnabas was selected for the purpose.
The same test that had been convincing in the case of
Cornelius satisfied Barnabas in Antioch: he saw the grace
of God. Then he proceeded to exhort and encourage them,
which he was qualified to do because the Divine Spirit
was in him. Sparing as Luke is of words, he feels bound
to state that Barnabas was qualified by grace for the work
(see p. 174). The result of his course of ministration[1] was
a great increase to the congregation.

Mindful of his former short experience of Saul, Barnabas
bethought himself that he was well suited to the peculiar
circumstances of the Antiochian congregation: and he
accordingly went to Tarsus, and brought Saul back with
him to Antioch. This journey must apparently have been
made in the early months of A.D. 43; and the rest of
that year was spent by the two friends in Antioch. The
date shows that the early stages of Christian history in
Antioch were slow. The congregation must have grown
insensibly, and no marked event occurred, until the attention
of the Church in Jerusalem was called to its existence. The
one important fact about it was that it came into existence
in this peculiar way. But with the advent of Barnabas and
Saul, its history enters on a new phase. It became the
centre of progress and of historical interest in the Church.

It lies in Luke's style to give no reason why Barnabas
summoned Saul to Antioch. This historian records the

---

[1] παρεκάλει, *imperfect.*

essential facts as they occurred; but he does not obtrude on the reader his own private conception as to causes or motives. But we cannot doubt that Barnabas, who became Saul's sponsor at Jerusalem (IX 27), and related to the Apostles the circumstances of his conversion, knew that God had already called him "to preach Him among the Gentiles" (*Gal.* I 16), and recognised that this congregation of the Gentiles was the proper sphere for Saul's work. We find in Barnabas's action the proof of the correctness of Paul's contention in *Epist. Gal.*, that his aim as an Apostle had been directed from the first towards the Gentiles; his sphere was already recognised.

As we shall see later, Paul must have spent nearly eight years at Tarsus. Why are these eight years a blank? Why were they such a contrast to the crowded hours of the period that was just beginning? On our hypothesis as to the meaning of Luke's silence, we conclude that Paul was still not fully conscious of the full meaning of his mission; he was still bound in the fetters of Judaic consistency, and acted as if the door of the synagogue was the portal through which the Nations must find their way into the Church. He had not yet learned, or at least he had not yet so fully shaken himself free from the prejudices of education and tradition as to act on the knowledge, that God "had opened a door of faith unto the nations" (XIV 27, p. 85).

A point in Luke's style here deserves note. He has mentioned in IX 30 that Saul was sent away to Tarsus; and he now takes up the thread from that point, saying that Barnabas went to Tarsus to seek for Saul. He implies that the reader must understand Tarsus to have been Saul's head-quarters during the intervening period. Not merely does XI 25 require one to look back, but also IX 30

requires one to look forward ; each is the complement of
the other, and the two together hit off a long period during
which no critical event had to be recorded.   The same
period, together with the following year in Antioch, is
described by Paul himself, *Gal.* I 21, 22 : " Then I came
into the climes of Syria and Cilicia : and I continued to be
unknown by face to the churches of Judæa, but they only
heard say, ' He that once persecuted us now preacheth the
faith ' ".   Paul and Luke complete each other, and make
up a picture of over ten years of quiet work within the
range of the synagogue and its influence.

The words of *v.* 25 seem harsh until one takes them as
a direct backward reference to IX 30, and as implying a
statement about the intervening period.   The Bezan Com-
mentator, not catching the style of Luke, inserts an explanatory clause, " hearing that Saul is in Tarsus," which
rounds off the sense here by cutting away the necessity of
finding in XI 25 the completion of a period of history
whose beginning is recorded in IX 30.

The term " Christians " attests that the congregation
became a familiar subject of talk, and probably of gossip
and scandal, in the city ; for obviously the name originated
outside the brotherhood.   The Brethren, then, were talked
of in popular society as " they that are connected with
Christos " : such a title could not originate with the Jews,
to whom " the Christ " was sacred.   The name Christos
therefore must have been the most prominent in the
expressions by which the Greek Brethren described or
defined their faith to their pagan neighbours.   The latter,
doubtless, got no clear idea of what this Christos
was : some took Christos as one of the strange gods
whom they worshipped (XVII 18); others took him as

their leader (p. 254). In any case the name belongs to popular slang.

In accordance with the tendency of popular language to find some meaning for strange words, the strange term Christos was vulgarly modified to Chrêstos, the Greek adjective meaning " good, useful," which seemed to popular fancy a more suitable and natural name for a leader or a deity. " Chrêstians " was the form in which the name was often used ; and it occurs in inscriptions.

3. THE ANTIOCHIAN COLLECTION FOR THE POOR OF JERUSALEM. (XI 27) AND AT THIS PERIOD THERE CAME DOWN FROM JERUSALEM PROPHETS TO ANTIOCH. (28) AND THERE STOOD UP ONE OF THEM, AGABUS BY NAME, AND SIGNIFIED BY THE SPIRIT THAT THERE SHOULD BE GREAT FAMINE OVER ALL THE WORLD ; WHICH CAME TO PASS IN THE DAYS OF CLAUDIUS. (29) AND THE DISCIPLES ACCORDING TO THE MEANS OF THE INDIVIDUAL ARRANGED TO SEND CONTRIBUTIONS FOR RELIEF TO THE BRETHREN SETTLED IN JUDÆA. (30) AND THIS TOO THEY DID, AND DESPATCHED *the relief* TO THE ELDERS BY THE HAND OF BARNABAS AND SAUL. (XII 25) AND BARNABAS AND SAUL FULFILLED THE MINISTRATION OF RELIEF, AND RETURNED FROM JERU-SALEM BRINGING AS COMPANION JOHN SURNAMED MARK.

Luke's brief statement about the famine is declared by Dr. Schürer to be unhistorical, improbable, and uncorro-borated by other evidence.[1] Opinions differ widely ; for the famine seems to me to be singularly well attested, considering the scantiness of evidence for this period. Suetonius alludes to *assiduæ sterilitates* causing famine-

---

[1] *Eine ungeschichtliche Generalisirung,* and again, *ist, wie an sich unwahrscheinlich, so auch nirgends bezeugt (Jüd. Volk* I p. 474).

prices under Claudius, while Dion Cassius and Tacitus speak of two famines in Rome, and famine in Rome implied dearth in the great corn-growing countries of the Mediterranean ; Eusebius mentions famine in Greece, and an inscription perhaps refers to famine in Asia Minor.[1] Thus wide-spread dearth over the Roman world is fully attested independently ; beyond the Roman world our evidence does not extend. Dr. Schürer seems to require a distinct statement that a famine took place in the same year all over Europe, Asia, and Africa. But that is too hard on Luke, for he merely says that famine occurred over the whole (civilised) world in the time of Claudius : of course the year varied in different lands.

The great famine in Palestine occurred probably in A.D. 46. The commentators as a rule endeavour, by straining Josephus, or by quoting the authority of Orosius, to make out that the famine took place in 44, and even that it occasioned the persecution by Herod.

The eagerness to date the famine in 44 arises from a mistake as to the meaning and order of the narrative of *Acts*. Between XI 30 and XII 25 there is interposed an account of Herod's persecution and his miserable death, events which belong to the year 44 ; and it has been supposed that Luke conceives these events as happening while Barnabas and Saul were in Jerusalem. But that is not the case. Luke describes the prophecy of Agabus, and the assessment imposed by common arrangement on the whole congregation in proportion to their individual resources. Then he adds that this arrangement was carried out and the whole sum sent to Jerusalem. The

[1] Le Bas-Waddington no. 1162, *Studia Biblica* IV p. 52 f.

process thus described was not an instantaneous subscription The money was probably collected by weekly contributions, for the congregation was not rich, and coin was not plentiful in Syrian cities. This collection would take a considerable time, as we gather both from the analogy of the later Pauline contribution (p. 288), and from the fact that the famine was still in the future, and no necessity for urgent haste existed. The arrangements were made beforehand in full reliance on the prophecy ; but there is no reason to think that the money was used until the famine actually began, and relief was urgently needed. The manner of relief must, of course, have been by purchasing and distributing corn, for it would have shown criminal incapacity to send gold to a starving city; and the corn would not be given by any rational person, until the famine was at its height. When Sir Richard Wallace relieved the distress in Paris after the siege, he did not content himself with telegraphing money from London, nor yet with distributing gold to the starving people in Paris. He brought food and gave it. As he did, so we may be sure did the Antiochian delegates do ; and no rational person will suppose that the corn was brought to Jerusalem until the famine was actually raging. But in a land where transport was difficult, preparations took time ; and Luke states at the outset the general course of the preparations which the Divine revelation aroused.

Thereafter, before describing the actual distribution of relief in Jerusalem, the author's method requires him to bring down the general narrative of events in Jerusalem and Judæa to the point when the famine began ; and then at last he mentions the actual administering of the relief. He, therefore, tells about the persecution of Herod (which took place near the time when Agabus prophesied), and about Herod's death ; and then at last he mentions the execution of the Antiochian design and the return of the delegates to their own city.

As thus interpreted, Luke's chronology harmonises admirably with Josephus. Agabus came to Antioch in the winter of 43-44 ; and in the early part of 44 Herod's persecution occurred, followed by his death, probably in the autumn.   In 45 the harvest was probably not good, and provisions grew scarce in the country ; then, when the harvest of 46 failed, famine set in, and relief was urgently required, and was administered by Barnabas and Saul. It is an interesting coincidence that relief was given liberally in Jerusalem by Queen Helena (mother of Izates, King of Adiabene), who bought corn in Egypt and figs in Cyprus, and brought them to Jerusalem for distribution. She came to Jerusalem in 45, and her visit lasted through the season of famine ; she had a palace in Jerusalem.   The way in which she imparted relief to the starving people illustrates the work that Barnabas and Saul had to perform.

The service in Jerusalem must have occupied Barnabas and Saul for a considerable time.   They acted as administrators ($\delta\iota\acute{a}\kappa o\nu o\iota$) of the relief ; and it becomes evident how much is implied in the words of XI 29, XII 25 from the comparison of VI 1 " the daily ministration " of food to the poor.   The same term ($\delta\iota a\kappa o\nu\acute{\iota}a$) that is used in these cases is applied (with $\tau o\hat{\upsilon}$ $\lambda\acute{o}\gamma o\upsilon$ understood) to the steady constant work of a missionary or an apostle, XX 24, XXI 19, I 17, 25, VI 4.   The Antiochian delegates did not merely act as carriers of money ; they stayed in Jerusalem through the famine and acted as providers and distributors, using all the opportunity of encouraging and comforting the dis-

tressed that was thus afforded.   In this way Saul's second
visit to Jerusalem was an important moment in the development of the Church, and is related as such by Luke : it
united far-distant parts of the Church at a great crisis ; it
gave to the poor in Jerusalem the sense of brotherhood
with the Antiochian brethren, and to the Antiochian congregation that consciousness of native life and power which
comes only from noble work nobly done.   But for this
end it was necessary that the work should be done from
first to last by the Antiochian congregation, and that every
starving disciple in Jerusalem should realise that he owed
his relief to his brethren at Antioch.   Great part of the
effect would have been lost, if the delegates had merely
handed a sum of money to the leaders in Jerusalem to dis-
tribute ; and the author, who is so sparing of words, does
not fail to assure us that the two delegates " completed the
ministration " before they returned to Antioch.

It must be noticed that only the Elders at Jerusalem are
here mentioned, whereas in XV Paul and Barnabas were
sent to the Apostles and Elders.   The marked difference
may probably be connected with the author's conception of
the appropriate duties of each.   In XV, when a matter of
conduct and principle was in question, the Apostles were
primarily concerned ; but when it was a matter of the distribution of food, the Apostles were not concerned, for it was
right that they should not " serve tables," but " continue in
the ministry of the word " (VI 2-4).   It would have been
quite natural to say that the contributions were sent to the
congregation, or to the Brethren, in Jerusalem ; and it is
apparent that here the Elders represent the congregation of
Jerusalem as directors of its practical working, while in XV
the Apostles and Elders represent the Church in every aspect.

The omission of the Apostles in XI 29 is commonly explained on other grounds, not very honourable to them. Even Lightfoot says: "the storm of persecution had broken over the Church of Jerusalem. One leading Apostle had been put to death ; another, rescued by a miracle, had fled for his life. It is probable that every Christian of rank had retired from the city. No mention is made of the Twelve ; the salutations of the Gentile Apostles are received by 'the Elders'. They arrived charged with alms for the relief of the poor brethren of Jerusalem. Having deposited these in trustworthy hands, they would depart with all convenient speed." But Luke expressly says that the administration of the relief was performed in detail by the two Antiochian delegates (XII 25) ; and one can only marvel that Lightfoot ever stooped to the idea that they sneaked into the city and sneaked out hastily again, leaving the poor without a single "Christian of rank" to minister to them. Nor is there any good reason to think that the Apostles all fled from Jerusalem, and left the disciples to look after themselves. It was not men like that who carried Christianity over the empire within a few years. Such an act of cowardice should not be attributed to the Apostles without distinct evidence ; and here the evidence tells in the opposite direction : (1) at the far more serious persecution following the death of Stephen, "all were scattered abroad except the Apostles" (VIII 1): (2) it is implied that " James and the Brethren" were in Jerusalem, when Peter escaped from prison and retired (XII 17) ; and immediately after, Herod went away and the persecution was at an end. The author of *Acts* evidently had the impression that the guidance of affairs rested with the Apostles in Jerusalem ; and they are conceived by him as being there permanently, except when absent on a special mission.

It is not mere accidental collocation, that immediately on the return of Barnabas and Saul comes the record of the flourishing state of the Church in Antioch, with its band of prophets and teachers (XIII 1): the result of their noble work in Jerusalem was apparent in the fuller and more perfect manifestation of Divine power and grace to the Church in Antioch.

Further, when Paul had founded a group of new churches in the four provinces, Galatia, Asia, Macedonia, Achaia, he, as the crowning act of organisation, instituted a general collection among them for the poor at Jerusalem ; and arranged that representatives should go up along with himself to Jerusalem bearing the money. His object was both to strengthen the separate congregations by good work, and to strengthen the whole Church by bringing its scattered parts into personal relations of service and help. We cannot doubt that it was his experience of the immense effect produced by the first Divinely ordered contribution which led Paul to attach such importance and devote so much trouble to the organisation of the second general contribution ; and he uses the same word to indicate the management of the second fund that Luke uses of the first (διακονεῖν, II Cor. VIII 19).[1]

The preceding notes have shown how much is contained in the brief record of Luke : all the main points in the execution of the scheme of relief are touched in the few words XI 29, 30, XII 25. But we are not reduced to this single account of the mission to Jerusalem. Paul, in writing to the Galatians, also mentions it ; his reason for alluding to it lay in certain incidental and unessential facts that occurred at Jerusalem ; but he tells enough to show what

[1] See Mr. Rendall's admirable paper in *Expositor*, Nov., 1893.

was the primary object of the visit. In describing his intercourse with the older Apostles, he mentions his second visit to Jerusalem in the following terms (I expand the concise language of Paul to bring out the close-packed meaning) :—

(*Gal.* II 1) THEN IN THE FOURTEENTH YEAR *after it pleased God to call me*, I WENT UP AGAIN TO JERUSALEM WITH BARNABAS, AND TOOK TITUS ALSO AS COMPANION. (2) NOW *I may explain that* I WENT UP ON ACCOUNT OF A REVELATION (*which shows how completely my action was directly guided by the Divine will, and how independent it was of any orders or instructions from the Apostles*). AND I COMMUNICATED TO THEM WITH A VIEW TO CONSULTA-TION THE GOSPEL WHICH I CONTINUE PREACHING AMONG THE GENTILES, BUT *I did so* PRIVATELY TO THOSE WHO WERE RECOGNISED AS THE LEADING SPIRITS, *not publicly to the whole body of Apostles ; since the latter course would have had the appearance of consulting the official governing body, as if I felt it a duty to seek advice from them ; whereas private consultation was a purely voluntary act.* MY PUR-POSE IN THIS CONSULTATION WAS TO CARRY WITH ME THE LEADING SPIRITS OF THE CHURCH, SINCE MISUNDER-STANDING OR WANT OF COMPLETE APPROVAL ON THEIR PART MIGHT ENDANGER OR FRUSTRATE MY EVANGELISTIC WORK WHETHER IN THE FUTURE OR THE PAST, *if doubt or dispute arose as to the rights of my converts to full member-ship in the Church without further ceremony.* (3) NOW, *as I have touched on this point, I may mention parenthetically that* NOT EVEN WAS MY COMPANION TITUS, GREEK AS HE WAS, REQUIRED TO SUBMIT TO CIRCUMCISION, *much less was the general principle laid down that the Jewish rite was a necessary preliminary to the full membership of the*

Church. (4) FURTHER, THE OCCASION *of my consulting the leading Apostles* WAS BECAUSE OF CERTAIN INSINUAT-ING FALSE BRETHREN, WHO ALSO CREPT INTO OUR SOCIETY IN AN UNAVOWED WAY TO ACT THE SPY ON OUR FREEDOM (WHICH WE FREE CHRISTIANS CON-TINUE ENJOYING THROUGHOUT MY MINISTRY), IN ORDER TO MAKE US SLAVES *to the ritual which they count necessary.* (5) BUT NOT FOR AN HOUR DID WE YIELD TO THESE FALSE BRETHREN BY COMPLYING WITH THEIR IDEAS, OR EXPRESSING AGREEMENT WITH THEM ; AND OUR FIRMNESS THEN WAS INTENDED TO SECURE THAT THE GOSPEL IN ITS TRUE FORM SHOULD CONTINUE IN LASTING FREEDOM FOR YOU *to enjoy* (6) BUT FROM THE RECOGNISED LEADERS—HOW DIS-TINGUISHED SOEVER WAS THEIR CHARACTER IS NOT NOW THE POINT ; GOD ACCEPTETH NOT MAN'S PERSON —THE RECOGNISED LEADERS, I SAY, IMPARTED NO NEW INSTRUCTION TO ME ; (7) BUT, ON THE CONTRARY, PERCEIVING THAT I THROUGHOUT MY MINISTRY AM CHARGED SPECIALLY WITH THE MISSION TO FOREIGN (NON-JEWISH) NATIONS AS PETER IS WITH THE JEWISH MISSION—(8) FOR HE THAT WORKED FOR PETER TO THE APOSTOLATE OF THE CIRCUMCISION WORKED ALSO FOR ME TO BE THE MISSIONARY TO THE GENTILES— (9) AND PERCEIVING *from the actual facts* THE GRACE THAT HAD BEEN GIVEN ME, THEY, JAMES AND CEPHAS AND JOHN, THE RECOGNISED PILLARS OF THE CHURCH, GAVE PLEDGES TO ME AND TO BARNABAS OF A JOINT SCHEME OF WORK, OURS TO BE DIRECTED TO THE GENTILES, WHILE THEIRS WAS TO THE JEWS. (10) ONE CHARGE ALONE THEY GAVE US, TO REMEMBER THE POOR *brethren at Jerusalem,* A DUTY WHICH AS A

MATTER OF FACT I *at that time* MADE IT MY SPECIAL
OBJECT TO PERFORM.

As is pointed out elsewhere in full detail, the concluding
sentence defines the object which Paul carried out in
Jerusalem : other events were incidental.   This journey,
therefore, is declared in *Epist. Gal.* to have been made
"according to revelation," and in *Acts* the exact circumstances of the revelation are narrated ; the object of the
visit is described in *Acts* as being to relieve the distress of
the poor brethren in Jerusalem, and in *Epist. Gal.* Paul says
he directed his attention specially to helping the poor
brethren ; another purpose is said in *Epist. Gal.* to have
been achieved on this journey, *v.* 3, but Paul immediately
adds that this other purpose was carried out as a mere
private piece of business, and implies thereby that it was
not the primary or official purpose of the journey.

How graceful and delicate is the compliment which the
older Apostles paid to Paul ! "the only advice and instruction which we have to give is that you continue to do what
you have been zealously doing," so they spoke at the conclusion of his visit.   And in what a gentlemanly spirit
does Paul refer to that visit ! His object is to prove to
the Galatians that, on his visits to Jerusalem, he received
nothing in the way of instruction or commission from the
older Apostles ; and to do this he gives an account of his
visits.   When he comes to the second visit he might have
said in the tone of downright and rather coarse candour,
" So far from receiving on this occasion, I was sent by
Divine revelation to be the giver ".   But not even in this
hot and hasty letter does he swerve from his tone of respect
and admiration, or assume in the slightest degree a tone of
superiority to Peter and James.   The facts are all there to

show the real situation; but they are put so quietly and allusively (the revelation in verse 2, the object in verse 10), as to avoid all appearance of boasting in what was really a very legitimate cause of satisfaction, and even of self-gratulation. It is precisely because on his second visit Paul was so obviously not the recipient, that he appeals to it with such perfect confidence as proving his independence.

Here as everywhere we find that *Acts* supplements and explains the incidents and arguments used by Paul in his letter. And we see that the influence which we have just ascribed to the visit in promoting the unity and solidarity of the whole Church is fully confirmed by Paul in verse 9; it resulted in a formal recognition by the older Apostles of the co-ordinate Apostolate of the two Antiochian delegates.

The same party in the Church which had criticised Peter's conduct to Cornelius, was discontented with the conduct of Barnabas and Saul to their companion, Titus; but in the circumstances their discontent did not take public action, though it was so apparent as to put Saul on his guard, and once more they seem to have acquiesced in an exceptional case, as they did in that of Cornelius. But it was now becoming evident that two distinct and opposed opinions existed in the Church, and were likely to come to open conflict; and Saul privately satisfied himself that the leaders were in agreement with himself on the subject of difference.

But why is *Acts* silent about this? Simply because it never came to an open discussion, and therefore did not reach the proper level of importance. Luke confines himself to the great steps in development. Nor is it strange that Titus is not mentioned by Luke. In carrying the relief to Jerusalem, it is obvious that Barnabas and Saul must have had assistants. The work was one of considerable magnitude, and involved a good deal of organisation. We may gather from Luke that the two envoys were entrusted with the management ; but the whole details of purchase, transport, and distribution lie outside of his conception and plan. The essential fact for his purpose was that relief was sent by the congregation in Antioch (XI 30), and its distribution personally carried out by Paul and Barnabas in Jerusalem (XII 25) ; and he tells us no more. In his letter Paul says that Titus was a privately selected associate and not an official ; and we may confidently add that he was one of the assistants who were needed to carry out the work described in *Acts* (see also p. 170).

The only strange fact in reference to Titus, is that he nowhere appears in *Acts ;* and that is equally hard to explain on every theory. Clearly he played a considerable part in the early history of the Church (as Luke himself did) ; and, on our hypothesis of Luke's historical insight and power of selecting and grouping details, the complete omission of Titus's name must be intentional, just as the silence about Luke is intentional. A suggestion to explain the omission is made on p. 390.

The situation on this visit is strikingly different from that described in *Acts* XV as existing at the next visit (see Chap. VII). Paul has here private communications with the three leading Apostles in prudent preparation against future difficulties. In the later stage, public meetings to hear the recital of his and Barnabas's experiences among the Gentiles are followed by a formal Council, in which " the leading Apostles stand forth as the champions of Gentile liberty ".

We find ourselves obliged to regard this visit as more

important than is generally believed. Canon Farrar, who may be quoted as a clear and sensible exponent of the accepted view, calls it " so purely an episode in the work of St. Paul, that in the Epistle to the Galatians he passes it over without a single allusion ". According to our view, if it had been a mere episode without influence on the development of the Church, Luke would have passed it unmentioned ; but it was a step of great consequence in the development of the Antiochian congregation and of the Church as a whole ; and therefore it required a place in this history.

The wonderful revelation described by Paul himself in his second letter to the Corinthians XII 2-4 took place in the fourteenth year before A.D. 56, when that letter was written ; and therefore probably occurred in 43 or 44. This brings us near the period when Agabus came to Antioch ; but all speculation is barred by the description : he " heard unspeakable words which it is not lawful for man to utter ". Another revelation, however, can with certainty be ascribed to this visit, and, specially, to its concluding days.

4. THE RETURN FROM JERUSALEM TO ANTIOCH. (XXII 17) WHEN I HAD RETURNED TO JERUSALEM, AND WHILE I PRAYED IN THE TEMPLE, I FELL INTO A TRANCE, (18) AND SAW HIM SAYING UNTO ME, " MAKE HASTE, AND GET THEE QUICKLY OUT OF JERUSALEM ; BECAUSE THEY WILL NOT RECEIVE OF THEE TESTIMONY CONCERNING ME ". (19) AND I SAID, " LORD, THEY THEMSELVES KNOW THAT I IMPRISONED AND BEAT IN EVERY SYNAGOGUE THEM THAT BE-LIEVED ON THEE : (20) AND WHEN THE BLOOD OF STEPHEN THY WITNESS WAS SHED, I ALSO WAS

STANDING BY, AND CONSENTING, AND KEEPING THE
GARMENTS OF THEM THAT SLEW HIM (*and therefore
they must see that some great thing has happened to con-
vince me*)". (21) AND HE SAID UNTO ME, "DEPART:
FOR I WILL SEND THEE FORTH FAR HENCE UNTO THE
NATIONS ".

Let us clearly conceive the probable situation at
that time. In the famine-stricken city it is not to be
supposed that Barnabas and Saul confined their relief to
professing Christians, and let all who were not Christians
starve. Christian feeling, ordinary humanity, and policy
(in the last respect Paul was as little likely to err as in
the others), alike forbade an absolute distinction. The
Antiochian delegates must have had many opportunities
of aiding their Jewish brethren, though they addressed
their work specially to their Brethren in the Church;
and the result must have been that they occupied a
position of peculiar advantage for the time, not merely
in the Church (where the respect and honour paid them
shines through *Gal.* II 1-10), but also in the city as a
whole. Now it was part of Paul's missionary method
not to insist where there was no opening, and not to
draw back where the door was open. It might well
seem that the remarkable circumstances of his mission
to Jerusalem, the revelation by which it was ordered,
and the advantage it secured to him in the city, were
the opening of a door through which he might power-
fully influence his own people. The thought could not
fail to occur to Paul; and the remarkable incident described in XXII 17-21 shows that it was in his mind.

This incident is usually assigned to the first visit which
Paul paid to Jerusalem after his conversion. But he does

not say or even imply that it was his first visit; and we must be guided by the suitability of the circumstances mentioned to the facts recorded about the various visits. Now Luke gives a totally different reason for his departure from Jerusalem at the first visit: he attributes it to the prudence of the Brethren, who learned that a conspiracy was made to slay him, and wished both to save him and to avoid the general danger that would arise for all, if persecution broke out against one. The revelation of XXII 18, to which Paul attributes his departure, suits the first visit very badly; but such discrepancy does not count for much with the modern interpreters, orthodox and "critical" alike, who, having achieved the feat of identifying the second visit of *Gal.* II 1-10 with the third visit of *Acts* XV (pp. 59, 154 f.), have naturally ceased to expect agreement between Luke and Paul on such matters. Accordingly, Lightfoot actually quotes the discrepancy between XXII 18 f. and IX 29 f. to illustrate and defend the discrepancy between *Gal.* II 2 and *Acts* XV 4.

Again, the reasoning of XXII 20, 21, is not suitable to the first visit. Paul argues that circumstances make him a peculiarly telling witness to the Jews of the power of Jesus: and the reply is that Jesus will send him far hence to the Nations. Now, the first visit was followed, not by an appeal to the Nations, but by many years of quiet uneventful work in Cilicia and Antioch, within the circle of the synagogue and its influence. But this revelation points to the immediate "opening of a door of belief to the Nations"; and that did not take place until Paul went to Paphos and South Galatia (XIV 27, pp. 41, 85).

To place this revelation on the first visit leads to

hopeless embarrassment, and to one of those discrepancies which the orthodox historians, like Lightfoot, labour to minimise, while the critical historians naturally and fairly argue that such discrepancies prove *Acts* to be not the work of Paul's pupil and friend, but a work of later origin. On this point I can only refer to what is said on p. 15; on the principle there laid down, we cannot connect XXII 17 f. with IX 28 f.

On the other hand this revelation suits excellently the state of matters which we have just described at the conclusion of the second visit. Paul was tempted by the favourable opportunity in Jerusalem; and his personal desire always turned strongly towards his Jewish brethren (*Rom.* IX 1-5). He prayed in the temple: he saw Jesus: he pleaded with Jesus, representing his fitness for this work: and he was ordered to depart at once, "for I will send thee forth far hence to the Nations". Thereupon he returned to Antioch; and in a few days or weeks a new revelation to the Antiochian officials sent him on his mission to the West, and opened the door of belief to the Nations.

One objection to this view is likely to be made. Many infer from XXII 18 that the visit was short. But there is no implication as to the duration of the visit. The words merely show that Paul was thinking of a longer stay, when the vision bade him hasten away forthwith. The second visit, according to Lightfoot's supposition, was even shorter than the first, but on our view it began when the failure of harvest in 46 turned scarcity into famine, and it probably lasted until the beginning of 47.

Our reference of XXII 17 to the second visit is corroborated by the reading of the two great uncial

MSS. in XII 25, "returned to Jerusalem": this seems to be an alteration made deliberately by an editor, who, because these passages referred to the same visit, tampered with the text of XII 25 to bring it into verbal conformity with XXII 17.

5. THE MISSION OF BARNABAS AND SAUL. (XIII I) NOW THERE WAS AT ANTIOCH, CONNECTED WITH "THE CHURCH,"[1] A BODY OF PROPHETS AND TEACHERS, BARNABAS, SYMEON (SURNAMED NIGER), AND LUCIUS (HE OF CYRENE), WITH MANAËN (FOSTER-BROTHER OF HEROD THE TETRARCH) AND SAUL. (2) AS THESE WERE LEADING A LIFE OF RELIGIOUS DUTIES AND FASTS, THE HOLY SPIRIT SAID, "SEPARATE ME BARNABAS AND SAUL FOR THE WORK WHEREUNTO I HAVE CALLED THEM". (3) THEN THEY (*i.e.*, *the Church*) HELD A SPECIAL FAST, AND PRAYED, AND LAID THEIR HANDS UPON THEM, AND GAVE THEM LEAVE TO DEPART.

A new stage in the development of the Antiochian Church is here marked. It was no longer a mere "congregation"; it was now "the Church" in Antioch; and there was in it a group of prophets and teachers to whom the grace of God was given.

There is indubitably a certain feeling that a new start is made at this point; but it is only through blindness to the style of a great historian that some commentators take this as the beginning of a new document. The subject demanded here a fresh start, for a great step in the development of the early Church was about to be narrated, "the opening of a door to the Gentiles" (XIV 27). The author emphasised this step beyond all others, because he was himself a Gentile; and the develop-

[1] Prof. Armitage Robinson, quoted in *Church in R. E.*, p. 52.

ment of the Church through the extension of Christian influence was the guiding idea of his historical work.

Probably the variation between the connecting particles (καί and τε) marks a distinction between three prophets, Barnabas, Symeon and Lucius, and two teachers, Manaën and Saul. In *Acts* VI 5, the list of seven deacons is given without any such variation; and it seems a fair inference that the variation here is intentional.[1] The distinction between the qualifications required in prophets and in teachers is emphasised by Paul in I *Cor.* XII 28. As regards Barnabas and Saul their difference in gifts and qualifications appears clearly in other places. Everywhere Saul is the preacher and teacher, Barnabas is the senior and for a time the leader on that account.

There is a marked distinction between the general rule of life in *v.* 2, and the single special ceremony in *v.* 3. An appreciable lapse of time is implied in *v.* 2: after the two envoys returned from Jerusalem, the regular course of Church life went on for a time; and, so long as everything was normal, the historian finds nothing to relate. The prophets and teachers had regular duties to which their energies were devoted; and they practised in their life a certain regular rule of fasting. They were not like the Elders, who were chosen as representative members of the congregation; they were marked out by the Divine grace as fitted for religious duties in the congregation. The "work" in *v.* 2 is defined in the subsequent narrative (XIII 41, XIV 26, XV 3, 38, etc.) as preaching the Gospel in new regions outside of the province Syria and Cilicia, in which there already existed Christian communities.

What is the subject in *v.* 3? It cannot be the five

---

[1] Compare Mr. Page's note on the grouping of the list in I 13.

officials just mentioned, because they cannot be said to lay their hands on two of themselves. Evidently some awkward change of subject takes place ; and the simplest interpretation is that the Church as a whole held a special service for this solemn purpose. *Codex Bezæ* makes all clear by inserting the nominative " all" (πάντες) ; and on our view this well-chosen addition gives the interpretation that was placed in the second century on a harsh and obscure passage. Similarly in XV 2 it is meant that the congregation appointed the delegates to Jerusalem; and the reader is expected to supply the nominative, though it has not occurred in the immediately preceding sentence. It seemed to the author so obvious that such action was performed by universal consent, that he did not feel any need to express the nominative. Such a way of thinking was possible only at a very early time. During the second century (if not even earlier) the action of officials began to supersede that of the whole congregation in such matters ; and, when even a beginning had been made, it could no longer be assumed as self-evident that such actions as XIII 3, XV 2, were performed by the congregation ; and the writer would necessarily express the nominative. The Bezan Reviser belonged to ,the period when the change had begun and the need of expressing the nominative was felt ; but he lived before the time when official action had regularly superseded that of the congregation, for in that case he would have taken the officials in this case to be the agents (as many modern commentators understand the passage).

What was the effect of the public ceremony described in *v.* 3 ? The high authority of Lightfoot answers that it constituted Barnabas and Saul as Apostles. He acknow-

ledges that Saul's "conversion may indeed be said in some
sense to have been his call to the Apostleship. But the
actual investiture, the completion of his call, took place
some years later at Antioch (*Acts* XIII 2)." He considers
that Barnabas and Saul were only prophets before this,
and did not become Apostles until they were elevated to
that rank by their "consecration to the office" at Antioch
(*Ed. Galat.* p. 96).

Our view, on the contrary, is that Barnabas and Saul
were Apostles before this. The Apostle was always appointed by God and not by the Church. The proof of
Apostleship lay in the possession of apostolic message and
powers, conversion of others and performance of signs.
It is an historical anachronism to attribute to this period
such belief in the efficacy of a Church-ceremony. Moreover, in XXII 17, 21, and XXVI 17, Paul claims to have
been an Apostle from his conversion, and represents his
work in Cilicia and Syria as an Apostolate. In *Gal.* I he
declares that his message came direct from God at his
conversion. Further, there is no sign in XIII 2, 3, that this
"consecration" by the Church was more efficacious than
the original Divine call : the ceremony merely blessed
Barnabas and Saul for a special work, which was definitely
completed in the next three years. In XIV 26 the work
for which they had been committed to the grace of God in
XIII 2 is declared to be fulfilled ; and they returned to
their ordinary circle of duties in the Church at Antioch.

The last word in verse 3 should not be "sent them away"
(as in the Authorised and Revised Versions). The Spirit
sent them away (verse 4) ; and the Church released them
from their regular duties and bade them "God-speed". The
Greek verb (ἀπέλυσαν, like the Latin *dimittere*) is used of

the superior giving his visitor leave to depart (for a visitor in the East is considered to be paying his respects, and does not presume to depart without formal permission to go), or of a host allowing his guests to depart, or of a commanding officer giving soldiers honourable dismissal after their term of service. The correct rendering of this term will prove important at a later stage (p. 155).

Note. Date of the famine. Orosius VII 6 puts it in the fourth year of Claudius, which began January 25, A.D. 44. But Orosius's dates at this point are put one year too early owing to a mistake in adapting to Claudius's years a series of events arranged in his authority according to a different system of chronology; this kind of mistake is known to have been frequently made by ancient chroniclers, and is proved in Orosius's case by the fact that he assigns to the tenth year of Claudius a famine at Rome which Tacitus *Ann.* XII 43 places in A.D. 51. We therefore take Orosius as an authority for dating the commencement of the famine in 45. Josephus mentions the famine as having occurred while Tiberius Alexander was procurator of Judæa; and there is general agreement that Alexander's administration lasted from 46 to 48 : though the time when it began was not *absolutely* certain, July 45 is the earliest admissible date, and 46 is far more probable: his predecessor Cuspius Fadus was sent by Claudius in 44, and a good deal occurred during his office. But Josephus also mentions the famine in connection with Queen Helena's arrival in 45. Helena, however, seems to have remained a considerable time, and Josephus's words are in perfect accord with our view that scarcity began with a bad harvest in 45.

In the preceding chapter, Lightfoot's view is quoted according to his edition of *Gal.*, where he says that Barnabas and Saul had come to Jerusalem and returned to Antioch before Herod's death. Since the chapter was in type, I notice that in a posthumous essay "printed from lecture notes" he dates the famine 45; but that seems hardly consistent with his edition, and as he republished his edition without change throughout his life, it must represent his mature opinion. Perhaps he means that Paul and Barnabas brought the famine-money to Jerusalem a year or more before the famine began, which we cannot accept as a natural or a useful procedure.

CHAPTER IV

THE MISSIONARY JOURNEY OF BARNABAS AND SAUL

1. CYPRUS AND SALAMIS. (XIII 4) THEY ACCORD-
INGLY, BEING SENT FORTH BY THE HOLY SPIRIT, CAME
DOWN TO *the harbour* SELEUCEIA, AND THENCE SAILED
AWAY TO CYPRUS; (5) AND WHEN THEY REACHED
SALAMIS THEY BEGAN TO PROCLAIM THE WORD OF GOD
IN THE SYNAGOGUES OF THE JEWS; AND THEY HAD
JOHN ALSO AS A SUBORDINATE. (6) AND THEY MADE A
missionary PROGRESS THROUGH THE WHOLE ISLAND
UNTIL *they reached* PAPHOS.

The harbour is mentioned, according to Luke's common
custom (XIV 25, XVIII 18, XVI 11). When he has
once mentioned the harbour of any city, he omits it on a
subsequent occasion (cp. XX 6 with XVI 11). The
failure to name the harbour of Berœa is remarkable
(XVII 14); doubtless there is some reason for it.

As they were able to make the harbour of Salamis, on
the south coast, they were not impeded by westerly winds,
which commonly blew throughout the summer (see p. 298).
With such winds, they would have run for the Cilician
coast, and worked along it westward with the aid of land-
breezes and the current (p. 299), till they could run across
to the north coast of Cyprus, as Barnabas had to do on his
next journey (if the *Periodoi Barnabæ* can be trusted). But

they probably started on the opening of the sailing season (March 5).

John Mark is brought before the reader's notice here in a curiously incidental way. He came with Barnabas and Saul from Antioch (see XII 25); why should he not be mentioned at the outset? A superficial view might see want of method in this apparently haphazard reference to the third traveller. But surely the object is to emphasise the secondary character of John Mark, in view of what was to happen in Pamphylia: he was not essential to the expedition; he had not been selected by the Spirit; he had not been formally delegated by the Church of Antioch; he was an extra hand, taken by Barnabas and Saul on their own responsibility. This obviated the criticism that the delegation consisted of three persons, and that Mark's retirement from Pamphylia was fatal to the official and representative character of the rest of the mission—a criticism which may probably have been actually used in the subsequent rather bitter controversy described in XV. This might have been formally and expressly set forth at an earlier stage; but the historian briefly expresses it by saying nothing about John Mark until he appears incidentally as a supernumerary and subordinate. The silence is singularly expressive, and therefore carefully calculated.

There must have been a large Jewish colony in Salamis, with more synagogues than one. Cypriote Jews are often mentioned in *Acts* (IV 36, XI 20, XXI 16); and Barnabas himself was a Cypriote. The practice of Saul always had been to go first to the synagogues; and up to the present time there is no reason to think that he had directly addressed the Gentiles except as hearers in the synagogue.

His procedure here is exactly as at Damascus, where he proceeded to preach in the synagogues immediately after his conversion (IX 20). It was right that the first offer should be addressed to the Jews (XIII 46). Moreover he was always sure of a good opening for his Gentile mission among the " God-fearing," who formed part of his audience in every synagogue.

In *v.* 6 how briefly the work of a considerable period is summed up! Four Greek words (διελθόντες ὅλην τὴν νῆσον) contain all that is said about a missionary journey throughout the island. We understand from this brevity that there was no important fact for the historian's purpose. The passage is a typical one: the same formula occurs with slight variations in many later parts of the narrative; and in this first case its meaning is specially clear, so that it throws its light on all the subsequent examples (which is, of course, intended by the historian). Doubtless the process which has just been described at Salamis is intended to apply everywhere. In each city where there was a settlement of Jews, the missionaries preached in the synagogue.

Further, the Cypriote Jews were not unfavourable to the new teaching. The influence and example of Barnabas were naturally effective with his fellow-countrymen. Moreover, the Word had already been preached in Cyprus not long after Stephen's martyrdom XI 19, and converts had been made. There was therefore a small audience ready to listen to the travelling preachers in several, perhaps in all, of the Cyprian cities. Finally, the doctrine that was preached was probably not such as to rouse strong feeling among the Jews; and, so long as the Gentiles were not specially appealed to and set on an equality with the Jews, the early Pauline teaching is not said to have caused more ill-will than the preaching of the older Apostles.

But we may also probably make some negative inferences. There was no specially marked effect; no sign of the Divine guidance or power was manifested ; and the address was made only through the synagogues and nowhere directly to the Gentiles. These are the points on which the historian always lays special stress; signs of the Divine power were the guarantee of Paul's Divine mission, and the steps by which Paul turned more and more decidedly to the Gentiles marked the stages in history as Luke conceived it.

We conclude, then, that the silence observed with regard to the Cyprian evangelisation is not due to mere ignorance on the part of the historian or to want of authorities, but to deliberate plan. On the scale on which his work was planned, and his incidents selected, there was nothing more to say.

The Apostles are said to have made a preaching tour through the whole island. In a writer so sparing of words as Luke, the addition of the word " whole " is important. We cannot press it so far as to suppose that they went through every place in the island. Its force may probably be best seen by supposing it were omitted : in that case the Greek (διελθόντες τὴν νῆσον ἄχρι Πάφου) would permit the interpretation that after landing at Salamis they went along the direct road to Paphos, preaching at convenient places. The word "whole" is probably intended to bring out clearly that they made a complete tour of the Jewish communities in the island, preaching in each synagogue.

2. PAPHOS. (XIII 6) AND WHEN THEY HAD GONE THROUGH THE WHOLE ISLAND UNTO PAPHOS, THEY FOUND A CERTAIN MAN, MAGIAN, PROPHET OF LIES, JEW, BY NAME BAR-JESUS, (7) WHO WAS IN THE COMPANY OF THE PROCONSUL, SERGIUS PAULUS, A MAN OF UNDER-

STANDING. THE PROCONSUL SUMMONED TO HIS PRES-
ENCE BARNABAS AND SAUL, AND SOUGHT [1] TO HEAR
THE WORD OF GOD.   (8) AND THERE STOOD FORTH
AGAINST THEM THE MAGIAN, ETOIMAS (*Son of the Ready*),
FOR SO IS THIS NAME TRANSLATED, SEEKING TO DIVERT
THE PROCONSUL FROM THE FAITH.   (9) BUT SAUL, OTHER-
WISE PAUL, FILLED WITH THE HOLY SPIRIT, LOOKED
FIXEDLY AT HIM, (10) AND SAID, "O FULL OF ALL GUILE
AND ALL VILLANY, THOU SON OF THE DEVIL, THOU
ENEMY OF ALL RIGHTEOUSNESS, WILT THOU NOT CEASE
TO PERVERT THE RIGHT WAYS OF THE LORD?   (11) AND
NOW, BEHOLD THE HAND OF THE LORD IS UPON THEE,
AND THOU SHALT BE BLIND, NOT SEEING THE SUN FOR
A SEASON." AND IMMEDIATELY THERE FELL ON HIM A
MIST AND A DARKNESS ; AND HE WENT ABOUT SEEKING
SOME TO LEAD HIM BY THE HAND.   (12) THEN THE
PROCONSUL, WHEN HE SAW WHAT WAS DONE, BELIEVED,
BEING STRUCK TO THE HEART AT THE TEACHING OF
THE LORD.

We notice, first, the accuracy of the title proconsul, applied to the governor of Cyprus.   The remarkable incident
that follows is connected with a definite individual, who is
named and characterised.   He was Sergius Paulus, a man
of ability.[2]   A Greek inscription of Soloi[3] on the north
coast of Cyprus is dated "in the proconsulship of Paulus,"
who probably is the same governor that played a part in
the strange and interesting scene now to be described.

[1] In classical Greek the meaning would be "put questions to
them " ; and perhaps that is the sense here.

[2] ξυνετός (in Attic) " of practical ability," σοφός " cultivated ".

[3] Found and made known by General Cesnola : but more accurately
and completely published in Mr. D. G. Hogarth's *Devia Cypria*, p. 114.

The order and style of narrative adopted in this incident is noteworthy in itself, and instructive in regard to the author's plan and his conception of history. He directs the reader's attention first to the prominent figure round whom the incident is centred: "in Paphos they found a certain Bar-jesus". Nothing is said about the length of residence in Paphos, nor about the conduct of the missionaries in the earlier part of their visit. Before anything else is mentioned about Paphos, Bar-jesus is named, and then it is explained who he was and how the missionaries came in contact with him. The order of narrative does not follow the order of time, but is guided by the special interest felt by the author, *i.e.*, he seizes first the detail or the personage that is most important in his eyes.

If we attempt to follow the order of development in time, the incident might be thus described. The missionaries came to Paphos. There they began preaching in the synagogues as they had done in other cities. They soon acquired notoriety and were talked about through the city; and the report about these strangers who were teaching a new kind of philosophy reached the Roman governor's ears. The governor was a highly educated man, interested in science and philosophy; and his attention was caught by the report of the two strangers, who were giving public teaching in rhetoric and moral philosophy (p. 271).

Travellers of that class were well known at the time. Those who aimed at high rank and fame as teachers of philosophy often travelled through the great cities of the Empire, giving public demonstrations of their skill: thus they became famous, and were accepted finally in some of the great universities as established teachers and Professors of Philosophy or Morals.

The governor, Sergius Paulus, then invited or commanded—a Roman proconsul's invitation was equivalent
to a command—the two travellers to his court, and sought
to hear a specimen of their skill and a demonstration of
their philosophy on the subject which, as he had been informed, was their favourite topic, the nature of God and
His action towards human beings. The exposition which
they gave seemed to him striking and excellent; and the
marked effect which it produced on him was apparent to
all who were in his train (who in Roman language would
be termed his *comites*). Among these was a Jew, Etoimas
Bar-jesus by name, a man skilled in the lore and the un-
canny arts and strange powers of the Median priests or
magi. On *v.* 6 see p. 115.

It is often said that the governor was "under the influence
of" the Magian; implying the view that the mind of
Sergius Paulus was dominated by Bar-jesus, but that the
Roman, deeply impressed by the way in which Paul seemed
to overpower the Magian, recognised the new master as
more powerful than the old, and thus passed under the
influence of a better teacher. This account seems to me
not to be consistent with the text, and to give a far too unfavourable conception of the governor's character; while it
certainly conveys rather a vulgar idea of the way in which
Paul's teaching first affected the Roman world. According
to the conception of Luke's method as a historian, which
guides us in this attempt to realise the facts, the words of
Acts require a different interpretation. The author, who is
singularly delicate, concise, and appropriate in his use of
language, would not have praised Sergius Paulus as "a
man of understanding," when describing the relation in
which the Magian stood to him, if he had understood

that the Roman was "under the influence of" the false prophet. Either we must say that the author scatters his words heedlessly on the page, or we must understand that these words of praise coming at that precise point exclude any idea of weak submission to the strong personality of the Magian. Moreover the Greek words express the simple fact that the Magian was one of the train of *comites* who always accompanied a Roman governor. Some of these were personal friends who came with him from Rome, others were young Romans of rank who thus gained an insight into administrative life (which as yet they were too young to enter on), others were in official attendance on the governor, and others were provincials, men of letters or of scientific knowledge or of tastes and habits that rendered them agreeable or useful to the great man.

There is also no reason to think that the Magian was an inmate of the proconsul's house. The words do not imply that ; and the facts in no way suggest it.

3. THE MAGIAN AND THE APOSTLE. To us the Roman governor is the prominent figure in this scene ; and his attitude towards the new teaching is what interests us most. But in the estimation of Luke, the Magian is the most important character, next to Paul ; and therefore the reader's attention is directed first upon him. His prominence is perhaps due to different estimate of historical importance : ancient views on this subject differ from modern. But is it not more probable that Luke is justified in his view? It is clear that the Magian was here the representative of a system and a religion ; and that his discomfiture was in itself a wide-reaching triumph. He is commonly said to be a magician. a mere " Jewish impostor" ;

and he is compared to the modern gipsy teller of fortunes. Such comparisons, while having a certain element of truth, are misleading, and give a false idea of the influence exerted on the Roman world by Oriental personages like this Magian. The Magian represented in his single personality both the modern fortune-teller and the modern man of science ; and he had a religious as well as a merely superstitious aspect to the outer world.

No strict line could then be drawn between lawful honourable scrutinising of the secret powers of Nature and illicit attempts to pry into them for selfish ends, between science and magic, between chemistry and alchemy, between astronomy and astrology. The two sides of investigation passed by hardly perceptible degrees into one another : and the same man might be by times a magician, by times the forerunner of Newton and Thomson (Lord Kelvin). It was not possible in the infancy of knowledge to know where lay the bounds between the possible and the impossible, between the search for the philosopher's stone or the elixir of life and the investigation of the properties of argon or the laws of biology. It was not possible then : he would be rash who would say that it is possible now. A writer may venture on many prophecies about the future of science to-day, for which he would have been ridiculed as an impostor or a dreamer twenty years ago ; and doubtless there are things he must not say now, which will be said soon.

It is certain that the priests of some Eastern religions possessed very considerable knowledge of the powers and processes of nature ; and that they were able to do things that either were, or seemed to be, marvellous. Which of these alternatives was true is a point on which individual judgments will vary widely ; but my own experience makes me believe that, so far as influence over human or animal nature and life was concerned, their powers were wonderful. It is natural that the Magian's knowledge and powers should have made him a striking and interesting personality ; and a person like the proconsul, keenly interested in nature and philosophy, would enjoy his society.

The influence of this Eastern religion—one nature with many varieties—was widely spread ; and it was inevitable that the new religion, which was strongly opposed to its methods of dominating its votaries and crushing their personality and individuality, should often be brought in collision with its teachers. Bar-jesus represented the strongest influence on the human will that existed in the Roman world, an influence which must destroy or be destroyed by Christianity, if the latter tried to conquer the Empire. Herein lies the interest of this strange scene ; and we cannot wonder that to Luke, familiar with the terrible power of that religion, the Magian seemed the prominent figure round whom the action moved.

At Philippi, and at Ephesus also, collisions took place between the two influences, of slavery and of freedom for the human mind ; but neither was so impressive as this at Paphos.

It is characteristic of the simple and natural evolution of the incidents, that no calculation of these great issues is represented as influencing the drama.   Human action is swayed for the most part by trivial motives ; and the Magian here was actuated chiefly by the fear of losing his prominent place in the governor's train. His position as friend and associate (*amicus* and *comes* were the technical terms to denote his position) of the governor was an honourable one, gratifying at once to ambition, to vanity, and to worse passions. In this position he could learn a great deal about people and events. In the East it is always believed that the governor's friend may influence his judgment ; and every suppliant, every litigant, and every criminal tries to propitiate or to bribe the friend. We cannot tell in what proportion the more noble and the baser motives were mixed in the Magian's mind ; but they all lie on the surface of the situation, and each had doubtless some effect on him. He saw in the new teachers mere rivals trying to supplant him ; and human nature could not accept defeat without a struggle.

Another point of method to note in the narrative is that no reason is stated for the Magian's opposition. It is a general rule throughout *Acts* that facts alone are stated, and causes left to the reader to gather from the facts : the author sees the causes so clearly that he does not think of stating them. In this case he even omits part of the sequence of facts : he does not say that the Apostles expounded their views, but leaves the reader to understand that the proconsul's desire was obeyed ; and the words of verses 8, 10 ("seeking to turn aside the proconsul from the faith," and "pervert the right ways of the Lord") imply that the exposition was made. Then we may be certain that the Magian would not so far violate politeness and the respect due to the proconsul as to interrupt them, unless he had seen that a marked effect was produced on the governor's mind ; and he interfered from fear that, if he did not put the strangers down or turn them into ridicule, they might supplant himself in the governor's society.

This view of the situation lies implicit in the text ; and it is put explicitly by the *Bezan* Reviser, who makes

Bar-jesus "stand forth in opposition to them, seeking to divert the proconsul from the faith, *because he was listening with much pleasure to them*".   If the added words are a gloss, they are inserted with great skill and judgment.   But to me they appear to be an addition, inserted to make the narrative simpler and easier : the author, as usual, left the reason unstated.

4. SAUL, OTHERWISE PAUL. The name Paul, here applied for the first time by the historian to the person whom he has hitherto called Saul, has given rise to much discussion and many theories. We shall not begin by theorising as to the names of this individual, but by inquiring what was the meaning of that very common formula, " Saul, otherwise Paul " (Σαῦλος ὁ καὶ Παῦλος), in the society of the Eastern provinces ; and shall then apply the results to this case.

The custom which was thus expressed seems to have originated in the bilingual governments and countries of the later centuries B.C. (or, at least, to have become common and familiar then). At that time Greece had gone forth to conquer the East ; and a varnish of Greek culture was spread over many non-Greek races, affecting the richer and the educated classes of the natives, but hardly reaching the mass of the people. Then it was the fashion for every Syrian, or Cilician, or Cappadocian, who prided himself on his Greek education and his knowledge of the Greek language, to bear a Greek name ; but at the same time he had his other name in the native language, by which he was known among his countrymen in general. His two names were the alternative, not the complement, of each other ; and the situation and surroundings of the moment, the *rôle* which he was playing for the time being, determined which name he was called by. In a Greek house he played the Greek, and bore the Greek name : in a company of natives, he was the native, and bore the native name. He did not require both to complete his legal designation, as a Roman required both *nomen* and *prænomen*. His Greek name, taken alone, was a full legal designation in a Greek court.

This has an obvious bearing on the case of " Saul, otherwise Paul ". In the earlier part of this book he has been a Jew among Jews ; and we have seen only his Hebrew name. Nothing has hitherto transpired to show that he was anything but " Hebrew sprung from Hebrews ". In Cyprus he went through the country city by city, synagogue by synagogue : and he was the Jew in all. But here he is in different surroundings : he stands in the hall of the proconsul, and he answers the questions of the Roman official. The interview, doubtless, began, as all interviews between strangers in the country still begin, with the round of questions : What is your name? (or who are you?) Whence come you? What is your business? The type is seen in the question of the Cyclops to Ulysses (*Odyssey* IX 252) : "Strangers, who are ye? Whence sail ye over the wet ways? On some trading enterprise, or at adventure do ye rove?"

To these questions how would Saul answer? After his years of recent life as a Jew, filled with the thought of a religion that originated among Jews, and was in his conception the perfected form of Jewish religion, did he reply : " My name is Saul, and I am a Jew from Tarsus "? First, let us see what he himself says as to his method of addressing an audience (I *Cor.* IX 20 f.), "to the Jews I made myself as a Jew that I might gain Jews ; to them that are under the law as under the law (though not myself under the law) ; to them that are without the law as without the law ; I am become all things to all men ; and I do all for the Gospel's sake ". We cannot doubt that the man who wrote so to the Corinthians replied to the questions of Sergius Paulus, by designating himself as a Roman, born at Tarsus, and named Paul. By a marvellous stroke of historic brevity, the author sets before us the past and the present in the simple words : " Then Saul, otherwise Paul, fixed his eyes on him and said ".

The double character, the mixed personality, the Oriental teacher who turns out to be a freeborn Roman, would have struck and arrested the attention of any governor, any person possessed of insight into character, any one who had even an average share of curiosity. But to a man with the tastes of Sergius Paulus, the Roman Jew must have been doubly interesting ; and the orator or the preacher knows how much is gained by arousing such an interest at the outset.

Coming forward in this character and name, Paul was taking a momentous step, the importance of which was fully marked in the narrative. In the first place, he was taking the leading place and guiding the tone of the interview instead of being, as heretofore, the subordinate following Barnabas. Hence in the narrative we find that Barnabas introduced Saul to the Apostles ; Barnabas brought Saul to Antioch ; Barnabas and Saul carried the Antiochian alms to Jerusalem ; Barnabas and Saul brought back John Mark with them from Jerusalem ; Barnabas was first and Saul last in the body of prophets and teachers of the Church at Antioch ; Barnabas and Saul were selected by the Spirit ; and Barnabas and Saul were

invited to the proconsul's presence. But now Paul took
this new departure, and Paul and his company sailed away
from Paphos to Pamphylia ; Paul and Barnabas addressed
the Gentiles in Antioch ; Paul and Barnabas disputed with
the Judaising party on their return to Syrian Antioch ; and
henceforth the regular order places Paul first. There are
only two exceptions to this rule, and these serve to bring
out its true character more clearly.

(1) In the Council at Jerusalem, and in the letter of the
Apostles and Elders, XV 12, 25, the order is Barnabas and
Paul ; but there we are among Jews, who follow the order of
seniority and Jewish precedence. The only surprising thing
here is that they use the name Paul, not the Hebrew Saul.
We can only infer from that that the Greek-speaking Jews
generally used the name Paul (compare p. 169), and
that the historian's use of the name Saul in the earlier part
of this narrative was deliberately chosen to emphasise the
contrast between Paul's earlier and his later manner.

(2) In the episode where the two Apostles were worshipped at Lystra, Barnabas is named first as Zeus the
chief god, and Paul next as Hermes the messenger. But
the same qualities which mark out Paul to us as the leader,
marked him out to the populace of Lycaonia as the agent
and subordinate. The Western mind regards the leader as
the active and energetic partner ; but the Oriental mind
considers the leader to be the person who sits still and
does nothing, while his subordinates speak and work for
him. Hence in the truly Oriental religions the chief god
sits apart from the world, communicating with it through
his messenger and subordinate. The more statuesque
figure of Barnabas was therefore taken by the Orientals
as the chief god, and the active orator, Paul, as his

messenger, communicating his wishes to men. Incidentally, we may notice both the diametrical antithesis of this conception of the Divine nature to the Christian conception, and also the absolute negation of the Oriental conception in Christ's words to His Disciples, " whosoever would become great among you shall be your minister ; and whosoever would be first among you shall be your servant " (*Matt.* XX 26).

How delicate is the art which by simple change in the order of a recurring pair of names, and by the slight touch at the critical moment, " Saul, otherwise Paul," suggests and reveals this wide-reaching conception in Luke's mind of historical development !

In the second place, when Paul thus came forward under his new aspect and personality, he was inaugurating a new policy. He was appealing direct for the first time to the Græco-Roman world as himself a member of that world. This is put plainly in XIV 27 as the great innovation and the great fact of the journey : as soon as Paul and Barnabas returned to Syrian Antioch, they made a report to the assembled Church " of all things that God had done with them, and how He had opened a door of faith unto the Gentiles ". The first stage in the admission of the Gentiles to the Christian Church was taken long before this journey. But the full implication of the Apostolate to the Gentiles was not even by Paul himself realised for many years. The second stage was achieved on this journey, and the historian fixes the psychological moment precisely at the point where the Apostles faced the Magian in the presence of the proconsul of Cyprus. Amid the conflict of the two religions before the Roman governor, Paul stepped forward in his character of citizen of the Empire ; and his act was followed by that transport of power, which attested the grace that was given to the bold innovator, and the Divine approval and confirmation of his step. On former occasions the grace that was evident in Antioch confirmed the high character of the Antiochian Brotherhood in the eyes of Barnabas (*Acts* XI 23), and the grace that was given Paul had justified his apostolate in the eyes of James, Peter and John (*Gal.* II 9).

Such is the situation in which we stand when we transport ourselves in thought to the time and the country where the events took place, and take the few brief words of Luke in the sense which they bore to the men of his time. But now let us turn from this picture to see what is made of the scene by the critic, who sits in his study and writes as if the men of this book were artificial figures and not real human beings. Weizsäcker, one of the most distinguished of modern German scholars, finds in this delicacy of language nothing but a sign of double authorship. The late author, he says, used two earlier authorities, one of whom employed the name Saul, while the other designated the Apostle as Paul, and *by a mere conjecture* he puts the change at this point. Weizsäcker emphasises this view that the point was selected by an arbitrary conjecture, and that any other point might have been chosen equally well. It might almost seem that, in a statement like this, the learned professor is taking his fun off us, and is experimenting to see how much the world will accept at the mouth of a deservedly famous scholar without rebelling.

Mr. Lewin states better than almost any other the force of this passage when he says : " The dropping of the Jewish, and the adoption of a Roman name, was in harmony with the great truth he was promulgating—that henceforth the

partition between Jew and Gentile was broken down". He
then asks, " Why is not the name of Paul introduced when
he first left Antioch to commence his travels?" and after
he has in a rather hesitating way suggested some quite unsuitable occasions as possible for the change, he rightly
concludes, " It occurs more naturally immediately afterwards when Saul stands forth by himself and becomes the
principal actor".

The marvels described in *Acts* concern my present purpose only in so far as they bear upon the historical effect
of the narrative. In themselves they do not add to, but
detract from its verisimilitude as history. They are difficulties; but my hope is to show first that the narrative
apart from them is stamped as authentic, second that they
are an integral part of it. To study and explain them does
not belong to me. Twenty years ago I found it easy to
dispose of them ; but now-a-days probably not even the
youngest among us finds himself able to maintain that we
have mastered the secrets of nature, and determined the
limits which divide the unknown from the impossible.
That Paul believed himself to be the recipient of direct revelations from God, to be guided and controlled in his
plans by direct interposition of the Holy Spirit, to be enabled by the Divine power to move the forces of nature in a
way that ordinary men cannot, is involved in this narrative.
You must make up your own minds to accept or to reject
it , but you cannot cut out the marvellous from the rest, nor
can you believe that either Paul or this writer was a mere
victim of hallucinations. To the men of that age only what
was guaranteed by marvellous accompaniments was true ;
to us unusual accompaniments tend to disprove truth. The
contrast between the ages is *himmelweit*.

The marvellous is indissolubly interwoven—for good or for bad—with this narrative, and cannot be eliminated. Do the marvellous adjuncts discredit the rest of the narrative, or does the vividness and accuracy of the narrative require us to take the marvels with the rest and try to understand them ? Every one must answer the question for himself.

CHAPTER V

FOUNDATION OF THE CHURCHES OF GALATIA

1. PAMPHYLIA. (XIII 13) AND PAUL AND HIS COM-
PANY SET SAIL FROM PAPHOS AND CAME TO PERGA
IN *the province* PAMPHYLIA. AND JOHN DEPARTED
FROM THEM, AND RETURNED TO JERUSALEM; (14) BUT
THEY WENT ACROSS FROM PERGA AND ARRIVED AT
PISIDIAN ANTIOCH.

The phrase " Perga of Pamphylia " is not intended to
distinguish this Perga from others (cp. XXI 39) : there was
no other city of the same name. Nor is it a mere piece of
geographical information : this historian has no desire to
teach the reader geography. The sense is " they proceeded
to Pamphylia, to the special point Perga " ; and the intention
is to define their next sphere of work as being Pamphylia.
This sense would have naturally been understood by every
one, were it not that no missionary work was actually done
in Pamphylia, for the next fact mentioned is that John left
the party, and the others went on to Pisidian Antioch ; and
the conclusion has sometimes been drawn hastily that
Pamphylia had never been contemplated as a mission-field,
and was merely traversed because it lay between Cyprus and
Antioch. But the plain force of the words must be accepted
here, for it lies in the situation that Pamphylia was the
natural continuation of the work that had been going on,

first in Syria and Cilicia for many years, and next in Cyprus. They went to Pamphylia to preach there, and, as they did not actually preach there, something must have occurred to make them change their plan. Further, the reason for this change of plan must have been merely a temporary one, for they preached in Pamphylia on their return journey.

We are justified in connecting with this change of plan the one fact recorded about the missionary party in Pamphylia: John left them in circumstances that made a deep and painful impression on Paul, and remained rankling in his mind for years (XV 38). The historian places together in a marked way the departure of John and the onward journey of the others without preaching in Pamphylia. Now, as we have seen, it does not lie in this historian's manner to state reasons ; he rarely says that one event was the cause of another, but merely states the facts side by side, and leaves the reader to gather for himself the causal connection between them.

Other reasons, which need not be repeated here, point to the same conclusion, that a change of plan was the reason why John abandoned the expedition. He conceived that the new " proposal was a departure from the scheme " with which they had been charged, " carrying their work into a region different in character and not contemplated by the Church ".

Further, we observe that the country between Perga and Pisidian Antioch is not mentioned ; the journey is not even summed up briefly as the Cyprian journey between Salamis and Paphos was described (XIII 6) : it is simply said that " they went across (the intervening mountain lands of Taurus) to Antioch," as in XVIII 27 Apollos "conceived the intention to go across (the intervening Ægean Sea) to Achaia". On our hypothesis that the narrative is singularly exact in expression, and that the slightest differences are significant, we gather that the journey to Antioch was a mere traversing of the country without preaching, with the view of reaching Antioch. On the other hand, it is stated that the return journey some years later from Antioch to Perga was a preaching journey, though no marked effects are recorded on it.

Again, it is a rule in this historian's clear and practical style, that when Paul is entering (or intending, even though unsuccessfully, to enter) a new field of missionary enterprise, the field is defined (as in *v.* 4); and the definition usually takes the form of a Roman provincial district. This will become apparent as the narrative proceeds, and the inferences that can be drawn from the form of definition or absence of definition in each case will illustrate and give precision to the rule. It is, I believe, a fair inference from the want of any indication of a wider sphere that when the travellers went to Pisidian Antioch, they had not in mind a wider field of work than the city : they went to Pisidian Antioch and not to the province Galatia, in which it was included.

The name is rightly given as Pisidian Antioch in the great MSS. ; the form "Antioch of Pisidia" is a corruption. Besides other reasons, Antioch was not considered by Luke to be in Pisidia (p. 124).

The facts, then, which can be gathered from the narrative of *Acts* are these. Paul and his companions came to Perga with the view of evangelising the next country on their route, a country similar in character to and closely connected in commerce and racial type with Cyprus and Syria and Cilicia. For some reason the plan was altered, and they passed rapidly over the Pamphylian lowlands and the Pisidian mountain-lands to Antioch, postponing the evangelisation of these districts till a later stage of their journey. They went to Antioch for some reason which concerned only that city, and did not contemplate as their object the evangelisation of the province to which it belonged. John, however, refused to participate in the changed programme, presumably because he disapproved of it. His refusal seems to have been felt as a personal slight by Paul, which suggests that the change of plan was in some way caused by Paul. What then was the reason? Is any clue to it given in any other part of *Acts* or in the words of Paul himself?

In passing from Perga to Pisidian Antioch, the travellers passed from the Roman province Pamphylia to the Roman province Galatia, and the rest of their journey lay in Galatia until they returned to Perga. Now, we possess a letter written by Paul to the Churches of Galatia, in which he says: "Ye know that it was by reason of physical infirmity that I preached the Gospel unto you on the first-of-my-two-visits; and the facts of my bodily constitution which were trying to you were not despised nor rejected by you, but ye received me as a messenger of God". We learn, then, from Paul himself that an illness (we may confidently say a serious illness) was the occasion of his having originally preached to the churches of Galatia. The words do not necessarily imply that the illness began in Galatia; they are quite consistent with the interpretation that the illness was the reason why he came to be in Galatia and had the opportunity of preaching there; but they imply that the physical infirmity lasted for some considerable time, and was apparent to strangers, while he was in Galatia.

Here we have a reason, stated by Paul himself, which fully explains all the curious phenomena of the text of *Acts*. Paul had a serious illness in Pamphylia, and on that account he left Perga and went to Antioch. It is unnecessary to repeat the argument that this is in perfect agreement with the known facts. Any constitutional weakness was liable to be brought out by "the sudden plunge into the enervating atmosphere of Pamphylia" after the fatigue and hardship of a journey on foot through Cyprus, accompanied by the constant excitement of missionary work, culminating in the intense nervous strain of the supreme effort at Paphos. The natural and common treatment for such an illness is to go to the higher ground of the interior; and the situation of Antioch (about 3600 ft. above the sea, sheltered by mountains on the north and east, and overlooking a wide plain to the south and south-west), as well as its Jewish population, and commercial connection with the Pamphylian coast-cities, made it a very suitable place for Paul's purpose.

But why then did the historian not state this simple fact? It lies out of his purpose and method to notice such personal details. He states in the briefest possible form the essential facts of the evangelisation of the world; and everything else he passes over as of ephemeral nature. We are dealing with a first century, and not a nineteenth century historian,—one who had not the eager desire to understand causes and reasons which characterises the present day, one who wrote for a public that was quite satisfied with a statement of facts without a study of causes. There is too much tendency to demand from the first century writers an answer to all the questions we should like to put.

Moreover, Luke passes very lightly over the sufferings and the dangers that Paul encountered ; many he omits entirely, others he mentions without emphasising the serious nature of the case (p. 279 f.).

It is plain that Paul at the moment felt deeply wounded. The journey which he felt to be absolutely necessary in the interests of future work was treated by Mark as an abandonment of the work ; and his sensitive nature would consider Mark's arguments, plausible as they were in some respects, as equivalent to a declaration of want of confidence. But that feeling, though it lasted for some years, was not of the permanent nature which would put it on the same plane as the facts recorded by Luke. Who can think that Paul would have desired permanent record of his illness and Mark's desertion ? And his desire on a matter personal to himself would be Luke's law.

2. THE "THORN IN THE FLESH". The character of the Pamphylian country, not merely in its modern half-cultivated condition, but at all times, must have been enervating and calculated to bring out any latent weakness of constitution. Now it is a probable and generally accepted view that the " physical weakness," which was the occasion why Paul preached to the Galatians, was the same malady which tormented him at frequent intervals. I have suggested that this malady was a species of chronic malaria fever ; and, in view of criticisms, it is necessary to dwell on this point ; for I have incurred the blame of exaggerating an ephemeral attack. The question is put whether such an illness "could reasonably have called forth their contempt and loathing ".[1]

---

[1] *Expositor*, Dec., 1893, p. 417.

A physical weakness, which recurs regularly in some situation that one is regularly required by duty to face, produces strong and peculiar effect on our human nature. An attentive student of mankind has caught this trait and described it clearly in one of the characters whom his genius has created. I quote from Charles Reade's description of a clergyman engaged in warfare against the barbarity of prison discipline, upon whom every scene of cruelty which he had often to witness produced a distressing physical effect, sickness and trembling. "His high-tuned nature gave way. He locked the door that no one might see his weakness ; and, then, succumbing to nature, he fell first into a sickness and then into a trembling, and more than once hysterical tears gushed from his eyes in the temporary prostration of his spirit and his powers. Such are the great. Men know their feats, but not their struggles." The feeling of shame at this weakness is several times described in the course of the narrative (*It is Never too Late to Mend*); and, when at last nature, on the verge of a more serious physical prostration, ceased to relieve itself in this painful way, " he thanked Heaven for curing him of that contemptible infirmity, so he called it ". Yet that weakness did not prevent the sufferer from facing his duty, but only came on as a consequence ; and it could be hidden within the privacy of his chamber. Let the reader conceive the distress and shame. of the sufferer, if the weakness had prostrated him before his duty was finished, and laid him helpless before them all when he required his whole strength. Surely he would have " besought the Lord that it might depart from " him, and regarded it as " a messenger of Satan sent to buffet him " (II *Cor.* XII 7, 8).

Now, in some constitutions malaria fever tends to recur

in very distressing and prostrating paroxysms, whenever one's energies are taxed for a great effort. Such an attack is for the time absolutely incapacitating : the sufferer can only lie and feel himself a shaking and helpless weakling, when he ought to be at work. He feels a contempt and loathing for self, and believes that others feel equal contempt and loathing.

Charles Reade's hero could at least retire to his room, and lock the door, and conceal his weakness from others ; but, in the publicity of Oriental life, Paul could have no privacy. In every paroxysm, and they might recur daily, he would lie exposed to the pity or the contempt of strangers. If he were first seen in a Galatian village, or house, lying in the mud on the shady side of a wall for two hours shaking like an aspen leaf, the gratitude that he expresses to the Galatians, because they " did not despise nor reject his infirmity," was natural and deserved.

Fresh light is thrown on this subject by an observation of Mr. Hogarth, my companion in many journeys. In publishing a series of inscriptions recording examples of punishment inflicted by the God on those who had approached the sanctuary in impurity, he suggests that malarial fever was often the penalty sent by the God. The paroxysms, recurring suddenly with overpowering strength, and then passing off, seemed to be due to the direct visitation of God. This gives a striking effect to Paul's words in *Gal.* IV 14, " you did not despise nor reject my physical infirmity, but received me as an angel of God " : though the Galatians might have turned him away from their door as a person accursed and afflicted by God, they received him as God's messenger. The obvious implication of this passage has led many to the view that Paul's malady was epilepsy, which was also attributed to the direct visitation of God.

A strong corroboration is found in the phrase : " a stake in the flesh," which Paul uses about his malady (II *Cor.* XII 7). That is the peculiar headache which accompanies the paroxysms : within my experience several persons, innocent of Pauline theorising, have described it as " like a red-hot bar thrust through the forehead ".   As soon as fever connected itself with Paul in my mind, the "stake in the flesh" impressed me as a strikingly illustrative metaphor ; and the oldest tradition on the subject, quoted by Tertullian and others, explains the " stake in the flesh " as headache.

The malady was a " messenger of Satan ".   Satan seems to represent in Pauline language any overpowering obstacle to his work, an obstacle which it was impossible to struggle against : so Satan prevented him from returning to Thessalonica, in the form of an ingenious obstacle, which made his return impossible for the time (p. 230).   The words " messenger sent to buffet me," imply that it came frequently and unexpectedly, striking him down with the power of the Enemy.

The idea that the malady was an affection of the eyes, resulting from blinding at his conversion, seems inadequate in itself, unsuitable to his own words, and contradicted by the evidence as to the power of his eyes (p. 38).

Paul describes the malady as sent to prevent him from " being exalted overmuch by reason of the exceeding greatness of the revelations " which had been granted to him ; and he clearly implies that it came later than the great revelation, when " he was caught up even to the third heaven " about 43 A.D. (p. 60).   The malady certainly did not begin long before this journey; and the attack in Pamphylia may perhaps have been the first

3. THE SYNAGOGUE IN PISIDIAN ANTIOCH. (XIII 13) JOHN DEPARTED FROM THEM AND RETURNED TO JERUSALEM ; (14) BUT THEY WENT ACROSS FROM PERGA AND ARRIVED AT PISIDIAN ANTIOCH. AND THEY WENT INTO THE SYNAGOGUE ON THE SABBATH DAY, AND SAT DOWN ; (15) AND AFTER THE READING OF THE LAW AND THE PROPHETS, THE ARCHISYNAGOGOI SENT TO THEM SAYING, " GENTLEMEN, BRETHREN, IF THERE IS IN YOU A WORD OF ENCOURAGEMENT TO THE PEOPLE, SAY ON ". (16) AND PAUL STOOD UP AND MADE A GESTURE WITH HIS HAND AND SPOKE. . . . (42) AND AS THEY WENT OUT, THEY BESOUGHT THAT THESE WORDS MIGHT BE SPOKEN TO THEM THE NEXT SABBATH. (43) NOW, WHEN THE SYNAGOGUE BROKE UP, MANY OF THE JEWS AND OF THE GOD-FEARING PROSELYTES FOLLOWED PAUL AND BARNABAS : WHO, SPEAKING TO THEM, URGED THEM TO CONTINUE IN THE GRACE OF GOD. (44) AND THE NEXT SABBATH ALMOST THE WHOLE CITY WAS GATHERED TOGETHER TO HEAR THE WORD OF GOD. (45) BUT WHEN THE JEWS SAW THE MULTITUDES, THEY WERE FILLED WITH JEALOUSY, AND CONTRADICTED THE THINGS WHICH WERE SPOKEN BY PAUL, AND BLASPHEMED. (46) AND PAUL AND BARNABAS SPAKE OUT BOLDLY AND SAID, " IT WAS NECESSARY THAT THE WORD OF GOD SHOULD FIRST BE SPOKEN TO YOU. SEEING YE THRUST IT FROM YOU, AND JUDGE YOURSELVES UNWORTHY OF ETERNAL LIFE, LO, WE TURN TO THE GENTILES." . . . (48) AND AS THE GENTILES HEARD THIS, THEY WERE GLAD AND GLORIFIED THE WORD OF GOD : AND AS MANY AS WERE ORDAINED TO ETERNAL LIFE BELIEVED. (49) AND THE WORD OF THE LORD WAS SPREAD ABROAD THROUGHOUT

ALL THE REGION. (50) BUT THE JEWS URGED ON THE DEVOUT WOMEN OF HONOURABLE ESTATE, AND THE CHIEF MEN OF THE CITY, AND STIRRED UP A PERSECU-TION AGAINST PAUL AND BARNABAS, AND CAST THEM OUT OF THEIR BORDERS. (51) BUT THEY SHOOK OFF THE DUST OF THEIR FEET AGAINST THEM, AND CAME UNTO ICONIUM. (52) AND THE DISCIPLES WERE FILLED WITH JOY AND WITH THE HOLY GHOST.

The route between Perga and Pisidian Antioch, with its " perils' of rivers, perils of robbers," and the later legend connected with the journey across the Pisidian mountains by the city which still bears the Apostle's name, is de-scribed elsewhere, and need not here detain us.

The usual punctuation of *vv.* 13, 14, seems to arise from the idea that Paul's sermon was delivered on the first Sab-bath after he reached Antioch. So, Conybeare and How-son say, " a congregation came together at Antioch on the Sabbath which immediately succeeded the arrival of Paul and Barnabas ". It seems, however, not possible that such powerful effect as is described in *v.* 44 should have been produced on the whole city within the first ten days after they arrived in Antioch. Moreover, when Paul's teaching had become more definite and pronounced, he preached three successive Sabbaths to the Jews at Thessalonica (p. 228), and it seems implied that the rupture took place there unusually soon ; hence, at this time, when he had been preaching for years in the Jewish synagogues of Cilicia, Syria and Cyprus, it is improbable that the quarrel with the Jews of Antioch took place on the second Sabbath.

But, when the passage is properly punctuated, there re-mains nothing to show that Paul's speech was delivered on his first Sabbath in Antioch. Nothing is said as to the first days of the Apostles' stay in the city. We are to understand, according to the rule already observed (p. 72 f.), that the usual method was pursued, and that some time passed before any critical event took place. As at Paphos, the fame of the new teachers gradually spread through the city. The historian gives an address to the synagogue with an outline of the teaching which produced this result ; the address delivered on a critical Sabbath, after feeling had already been moved for some time, may well have remained in the memory or in the manuscript diary of somé of the interested hearers, and thus been preserved. We make it part of our hypothesis that Luke took his task as a historian seriously, and obtained original records where he could.

Paul's address to the assembled Jews and proselytes was doubtless suggested by the passages, one from the Law, one from the Prophets, which were read before he was called to speak. It has been conjectured that these passages were *Deut.* I and *Isaiah* I, which in the Septuagint Version contain two marked words employed by Paul : the Scriptures were probably read in Greek in this synagogue of Grecised Jews (see pp. 84, 169). *Deut.* I naturally suggests the historical retrospect with which Paul begins ; and the promise of remission of sins rises naturally out of *Isaiah* I 18. Dean Farrar mentions that " in the present list of Jewish lessons, *Deut.* I-III 22 and *Isaiah* I 1-22 stand forty-fourth in order ". That list is of decidedly later origin ; but probably it was often determined by older custom and traditional ideas of suitable accompaniment.

The climax of the address passed from the historical survey (with its assurance of unfailing Divine guidance for the Chosen People) to the sending of Jesus, who had been slain by the rulers of Jerusalem (" because they knew Him not, nor the voices of the prophets which are read every Sabbath," *v.* 27), but whom God had raised from the dead. Then follow the promise and the peroration—

(XIII 38) BE IT KNOWN UNTO YOU THEREFORE, BRETHREN, THAT THROUGH TIIIS MAN IS PROCLAIMED UNTO YOU REMISSION OF SINS ; (39) AND BY HIM EVERY ONE THAT BELIEVETH IS JUSTIFIED FROM ALL THINGS, FROM WHICH YE COULD NOT BE JUSTIFIED BY THE LAW OF MOSES. (40) BEWARE, THEREFORE, LEST TIIAT COME UPON YOU, WHICH IS SPOKEN IN THE PROPHETS ; " BEHOLD, YE DESPISERS, AND WONDER, AND PERISH ; FOR I WORK A WONDER IN YOUR DAYS ".

This outspoken declaration that the Judaic system was superseded by a higher message from God is not said to have hurt the feelings of the Jews who were present. Paul was invited to continue his discourse on the following Sabbath ; many of the audience, both Jews and proselytes, followed the Apostles from the synagogue ; and both Paul and Barnabas addressed them further, and emphasised the effect of the previous address.

There must have been something in the situation or in the supplementary explanations given by Paul and Barnabas, which made his words specially applicable to the Gentiles ; and a vast crowd of the citizens gathered to hear Paul on the following week. Paul's address on this occasion is not given. It was in all probability addressed pointedly to the Antiochians, for violent opposition and contradiction and jealousy were roused among the Jews. We may fairly infer that the open door of belief for the whole world irrespective of race was made a prominent topic; for the passion which animated the Jewish opposition is said to have been jealousy. The climax of a violent scene was the bold declaration of Paul and Barnabas that they "turned to the Gentiles, since the Jews rejected the Gospel".

In this scene the same fact that was observed at Paphos came out prominently. The eager interest and the invitation of the general population stimulated Paul; and his ideas developed rapidly. The first thoroughly Gentile congregation separate from the synagogue was established at Pisidian Antioch. Where he saw no promise of success, he never persisted; but where "a door was opened unto him," he used the opportunity (I *Cor.* XVI 9, II *Cor.* II 12).

The influence attributed to the women at Antioch, *v.* 50, is in perfect accord with the manners of the country. In Athens or in an Ionian city, it would have been impossible (p. 252).

4. THE CHURCH AT PISIDIAN ANTIOCH. The deep impression that had already been produced on the general population of Antioch was intensified when the preaching of Paul and Barnabas began to be addressed to them directly and exclusively. The effect was now extended to the whole *Region*. This term does not indicate the lands immediately around the fortifications of Antioch, and belonging to that city. The free population of those lands were citizens of Antioch; and the term "city," according to the ancient idea, included the entire lands that belonged to it, and not the mere space covered by continuous houses and a fortified wall. "A city was not walls, but men;" and the saying had a wider and more practical meaning to the ancients than is generally taken from it in modern times. The phrase that is here used, "the whole *Region*," indicates some distinct and recognised circle of territories.

Here we have a fact of administration and government

assumed in quiet undesigned fashion : Antioch was the centre of a *Region*.　This is the kind of allusion which affords to students of ancient literature a test of accuracy, and often a presumption of date.　I think that, if we put this assumption to the test, we shall find (1) that it is right, (2) that it adds a new fact, probable in itself but not else-where formally stated, about the Roman administration of Galatia, (3) that it explains and throws new light on several passages in ancient authors and inscriptions.　Without discussing the subject too elaborately, we may point out the essentials.

My friend Prof. Sterrett, of Amherst, Massachusetts, has discovered and published an inscription of Antioch, which speaks of a "regionary centurion" (ἑκατοντάρχην ῥεγεωνά-ριον), evidently a military official charged with certain duties (probably in the maintenance of peace and order) within a certain *Regio* of which Antioch was the centre.

Partly to guard against a possible objection, partly to show how much may depend on accuracy in a single letter, it may be added that Prof. Sterrett in publishing this in-scription makes a conjectural alteration, which would deprive us of the help that the inscription gives.　He prints (λ)εγεωνάριον ; but this is an arbitrary change in violation of his own copy.

Thus we have epigraphic authority to prove that Antioch under the Roman administration was the centre of a *Region*.　Further, we can determine the ex-tent and the name of that *Region*, remembering always that in a province like Galatia, where evidence is lamentably scanty, we must often be content with reasonable prob-ability, and rarely find such an inscription as Prof. Sterrett's to put us on a plane of demonstrated certainty.

It is natural in the administration of so large a province as Galatia, and there are some recorded proofs, that a certain number of distinct *Regiones* (or χῶραι) existed in Southern Galatia. To quote the exact names recorded, we have *Phrygia* or Φρυγία χώρα, *Isauria* or Ἰσαυρικὴ (χώρα), Pisidia, Lycaonia or Γαλατικὴ χώρα (with τῆς Λυκαονίας understood, denoting the Roman part of Lycaonia in contrast with *Lycaonia Antiochiana* or Ἀντιοχιανὴ χώρα, the part of Lycaonia ruled by King Antiochus). There can be no doubt that Pisidian Antioch (strictly "a Phrygian city towards Pisidia") was the centre of the *Region* called Phrygia in inscriptions enumerating the parts of the province, and "the Phrygian Region of (the province) Galatia" in *Acts* XVI 6, or "the Phrygian Region" XVIII 23. This central importance of Antioch was due to its position as a Roman Colony, which made it the military and administrative centre of the country.

Thus, without any formal statement, and without any technical term, but in the course of a bare, simple and brief account of the effects of Paul's preaching, we find ourselves unexpectedly (just as Paul and Barnabas found themselves unintentionally) amid a Roman provincial district, which is moved from the centre to the extremities by the new preaching. It is remarkable how the expression of Luke embodies the very soul of history (p. 200).

A certain lapse of time, then, is implied in the brief words of *v.* 49. The process whereby the whole region was influenced by the Word must have been a gradual one. The similar expression used in XIX 10 may serve as a standard of comparison: there, during a period of two years in Ephesus, "all they which dwelt in Asia heard the Word". The sphere of influence is immensely wider in that case;

but the process is the same.   Persons from the other cities
came to Antioch as administrative centre, the great garrison
city, which was often visited by the Roman governor and
was the residence of some subordinate officials : they came
for law-suits, for trade, for great festivals of the Roman
unity (such as that described in the *Acta* of Paul and
Thekla).[1]   In Antioch they heard of the new doctrine ;
some came under its influence ; the knowledge of it was
thus borne abroad over the whole territory ; probably small
knots of Christians were formed in other towns.

How long a period of time is covered by *v.* 49 we cannot
tell with certainty ; but it must be plain to every one that
the estimate of the whole residence at Antioch as two to
six months, is, as is elsewhere said, a minimum.

It may be observed that in the Antiochian narrative a
period of some weeks is passed over in total silence, then
thirty-three verses are devoted to the epoch-making events
of two successive Sabbaths, and then another considerable
period is summed up in *v.* 49.

The action by which Paul and Barnabas were expelled
from Antioch has been fully described elsewhere.   The
expulsion was inflicted by the magistrates of the city, and
was justified to their minds in the interests of peace and
order.   It was not inflicted by officials of the province,
and hence the effect is expressly restricted by the historian
to Antiochian territory.   Slight as the details are, they
suit the circumstances of the time perfectly.

A slight addition made in *Codex Bezæ* at this point
presents some features of interest.   In the Approved Text
the Jews " roused persecution " against the Apostles ; but
in the *Codex* they roused " great affliction and persecution ",

---

[1] *Church in R. E.*, p. 396; *Cities and Bishoprics*, p. 56.

The additional words are not characterised by that delicate precision in the choice of terms which belongs to Luke. " Affliction " (θλίψις) refers more to the recipient, " persecution " (διωγμός) to the agent ; hence the "to rouse persecution " is a well-chosen phrase, but " to rouse affliction " is not. The words of *Codex Bezæ* have been added under the influence of the enumeration of his sufferings given by Paul in II *Cor.* XI 23 (cp. II *Tim.* III 11). The disproportion between that list and the references to physical sufferings in *Acts* led to a series of additions, designed to bring about a harmony between the two authorities.

In the additions of this kind made to *Codex Bezæ* we have the beginnings of a Pauline myth. There is nothing in which popular fancy among the early Christians showed itself so creative as the tortures of its heroes. The earliest *Acta* of martyrs contain only a moderate amount of torture, such in kind as was inseparable from Roman courts of justice ; as time passed, these tortures seemed insufficient, and the old *Acta* were touched up to suit what the age believed must have taken place. Where we possess accounts of a martyrdom of different dates, the older are less filled with sufferings than the later. A similar process of accretion to *Acts* was actually beginning, but was checked by the veneration that began to regard its text as sacred.

Luke passes very lightly over Paul's sufferings : from II *Tim.* III 11, we see that he must have endured much. He was three times beaten with the rods of lictors before A.D. 56 (II *Cor.* XI 25). Now, since the Roman governors whom he met were favourable to him, these beatings must have taken place in " colonies," whose magistrates were attended by lictors. It is probable that the persecution which is mentioned in Antioch, and hinted at in Lystra, included beating by lictors. It is noteworthy that the magistrates of these two cities are not expressly mentioned, and therefore there was no opportunity for describing their action. The third beating by lictors was in Philippi, also a colony.

Similarly it can hardly be doubted that some of the five occasions on which Paul received stripes from the Jews were in the Galatian cities, where some Jews were so active against him.

5. ICONIUM. (XIV 1) AND IT CAME TO PASS IN ICONIUM AFTER THE SAME FASHION *as in Antioch* THAT THEY ENTERED INTO THE SYNAGOGUE OF THE JEWS AND SO SPAKE THAT A GREAT MULTITUDE, BOTH OF JEWS AND OF GREEKS, BELIEVED. (2) BUT THE DISAFFECTED AMONG THE JEWS STIRRED UP AND EXASPERATED THE MINDS OF THE GENTILES AGAINST THE BRETHREN. (4) AND THE POPULACE WAS DIVIDED ; AND PART HELD WITH THE JEWS AND PART WITH THE APOSTLES. (5) AND WHEN THERE WAS MADE AN ONSET BOTH OF THE GENTILES AND OF THE JEWS WITH THEIR RULERS, TO ENTREAT THEM SHAMEFULLY, AND TO STONE THEM, (6) THEY BECAME AWARE OF IT, AND FLED INTO LYCAONIA.

According to the reading of the MSS., the narrative of these incidents is obscure ; and it is hard to believe that the text is correct. In *v.* 1 the great success of the preaching is related, while in *v.* 2 the disaffected Jews rouse bitter feeling against the Apostles (the *aorists* implying that the efforts were successful). Then in *v.* 3 we are astonished to read, as the sequel of the Jewish action, that the Apostles remained a long time preaching boldly and with marked success : and finally, in *v.* 4, the consequences of the Jewish action are set forth. It is therefore not surprising that the critics who look on *Acts* as a patchwork have cut up this passage. It must be conceded that appearances in this case are in their favour, and that the correctness and originality of the narrative can hardly be defended without the supposition that some corruption has crept into it ; but the great diversity of text in the various MSS. and Versions is, on ordinary critical principles, a sign that some corruption did take place at a very early date.

The close relation of *vv.* 2 and 4 is patent ; and Spitta's hypothesis of a primitive document containing *vv.* 1, 2, 4, 5, 6, 7, gives a clear and excellent narrative. Only, in place of his improbable theory that *v.* 3 is a scrap from an independent and complete narrative, I should regard it as an early gloss, similar to the many which have crept into the Bezan Text. The emphasis laid on the marvel at Lystra, which perhaps implies that it was the first sign of special Divine favour in the Galatian work (p. 115), may corroborate this view to some extent. Marvels and tortures are the two elements which, as time goes on, are added to the story of every saint and martyr ; the Bezan Text of this passage shows a further addition of the same type (p. 113), and is distinguished by numerous additions telling of the Divine intervention in Paul's work. All such additions, probably, grew in the popular belief, and then became attached as true facts to the original text.

The Bezan Text of 2, 3, is a good example of its character as a modernised and explanatory edition of an already archaic and obscure text. The discrepancy between *v.* 2 and *v.* 3 called for some remedy, which was found in the supposition that there were two tumults in

Iconium : on this supposition *v.* 2 was interpreted of the first tumult, and a conclusion, "and the Lord soon gave peace," was tacked on to it. The narrative then proceeds, after the renewed preaching of *v.* 3, to the second tumult of *vv.* 4, 5 (p. 113). The double tumult lent itself well to the growing Pauline myth, which sought to find occasion for the sufferings and persecutions of II *Cor.* XI.

But, if there were two stages in the Iconian narrative in its original uncorrupted form, we might reasonably argue from the words "*in the same way (as at Antioch),*" that the two stages were (1) successful preaching in the synagogue, brought to a conclusion by the jealousy and machinations of the Jews ; (2) Paul and Barnabas turned to the Gentile population exclusively and were remarkably successful among them. But conjectural alteration of the text would be required to elicit that meaning ; and we cannot spend more time here on this passage.

It is to be noted that no effect on the *Region* around Iconium is mentioned. According to our hypothesis we must recognise the difference from the narrative at Antioch, where the wide-spread effect is emphasised so strongly. The difference is natural, and the reason is clear, when we consider the difference between the two cities : Antioch was the governing centre of a wide *Region* which looked to it for administration, whereas Iconium was a comparatively insignificant town in the *Region* round Antioch.

Again, when Paul and Barnabas went from Antioch to Iconium, they were not going to a new district, but to an outlying city of the same district ; hence there is no definition of their proposed sphere of duty. They were expelled from Antioch, and they came to Iconium. The case was very different when they found it expedient to leave Iconium. They then had to cross the frontier to a new *Region* of the same province, which began a few miles south and east from Iconium. The passage to a new *Region* and a new sphere of work is clearly marked in the text.

6. THE CITIES OF LYCAONIA. (XIV 6) *Paul and Barnabas* FLED UNTO THE CITIES OF LYCAONIA, LYSTRA AND DERBE, AND THE SURROUNDING REGION ; (7) AND THERE THEY WERE ENGAGED IN PREACHING THE GOSPEL.

The expression used in XIV 6 is remarkable (p. 90) : "they fled into Lycaonia, especially to the part of it which is summed up as the cities, Lystra and Derbe, and the surrounding *Region* ". To understand this we must bear in mind that the growth of cities in Central and Eastern Asia Minor was connected with the spread of Greek civilisation ; and in the primitive pre-Greek condition of the country there were no cities organised according to the Greek system, and hardly any large settlements, except the governing centres, which were, however, Oriental towns, not Greek cities. Now, in *v.* 6 a *Region* comprising part of Lycaonia is distinguished from the rest as consisting of two cities and a stretch of cityless territory (*i.e.*, territory organised on the native pre-Greek village system).

Here, as in XIII 14, we have one of those definite statements, involving both historical and geographical facts, which the student of ancient literature pounces upon as evidence to test accuracy and date. Is the description accurate ? If so, was it accurate at all periods of history, or was it accurate only at a particular period ? To these questions we must answer that it was accurate at the period when Paul visited Lycaonia ; that it was accurate at no other time except between 37

and 72 A.D. ; and that its only meaning is to distinguish
between the Roman part of Lycaonia and the non-
Roman part ruled by Antiochus. It is instructive as
to Luke's conception of Paul's method, and about
Luke's own ideas on the development of the Christian
Church, that he should here so pointedly define the
Roman part of Lycaonia as the region to which Paul
went and where he continued preaching.

In modern expression we might call this district
" Roman Lycaonia " ; but that would not be true to
ancient usage. Territory subject to Rome was not
termed *ager Romanus* (p. 347), but was designated
after the province to which it was attached ; and this
district was *Galatica Lycaonia*, because it was in the
province Galatia. It was distinguished from " *Lycaonia
Antiochiana*," which was ruled by King Antiochus.

Such was official usage ; but we know the capricious-
ness of popular nomenclature, which often prefers some
other name to the official designation. The inhabitants
of the Roman part spoke of the other as " the
Antiochian Region " (᾽Αντιοχιανὴ χώρα), and the people
of the latter spoke of the Roman part as the
" Galatic Region " (Γαλατικὴ χώρα). It was unnecessary
for persons who were living in the country to be more
precise. Now this *Region* of Roman or Galatic Lycaonia
is three times mentioned in *Acts*. (1) In XIV 7 it is
defined by enumerating its parts ; and as Paul goes
to it out of Phrygia, it is necessary to express that
he went into Lycaonia : the advice which the Iconians
gave him would be to go into Lycaonia. (2) In XVI
1-3 the writer does not sum up the district as a whole,
for his narrative requires a distinction between the brief

visit to Derbe and the long visit to Lystra. (3) In XVIII 23, as he enters the Roman Region from the "Antiochian Part," the writer uses the name which Paul would use as he was entering it, and calls it "the Galatic Region". This is characteristic of *Acts :* it moves amid the people, and the author has caught his term in many a case from the mouth of the people. But this is done with no subservience to vulgar usage ; the writer is on a higher level of thought, and he knows how to select those popular terms which are vital and powerful, and to reject those which are vulgar and inaccurate : he moves among the people, and yet stands apart from them.

The subsequent narrative makes it clear that Paul visited only Lystra and Derbe. Why, then, should the author mention that Paul proceeded "to Lystra and Derbe and the *Region* in which they lie"? The reason lies in his habit of defining each new sphere of work according to the existing political divisions of the Roman Empire.

It is characteristic of Luke's method never formally to enunciate Paul's principle of procedure, but simply to state the facts and leave the principle to shine through them ; and here it shines clearly through them, for he made the limit of Roman territory the limit of his work, and turned back when he came to Lystra. He did not go on to Laranda, which was probably a greater city than Derbe at the time, owing to its situation and the policy followed by King Antiochus. Nor did he go to the uncivilised, uneducated native villages or towns of Roman Galatia, such as Barata.

Accordingly, the historian in the few words (XIV 6, 7) assumes and embodies the principle which can be recognised as guiding Paul's action, *viz.*, to go to the Roman world, and especially to its great cities. There is no more emphatic proof of the marvellous delicacy in expression that characterises the selection of words in *Acts*,—a delicacy that can spring only from perfect knowledge of the characters and actions described.

But the passage, not unnaturally, caused great difficulties to readers of the second century, when the bounds of Galatia had changed, and the remarkable definition of XIV 6 had become unintelligible. It was then gathered from these words that some preaching took place in " the region round about," and the explanation was found in the later historical fact (which we may assume unhesitatingly as true), that converts of Paul carried the new religion over the whole region. This fact, got from independent knowledge, was added to the text, and thus arose the " Western " Text, which appears with slight variations in different authorities. In *Codex Bezæ* the result is as follows (alterations being in italics) :—

"(4) AND THE POPULACE *remained divided*, SOME TAKING PART WITH THE JEWS, AND SOME WITH THE APOSTLES, *cleaving to them through the word of God.* (5) *And again the Jews, along with the Gentiles, roused persecution for the second time, and having stoned them they cast them out of the city;* (6) *and fleeing they came into Lycaonia, to a certain city called* LYSTRA, AND DERBE, AND THE *whole* SURROUNDING REGION ; (7) AND THEY WERE THERE ENGAGED IN PREACHING, *and the entire population was moved at the teaching;* but Paul and Barnabas continued in Lystra.*"

In this text the Pauline myth has been considerably developed. The disciples cling to the Apostles, are per-

secuted with them, accompany their flight, and preach
in the surrounding *Region*, while Paul and Barnabas
spent their time at Lystra. But the enlarged text moves
in the atmosphere of the second century. It gives us an
idea of the difficulties besetting the study of *Acts* even
then, owing to the changes that had occurred in the
surroundings of the events narrated ; and it shows that
these difficulties were not ignored and the text accepted
as inspired and above comprehension, but facts of history
were applied to explain the difficulties.

Accepted Text.

7. LYSTRA. (XIV 8) AND
AT LYSTRA THERE SAT A
CERTAIN MAN IMPOTENT
IN HIS FEET, A CRIPPLE
FROM HIS BIRTH, WHO
NEVER WALKED. (9) THIS
MAN WAS A HEARER OF
PAUL'S PREACHING, WHO,
LOOKING FIXEDLY ON HIM
AND SEEING THAT HE HAS
THE FAITH THAT BELONGS
TO SALVATION, (10) SAID,
WITH A LOUD VOICE,
"STAND UP ON THY FEET
UPRIGHT". AND HE LEAPED,
AND BEGAN TO WALK.

Bezan Text.

(8) AND THERE WAS
THERE A CERTAIN INFIRM
MAN SITTING, IMPOTENT IN
HIS FEET, WHO FROM HIS
BIRTH NEVER WALKED. (9)
THIS MAN LISTENED
GLADLY TO PAUL'S
SERMON, AND HE WAS IN
THE FEAR OF GOD. AND
PAUL, LOOKING FIXEDLY
AT HIM, AND DISCERNING
THAT HE HAS THE FAITH
THAT BELONGS TO SALVA-
TION, (10) SAID, WITH A
LOUD VOICE, "I SAY UNTO
THEE IN THE NAME OF
THE LORD JESUS CHRIST,
STAND ON THY FEET UP-
RIGHT, AND WALK". AND
IMMEDIATELY ON THE
MOMENT HE LEAPED UP,
AND BEGAN TO WALK.

In *v.* 8 we observe the marked emphasis laid on the real physical incapacity of the lame man. Though Luke, as a rule, carries brevity even to the verge of obscurity, here he reiterates in three successive phrases, with growing emphasis, that the man was really lame. The three phrases are like beats of a hammer : there is no fine literary style in this device, but there is real force, which arrests and compels the reader's attention. Luke uses the triple beat in other places for the same purpose, *e.g.*, XIII 6, " Magian, false prophet, Jew," and XVI 6, 7 (according to the true text, p. 196).

The author therefore attached the utmost importance to this point. The man was no mendicant pretender, but one whose history from infancy was well known. The case could not be explained away : it was an incontestable proof of the direct Divine power working through Paul and guaranteeing his message to the Galatic province as of Divine origin. The sign has extreme importance in the author's eyes as a proof that Paul carried the Divine approval in his new departure in Galatia, and we can better understand its importance in his eyes if it were the first which he had to record on distinct evidence (p. 108) ; but he attributes to it no influence in turning the people to Christianity. The result was only to persuade the populace that the deities whom they worshipped had vouchsafed to visit their people ; and at Malta the same result followed from the wonders which Paul wrought. The marvels recorded in *Acts* are not, as a rule, said to have been efficacious in spreading the new religion ; the marvel at Philippi caused suffering and imprisonment ; to the raising of Eutychus no effect is ascribed. The importance of these events lies rather in their effect on the mind of the Apostles themselves, who accepted them as an encouragement and a confirmation of their work. But the teaching spread by convincing the minds of the hearers (XIII 12).

The Bezan Text adds several details which have the appearance of truth. The most important is that the lame man was "in the fear of God," *i.e.*, he was a pagan of Lystra who had been attracted to Judaism before he came under Paul's influence: after some time Paul recognised him as a careful hearer (ἤκουεν, corrupted ἤκουσεν in the Bezan Text) and a person inclined towards the truth. Several other authorities give the same statement at different points and in varying words; and it therefore has the appearance of a gloss that has crept into the text in varying forms. It has however all the appearance of a true tradition preserved in the Church; for the idea that he was a proselyte is not likely to have grown up falsely in a Gentile congregation, nor is it likely to have lasted long in such a congregation, even though true. It is therefore a very early gloss.

8. THE APOSTLES AS GODS. (11) AND THE MULTITUDE, SEEING WHAT PAUL DID, LIFTED UP THEIR VOICE IN THE LYCAONIAN TONGUE, SAYING, "THE GODS HAVE TAKEN THE FORM OF MEN AND HAVE COME DOWN TO US"; (12) AND THEY CALLED BARNABAS ZEUS, AND PAUL HERMES.

Accepted Text.	*Bezan Text.*
(13) AND THE PRIEST OF ZEUS, THE GOD BEFORE THE CITY, BROUGHT OXEN	(13) AND THE PRIESTS OF THE GOD, "ZEUS BEFORE THE CITY."

AND GARLANDS TO THE GATES, AND INTENDED TO OFFER SACRIFICE ALONG WITH THE MULTITUDES. BROUGHT OXEN AND GARLANDS TO THE GATES, AND INTENDED TO MAKE SACRIFICE BEYOND *the usual ritual* ALONG WITH THE MULTITUDES.

(14) AND HEARING, THE APOSTLES BARNABAS AND PAUL RENT THEIR GARMENTS AND RAN HASTILY OUT AMONG THE CROWD, (15) SHOUTING AND SAYING, "SIRS, WHAT IS THIS YE DO? WE ALSO ARE MEN OF LIKE NATURE TO YOU, BRINGING YOU THE GLAD NEWS TO TURN FROM THESE VAIN ONES TO GOD THE LIVING, WHICH MADE THE HEAVEN AND THE EARTH AND THE SEA AND EVERYTHING IN THEM. ARE MEN OF LIKE NATURE TO YOU, BRINGING YOU THE GLAD NEWS OF THE GOD, THAT YOU MAY TURN FROM THESE VAIN ONES TO THE GOD, THE LIVING, WHICH MADE THE HEAVEN AND THE EARTH AND THE SEA AND EVERYTHING IN THEM.

(16) WHO IN THE BYGONE GENERATIONS LEFT ALL THE NATIONS TO GO IN THEIR OWN WAYS. (17) AND YET HE LEFT NOT HIMSELF WITHOUT WITNESS, IN THAT HE DID GOOD, GIVING YOU FROM HEAVEN RAINS AND FRUITFUL SEASONS, FILLING YOUR HEARTS WITH FOOD AND GLADNESS." (18) AND, SAYING THIS, THEY SCARCE RESTRAINED THE MULTITUDES FROM DOING SACRIFICE UNTO THEM.

In *v.* 12 the Accepted Text contains a gloss, which is rightly omitted in one old Latin Version (*Fl.*).

Paul is here the Messenger of the Supreme God (p. 84): he says in *Gal.* IV 14, "ye received me as a Messenger of

God ". The coincidence, as Prof. Rendel Harris points out, is interesting.

The Bezan Text has in several details the advantage of local accuracy—the plural "priests," the title "Zeus before the city," the phrase "the God," the "extra-sacrifice". Dr. Blass rejects the Bezan reading "priests" on the ground that there was only one priest of a single god; but there was regularly a college of priests at each of the great temples of Asia Minor. The "God before the city" had in almost every case been seated in his temple when there was no city; and he remained in his own sacred place after civilisation progressed and a Greek or Roman city was founded in the neighbourhood. According to the Bezan Text the proposed sacrifice was an extra beyond the ordinary ritual which the priests performed to the God. This sense of ἐπιθύειν does not occur elsewhere, but seems to lie fairly within the meaning of the compound.

Dr. Blass, who is usually so enthusiastic a supporter of the Western Text, rejects these three variations; but they add so much to the vividness of the scene, that one cannot, with him, regard them as mere corruptions.

In Asia Minor the great God was regularly termed by his worshippers "the God"; and Paul, who introduces the Christian God to his Athenian audience as "the Unknown God," whom they have been worshipping, might be expected to use the familiar term "the God" to the Lystran crowd. Here, probability favours the originality of the Bezan Text.

There remain some serious difficulties in this episode: Dr. Blass rejects the idea of some commentators that the sacrifice was prepared at the gates of the temple; and explains that the priests came from the temple before the city to the gates of the city. But in that case Lukan usage would lead us to expect πύλη (cp. IX 24, XVI 13), rather than πυλών (cp. X 17, XII 13, 14).   Another difficulty occurs in *v*. 14.   Dr. Blass's explanation is that the Apostles had gone home after healing the lame man, and there heard what was going on and hurried forth from their house.   This explanation is not convincing.   Probably a better knowledge of the localities might make the narrative clearer : it has been for years a dream of mine to make some excavations at Lystra, in the hope of illustrating this interesting episode. One suggestion, however, may be made.   The college of priests probably prepared their sacrifice at the outer gateway of the temple-grounds, because, being no part of the ordinary ritual, it could not be performed on one of the usual places, and because they wished the multitudes to take part; whereas sacrifice at the city-gates seems improbable for many reasons.   Then as the day advanced, the Apostles, who were continuing their missionary work, heard that the priests and people were getting ready to celebrate the Epiphany of the Gods ; and they hurried forth from the city to the temple.

The use of the Lycaonian language shows that the worshippers were not the Roman *coloni*, the aristocracy of the colony, but the natives, the less educated and more superstitious part of the population (*incolæ*, p. 218).

9. DERBE.   (XIV 19) AND   THERE   CAME   JEWS FROM ANTIOCH AND ICONIUM ; AND THEY PERSUADED THE MULTITUDES AND STONED PAUL AND DRAGGED *his body* OUT OF THE CITY, CONSIDERING THAT HE WAS DEAD.   (20) BUT, WHEN THE DISCIPLES ENCIRCLED HIM, HE STOOD UP AND WENT INTO THE CITY ; AND ON THE MORROW HE WENT FORTH WITH BARNABAS TO DERBE.   (21) AND THEY PREACHED THE GLAD NEWS TO THAT CITY AND MADE MANY DISCIPLES.

It is interesting to observe the contrast between the emphasis of XIV 8 and the cautiousness of statement in XIV 19. The writer considered that there was full evidence as to the real condition of the lame man ; but all that he can guarantee in XIV 19 is that his persecutors considered Paul to be dead : and beyond that he does not go. As usual, he simply states the facts, and leaves the reader to judge for himself. A writer who tried to find marvels would have found one here, and said so.

In Derbe nothing special is recorded : the same process went on as in previous cases. Here on the limits of the Roman province the Apostles turned. New magistrates had now come into office in all the cities whence they had been driven ; and it was therefore possible to go back.

10. ORGANISATION OF THE NEW CHURCHES. (XIV 21) THEY RETURNED TO LYSTRA AND TO ICONIUM AND TO ANTIOCH, (22) CONFIRMING THE SOULS OF THE DISCIPLES, EXHORTING THEM TO CONTINUE IN THE FAITH, AND THAT THROUGH MANY TRIBULATIONS WE MUST ENTER INTO THE KINGDOM OF GOD. (23) AND WHEN THEY HAD APPOINTED FOR THEM ELDERS IN EVERY CHURCH, AND HAD PRAYED WITH FASTING, THEY COMMENDED THEM TO THE LORD, ON WHOM THEY HAD BELIEVED.

On the return journey the organisation of the newly founded churches occupied Paul's attention. It is probable that, in his estimation, some definite organisation was implied in the idea of a church ; and until the brotherhood in a city was organised, it was not in the strictest sense a church. In this passage we see that the fundamental part of the Church organisation lay in the appointment of Elders (πρεσβύτεροι). In XIII 1 we found that there were prophets and teachers in the Antiochian church ; here nothing is said about appointing them, but the reason indubitably is that prophets and teachers required Divine grace, and could not be appointed by men : they were accepted when the grace was found to have been given them.

Paul used the word Bishops (ἐπίσκοποι) as equivalent to Elders. This is specially clear in XX, where he summoned the Ephesian Elders, *v.* 17, and said to them : "the Holy Spirit hath made you Bishops," verse 28. It is therefore certain that the " Bishops and Deacons" at Philippi (*Phil.* I 1) are the Elders and Deacons, who were the constituted officials of the Church. The Elders are also to be understood as "the rulers " (προιστάμενοι) at Rome and Thessalonica (*Rom* XII 8, I *Thess.* V 12). Both terms, Elders and Bishops, occur in the Epistles to Titus and Timothy ; but it is plain from *Tit.* I 5-7 that they are synonymous.

It is clear, therefore, that Paul everywhere instituted Elders in his new Churches ; and on our hypothesis as to the accurate and methodical expression of the historian, we are bound to infer that this first case is intended to be typical of the way of appointment followed in all later cases. When Paul directed Titus (I 5) to appoint Elders in each Cretan city, he was doubtless thinking of the same method which he followed here. Unfortunately, the term used (χειροτονήσαντες) is by no means certain in meaning ; for, though originally it meant *to elect by popular vote*, yet it came to be used in the sense *to appoint* or *designate* (*e.g.,* Acts X 41). But it is not in keeping with our conception of the precise and often pragmatically accurate expression of Luke, that he should in this passage have used the term χειροτονή- σαντες, unless he intended its strict sense. If he did not mean it strictly, the term is fatally ambiguous, where definiteness is specially called for. It must, I think, be allowed that the votes and voice of each congregation were considered; and the term is obviously used in that way by Paul, II *Cor.* VIII 19.

It is also apparent that a certain influence to be exercised by himself is implied in the instructions given to Titus (I 5); but those instructions seem only to mean that Titus, as a sort of presiding officer, is to nstruct the people what conditions the person chosen nust satisfy, and perhaps to reject unsuitable candidates. Candidature, perhaps of a merely informal character, is implied in I *Tim.* III 1; but, of course, if election has any scope at all, candidature goes along with it.

The procedure, then, seems to be not dissimilar to Roman elections of magistrates, in which the presiding magistrate subjected all candidates to a scrutiny as to their qualifications, and had large discretion in rejecting those whom he considered unsuitable.

Finally, it is stated in XX 28 that the Holy Spirit made men Bishops; but this expression is fully satisfied by what may safely be assumed as the final stage of the appointment, *viz.*, the Bishops elect were submitted to the Divine approval at the solemn prayer and fast which accompanied their appointment. This meeting and rite of fasting, which Paul celebrated in each city on his return journey, is to be taken as the form that was to be permanently observed (cp. XIII 3).

These inferences seem to follow naturally from the authorities to whom we have restricted ourselves.

The use of the first person plural in *v.* 22 is not personal, but general ; Paul impressed on them the universal truth that "we Christians" can enter the kingdom of God by no other path than that of suffering. At the same time the author, by using the first person, associates himself with the principle, not as one of the audience at the time, but as one who strongly realised its truth. This is one of the few personal touches in *Acts ;* and we must gather from it that, at the time when he was writing, the principle was strongly impressed on him by circumstances. I can understand this personal touch, in comparison with the studious suppression of personal feelings and views throughout *Acts*, in no other way than by supposing that Luke was composing this history during a time of special persecution. On that supposition the expression is luminous ; but otherwise it stands in marked contrast to the style of *Acts*. Now evidence from a different line of reasoning points to the conclusion that Luke was writing this second book of his history under Domitian, the second great persecutor (Ch. XVII).

11. PISIDIA AND PAMPHYLIA. (XIV 24) AND HAVING MADE A MISSIONARY JOURNEY THROUGH PISIDIA, THEY CAME INTO PAMPHYLIA ; (25) AND AFTER HAVING SPOKEN THE WORD IN PERGA, THEY CAME DOWN TO *the harbour* ATTALEIA ; (26) AND FROM THENCE THEY SAILED AWAY TO ANTIOCH, WHENCE THEY HAD BEEN COMMITTED TO THE GRACE OF GOD FOR THE WORK WHICH THEY FULFILLED. (27) AND REACHING ANTIOCH, AND HOLDING A MEETING OF THE

CHURCH, THEY PROCEEDED TO ANNOUNCE ALL THAT GOD DID WITH THEM, AND THAT HE OPENED TO THE NATIONS THE GATE OF BELIEF (see p. 85).

Next, the journey goes on from Antioch (*v.* 21), leading first into Pisidia, a *Region* of the province Galatia, and then into the province Pamphylia. It is clearly implied that Pisidian Antioch was not in Pisidia ; and, strange as that seems, it is correct (p. 104). Any Church founded in Pisidia would rank along with those founded in Galatic Phrygia and Galatic Lycaonia as one of "the Churches of Galatia"; but neither Pisidia nor Pamphylia plays any further part in early Christian history. There was, however, a Pauline tradition at Adada.

Attaleia seems to be mentioned here solely as the port of departure (though they had formerly sailed direct up the Cestrus to Perga). Not catching Luke's fondness for details connected with the sea and harbours (p. 20), the Bezan Reviser reads : "they came down to Attaleia, giving them the good news".

12. THE CHURCHES. In Lukan and Pauline language two meanings are found of the term *Ecclesia.* It means originally simply "an assembly"; and, as employed by Paul in his earliest Epistles, it may be rendered "the congregation of the Thessalonians". It is then properly construed with the genitive, denoting the assembly of this organised society, to which any man of Thessalonica may belong if he qualifies for it. The term *Ecclesia* originally implied that the assembled members constituted a self-governing body like a free Greek city (πόλις). Ancient religious societies were commonly organised on the model of city organisation. The term was adopted in the Septuagint, and came into ordinary use among Grecian Jews.

Gradually Paul's idea of "the Unified Church" became definite; and, with the true philosophic instinct, he felt the need of a technical term to indicate the idea. *Ecclesia* was the word that forced itself on him. But in the new sense it demanded a new construction; it was no longer "the church of the Thessalonians," but "the Church in Corinth"; and it was necessarily singular, for there was only one Church.

The new usage grew naturally in the mind of a statesman, animated with the instinct of administration, and gradually coming to realise the combination of imperial centralisation and local home rule, which is involved in the conception of a self-governing unity, the Universal Church, consisting of many parts, widely separated in space. Each of these parts must govern itself in its internal relations, because it is distant from other parts, and yet each is merely a piece carved out of the homogeneous whole, and each finds its justification and perfect ideal in the whole. That was a conception analogous to the Roman view, that every group of Roman citizens meeting together in a body (*conventus Civium Romanorum*) in any part of the vast Empire formed a part of the great conception " Rome," and that such a group was not an intelligible idea, except as a piece of the great unity. Any Roman citizen who came to any provincial town where such a group existed was forthwith a member of the group; and the group was simply a fragment of " Rome," cut off in space from the whole body, but preserving its vitality and self-identity as fully as when It was joined to the whole, and capable of re-uniting with the whole as soon as the estranging space was annihilated. Such was the

Roman constitutional theory, and such was the Pauline theory. The actual working of the Roman theory was complicated by the numberless imperfect forms of citizenship, such as the provincial status (for the provincials were neither Romans nor foreigners ; they were in the State yet not of the State), and other points in which mundane facts were too stubborn ; and it was impeded by failure to attain full consciousness of its character. The Pauline theory was carried out with a logical thoroughness and consistency which the Roman theory could never attain in practice ; but it is hardly doubtful that, whether or not Paul himself was conscious that the full realisation of his idea could only be the end of a long process of growth and not the beginning, his successors carried out his theory with a disregard of the mundane facts of national and local diversity that produced serious consequences. They waged relentless war within the bounds of the Empire against all provincial distinctions of language and character, they disregarded the force of associations and early ties, and aimed at an absolute uniformity that was neither healthy nor attainable in human nature. The diversities which they ejected returned in other ways, and crystallised in Christian forms, as the local saints who gradually became more real and powerful in the religious thought and practice of each district than the true Christian ideas ; and, as degeneration proceeded, the heads of the Church acquiesced more and more contentedly in a nominal and ceremonial unity that had lost reality.

As is natural, Paul did not abandon the old and familiar usage of the term *Ecclesia*, when the new and more technical usage developed in his mind and language. The process is apparent in *Gal.* I 13, where the new sense occurs, though hardly as yet, perhaps, with full consciousness and intention. Elsewhere in that letter the term is used in the old sense, "the Churches *of* Galatia". In I *Cor.* I 2 the new sense of *Ecclesia* is deliberately and formally employed.

The term *Ecclesia* is used in *Acts* in both these ways, and an examination of the distinction throws some light on the delicacy of expression in the book. It occurs in the plural sense of "congregations" or "every congregation" in XIV 23, XV 41, XVI 5. In each of these cases it is used about Paul's work in the period when he was employing the term in its earlier sense; and there is a fine sense of language in saying at that period that Paul went over the congregations which he had founded in Syria and Cilicia and in Galatia. In all other cases (in the Eastern Text at least), Luke uses *Ecclesia* in the singular, in some cases markedly in the sense of the Unified Church (*e.g.*, IX 31), in some cases as "the Church in Jerusalem" (VIII 1), and in some cases very pointedly "the Church in so far as it was in Jerusalem" or "in Antioch" (XI 22, XIII 1); and in some cases where the sense "congregation" might be permitted by the context, the sense of "the Church" gives a more satisfactory meaning.

The author, therefore, when he speaks in his own person, stands on the platform of the developed Pauline usage, and uses *Ecclesia* in the sense of "the single Unified Church," but where there is a special dramatic appropriateness in employing the earlier Pauline term to describe Paul's work, he employs the early term.

An exception occurs to this rule, in an addition of the Bezan Text, according to which Apollos went to Achaia and contributed much to strengthening the congregations (ταῖς ἐκκλησίαις). We have here not the original words of Luke, but an addition (as I believe, trustworthy in point of fact) made by a second century Reviser, imitating passages like XV 41, XVI 5, *Gal.* I. 2, 22. This case stands in close analogy to IX 31, where many authorities have (*Codex Bezæ* is defective) "the *Ecclesiai* throughout the whole of Judæa and Galilee and Samaria," but the singular is used in the Accepted Text founded on the great MSS.

Note 1. Date. On our view this journey began in March 47, and ended about July or August 49.

Note 2. Declension of *Lystra*. The variation in the declension of the word *Lystra*[1] is sometimes taken as a sign that the author employed two different written authorities (in one of which the word was declined as feminine singular and in the other as neuter plural), and followed them implicitly, using in each case the form employed in the authority whom he was following at the moment. This suggestion has convinced neither Spitta nor Clemen, who both assign XVI 1-3 to one author. Only the most insensate and incapable of compilers would unawares use the double declension twice in consecutive sentences. The author, whoever he was and whenever he lived, certainly considered that the proper declension of the name was Λύστροις, Λύστραν; and the only question is this: was

---

[1] Accusative Λύστραν XIV 6, XVI 1, dative Λύστροις XIV 8, XVI 2.

that variation customary in the Lystran Greek usage?
If it was customary, then its employment in *Acts* is a
marked proof of first-hand local knowledge, and if it
was not customary, the opposite. We have unfortunately
no authorities for the Lystran usage : the city name
occurs in the inscriptions only in the nominative case,
Lustra. It is certain that many names in Asia Minor,
such as Myra, etc., occur both in feminine singular and in
neuter plural ; but there is no evidence as to any local
usage appropriating certain cases to each form. Excavations on the site may yield the needed evidence to test
the accuracy of this detail.

One indirect piece of evidence may be added. Myra
is an analogous name. Now the local form of accus. was
Μύραν, for the Turkish Dembre comes from τὴν Μβρα(ν),
i.e. (εἰς) τὴν Μύραν. [It is most probable that in XXVII 5
Μύραν (or Μύρραν) should be read, not Μύρα.] I know no
evidence as to the local form of the dative ; but the genitive
appears as Μύρων in the signatures of bishops.

Incidentally we notice that the name of the city is spelt
Lustra, not *Lystra* (like Prymnessos), on coins and inscriptions. That is an indication of Latin tone, and of the
desire to make the city name a Latin word. People who
called their city *Lustra* would have distinguished themselves pointedly from the Lycaonians, the subjects of
King Antiochus and mentioned in that way on his coins.

CHAPTER VI

ST. PAUL IN GALATIA

ι. THE .IMPERIAL AND THE CHRISTIAN POLICY
When Paul passed out of Pamphylia into Galatia, he
went out of a small province, which was cut off from the
main line of historical and political development, into a
great province that lay on that line. The history of
Asia Minor at that time had its central motive in the
transforming and educative process which the Roman
imperial policy was trying to carry out in the country.
In Pamphylia that process was languidly carried out
by a governor of humble rank; but Galatia was the
frontier province, and the immense social and educational
changes involved in the process of romanising an
oriental land were going on actively in it. We proceed
to inquire in what relation the new Pauline influence
stood to the questions that were agitating the province.

What, then, was the character of Roman policy and
the line of educational advance in the districts of Galatic
Phrygia and Galatic Lycaonia; and what were the
forces opposing the Roman policy?

The aim of Roman policy may be defined as the
unification and education in Roman ideas of the province; and its general effect may be summed up under
four heads, which we shall discuss in detail, comparing
in each case the effect produced or aimed at by the

Church. We enumerate the heads, not in (rder of importance, but in the order that best brings out the relation between Imperial influence and Church influence:
(1) relation to Greek civilisation and language : (2) development of an educated middle class : (3) growth of unity
over the Empire : (4) social facts.

(1) The Roman influence would be better defined as
" Græco-Roman ".   Previous to Roman domination, the
Greek civilisation, though fostered in the country by the
Greek kings of Syria and Pergamos, who had successively
ruled the country, had failed to affect the people as a body ;
it had been confined to the coast valleys of the Hermus,
Cayster, Mæander and Lycus, and to the garrison cities
founded on the great central plateau by the kings to
strengthen their hold on the country.   These cities were
at the same time centres of Greek manners and education ;
their language was Greek ; and, in the midst of alien
tribes, their interests naturally coincided with those of the
kings who had founded them.

The Roman Government, far from being opposed to
Greek influence, acted in steady alliance with it.   It
adopted the manners of Greece, and even recognised the
Greek language for general use in the Eastern provinces.   Rome was so successful, because she almost
always yielded to the logic of facts.   The Greek influence
was, on the whole, European and Western in character ;
and opposed to the oriental stagnation which resisted
Roman educative efforts.   Rome accepted the Greek
language as her ally.   Little attempt was made to
naturalise the Latin language in the East ; and even the
Roman colonies in the province of Galatia soon ceased
to use Latin except on state occasions and in a few

formal documents. A Græco-Roman civilisation using the Greek language was the type which Rome aimed at establishing in the East.

The efforts of Rome to naturalise Western culture in Asia Minor were more successful than those of the Greek kings had been ; but still they worked at best very slowly. The evidence of inscriptions tends to show that the Phrygian language was used in rural parts of the country during the second and even the third century. In some remote and rustic districts.it persisted even until the fourth century, as Celtic did in parts of North Galatia.

The Christian influence was entirely in favour of the Greek language. The rustics clung longest to Paganism, while the Greek-speaking population of the cities adopted Christianity. It is not probable that any attempt was made to translate the Christian sacred books into Phrygian or Lycaonian; there is not even any evidence that evangelisation in these languages was ever attempted. The Christians seem to have been all expected to read the Scriptures in Greek. That fact was sufficient to put the Church, as regards its practical effect on society, on the same side as the romanising influence; and the effect was quite independent of any intentional policy. The most zealous enemy of the imperial Antichrist was none the less effective in aiding the imperial policy by spreading the official language. In fact, Christianity did far more thoroughly what the emperors tried to do. It was really their best ally, if they had recognised the facts of the case ; and the Christian Apologists of the second century are justified in claiming that their religion was essentially a loyal religion.

(2) The Empire had succeeded in imposing its languages

on the central districts of Asia only so far as education spread. Every one who wrote or read, wrote and read Greek ; but those who could do neither used the native language. Hence inscriptions were almost universally expressed in Greek, for even the most illiterate, if they aspired to put an epitaph on a grave, did so in barbarous (sometimes unintelligible) Greek ; the desire for an epitaph was the first sign of desire for education and for Greek.

In education lay the most serious deficiency of the imperial policy. Rome cannot be said to have seriously attempted to found an educational system either in the provinces or in the metropolis. " The education imparted on a definite plan by the State did not go beyond instituting a regular series of amusements, some of a rather brutalising tendency" (*Church in R. E.*, p. 360). And precisely in this point, Christianity came in to help the Imperial Government, recognising the duty of educating, as well as feeding and amusing, the mass of the population. The theory of universal education for the people has never been more boldly and thoroughly stated than by Tatian (*ibid.* p. 345). " The weak side of the Empire—the cause of the ruin of the first Empire—was the moral deterioration of the lower classes : Christianity, if adopted in time, might have prevented this result."

Now, the classes where education and work go hand in hand were the first to come under the influence of the new religion. On the one hand the uneducated and grossly superstitious rustics were unaffected by it. On the other hand, there were "not many wise, not many mighty, not many noble " in the Churches of the first century, *i.e.*, not many professional teachers of wisdom and philosophy, not many of the official and governing class, not many of the hereditarily privileged class. But the working and thinking classes, with the students, if not the Professors, at the Universities, were attracted to the new teaching ; and it spread among them with a rapidity that seemed to many modern critics incredible and fabulous, till it was justified by recent discoveries. The enthusiasm of the period was on the side of the Christians ; its dilettantism, officialism, contentment and self-satisfaction were against them.

In respect of education Christianity appears as filling a gap in the imperial policy, supplementing, not opposing it—a position which, though it earns no gratitude and often provokes hatred, implies no feeling of opposition in the giver.

(3) Again, the main effort of Roman policy was directed towards encouraging a sense of unity and patriotism in the Empire. It discouraged the old tribal and national divisions, which kept the subject population in their pre-Roman associations, and substituted new divisions. Patriotism in ancient time was inseparable from religious feeling, and Roman policy fostered a new imperial religion in which all its subjects should unite, *viz.*, the worship of the divine majesty of Rome incarnate in human form in the series of the emperors and especially in the reigning emperor. Each province was united in a formal association for this worship : the association built temples in the great cities of the province, held festivals and games, and had a set of officials, who were in a religious point of view priests and in a political point of view officers of the imperial service. Everything that the imperial policy did in the provinces during the first century was so arranged as to encourage the unity of the entire Roman province ;

and the priests of the imperial religion became by insensible degrees a higher priesthood, exercising a certain influence over the priests of the other religions of the province. In this way a sort of hierarchy was created for the province and the empire as a whole ; the reigning emperor being the religious head, the Supreme Pontiff of the State, and a kind of sacerdotal organisation being grouped under him according to the political provinces.

As time passed, gradually the Christian Church grouped itself according to the same forms as the imperial religion, —not indeed through conscious imitation, but because the Church naturally arranged its external form according to the existing facts of communication and interrelation. In Pisidian Antioch a preacher had unique opportunities for affecting the entire territory whose population resorted to that great centre (p. 105). So Perga was a centre for Pamphylia, Ephesus for Asia. But the direct influence of these centres was confined to the Roman district or province. In this way necessarily and inevitably the Christian Church was organised around the Roman provincial metropolis and according to the Roman provincial divisions.

The question then is, when did this organisation of the Church begin ? I can see no reason to doubt that it began with Paul's mission to the West. It grew out of the circumstances of the country, and there was more absolute necessity in the first century than later, that, if the Church was organised at all, it must adapt itself to the political facts of the time, for these were much stronger in the first century. The classification adopted in Paul's own letters of the Churches which he founded is according to provinces, Achaia, Macedonia, Asia, and

Galatia. The same fact is clearly visible in the narrative of *Acts*: it guides and inspires the expression from the time when the Apostles landed at Perga. At every step any one who knows the country recognises that the Roman division is implied. There is only one way of avoiding this conclusion, and that is to make up your mind beforehand that the thing is impossible, and therefore to refuse to admit any evidence for it.

The issue of events showed that the Empire had made a mistake in disregarding so completely the existing lines of demarcation between tribes and races in making its new political provinces. For a time it succeeded in establishing them, while the energy of the Empire was still fresh, and its forward movement continuous and steady. But the differences of tribal and national character were too great to be completely set aside; they revived while the energy of the Empire decayed during the second century. Hence every change in the bounds of the provinces of Asia Minor from 138 onwards was in the direction of assimilating them to the old tribal frontiers; and at last in 295 even the great complex province Asia was broken up after 428 years of existence, and resolved into the old native districts, Lydia, Caria, Phrygia, etc.; and the moment that the political unity was dissolved there remained nothing of the Roman Asia. But the ultimate failure of the Roman policy must not blind us to the vigour and energy with which that policy was carried out during the first century. "Asia" and "Galatia" were only ideas, but they were ideas which the whole efforts of Roman government aimed at making into realities.

(4) There was another reason why the power of the

new religion was necessarily thrown on the side of the
Roman policy. Greek civilisation was strongly opposed
to the social system that was inseparably connected with
the native religion in all its slightly varying forms in
different localities. The opposition is as old as the
landing of the earliest Greek emigrants on the Asian
coasts : the colonists were the force of education, and
progress and freedom, the priests arrayed against them
the elements that made for stagnation and priest-ridden
ignorance and slavery. Throughout Greek history the
same opposition constantly appears. The Phrygian religion
was always reckoned as the antithesis of Hellenism. That
is all a matter of history, one might say a commonplace
of history. But the same opposition was necessarily
developed in the Romanisation of the provinces of Asia
Minor. The priests of the great religious centres were
inevitably opposed to the Roman policy ; but their power
was gone, their vast estates had become imperial property,
and their influence with the population was weakened
by the growth of the Greek spirit. This subject might
be discussed at great length ; but I must here content
myself with referring to the full account of the districts in
my *Cities and Bishoprics of Phrygia.*

In this conflict there can be no doubt on which side
the Christian influence must tell. When we consider the
social system which was inculcated as a part of the native
religion, it is evident that every word spoken by Paul
or Barnabas must tell directly against the prevalent
religion, and consequently on the side of the Roman
policy. It is true that in moral tone the Greek society
and religion were low, and Christianity was necessarily
an enemy to them. But Greek religion was not here

present as the enemy. The native religion was the active enemy; and its character was such that Greek education was pure in comparison, and the Greek moralists, philosophers, and politicians inveighed against the Phrygian religion as the worst enemy of the Greek ideals of life. Greek society and life were at least founded on marriage; but the religion of Asia Minor maintained as a central principle that all organised and settled social life on the basis of marriage was an outrage on the free unfettered divine life of nature, the type of which was found in the favourites of the great goddesses, the wild animals of the field and the mountains. The Greek and Roman law which recognised as citizens only those born from the legitimate marriage of two citizens had no existence in Phrygian cities.

Thus in Galatia the Græco-Roman education, on the side of freedom, civilisation and a higher social morality, was contending against the old native religious centres with their influential priestly colleges, on the side of ignorance, stagnation, social anarchy, and enslavement of the people to the priests. Christian influence told against the latter, and therefore in favour of the former.

In all these ways Christianity, as a force in the social life of the time, was necessarily arrayed on the side of the Roman imperial policy. "One of the most remarkable sides of the history of Rome is the growth of ideas which found their realisation and completion in the Christian Empire. Universal citizenship, universal equality of rights, universal religion, a universal Church, all were ideas which the Empire was slowly working out, but which it could not realise till it merged itself in Christianity." "The path of development for the Empire lay in accepting the religion which offered it the possibility of completing its organisation."

With the instinctive perception of the real nature of the case that characterises the genius for organisation, Paul from the first directed his steps in the path which the Church had to tread. He made no false step, he needed no tentatives before he found the path, he had to retract nothing (except perhaps the unsuccessful compromise embodied in the Decree of the Apostolic Council, pp. 172, 182). It is not necessary to assert or to prove that he consciously anticipated all that was to take place; but he was beyond all doubt one of those great creative geniuses whose policy marks out the lines on which history is to move for generations and even for centuries afterwards.

It is apparent how far removed we are from a view, which has been widely entertained, "that there was an entire dislocation and discontinuity in the history of Christianity in Asia Minor at a certain epoch; that the Apostle of the Gentiles was ignored and his teaching repudiated, if not anathematised"; and that this anti-Pauline tendency found in "Papias a typical representative". Like Lightfoot, whose summary we quote, we must reject that view. We find in the epitaph of the second-century Phrygian saint, Avircius Marcellus, a proof of the deep reverence retained in Asia Minor for St. Paul: when he travelled, he took Paul everywhere with him as his guide and companion.

These considerations show the extreme importance of the change of plan that led Paul across Taurus to Pisidian Antioch. So far as it is right to say that any single event is of outstanding importance, the step that took Paul away from an outlying corner and put him on the

main line of development at the outset of his work in
Asia Minor, was the most critical step in his history. It
is noteworthy that the historian, who certainly understood
its importance, and whose sympathy was deeply engaged
in it, does not attribute it to Divine suggestion, though he
generally records the Divine guidance in the great crises
of Paul's career; and it stands in perfect agreement with
this view, that Paul himself, when he impresses on the
Galatian Churches in the strongest terms his Divine commission to the Gentiles, does not say that the occasion of
his going among them was the Divine guidance, but expressly mentions that an illness was the cause why he
preached among them at first.

Now, every reader must be struck with the stress that
is laid, alike by Paul and by Luke, throughout their
writings, on the Divine guidance. They both find the
justification of all Paul's innovations on missionary enterprise in the guiding hand of God. We demand that there
should be a clear agreement in the occasions when they
discerned that guidance; and in this case the South-
Galatian theory enables us to recognise a marked negative
agreement.

Further, there is evidently a marked difference between
the looser way of talking about " the hand of God " that
is common in the present day, and the view entertained
by Paul or Luke. Where a great advantage results from
a serious illness, many of us would feel it right to recognise
and acknowledge the " guiding hand of God "; but it is
evident that, when Luke or Paul uses such language as
" the Spirit suffered them not," they refer to some definite
and clear manifestation, and not to a guidance which became apparent only through the results. The superhuman

element is inextricably involved in Luke's history and in Paul's letters.

All that has just been said is, of course, mere empty verbiage, devoid of any relation to Paul's work and policy in Galatia, if the Churches of Galatia were not the active centres of Roman organising effort, such as the colonies Antioch and Lystra, or busy trading cities like Claud-Iconium and Claudio-Derbe, but Pessinus and some villages in the wilderness of the Axylon (as Professor Zöckler has quite recently maintained). Lightfoot saw the character of Paul's work, and supposed him to have gone to the great cities of North Galatia, and specially the metropolis Ancyra; but the most recent development of the North-Galatian theory denies that Paul ever saw the Roman central city.

2. THE JEWS IN ASIA AND SOUTH GALATIA. In Cyprus, Barnabas and Saul had confined themselves within the circle of the synagogue, until Paul stepped forth from it to address the Roman proconsul. In entering Galatia Paul was passing from Semitic surroundings into a province where Greek was the language of all even moderately educated persons, and where Græco-Roman manners and ideas were being actively disseminated and eagerly assimilated by all active and progressive and thoughtful persons. How then did Paul, with his versatility and adaptability, appear among the Galatians, and in what tone did he address them?

At first he adhered to his invariable custom of addressing such audience as was found within the synagogue. There was a large Jewish population in the Phrygian district of Galatia, as well as in Asian Phrygia (which Paul entered and traversed at a later date XIX 1). According to Dr.

Neubauer (*Géographie du Talmud*, p. 315), these Jews had to a considerable extent lost connection with their country, and forgotten their language; and they did not participate in the educated philosophy of the Alexandrian Jews: the baths of Phrygia and its wine had separated the Ten Tribes from their brethren, as the Talmud expresses it: hence they were much more readily converted to Christianity; and the Talmud alludes to the numerous con· verts.

It is much to be desired that this distinguished scholar should discuss more fully this subject, which he has merely touched on incidentally. The impression which he conveys is different from that which one is apt to take from the narrative in *Acts;* and one would be glad to have the evidence on which he relies stated in detail. But my own epigraphic studies in Phrygia lead me to think that there is much in what Dr. Neubauer has said; and that we must estimate Luke's account from the proper point. Luke was profoundly interested in the conflict between Paul and the Judaising party; and he recounts with great detail the stages in that conflict. That point of view is natural in one who had lived through the conflict, before the knot was cut by the destruction of Jerusalem in A.D. 70; but, though short, the struggle was far more severe than later scholars, who see how complete was Paul's triumph, are apt to imagine. Even to a writer of the second century, the conflict with the Judaisers could not have bulked largely in Church history. But to Luke that conflict is the great feature in the development of the Church. Hence he emphasises every point in the antagonism between Paul and the Judaisers; and his readers are apt to leave out of notice other aspects of the case. The Jews of Pisidian

Antioch are not represented as opposed to Paul's doctrines, but only to his placing the Gentiles on an equality with themselves (p. 101, XIII 45). A great multitude of the Iconian Jews believed (XIV 1). The few Jews of Philippi seem to have been entirely on Paul's side: they were probably to a great extent settlers who had come, like Lydia, in the course of trade with Asia Minor. In Berœa the Jews in a body were deeply impressed by Paul's preaching. In Thessalonica, however, the Jews were almost entirely opposed to him; and in Corinth it was nearly as bad, though the *archisynagogos* followed him. In Corinth the Jewish colony would certainly be in close and direct communication with Syria and Palestine by sea, more than with the Phrygian Jews of the land road; and it is probable that the same was the case in Thessalonica, though no facts are known to prove it.

From the recorded facts, therefore, it would appear that the Jews in central Asia Minor were less strongly opposed to Pauline Christianity than they were in Palestine. Further, the Asian and Galatian Jews had certainly declined from the high and exclusive standard of the Palestinian Jews, and probably forgotten Hebrew. In Lystra we find a Jewess married to a Greek, who cannot have come into communion with the Jews, for the son of the marriage was not submitted to the Jewish law (XVI 1-3). The marriage of a Jewess to a Gentile is a more serious thing than that of a Jew, and can hardly have come to pass except through a marked assimilation of these Jews to their Gentile neighbours. In Ephesus the sons even of distinguished priests practised magic, and exorcised demons in the name of Jesus (XIX 14); and Dr. Schürer has shown that gross superstitions were practised by the Jews of Thyatira. There seems, therefore, to be no real discrepancy between the evidence of Luke and Dr. Neubauer's inference about the Phrygian Jews from the Talmud.

Naturally the approximation between Jews and Gentiles in Phrygia had not been all on one side. An active, intelligent, and prosperous minority like the Jews must have exercised a strong influence on their neighbours. Evidence to that effect is not wanting in inscriptions (see *Cities and Bishoprics*, Chap. XIV); and we may compare the readiness with which the Antiochians flocked to the synagogue, XIII 43-4, and at a later time yielded to the first emissaries of the Judaising party in the Church (*Gal.* I 6). The history of the Galatian Churches is in the closest relation to their surroundings (p. 183).

3. TONE OF PAUL'S ADDRESS TO THE GALATIAN AUDIENCES. The only recorded sermon of Paul in Galatia was delivered in the synagogue at Antioch (p. 100). Thereafter he "turned to the Gentiles," and appealed direct to the populace of the city. Now Paul was wont to adapt himself to his hearers (p. 82). Did he address the people of Antioch as members of a nation (Phrygians, or, as Dr. Zöckler thinks, Pisidians), or did he regard them as members of the Roman Empire? We cannot doubt that his teaching was opposed to the native tendency as one of mere barbarism and superstition; and that he regarded them as members of the same Empire of which he was a citizen. Moreover, the Antiochians claimed to be a Greek foundation of remote time by Magnesian settlers: that is, doubtless, a fiction (of a type fashionable in the great cities of Phrygia), but it shows the tendency to claim Greek origin and to regard

national characteristics as vulgar. Finally, Antioch was now a Roman colony, and its rank and position in the province belonged to it as the representative of old Greek culture and modern Roman government amid uncultured rustic Pisidians and Phrygians. But some North Galatian theorists resolutely maintain that Paul could never appeal to its population as "men of the province Galatia," but only as " Pisidians ".

We possess a letter which Paul addressed to the Galatian Churches; but it was addressed to congregations which had existed for five years or more, and was written on a special occasion to rebuke and repress the Judaising tendency: it moves in a series of arguments against that tendency, and gives us little information as to the line Paul would take in addressing for the first time a pagan audience in one of the Galatian cities (see Ch. VIII).

In writing to the Corinthian Church Paul mentions that he had adopted a very simple way of appealing to them, and that his simple message was by some persons contrasted unfavourably with the more philosophical style of Apollos and the more ritualistic teaching of the Judaising Christians. But it is apparent (see p. 252) that Paul made a new departure in this respect at Corinth ; and we must not regard too exclusively what he says in that letter. Though the main elements of his message were the same from first to last (*Gal.* III 1, I *Cor.* II 2), yet it is natural and probable that there should be a certain degree of development in his method ; and in trying to recover the tone in which he first appealed to his Galatic audiences, we are carried back to a period in his career earlier than any of his extant letters.

The passages in *Acts* that touch the point are the

address to his worshippers at Lystra, the speech before the Areopagus at Athens, and, at a later time, the account which the Town-clerk at Ephesus gave of his attitude as a preacher.

The Town-clerk of Ephesus reminded the rioters that Paul had not been guilty of disrespect, either in action or in language, towards the patron and guardian goddess of the city. Chrysostom in the fourth century remarks that this was a false statement to suit the occasion and calm the riot ; it seemed to him impossible that Paul should refrain from violent invective against the false goddess, for the later Christians inveighed in merciless terms against the Greek gods, and (as every one who tries to understand ancient religion must feel) the Apologists from the second century onwards give a one-sided picture of that religion, describing only its worst features, and omitting those germs of higher ideas which it certainly contained. But we cannot suppose with Chrysostom that the clerk misrepresented the facts to soothe the popular tumult. The effect of his speech depended on the obviousness of the facts which he appealed to ; and it would defeat his purpose, if his audience had listened to speeches in which Paul inveighed against the goddess. If this speech is taken from real life, the clerk of Ephesus must be appealing to well-known facts (see p. 281 f.).

Next we turn to the speech at Athens. So far was Paul from inveighing against the objects of Athenian veneration that he expressly commended the religious feelings of the people, and identified the God whom he had come to preach with the god whom they were blindly worshipping. He did not rebuke or check their religious ideas, but merely tried to guide them ; he distinctly set forth the principle that the pagans were honestly striving to worship "the God that made the world and all things therein " (p. 251 f.).

In this speech Paul lays no emphasis on the personality of the God whom he sets forth : "*what* ye worship in ignorance, this set I forth unto you," and "we ought not to think that the *Divine nature* is like unto gold or silver or stone, graven by art and device of man". The popular philosophy inclined towards Pantheism, the popular religion was Polytheistic ; but Paul starts from the simplest platform common to both—there exists something in the way of a Divine nature which the religious try to please and the philosophers try to understand. That is all he seeks as a hypothesis to start from.

At Athens the speech was more philosophical in tone, catching the spirit of a more educated populace. At Lystra it was more simple, appealing to the witness they had of the God "who gives from heaven rain and fruitful seasons, filling your hearts with gladness". But the attitude is the same in both cases. "God who made the heaven and the earth in the generations gone by suffered all the nations to walk in their own ways" ; and "we bring you the good news that you should repent". That is the same tone in which at Athens he said, "The times of ignorance God overlooked ; but now He commandeth men that they should all everywhere repent".

There is one condition, however, on which Paul insisted from the first, at Athens and at Lystra and everywhere. The worship of idols and images was absolutely pernicious, and concealed from the nations the God whom they were groping after and trying to find : they must turn from these vain and dead gods to the God that lives. Hence the riot at Ephesus was got up by the tradesmen who made images of the Goddess Artemis in her shrine, and whose trade was threatened when the worship of images was denounced. But the denunciation of images was a commonplace of Greek philosophy; and the idea that any efficacy resided in images was widely regarded among the Greeks as a mark of superstition unworthy of the educated man. Paul stands here on the footing of the philosopher, not contravening the State laws by introducing new gods, but expounding to the people the true character of the living God whom they are seeking after.

Such was the way in which Paul introduced his Good Tidings to the peoples of the province Galatia. From this he went on step by step, and his method is summed up by himself, *Gal.* III 1, "Christ had been placarded before their eyes". Now was the opportunity granted them; "through this Man is proclaimed remission of sins" (XIII 38). But if they despised the opportunity they must beware (XIII 40-1), "inasmuch as He hath appointed a day in the which He will judge the world" (XVII 31).

Paul's teaching thus was introduced to his pagan audiences in the language of the purest and simplest theology current among educated men. He started from those thoughts which were familiar to all who had imbibed even the elements of Greek education. But even in the more advanced stage of his teaching he did not cut it off from the philosophy of the time. He never adopted that attitude of antagonism to philosophy which became customary in the second century, springing from the changed circumstances of that period. On the contrary, he says (*Col.* IV 5-6, *cf. Eph.* V 16): "Regulate with wisdom

your conduct towards the outside world, making your market
to the full from the opportunity of this life.   Let your conversation be always gracious, seasoned with the salt and
the refinement of delicacy, so as to know the suitable reply
to make to every individual."   As Curtius says, with his
own grace and delicacy of perception, the Attic salt is
here introduced into the sphere of Christian ethics.
Polished courtesy of address to all, was valued by Paul as
a distinct and important element in the religious life ; and
he advised his pupils to learn from the surrounding world
everything that was worthy in it, "making your market
fully from the occasion" (a thought very inadequately
expressed in the English Version, "redeeming the time,"
Col. IV 6).   But it is in *Phil.* IV 8 that his spirit is
expressed in the fullest and most graceful and exquisite
form, "whatsoever is true, whatsoever is holy, whatsoever
is just, whatsoever is pure, whatsoever is courteous, whatsoever is of fine expression, all excellence, all merit, take
account of these," wherever you find these qualities, notice
them, consider them, imitate them.

It is not the Jew who speaks in these and many other
sentences ; it is the educated citizen of the Roman world
attuned to the most gracious and polished tone of educated
society.   We can faintly imagine to ourselves the electrical
effect produced by teaching like this on the population of
the Galatian cities, on a people who were just beginning to
rise from the torpor of oriental peasant life and to appreciate
the beauty of Greek thought and the splendour of Roman
power.   They found in Paul no narrow and hard bigot to
dash from their lips the cup of education ; they found one
who guided into the right channel all their aspirations after
culture and progress, who raised them into a finer sphere of

thought and action, who showed them what wealth of meaning lay in their simple speculations on the nature of God, who brought within their grasp all that they were groping after. We can imagine how sordid and beggarly were the elements that Jewish ritual had to offer them in comparison; and we can appreciate the tone of Paul's letter to them, where his argument is to recall to their minds the teaching which he had given them on his former visit, to contrast with this freedom and graciousness and progress which he offered them the hard cut and dry life of Jewish formalism, and to ask who had bewitched them into preferring the latter before the former.[1]

It is remarkable that, alike at Lystra and Athens, there is nothing in the reported words of Paul that is overtly Christian, and nothing (with the possible exception of " the man whom he hath ordained ") that several Greek philosophers might not have said. That is certainly not accidental; the author of *Acts* must have been conscious of it; and it is a strong proof of their genuineness: no one would invent a speech for Paul, which was not markedly Christian. That remarkable omission is explained by some commentators in the speech at Athens (*e.g.*, Meyer-Wendt) as due to the fact that the speech was not completed; and yet they acknowledge that the speech is a rounded whole, and that all the specially Pauline ideas are touched in it. To look for an addition naming the Saviour is to ignore the whole character of the speech and the scene where it was delivered.

The same mark of genuineness occurs in the central episode of the romance of Thekla, when we disentangle

[1] Curtius's beautiful essay on *Paulus in Athen* has been constantly in the writer's mind in this and some other places.

the tale of her trials at Pisidian Antioch from the incongruous and vulgar additions by which it is disfigured. In the beautiful story as it was originally written, probably in the latter part of the first century, Thekla appeared to the mass of the Antiochian populace to be a devotee of "the God," bound by a rule of service given her by direct Divine command; and she commanded their sympathy, in so far as she represented their own cause; whereas, if she had been seen to be severing herself absolutely from their life and their religion, their sympathy would be incredible. In this character lies the proof of its early date: the episode in its original form is contrary to the tone of the second century.

Incidentally we notice what an anachronism it is to suppose that the attitude attributed in *Acts* to Paul could have been conceived by a second-century author! The tone of these speeches is of the first century, and not of the time when the Apologists were writing. In the first century Christianity and the current philosophy alike were disliked and repressed by the Flavian emperors, as favouring the spirit of unrest and dissatisfaction. But during the second, the Imperial Government and the popular philosophy were in league against the increasing power of the Church; and the tone of the speeches is incredible in a composition of that time.

CHAPTER VII

THE APOSTOLIC COUNCIL

1. ORIGIN OF THE COUNCIL. (XIV 27) WHEN PAUL AND BARNABAS WERE COME TO ANTIOCH AND HAD GATHERED THE CHURCH TOGETHER, THEY RE-HEARSED ALL THINGS THAT GOD HAD DONE WITH THEM, AND HOW THAT HE HAD OPENED A DOOR OF BELIEF UNTO THE NATIONS. (28) AND THEY TARRIED NO LITTLE TIME WITH THE DISCIPLES. (XV 1) AND CERTAIN PERSONS CAME DOWN FROM JUDÆA, AND TAUGHT THE BRETHREN, THAT "EXCEPT YE BE CIR-CUMCISED, AFTER THE CUSTOM OF MOSES, YE CANNOT BE SAVED". (2) AND WHEN PAUL AND BARNABAS HAD NO SMALL DISSENSION AND QUESTIONING WITH THEM, THEY (*i.e.*, *the Brethren*) APPOINTED THAT PAUL AND BARNABAS AND CERTAIN OTHER OF THEM SHOULD GO UP TO JERUSALEM ABOUT THIS QUESTION. (3) THEY, THEREFORE, BEING BROUGHT ON THEIR WAY BY THE CHURCH, PASSED THROUGH BOTH PHŒNICE AND SAMARIA, DECLARING THE CONVERSION OF THE NATIONS; AND THEY CAUSED GREAT JOY UNTO ALL THE BRETHREN.

A considerable lapse of time is implied in *v.* 28, during which Paul and Barnabas resumed their former duties at Antioch (XIII 1). Luke, as usual, states the lapse of time very vaguely, and it is impossible to estimate from his words the interval between Paul's return and the arrival of the envoys from Jerusalem (XV 1). If *v.* 28 includes only that interval, the Apostolic Council cannot have occurred before A.D. 50; but if, as is more likely (p. 256), *v.* 28 refers to the whole residence of Paul at Antioch before and after the Council, then probably the Council took place in the end of 49.

A difficulty (which is described in § 2) occurred at Antioch as to the obligation of the Gentile members of the Church to come under the full ceremonial regulations of the Jewish Law; and it was resolved to send delegates to the governing body of the Church in Jerusalem about this question. We cannot doubt that this resolution was acquiesced in by Paul; probably he even proposed it. Now, the resolution clearly involved the recognition that Jerusalem was the administrative centre of the Church; and this is an important point in estimating Paul's views on administration. With the vision of a statesman and organiser, he saw that the Church as a unified and organised body must have an administrative centre, and that a Church of separate parts could not be unified without such a centre, which should be not a governor over subordinates, but the head among equals; and his whole history shows that he recognised Jerusalem as necessarily marked out for the centre. Hence he kept before the attention of his new foundations their relation and duty to Jerusalem; and he doubtless understood the solitary injunction given him by the older Apostles on his second visit to Jerusalem (p. 57), as involving a charge to remember that duty.

Moreover, he had already communicated privately with

the recognised leaders in Jerusalem, and knew that their sentiments agreed with his own ; and he must have been fully alive to the great step in organisation which would be made, if Antioch set the example of referring such a question to authoritative decision in Jerusalem at a meeting where it was represented by delegates.

In the mission of Paul and Barnabas to Jerusalem it is noteworthy that the Divine action plays no part. The Church in Antioch resolved, and the Church sent them to Jerusalem, escorting them on their way. This is not accidental, but expresses the deliberate judgment of Paul and of Luke. The action that led up to the Council in Jerusalem and the ineffective Decree did not originate in Divine revelation.

The accepted view is different. There is a practically universal agreement among critics and commentators of every shade of opinion that the visit described as the third in *Acts* XV is the one that Paul describes as the second in *Gal.* II 1-10. Scholars who agree in regard to scarcely any other point of early Christian history are at one in this. Now, Paul says in his letter to the Galatians that he made his second visit in accordance with revelation. Lightfoot tries to elude the difficulty of identifying this second visit by revelation with the third visit without revelation recorded in *Acts* XV : he says (*Gal.*, p. 125), " here there is no contradiction. The historian naturally records the external impulse which led to the mission : the Apostle himself states his inward motive." He quotes " parallel cases which suggest how the one motive might supplement the other ". But the parallels which he quotes to support his view seem merely to prove how improbable it is. (1) He says that in *Acts* XIII 2, 4, Barnabas and Paul were sent forth by the Holy Spirit through a direct command ; while in XIII 3 they are sent away by the Church of Antioch. But that is not the proper force of XIII 3 (p. 67 f.) : the Church merely gave Barnabas and Saul freedom from their duties and leave to depart, while the Spirit " sent them out ". In XV 3, on the contrary, the Church is said to have initiated and completed the action. (2) He founds another parallel on the mistaken idea that XXII 17 and IX 29 f. refer to the same visit (p. 62).

The journey to Jerusalem occupied some time ; for in Phœnice and in Samaria the envoys took the opportunity of "describing in detail the turning of the Nations *to God*". Here, evidently, the newly accomplished step, "the opening of the door of faith to the Nations," is meant. The recital of the circumstances and results of the new step caused great joy. Now, Luke pointedly omits Judæa ; and his silence is, as often elsewhere, eloquent : the recital would cause no joy in Judæa. Accordingly, we are not to suppose that the joy was merely caused by sympathy with the spread of Christianity, in which the Judæan Brethren would doubtless rejoice as much as any. The joy of the people of Phœnice and Samaria was due to the news of free acceptance of Gentile converts : Paul, as he went, preached freely to all and invited all. When he did this in Phœnice and Samaria, it follows that he had been doing the same in Antioch since his return from Galatia : the door which had once been opened, XIV 27, remained permanently open.

2. THE DISPUTE IN ANTIOCH. The new departure in Galatia and Antioch—the opening of the door of faith to the Nations—forced into prominence

the question of the relations of Gentile to Jewish
Christians.

There had already been some prospect that this
question would be opened up during Paul's second visit
to Jerusalem (p. 56 f.); but for the moment the difficulty
did not become acute. The older Antiochian converts,
as we have seen, had all entered through the door of
the synagogue; and had necessarily accepted certain prohibitions as a rule of life. But the newly founded
Galatian Churches contained large numbers who had
joined Paul directly, without any connection with the
synagogue; in the face of Luke's silence on such a
crucial point we cannot think that Paul imposed on
them any preliminary conditions of compliance with
Jewish rules; and, if so, we must understand that the
same interpretation of "the open door" characterised
his action in Antioch, Phœnice and Samaria.

The Jews who had been settled for generations in the
cities of Syria and Asia Minor had lost much of their
exclusiveness in ordinary life (p. 143). Moreover, the
development of events in Antioch had been gradual;
and no difficulty seems to have been caused there at
first by this last step. We learn from Paul himself
(*Gal.* II 12 f.) that even Peter, already prepared to
some extent by his own bold action in the case of Cornelius, had no scruple in associating freely with the
Antiochian Christians in general. But the Jews of
Jerusalem were far more rigid and narrow; and when
some of them came down on a mission to Antioch
from the Church in Jerusalem, they were shocked by the
state of things which they found there. They could
not well take the ground that one Christian should not
associate with another; they put their argument in a

more subtle form, and declared that no one could become in the full sense a member of the Church, unless he came under the Jewish Law, and admitted on his body its sign and seal : the Nations could be received into the Church, but in the reception they must conform to the Law (XV 2). The question, it must be clearly observed, was not whether non-Jews could be saved, for it was admitted by all parties that they could, but how they were saved : did the path of belief lie through the gate of the Law alone, or was there a path of belief that did not lead through that gate ? Had God made another door to Himself outside of the Law of Moses ? Had He practically set aside that Law, and declared it of no avail, by admitting as freely them that disregarded it as them that believed and followed it ?

When the question was put in this clear and logical form, we can well believe that Jews as a rule shrank from all the consequences that followed from free admission of the Nations. We can imagine that some who had answered practically by associating with the Gentile Christians, repented of their action when its full consequences were brought before them. Only rare and exceptional natures could have risen unaided above the prejudices and the pride of generations, and have sacrificed their Law to their advancing experience. The record confirms what we see to be natural in the circumstances. Paul stood immovably firm ; and he carried with him, after some wavering, the leaders (but not the mass) of the Jewish Christians. This point requires careful study.

The occasion of the dissension at Antioch is thus described by our three authorities,—Luke, the Apostles at Jerusalem, and Paul himself.

Acts XV 1.	*Acts XV 24.*	*Gal. II 12.*
CERTAIN PERSONS CAME DOWN FROM JUDÆA AND TAUGHT THE BRETHREN, THAT "IF YE BE NOT CIRCUMCISED AFTER THE MANNER OF MOSES, YE CANNOT BE SAVED".	WE HAVE HEARD THAT CERTAIN PERSONS WHICH WENT FORTH FROM US HAVE TROUBLED YOU WITH WORDS, SUBVERTING YOUR SOULS [AND (*as v.* 28 *implies*) LAYING ON YOU GREATER BURDEN THAN THE FOUR NECESSARY POINTS OF RITUAL].	BEFORE THAT CERTAIN PERSONS CAME FROM JAMES, PETER USED TO EAT WITH THE GENTILES; BUT, WHEN THEY CAME, HE BEGAN TO DRAW BACK AND SEPARATE HIMSELF, FEARING THE CHAMPIONS OF CIRCUMCISION. (14) BUT I SAID UNTO CEPHAS BEFORE THEM ALL, "HOW COMPELLEST THOU THE NATIONS TO CONFORM TO JEWISH CEREMONIAL?"

It is noteworthy that Luke used the vague expression that " persons came down from Judæa," which is made more definite in *v.* 24 : the champions of circumcision who caused the dissension in Antioch had come on a mission from the Apostles in Jerusalem. Luke pointedly avoids any expression that would connect the leading Apostles with the action of these emissaries. They had been sent from Jerusalem : but in *v.* 24 the Apostles disclaim all responsibility for their action. While Luke gives all the materials for judging, the substitution of *Judæa* for *Jerusalem* in his narrative is very significant of his carefulness in the *minutiæ* of expression. It is in no sense incorrect (it puts the general name of the whole land in place of the city name), and it guards against a probable misconception in the briefest way.

The incidents described in *Gal.* II 11-14 are not usually referred to this period ; and it is therefore advisable to elicit from the words of Paul the precise situation as he conceives it. Certain persons had come to Antioch from James : James, the head of the Church in Jerusalem, here stands alone as " the local representative" of that Church (to borrow a phrase from Lightfoot, *Ed. Gal.* p. 365). These persons had found in Antioch a situation that shocked them, and they expressed their disapproval so strongly and effectively, that Peter shrank from continuing the free intercourse with Gentile Christians which he had been practising. What do we learn from the context as to their attitude ? They are styled "they of the circumcision"; and this phrase (as distinguished from the mere general expression of disagreement and dislike used about persons of the same class in *Gal.* II 4) implies that they actively championed that cause against Peter. The exact form of the argument which moved Peter is not stated explicitly by Paul in his hurried and impassioned narrative ; but we gather what it was from the terms of his expostulation with Peter. He said to him in public : " how compellest thou the Nations to Judaise ? " The words have no force unless Peter, convinced by the Judaistic envoys, had begun to declare that compliance with the Law was compulsory, before Gentiles could become members of the Church fully entitled to communion with it.

Accordingly, the situation described in *Gal.* II 11-14 is that which existed in Antioch after Paul's return from the Galatian Churches. In the first part of his letter to the Galatians, Paul recapitulates the chief stages in the development of the controversy between the Judaising party in the Church, the premonitory signs on his second visit to Jerusalem, and the subsequent open dispute with Peter in Antioch. The dispute occurred after Paul's second, but before his third, visit to Jerusalem, *i.e.*, either between *Acts* XII 25 and XIII 1, or between XIV 26 and XV 4. Now in XV 1 (cp. v. 24) envoys from James caused strife in Antioch ; and we can hardly think that envoys also came from James after XII 25, and caused exactly similar strife, which was omitted by Luke but recorded in *Gal.* II 12.

When the question was put distinctly in all its bearings and consequences before Peter, he was unable to resist the argument that Christians ought to observe the Law, as Christ had done, and as the Twelve did. On one or two occasions, indeed, Christ had been taunted with permitting breaches of the Law ; but His actions could be so construed only by captious hypercriticism. It is quite clear that Peter and the older Apostles did not for a time grasp the full import of Christ's teaching on this subject: the actual fact that He and they were Jews, and lived as such, made more impression on them than mere theoretical teaching. Barnabas, even, was carried away by the example of Peter, and admitted the argument that the Gentile Christians ought "to live as do the Jews".

Paul alone stood firm. The issue of the situation is not described by Paul; he had now brought down his narrative to the situation in which the Galatian defection arose; and his retrospect therefore came to an end, when he reached the familiar facts (p. 185 f.). We must estimate from the context the general argument and what was the issue. Obviously, the rebuke which Paul gave must have been successful in the case of Peter and Barnabas; the immediate success of his appeal to their better feelings constitutes the whole force of his argument to the Galatians. The power of his letter to them lies in this, that the mere statement of the earlier stages of the controversy is sufficient to show the impregnability of his position and the necessity of his free and generous policy: the narrow Judaising tyranny was self-condemned; Peter was wholly with him, and so was Barnabas; but the victory had been gained, not by listening to the older Apostles, but by obeying " the good pleasure of God, who called me by His grace to preach Him among the Gentiles ". If the hesitation of Peter and Barnabas had resulted in an unreconciled dispute, the force of Paul's argument is gone: he has urged at great length that the older Apostles were in agreement with him, and accepted him as the Apostle called to the Foreign Mission, as they were to the Jewish Mission; and, as the climax of his argument for equality of privilege, he says: " Peter and even Barnabas wavered for a moment from their course, when the gravity of its consequences, *viz.*, the supersession of the Judaic Law, was set plainly before them by some of their friends; but I pointed out Peter's error in one brief appeal from his present wavering to his own past action ".

From this analysis we see that the issue of the situation implied in *Gal.* II 11-14 is described in *Acts* XV 2, 7: Barnabas joined Paul in combating the Judaising party, and Peter championed the cause in emphatic and noble terms at the subsequent Council in Jerusalem. That follows naturally on the interrupted narrative of the Epistle: the history as related in *Acts* completes and explains the Epistle, and enables us to appreciate the force of Paul's argument and its instantaneous effect on the Galatian Churches.

It is an interesting point, that Peter used at the Council the argument in favour of freedom with which Paul had pressed him in Antioch. Paul said to him, "In practice thou, a Jew, livest as do the Gentiles; how then compellest thou the Gentiles to act according to the Jewish Law?" Struck with this argument, Peter puts it in a more general form to the Council, "Why put a yoke on them which neither we nor our fathers could bear?" It is true to nature that he should employ to others the argument that had convinced himself.

It must, however, be confessed that while *Galatians* leads up excellently to *Acts*, and gains greatly in force from the additional facts mentioned there, *Acts* is silent about the facts narrated in *Galatians*. The eye-witness's narrative gains from the historian and stands out in new beauty from the comparison; but here *Acts* seems to lose by being brought into juxtaposition with the narrative of the eye-witness. To our conception the omission of all reference to the wavering of Barnabas and Peter appears almost like the sacrifice of historic truth, and certainly loses a picturesque detail. But the difference of attitude and object, I think, fully explains the historian's selection amid the incidents of the controversy. For him picturesque details had no attraction ; and the swerving of all the Jews except Paul from the right path seemed to him an unessential fact, like hundreds and thousands of others which he had to leave unnoticed. The essential fact which he had to record was that the controversy raged, and that Paul and Barnabas championed the cause of freedom.

But, it may be objected, Barnabas had wavered, and it is not accurate to represent him as a champion along with Paul. We reply that Paul does not make it clear how far Barnabas had gone with the tide : the matter was one of tendency, more than of complete separation. Peter *began to* withdraw and separate himself[1] from familiar communion with the Gentile Christian : the resident Jews joined him in concealing their real sentiment and their ordinary conduct towards the non-Jewish members of the Church : even Barnabas was carried off his feet by the tide of dissembling. These words would be correct, if Barnabas had merely wavered, and been confirmed by Paul's arguments in private. Paul's public rebuke was not addressed to Barnabas, but only to Peter. There is a certain difficulty in the record ; but I confess that, after trying honestly to give full emphasis to the difficulty, I see no reason why we should not, as the issue of the facts in *Gal.* II 11-14, conceive Barnabas to have come forward as a thoroughgoing advocate of the Pauline doctrine and practice.

Moreover, the difficulty remains, and becomes far more serious, on the ordinary view that the incidents of

---

[1] *Imperfects*, not *aorists.*

Gal. II 11-14 occurred after the Council in Jerusalem. According to that view, Barnabas, when delegates came from Jerusalem (*Acts* XV 2, 24), resisted them strenuously, represented the cause of freedom as an envoy to Jerusalem, and obtained an authoritative Decree from the Apostles disowning the action of the delegates, and emphatically condemning it as " subverting your souls " : thereafter delegates came again from James, the same Apostle that had taken the foremost part in formulating the recent Decree ;[1] but this time Barnabas, instead of resisting, weakly yielded to their arguments.

Worse, almost, is the conduct of Peter in that view. When the case came up before the Council to be considered in all its bearings and solemnly decided, he, " after there had been much discussion " (in which we may be sure that the consequences were fully emphasised by the Judaising party), appeared as the most outspoken advocate of freedom, and declared that " we must not demand from them what we ourselves have been unable to endure ". Shortly after the Council (on that view), Peter went to Antioch and put in practice the principle of freedom for which he had contended at the Council. But " certain persons came from James," the same Apostle that had supported him in the Council ; these persons reopened the controversy ; and Peter abandoned his publicly expressed conviction, which in a formal letter was declared with his approval to be the word of the Holy Spirit.

We are asked to accept as a credible narrative this recital of meaningless tergiversation, which attributes to

---

[1] "The Apostolic letter seems to have been drawn up by him " (Lightfoot, *Ed. Gal.*, p. 112, II 12).

Peter and to Barnabas, not ordinary human weakness and inability to answer a grave issue at the first moment when it is presented to them, but conduct devoid of reason or sanity. Who can wonder that many who are asked to accept this as history, reply that one of the two authors responsible for the two halves of the recital has erred and is untrustworthy? For the truth of history itself one must on that theory distrust one of the two documents. That is not the faith, that is not the conduct, which conquered the world! The only possible supposition would be that the Apostles were men unusually weak, ignorant, and inconstant, who continually went wrong, except where the Divine guidance interposed to keep them right. That theory has been and is still held by some; but it removes the whole development of Christianity out of the sphere of history into the sphere of the supernatural and the marvellous, whereas the hypothesis on which this investigation is based is that it was a process intelligible according to ordinary human nature, and a proper subject for the modern historian.

It is true that Peter once before denied his own affirmed principles, but that was when he was younger, when he was a mere pupil, when a terrible strain was put on him; but this denial is supposed to have been made when he was in the maturity of his power, after he had experienced the quickening sense of responsibility as a leader of the Church for many years, and after his mind and will had been enlarged and strengthened at the great Pentecost (see p. 365).

Further, according to the view stated by Lightfoot, the feeble action of Peter and Barnabas in Antioch produced lasting consequences: it "may have prepared the way for the dissension between Paul and Barnabas which shortly afterwards led to their separation. From this time forward they never appear again associated together." If it was so serious, the total omission of it by Luke becomes harder to understand and reconcile with the duty of a historian ; whereas, if it was (as we suppose) a mere hesitation when the question was first put explicitly, it was not of sufficient consequence to demand a place in his history.

Peter's visit to Antioch was not of the same character as his visits to Samaria and other Churches at an earlier time, in which he was giving the Apostolic approval to the congregations established there. The first visit of Barnabas to Antioch, followed by the Antiochian delegation to Jerusalem (XI 28, XII 25), and the recognition of Paul and Barnabas as Apostles (*Gal.* II 9), had placed Antioch on a recognised and independent basis (XIII 1). In Luke's view, therefore, as in Paul's, Peter's visit was not a step in the development of the Church in Antioch, as Barnabas's had been.

3. THE COUNCIL. (XV 4) AND WHEN THEY WERE COME TO JERUSALEM, THEY WERE RECEIVED BY THE CHURCH AND THE APOSTLES AND THE ELDERS, AND THEY REHEARSED ALL THINGS THAT GOD HAD DONE WITH THEM. (5) BUT THERE ROSE UP CERTAIN OF THE SECT OF THE PHARISEES WHO BELIEVED, SAYING, "IT IS NEEDFUL TO CIRCUMCISE THEM, AND TO CHARGE THEM TO KEEP THE LAW OF MOSES". (6) AND THE APOSTLES AND THE ELDERS WERE GATHERED TOGETHER TO CONSIDER OF THIS MATTER. (7) AND WHEN THERE HAD BEEN MUCH DISCUSSION,

PETER ROSE AND SPOKE. . . . (12) AND ALL THE
MULTITUDE KEPT SILENCE ; AND THEY HEARKENED
UNTO BARNABAS AND PAUL, WHO REHEARSED WHAT
SIGNS AND WONDERS GOD HAD WROUGHT AMONG
THE NATIONS BY THEM. (13) AND AFTER THEY HAD
CEASED, JAMES SPOKE.

At Jerusalem there occurred in the first place a
general meeting of the Church as a whole to receive
and welcome the delegates. The Apostles and the
Elders are specified as taking part in the meeting ; and
the separate article before each name implies distinct
action of each body. At this meeting the delegates
explained the circumstances which had caused their
mission ; and the extreme members of the Judaising
party, who are described here as Pharisees, stated their
view forthwith.

A mark of the developed situation since Paul's last
visit must be noted in *v.* 4. Paul and Barnabas now
expound in a formal and public way all their missionary
experience ; but on their previous visit, Paul privately
submitted to the leaders of the Church his views as to
missionary enterprise.

Thereupon, a special meeting of the Apostles and the
Elders was held to consider the matter, and a long discussion took place. Peter delivered a speech in favour
of complete freedom for the new converts ; and the effect
which he produced was shown by the patient hearing
accorded to Barnabas and to Paul, as they recounted
the proofs of Divine grace and Divine action in the
Gentile congregations : these congregations fulfilled the
test that God was with them. Thus, the course of the
meeting was very similar to the discussion that followed

after the conversion of Cornelius (XI 1-18). The general sense was clearly against the claim of the extreme Judaistic party (called "them of the circumcision" XI 2, *Gal.* II 12).

But, while the champions of circumcision were clearly in the minority, apparently a decided feeling was manifest in favour of some concessions to the Jewish feeling and practice : the Nations were to be received into the Church, but the widened Church was not to be apart from and independent of the old Jewish community : it was to be " a rebuilding of the tabernacle of David ". To render possible a real unanimity of feeling, the Nations must accept the fundamental regulations of purity. The chairman's speech summed up the sense of the meeting in a way that was universally accepted. James, the recognised head of the Church in Jerusalem, said :—

(XV 14) SYMEON HATH REHEARSED HOW FIRST GOD TOOK CARE TO GATHER FROM AMONG THE NATIONS A PEOPLE FOR HIS NAME. (15) AND TO THIS AGREE THE WORDS OF THE PROPHETS : AS IT IS WRITTEN, (16) " I WILL BUILD AGAIN THE TABERNACLE OF DAVID, (17) THAT THE RESIDUE OF MEN MAY SEEK AFTER THE LORD, AND ALL THE NATIONS, OVER WHOM MY NAME IS PRONOUNCED," SAITH THE LORD, WHO MAKETH THESE THINGS (18) KNOWN FROM THE BEGINNING OF TIME.[1] (19) WHEREFORE MY VOICE IS THAT WE TROUBLE NOT THEM WHICH FROM AMONG THE NATIONS TURN TO GOD ; (20) BUT SEND INSTRUCTIONS TO THEM TO ABSTAIN FROM THE

[1] The Bezan Text, and many other authorities, have "saith the Lord who doeth this. (18) Known to the Lord from the beginning of time is His work."

POLLUTIONS OF IDOLS AND FROM MARRIAGE WITHIN THE DEGREES FORBIDDEN BY THE LAW, AND FROM WHAT IS STRANGLED, AND FROM *the use of* BLOOD *as food.* (21) FOR MOSES FROM ANCIENT GENERATIONS HATH IN EVERY CITY THEM THAT PREACH HIM, AS HE IS READ IN THE SYNAGOGUES EVERY SABBATH.

James grounds his advice for partial conformity on the fact, *v.* 21, that the Mosaic Law had already spread widely over the cities of the empire, and that the existing facts which facilitated intercourse between Jews and "God-fearing" pagans should be continued. He grounds his advice for freedom from the rest of the Law on the declared will of God, first by prophecy in time long past, and afterwards by revelation to Peter, that the Nations should be admitted to the tabernacle of David, from which he infers that their own duty is to make admission easy.

Incidentally we observe that James used the Septuagint Version, quoting loosely from *Amos* IX 11, 12, a passage where the telling point for his purpose occurs only in the Greek and not in the Hebrew Version.

Another point of development since Paul's second visit to Jerusalem must be noticed here. On the second visit, as Paul declares, the recognised leaders in Jerusalem gave him no advice and no instruction, except to remember the poverty of the brethren there. It would be hard to put that in more emphatic terms than he uses (p. 56). But on the third visit, the delegates bring a question for settlement, and receive from the recognised leaders in Jerusalem an authoritative response, giving a weighty decision in a serious matter of practical work, a decision that would have been epoch-making, if it had been permanently carried into effect. On the second visit the difficulty could be foreseen; between the second and third visit it became acute; at the third visit it was settled in a way that was a distinct rebuff to the Judaising party, but not a complete triumph for the party of freedom. It would not be honest to use the words of *Gal.* II 10 about the visit described in *Acts* XV.

Another contrast between the second and the third visit must be observed. The Church sent forth several delegates along with Paul and Barnabas on the third journey; but on the second they were the sole delegates. The common view, which identifies the second visit of *Gal.* II 1-10 with the third visit of *Acts* XV, is defended by its supporters on the ground that Titus, who went along with Paul (*Gal.* II 1), was one of the additional delegates mentioned, XV 2. This argument sins against the facts. In *Gal.* II 1 Titus is defined as a subordinate, and not as one of the delegates;[1] we have no reason to think that any subordinates went up to the Council, whereas it was necessary for the work of the second visit to use assistants. Moreover, we may be certain that, if Paul did take any subordinates with him to the Council, he was too prudent and diplomatic to envenom a situation already serious and difficult by taking an uncircumcised Greek with him. It was different on a later visit, when the authoritative decree had decided against circumcision, or on an earlier visit, before the question was raised; but when that question was under discussion, it would have been a harsh and heedless hurt to the susceptibilities of the other party,

[1] συμπαραλαβών, cp. XII 25 and pp. 59, 71, 177.

to take Titus with him ; and Paul never was guilty of such an act. The example of Timothy shows how far he went about this time in avoiding any chance of hurting Jewish feeling.

4. THE DECREE. (XV 22) THEN IT SEEMED GOOD TO THE APOSTLES AND ELDERS, WITH THE WHOLE CHURCH, TO CHOOSE MEN OUT OF THEIR COMPANY, AND SEND THEM TO ANTIOCH WITH PAUL AND BARNABAS, *namely*, JUDAS CALLED BARSABBAS, AND SILAS, CHIEF MEN AMONG THE BRETHREN. (23) AND THEY SENT A LETTER BY THEIR MEANS: "THE APOSTLES AND THE ELDERS [BRETHREN][1] UNTO THE BRETHREN WHICH ARE OF THE NATIONS IN ANTIOCH AND SYRIA AND CILICIA, GREETING. (24) FORASMUCH AS WE HAVE HEARD THAT CERTAIN WHICH WENT OUT FROM US HAVE TROUBLED YOU WITH WORDS, SUBVERTING YOUR SOULS; TO WHOM WE GAVE NO COMMANDMENT; (25) IT SEEMED GOOD UNTO US, HAVING COME TO ONE ACCORD, TO CHOOSE OUT MEN AND SEND THEM UNTO YOU WITH OUR BELOVED BARNABAS AND PAUL, (26) MEN THAT HAVE HAZARDED THEIR LIVES FOR THE NAME OF OUR LORD JESUS CHRIST. (27) WE HAVE SENT THEREFORE JUDAS AND SILAS, WHO THEMSELVES ALSO SHALL TELL YOU THE SAME THINGS BY WORD OF MOUTH. (28) FOR IT SEEMED GOOD TO THE HOLY SPIRIT, AND TO US, TO LAY UPON YOU NO GREATER BURDEN THAN THESE NECESSARY THINGS. (29) THAT YE ABSTAIN FROM THINGS SACRIFICED TO IDOLS, AND FROM BLOOD, AND FROM THINGS STRANGLED, AND FROM MARRIAGE WITHIN THE DEGREES; FROM WHICH

---

[1] Dr. Blass's explanation of this word as an accidental corruption is highly probable.

IF YE KEEP YOURSELVES, IT SHALL BE WELL WITH YOU. FARE YE WELL."

The Decree is, as Lightfoot says, a compromise. On the one hand the extreme Judaising party is entirely disowned and emphatically condemned, as " subverting the souls " of the Gentiles. But, on the other hand, part of the Law is declared to be obligatory; and the word selected is very emphatic (ἐπάναγκες). If this word be taken in its full sense, the Decree lacks unity of purpose and definiteness of principle; it passes lamely from side to side. Now it seems impossible to suppose that Paul could have accepted a Decree which declared mere points of ritual to be compulsory; and one of them he afterwards emphatically declared to be not compulsory (I *Cor.* VIII 4 f.). But those who had listened to the speeches of Peter and James, and were familiar with the situation in which the question had emerged, were prepared to look specially at the exordium with its emphatic condemnation of the Judaising party; and thereafter, doubtless, they took the concluding part as a recommendation, and regarded the four points as strongly advised in the interests of peace and unity.

But the real power of a law lies in its positive enactment; and most people would look only to what the Decree ordered. Now, whether or not the last sentences *must* bear the sense, they certainly *may* naturally bear the sense, that part of the Law was absolutely compulsory for salvation, and that the Nations were released from the rest as a concession to their weakness : " we lay on you no greater burden than these necessary conditions ". This seemed to create two grades of Christians : a lower class of weaker persons, who could not observe the whole Law, but only the compulsory parts of it, and a higher class, who were strong enough to obey the whole Law. The Gentile Christians were familiar in the pagan religions with distinctions of grade ; for stages of initiation into the Mysteries existed everywhere. It was almost inevitable that a Decree, which lays down no clear and formal principle of freedom, should in practice be taken as making a distinction between strong and weak, between more and less advanced Christians ; and it is certain that it was soon taken in that sense.

The question is often asked, why this letter was not addressed also to the Churches of Galatia ; and several answers are suggested. But the answer which seems obvious from our point of view is that the letter was addressed only to those who asked the question. The provincial organisation of the Church began through the compulsion of circumstances (p. 135) : there must either be a provincial organisation or no organisation. The principle, when it has been once stated, is self-evident. Circumstances made Antioch the centre of the Church in the province Syria and Cilicia ; and the address of this letter attests the recognition of that fact and its consequences.

Hence, when Paul went forth on his next journey, he did not communicate the Decree to the Churches in Syria and Cilicia, XV 41, because they had already received it, when it was first sent out. But, when he and Silas reached Galatia, "they delivered them the decrees for to keep, which had been ordained of the Apostles and Elders," XVI 4. But the Bezan Reviser, not understanding this delicate distinction, interpolated the statement in XV 41, that Paul and Silas "delivered the instructions of the Apostles and Elders ".

5. THE RETURN TO ANTIOCH. (XV 30) SO THEY, BEING SET FREE TO DEPART, CAME DOWN TO ANTI-OCH; AND HAVING GATHERED THE MULTITUDE TO-GETHER, THEY DELIVERED THE LETTER. (31) AND WHEN THEY HAD READ IT, THEY REJOICED AT THE ENCOURAGEMENT. (32) AND JUDAS AND SILAS ON THEIR OWN ACCOUNT ALSO, INASMUCH AS THEY WERE PROPHETS, ENCOURAGED THE BRETHREN AT GREAT LENGTH, AND CONFIRMED THEM. (33) AND AFTER THEY HAD SPENT SOME TIME, THEY WERE SET FREE BY THE BRETHREN TO DEPART IN PEACE TO THEM THAT SENT THEM FORTH; (34) *But it pleased Silas to abide there still.* (35) AND PAUL AND BARNABAS TARRIED IN ANTIOCH, TEACHING AND PREACHING THE WORD OF THE LORD, WITH MANY OTHERS ALSO. (36) AND AFTER CERTAIN DAYS PAUL SAID . . .

As in XI 24, so here, *v.* 32, the qualification of Judas and Silas for exhorting the congregation is carefully stated. Luke lays such evident stress on proper quali-fication, that he seems to have considered Divine gifts necessary in any one that was to address a congrega-tion (p. 45).

After the Council, Paul and Barnabas returned to their ordinary duties in Antioch, where the number of qualified prophets and teachers was now larger than in XIII 1. They remained there a short time (*v.* 36, cp. IX 19, 23). The second journey began probably in the spring of the year 50.

At some period *v.* 34 was deliberately omitted from the next, from the mistaken idea that *v.* 33 declared the

actual departure of Judas and Silas : but the officials of
the Church in Antioch (the Elders?) simply informed
Judas and Silas that their duties were concluded and
they were free to return home, and Silas did not avail
himself of the permission.   Considering how XII 25
prepares the way for XIII 5, we must hold that XV 34
is genuine and prepares for XV 40 ; and the fact that
the Bezan Reviser found 34 in the text and added to
it the comment "and Judas went alone," constitutes a
distinct proof of its genuineness.   It is not that any difficulty need be found in Paul selecting Silas from Jerusalem,
for Barnabas here takes Mark from Jerusalem (XIII 13).
But it is one of the points of Luke's style to furnish the
material for understanding a new departure, and the very
marked statement that Silas voluntarily remained, when
his official duty was declared to be at an end, makes the
next event much more intelligible (p. 176).   There is in
the sequence of thought 33-4 a certain harshness (characteristic of Luke when he wants to draw attention to a
point) ; and this led to the omission of 34 in the great
MSS. and by many modern editors.

6. THE SEPARATION OF PAUL AND BARNABAS.
(XV 36) AND AFTER SOME DAYS PAUL SAID UNTO
BARNABAS, "LET US RETURN NOW AND VISIT THE
BRETHREN IN EVERY CITY WHEREIN WE PROCLAIMED
THE WORD OF THE LORD, HOW THEY FARE".   (37)
AND BARNABAS WAS MINDED TO TAKE WITH THEM
JOHN ALSO, WHO WAS CALLED MARK.   (38) BUT PAUL
THOUGHT NOT GOOD TO TAKE WITH THEM HIM THAT
WITHDREW FROM THEM FROM PAMPHYLIA AND WENT
NOT WITH THEM TO THE WORK.   (39) AND THERE
AROSE A SHARP CONTENTION, SO THAT THEY PARTED

ASUNDER ONE FROM THE OTHER ; AND BARNABAS
TOOK MARK WITH HIM, AND SAILED AWAY UNTO
CYPRUS ; (40) BUT PAUL CHOSE SILAS AND WENT
FORTH, BEING COMMENDED BY THE BRETHREN TO THE
GRACE OF THE LORD : AND HE WENT THROUGH SYRIA
AND CILICIA, CONFIRMING THE CHURCHES.

Barnabas here passes out of this history. The tradition,
as stated in the apocryphal *Periodoi Barnabæ*, a very late
work, was that he remained in Cyprus till his death ; and
the fact that Mark reappears at a later stage without Barnabas, is in agreement. At any rate his work, wherever it
was carried on, did not, in Luke's estimation, contribute to
work out the idea of the organised and unified Church.
That idea was elaborated in Paul's work ; and the history
is guided by Paul's activity from the moment when he
began to be fully conscious of the true nature of his work.
Others contributed to the earlier stages, but, as it proceeded, all the other personages became secondary, and
Paul more and more the single moving genius.

The choice of Silas was, of course, due to his special
fitness for the work, which had been recognised during
his ministration in Antioch. Doubtless he had shown
tact and sympathy in managing the questions arising
from the relations of the Gentile Christians to the Jews.
His sympathies had also been shown by his preferring
to remain in the mixed and freer congregation in Antioch,
when he had been at liberty to return to Jerusalem.

The name Silas is a familiar diminutive of Silvanus ;
and the full and more dignified form is employed in
the superscription of the two letters to the Thessalonians.
Silvanus is a Latin name ; and Silas is implied in XVI 37
to have been a Roman citizen. It may, however, be

looked on as certain that he was a Hebrew, for only a Hebrew would have been a leading man among the Brethren at Jerusalem (XV 22). His double character, Hebrew and Roman, was in itself a qualification for a coadjutor of Paul ; and, doubtless, the Roman side of his character caused that freedom from narrow Judaistic pre- judice which shines through his action.

It appears from the term employed in *v.* 40 that Silas took the place of Barnabas, not of Mark. The latter was a mere unofficial companion in every case, as is shown by the word used.[1]   The verbs in the next few verses are all singular ; though it is clear that Silas is concerned in many of the actions.   The singular was preferred by Luke because certain of the actions were special to Paul, the choosing of Silas and of Timothy. There is a decided harshness in the narrative that follows, owing to the variation between the singular and the plural.   At some points in the action Paul monopolises the author's attention ; and probably the expression, harsh though it be grammatically, corresponds to the facts.   At the opening of the journey Paul alone is the subject : now at the opening the new comrade was un- trained to the work.   After a time the plural begins, XVI 4, and, wherever travelling is described, it is em- ployed ; but, when the direction given to missionary work is alluded to, Silas disappears, and Paul alone is the subject, XVII 2.

[1] συμπαραλαμβάνω XII 25, XV 37, p. 170.

CHAPTER VIII

HISTORY OF THE CHURCHES OF GALATIA.

1. THE VISIT OF PAUL AND SILAS. (XVI 1) AND HE CAME ALSO TO DERBE AND TO LYSTRA; AND BEHOLD A CERTAIN DISCIPLE WAS THERE NAMED TIMOTHY, THE SON OF A JEWESS WHICH BELIEVED; BUT HIS FATHER WAS A GREEK. (2) THE SAME HAD A GOOD REPUTATION AMONG THE BRETHREN THAT WERE IN LYSTRA AND ICONIUM. (3) HIM WOULD PAUL HAVE TO GO FORTH WITH HIM; AND HE TOOK AND CIRCUMCISED HIM BECAUSE OF THE JEWS THAT WERE IN THOSE PARTS, FOR THEY ALL KNEW THAT HIS FATHER WAS A GREEK. (4) AND AS THEY WERE PASSING THROUGH THE CITIES, THEY *in each* DELIVERED THEM THE DECREES FOR TO KEEP, WHICH HAD BEEN ORDAINED OF THE APOSTLES AND ELDERS THAT WERE AT JERUSALEM. (5) THE CHURCHES THEN WERE STRENGTHENED IN THE FAITH, AND INCREASED IN NUMBER DAILY. (6) AND THEY MADE A MISSIONARY PROGRESS THROUGH THE PHRYGIAN REGION OF *the province* GALATIA (*the Phrygo-Galatic Region*).

In *v.* 1 it is implied that Derbe and Lystra are a pair, constituting a district (p. 110). The work of this journey is divided according to districts: (1) Syria and Cilicia, a single Roman province ; (2) Derbe and Lystra, a *region* of the province Galatia, which is here indicated by its two cities as the most convenient way, because in one of them a considerable halt had to be described ; (3) the Phrygian region of the province Galatia ; (4) Asia, where preaching was forbidden, was traversed transversely to its north-western point after an unsuccessful effort to enter the province Bithynia for missionary purposes. Between Cilicia and Derbe the great realm of Antiochus is omitted from the narrative, as being a non-Roman territory and out of Paul's plans.

Derbe and Lystra are grouped together as a *Region*, but the author dwells only on Lystra. The only reason why they are grouped together and separated from the districts that precede and follow, lies in the Roman classi-fication, which made them a group. But in order to mark that Lystra alone is referred to in the sequel, the historian repeats the preposition before it : "he came to Derbe and to Lystra ".

In *v.* 2 Lystra and Iconium are grouped together as the district where Timothy was well known. It is implied that he was not known at Derbe. This again is true to the facts of commerce and intercourse. Lystra is much nearer Iconium than it is to Derbe ; and geographically, Lystra goes along with Iconium, while Derbe goes with Laranda and that part of Lycaonia. Neither blood nor Roman classification could prevent commerce from running in its natural channels (XIV 19). The nearest city to Iconium was Lystra, and the nearest to Lystra was Iconium ; and the relations between them must always be close.

The historian is careful to add in this case, as he does

about the Seven Deacons (VI 3), about Cornelius (X 22, cp. 2), and as Paul does about Ananias (XXII 12), and as is implied in I 21, that Timothy had so lived as to bear a good character in the district where he was known. It is not meant that Paul went about taking the opinion of Lystra and Iconium about Timothy, any more than it is meant in X 22 that Cornelius's messengers went collecting evidence about him all over Palestine : we may be sure that in such a selection Paul depended on his own insight, guided perhaps by Divine approval. The author adds this information about the good repute of Timothy, because he considered good repute one of the conditions of appointment to any office however humble in the Church. He is interested in all questions of organisation ; and we may compare what he says about the qualification of preachers (pp. 45, 174). As a point of literary style we note that the event of a new and important character is marked by an unusually detailed account of him.

We infer from the expression that in *vv.* 1-3 Paul and Silas have not gone beyond Lystra ; and that it is a misconception to think that in *v.* 2 Paul is in Iconium. At Lystra Paul felt that, along the route which he intended to take, the Jews knew Timothy's father to be a Greek : he was going along a frequented route of trade, on which were colonies of Jews in communication with each other, for there can be no doubt that his plan was to go by Iconium and Antioch into Asia. The opinion has sometimes been held that at this point Paul abandoned the visitation of his Churches as contemplated in XV 36; and that "the fact that God put this companion in his way served as a warning to him to go direct from

Lykaonia to a new mission-field " (see Weiss's note
on XVI 2). But, on the contrary, our view is that,
when Luke records any deliberately formed intention
on Paul's part, he leaves us to understand that it was
carried out, if no intimation to the contrary is given
(p. 342); and that Timothy here was taken as companion
for the route as first planned, to fill the place of John
Mark on the previous journey. There seems no reason
to think (as Blass does) that one or more subordinates
accompanied Paul from Syrian Antioch. It is not improbable that Paul, owing to previous experience, thought
of Timothy as a companion even before he left Antioch.

Paul then proceeded on his intended route through
the Phrygian *Region* of the province, whose two cities
visited on the previous journey were Iconium and Pisidian
Antioch. The cities are not specially named, as nothing
striking or important occurred in either. It is implied
that no Church had been founded on the former journey
in Pisidia or Pamphylia; and hence Paul had no
Churches to review and confirm there. The reference
to Pisidia (a *Region* of the province Galatia) in XIV 24
does not suggest that any success was attained there;
and we may find in the list of I *Peter* I 1 a clear proof
that there was no Church in Pamphylia at a date considerably later. That list is clearly intended to exhaust
the Church in Asia Minor; and it mentions every province except Lycia and Pamphylia (which, therefore, did
not yet contain any Churches, and seem to have long
resisted Christianity), and Cilicia, which was part of Syria.
The list, incidentally, shows that already in the first
century a certain coherence was perceptible between the
various Churches of Asia Minor, as distinguished from

Syria and Cilicia. That springs naturally from the political conditions, and it grew stronger as time passed, until the two divisions became the patriarchates of Constantinople and of Antioch.

At this point Luke inserts an account of Paul's action in the cities through which he was making his way. It is in his style to put this account near the beginning and expect the reader to apply it in all subsequent cases (p. 72). It does not apply to Cilicia (p. 173), and could not therefore be given sooner. In each city Paul and Silas delivered the Decree, and urged the Gentile converts to observe the necessary points of Jewish ritual; and everywhere the congregations were vigorous and growing. We cannot mistake the emphasis laid by the historian on Paul's loyal determination to carry out the Apostolic Decree. and his anxiety to go as far as was honestly possible in the way of conciliating the Jews: that is in keeping with his view that the entire blame for the rupture between Paul and the Jews lay with the latter. But, if Paul was so anxious at this time to recommend the Decree to his converts, why does he never refer to it in any of his subsequent letters, even where he touches on points that were formally dealt with in the Decree, and why does he give advice to the Corinthians about meat offered to idols, which certainly strains the Decree to the utmost, if it be not actually inconsistent with it? The explanation lies in the immediate consequences of his action in the Galatian Churches.

2. THE DESERTION OF THE GALATIANS. Soon after Paul left the province Galatia, there came to it missionaries of the Judaising party, who taught the Galatian Churches to take that view of the Apostolic Decree which

we have described on p. 172 f. They pointed out that
Paul himself recognised the principle that circumcision was
needed for the higher grade of Christian service ; for when
he selected Timothy for a position of responsibility in the
Church, he, as a preliminary, performed the rite on him ;
and they declared that thereby he was, in effect, " preaching circumcision" (*Gal.* V 11). Further, they threw
doubt on his sincerity in this act ; and insinuated that he
was reluctantly complying with necessity, in order to
"conciliate and ingratiate himself with" the mass of the
Church (see Lightfoot on *Gal.* I 10). Above all they insisted on the existence of the two grades of Christians ;
they pointed out that Paul had himself delivered and
recommended the Apostolic Decree which recognised the
distinction of weaker and stronger Brethren ; and they
urged the Galatians to strive to attain to the higher, and
not rest content with the lower grade, which was a mere
concession to weakness.

Such teaching found a ready response in the minds of
the Galatian Christians. Many of them had first heard
Paul preaching in the synagogue, many had come under
the influence of Judaism to some extent even before Paul
entered Galatia ; all were ready to accept the belief that,
as the Jews were always the first in Paul's own plans,
and as Christianity came from the Jews, therefore it was
right to imitate the Jews (p. 144). It was precisely the
most enthusiastic and devoted, who would be eager to rise
to the highest and most difficult stage of Christian life.

Further, the Judaistic emissaries urged that Paul was
merely the messenger and subordinate of the Twelve, that
these original Apostles and leaders of the Church must
be accepted as the ultimate guides, and that where Paul

swerved from their teaching he was in error; and they claimed likewise to be the messengers come direct from the Twelve to communicate their latest views. Paul had recently delivered the Decree of the older Apostles; and now later messengers supplemented and elucidated the Decree.

3. LETTER TO THE CHURCHES OF GALATIA. Paul saw that his vision of the Church that should unite the civilised world was a vain dream, if it were to be bound by the fetters of Judaism; and he felt, as soon as he heard of this defection, that it must be met at once. If these Churches, his first foundations towards the west, were to pass under the party of slavery, his work was ruined at its inception : the blow to his policy and his influence was ruinous. One of the arguments by which the change had been produced was especially galling to him : his efforts at conciliation were taken advantage of to distort his motives, and to represent him as inconsistent and temporising, and his attempts to soothe the prejudices of the Judaistic party were treated as attempts at compromise. Hence he bursts forth at the outset in a strain of terrific vehemence (which I purposely give as far as possible in Lightfoot's language): " Though we (*i.e.*, *Silas and I*), or an angel from heaven, should preach unto you any gospel other than that which we preached unto you, let him be accursed. As we have told you before, so now once more I say, if any man preacheth unto you any gospel other than that which ye received, let him be anathema. What! does my boldness startle you? Is *this*, I ask, the language of a time-server? Will any one say *now* that, careless of winning the favour of God, I seek to conciliate men, to ingratiate myself with men? I speak thus strongly; for my

language shall not be misconstrued, shall wear no semblance
of compromise " (*Gal.* I 8-10). And towards the end of his
letter he returns to the same point : " What ! do *I*, who
have incurred the deadly hatred of the Judaisers, who am
exposed to continual persecution from them, do *I* preach
circumcision ? If so, why do they persecute me ? Surely
what scandalises them in my teaching, the crucifixion with
its atonement for sin, has been done away with, if I have,
as they say, taken to their method, and begun to preach
circumcision " (V 11).

Satisfied with the vehemence of the first outburst, and
the sarcasm of the second, Paul wastes no argument
to prove that he has been consistent throughout. He
knows that the Galatic Churches *cannot* really believe that
part of his adversaries' arguments : they feel in their
hearts that he has always been true to the first Gospel ;
and he proceeds to remind them of its origin and its hold
on them, in order to enforce the conclusion that they
must cling to the first Gospel, whoever it be that preaches
any other. His argument, therefore, is directed to show
that he came among them in the beginning with a
message direct from God : " the Gospel which was
preached by me is not after man " (I 11): "it came
to me through revelation of Jesus". Then he proceeds
to show, by appealing to the facts, that he had not had
the opportunity of learning anything from the recognised
pillars of the Church. When it pleased God to reveal
Jesus in him, bitter enemy of the Church as he was, he
" conferred not with flesh and blood," but went away
for solitary meditation into Arabia. He was made by
God His Apostle to the Nations years before he conferred
with any of the Apostles. Twice at a later date did

he go up to Jerusalem, in one case remaining fifteen days and seeing only Peter and James, in the second going up at the Divine command to help the poor at Jerusalem (II 10)—on which occasion, as a matter of fact, no injunction was laid on his Greek assistant Titus to accept the Judaic rite—and receiving the recognition of his Apostleship, but no instruction, from the heads of the Church (p. 56 f.).

Here in passing let us ask the question, Did Paul in this autobiographical sketch, given in such solemn yet vehement style, with the oath by God that he is not deceiving them—did Paul, I say, omit to mention that he had paid another visit to Jerusalem between the two that he describes? The question seems almost an insult; yet many scholars of the highest order consider that he here leaves out of sight the visit described by Luke, XI 28-30, and XII 25. I confess that, after studying all that the orthodox scholars say on this point I find a higher conception of Paul's character and truthfulness in the position of the critics who conclude that Luke utterly misconceived the sequence of events in early Christian history and interpolated an intermediate visit where no visit occurred, than in Bishop Lightfoot's position that "of this visit Paul makes no mention here". Paul's argument is founded on the rarity of his visits, and his aim is to show that on these visits he received no charge from the Twelve. Reason and truth rebel against the idea that he left out the middle visit. If he passed over part of the facts here, what situation can be imagined in which he would feel obliged to tell all the facts? And on that supposition, that Paul omitted a fact so essential to his purpose and to honest autobiography, the entire body of orthodox scholars have built up their theory of early Church history! It cannot be! Luke's second visit must be Paul's second visit; and when we build boldly on that plain foundation, the history rises before us in order and symmetry.

But further, it is obvious that Paul appeals with absolute confidence to this second visit as proving his case: he evidently conceives that he has merely to recall the facts to the Galatians in order to make all clear. Now, there is one situation in which a man is obviously not receiving from others, and that is when he is actually giving to them: that was the situation on the second visit according to Luke, and that explains Paul's confidence in appealing to his second visit.

Again, Paul knew that he had clever and skilful arguers to contend against. How could he expose himself to the retort that he was missing out the intermediate visit to Jerusalem? How could he feel confident that the Galatians, who had already shown themselves so liable to be deceived by specious arguments, would be able at once to reply to that obvious retort?

Finally, Paul, as an honest and rational man, could not appeal to the events of the third visit according to Luke, as proving beyond question that he received on that occasion no charge from the Apostles. He *did* receive a charge then, and he delivered that charge to the Churches.

Why, then, it may be objected, does Paul not mention his third visit? The answer is obvious. He is engaged in proving that, when he gave his first message to the Churches of Galatia, he had never received any charge from the older Apostles. His whole point is: "Cleave to my first message, which came direct from God: if Silas and I afterwards said anything inconsistent with that message, we are accursed ". The third visit to Jerusalem did not take place until after the Galatian Churches were founded, and therefore it could find no place in the autobiographical retrospect of I 12-II 10; but it is clearly implied in the scornful and impetuous sentence, I 8 : " Even if Silas and I (as these emissaries have been telling you), if an angel from heaven, should preach to you a Gospel contrary to that which we originally preached to you, a curse be upon us ".

After this autobiographical sketch, Paul refers to an instance which showed very strongly his independence in face of the leading Apostle Peter, and then passes on to the third and main argument of his adversaries, founded on the supposed grades in Christian life. His line of reply is to bring out in various ways the truth that the Judaistic form is the lower stage, and the Gospel of freedom which had been delivered to the Galatians the higher stage. The Law alone was not sufficient for salvation, inasmuch as Christ had died to supplement its deficiency; therefore life according to the Law could not be the highest stage of Christian life. How could the Galatians be so foolish as to think that, having begun in the Spirit, their higher stage of development would be in the flesh (III 3)? The Christians who have entered through the Spirit are the children of the free woman, but the Judaistic Christians are the children of the bond woman and lower in rank (IV 31). The latter may rise to be free, but, if the former sink under bondage to the Law, they sacrifice their Christianity. The Judaistic Christians are children under care of a pedagogue, who have to be raised by Christ to the full growth and freedom (III 23-4). In a variety of

other striking and impressive figures the superiority of
the free to the Judaistic Christians is illustrated.   It
cannot be said that there is any reasoning or argument :
illustrations are used to bring the Galatians to a clear
consciousness of what they have in their own minds.
Argument is too external a process ; Paul merely points
out to the Galatians that "they already know ".

As a whole, the letter is an eloquent and powerful claim
for freedom of life, freedom of thought, freedom of the
individual from external restrictions and regulations,
freedom for all to work out their own salvation and develop
their own nature: "Ye were called for freedom" (V 13).
And towards the conclusion this turns to a glorification of
love.   Their freedom is freedom to do right, not freedom
to do everything ; "the whole Law is fulfilled in one word,
even in this : Thou shalt love thy neighbour as thyself"
(V 14).   Selfishness, *i.e.,* "the flesh," is the absolute antithesis of love, *i.e.,* " the Spirit " ; and the receiving of Christ
is " crucifying the flesh with the passions thereof" (V 24).
The essence of the true life lies neither in observing the
Law nor in being above the Law, but in building anew
one's nature (VI 15).

4. THE DATE OF THE GALATIAN EPISTLE, though
out of chronological order, may be considered here.   The
defection of the Galatians occurred shortly after Paul's
second visit (not shortly after his first visit, as Lightfoot
strangely takes it, I, 6, p. 42).   He spent the summer of 50
among them ; and the Judaic emissaries may have come in
the summer of 51 or 52.   But, amid the sudden changes of
plan on his journey, Paul could not receive many letters
from Galatia.   Moreover, his epistle seems to imply the
possession of full knowledge, such as could not be gained

from a mere letter: if the Galatians wrote to him, it is most improbable that they explained their changed attitude and all the reasons for it. No! Paul's information comes from the personal report of a trusty messenger; and the obvious suitability of Timothy for the duty occurs at once to one's mind. Further, it is clear that Timothy was with Paul during a considerable part of the stay in Corinth, for he joined in the greeting at the opening of both letters to Thessalonica. It is therefore hardly possible that he could have gone home, visited his friends, satisfied himself as to the condition of the Churches, and returned to Corinth before Paul left that city. Moreover, if Paul heard at that time, it is not probable that he would have spent so much time on a voyage to Jerusalem and a visit to Syrian Antioch before visiting personally the wavering Churches.

We conclude, then, that Timothy went to pay a visit to his friends, not before the latter part of Paul's stay in Corinth; and, when he found out the real state of affairs in South Galatia, he went to meet Paul with the news. Owing to Paul's movements, there are only two places where Timothy could have met him,—Ephesus and Syrian Antioch. The former is most unlikely, for, if Timothy left Corinth some months before Paul, he could have no assurance of meeting him there, where he merely called in passing. It is probable, then, that he brought his report to Paul at Syrian Antioch after the fourth visit to Jerusalem (p. 265). With the entire want of definite evidence, we cannot get beyond this estimate of probabilities; and it is most likely that Timothy stayed with Paul during the whole of his residence at Corinth, sailed with him as far as Ephesus, and landed there in order to go home on a visit to his friends, while Paul went on to Jerusalem. We shall at a later stage find that Paul often sent deputies to inspect his Churches ; and their reports often drew forth an Epistle to correct an erring Church (pp. 275, 284).

In this way, when Paul reached Syrian Antioch, or immediately after he reached it, at the end of his visit to Cæsareia and Jerusalem, he found Timothy waiting with the disheartening news, in the summer of 53 : and at once he sat down and wrote the letter which has been preserved to us.

One question remains. Why was Paul content with writing ? Why did he not start at once himself ? Personal intervention is always more effective in such cases. But, in the first place, a letter would certainly travel faster than Paul could get over the ground ; and he would not lose a moment in letting the Galatians hear what he thought. In the second place, he could hardly sacrifice the opportunity of reviewing the Churches in Syria and Cilicia that lay on his way : everywhere he would be besieged with entreaties to stay for a little, and he could not well hurry past them without at least a brief stay of one or two days in each. Finally there are frequently reasons which make it impossible to hurry away on a serious journey like that from Syria to South Galatia. Paul was only human.

When Paul wrote the letter he must, on our view, have been intending to arrive very soon after his letter. It may be asked why he makes no reference to this intention. But we should rather ask, if, according to the ordinary view, he were not coming immediately, why he did not make some explanatory statement of the reasons that compelled him at such a crisis to be content with a letter and to do without a visit (p. 275 f.). The messenger who carried the letter carried also the news that Paul was following close after, as fast as his necessary detentions at Antioch and other cities on the way permitted ; and part of the effect of the letter lay in the fact that the writer was going to be present in person very soon.

The Epistle to the Galatians, therefore, belongs to A.D. 53, and was written just when he was starting on his third journey, but before he had begun that scheme of a general contribution among all his new Churches which is so prominent in the three following letters, I, II *Cor.* and *Rom.*

To this date one objection may perhaps be urged : in IV 10, Paul asks, " Are ye observing days and months and seasons and years ? " It has been urged that this implies that the Sabbatical year 54-55 was observed by the Galatians when the letter was written. But Lightfoot has rightly rejected this argument: Paul asks in sarcasm : " Are ye observing the whole series of institutions ? are ye taking up anew a ritual like that of paganism from which you were set free ? "

5. THE LATER HISTORY OF THE CHURCHES OF GALATIA is obscure. They took part in the contribution raised by the Pauline Churches for the poor brethren at Jerusalem (p. 286 f.), and were represented in the delegation that carried it to Jerusalem. Thereafter history ends, and tradition alone preserves some scraps of information about Antioch, Iconium and Lystra. Derbe alone is not mentioned either in the tradition (so far as my knowledge extends) or in the history of the Church until we come down to A.D. 381, when its bishop Daphnus was present at the Council of Constantinople. The only hope of further information about the four Churches lies in

archæology; but unless the spade can be brought to supplement the too scanty records that remain above ground, little can be hoped for.[1]

[1] The Christian antiquities of Antioch and Iconium will be discussed at some length in my *Cities and Bishoprics of Phrygia*. If my dream of excavating the deserted sites of Derbe and Lystra be ever realised, they would form the subject of a special treatise.

CHAPTER IX

THE COMING OF LUKE AND THE CALL INTO MACEDONIA

1. A C R O S S A S I A. (XVI 6) AND THEY, HAVING MADE A PROGRESS THROUGH THE PHRYGIAN REGION OF *the province* GALATIA, AND HAVING BEEN PREVENTED BY THE HOLY SPIRIT FROM SPEAKING THE WORD IN *the province* ASIA, (7) AND HAVING REACHED A POINT OVER AGAINST MYSIA (*or, perhaps, on the skirts of Mysia*), WERE ATTEMPTING TO MAKE THEIR WAY INTO *the province* BITHYNIA; AND THE SPIRIT OF JESUS SUFFERED THEM NOT; (8) AND, NEGLECTING MYSIA, THEY CAME DOWN TO *the harbour* TROAS. (9) AND A VISION APPEARED TO PAUL BY NIGHT: THERE WAS A CERTAIN MAN, A MACEDONIAN, STANDING, AND EXHORTING HIM AND SAYING, "COME OVER TO MACEDONIA, AND HELP US". (10) AND WHEN HE SAW THE VISION, IMMEDIATELY WE SOUGHT TO GO OUT *from Asia* INTO *the province* MACEDONIA, ASSUREDLY GATHERING THAT "GOD HAS SUMMONED US TO BRING THE GOOD NEWS TO THEM".

Paul and his companions made a missionary progress through the Phrygian *Region* of the province Galatia (p. 104), and then crossed the frontier of the province Asia: but here they were prevented from preaching, and the prohibition was made absolute for

(194)

the entire province. They therefore kept to the north across Asian Phrygia with the intention of entering the adjoining Roman province Bithynia ; but when they came opposite Mysia, and were attempting to go out of Asia into Bithynia, the Spirit of Jesus suffered them not. They therefore kept on towards the west through Mysia, without preaching in it (as it was part of Asia), until they came out on its western coast at the great harbour of Alexandria Troas.

The expression marks clearly the distinction between the prohibition to preach in Asia, while they were actually in it, and the prohibition even to set foot in Bithynia. It was necessary for them to cross Asia in order to fulfil the purpose for which they were about to be called.

The geographical facts of this paragraph are stated with great clearness in the text followed by the Authorised Version and the older editions ; but the reading which they give is founded on Manuscripts of an inferior class (while the great MSS. have a different text), and is characterised by the sequence of three participial clauses, a sequence almost unique in Luke's writings, and therefore suspected and altered. But the strange form of construction by a succession of participles suits so perfectly the strange and unique character, the hurry, and the deep-lying emotion of the passage (see § 2) that, as Lightfoot's judgment, *Bibl. Essays*, p. 237, perceived, the inferior MSS. must here be followed. The text of the great MSS., though it does not quite conceal the feeling of the passage, yet obscures it a little, and, by approximating more to Luke's ordinary form of sentence, loses that perfect adaptation of form to sense, which so

often strikes us in this history. We have already noticed,
p. 115, that Luke loves the triple iteration of successive
words or clauses to produce a certain effect in arresting
attention.

The reading of the inferior MSS. suits the South-
Galatian theory admirably ; but that fact never weighed
with me for a moment in the choice. As long as
the question between the two theories was alone
concerned, the thought of following the inferior MSS.
did not even present itself : I followed the great MSS.
and interpreted them in the best way possible, neither
looking aside nor feeling the slightest wish to adopt
the rival text. But when the question of literary
feeling came up, after the delicate adaptation of expression to emotion throughout *Acts* gradually revealed itself,
it became clear that here the choice lay between a cast
of sentence unusual in this author, and one that was
quite in his ordinary style, in a place where the feeling
and the facts were strange and unique : hesitation was
then impossible : the unusual emotion demanded the
unusual expression. See note, p. 211 f.

In this passage the distinction observed by Luke between Roman provincial designations and the older
national names is specially clear. Wherever he mentions
districts of mission work, he classifies according to the
existing political (Roman) divisions (as here, the Phrygo-
Galatic Region, Asia, Bithynia, Macedonia) ; but where
he is simply giving geographical information, he either
uses the pre-Roman names of lands (*e.g.*, Mysia), or omits
the land from his narrative.

The " neglecting " of Mysia is a remarkable expression,
one of those by which Luke compels attention at a critical

point. As a rule he simply omits a country where no preaching occurred (p. 90 f.); but here he accumulates devices to arrest the reader. His effects are always attained, not by rhetorical devices, but by order and marshalling of facts; and here, in a missionary tour, the " neglecting " of a great country is a fact that no one can pass over. Not catching the intention, many understand " passing without entering " (παρελθόντες): Dr. Blass rightly sees that a traveller cannot reach Troas without crossing Mysia; but he goes on to alter the text, following the Bezan reading (διελθόντες; see p. 235).

The journey across Mysia led naturally down the course of the river Rhyndacos, and past the south shore of the great lakes. A tradition that Paul had travelled by the sacred town of the goddess Artemis at the hot springs of the river Aisepos can be traced as early as the second century, accompanied with the legend that he had founded a chapel in the neighbourhood. If he went down the Rhyndacos, it is practically certain that he must have passed close to, or through, Artemaia on his way to the great harbour. Under the influence of this tradition, the Bezan Reviser changed the text of *v.* 8, reading "making a progress through Mysia". But evangelisation on the journey across Mysia was forbidden, *v.* 6. The tradition, however, is interesting; and there is further trace of very early foundations in this quarter, which will be treated elsewhere.

The rapid sweep of narrative, hurrying on from country to country, is the marked feature of this paragraph; yet it merely places before us the facts, as Paul's missionary aims found no opening, and he was driven on and on. But, on the current North-Galatian theory, this effect, which is obviously intended, is got, not by simply stating facts, but by slurring over one of Paul's greatest enterprises, the evangelisation of North Galatia and the founding of several Churches in a new mission district. But the first words of *v.* 6 describe a progress marked by no great events, a steady continuance of a process fully described in the context (p. 72).

2. THE CALL INTO MACEDONIA. This is in many respects the most remarkable paragraph in *Acts*. In the first place the Divine action is introduced three times in four verses, marking and justifying the new and great step which is made at this point. In XIII 1-11 also the Divine action is mentioned three times, leading up to the important development which the author defines as "opening the door of belief to the Nations"; but in that case there were only two actual manifestations of the Divine guidance and power. Here on three distinct occasions the guidance of God was manifested in three different ways—the Holy Spirit, the Spirit of Jesus, and the Vision—and the three manifestations all lead up to one end, first forbidding Paul's purpose of preaching in Asia, then forbidding his purpose of entering Bithynia, and finally calling him forward into Macedonia. Now, amid "the multitude of the revelations" (II *Cor.* XII 7) granted to Paul, Luke selects only those which have a distinct bearing on his own purpose as an historian, and omits the vast majority, which were all important in their influence on Paul's conduct and character. What is the reason for his insistence in this case?

It is not easy to account on strictly historical grounds for the emphasis laid on the passage to Macedonia.

Lightfoot, in his fine essay on " the Churches of Macedonia," recognises with his usual insight that it is necessary to acknowledge and to explain that emphasis ; but his attempt cannot be called successful. As he himself acknowledges, the narrative gives no ground to think that the passage from Troas to Philippi was ever thought of by Luke as a passage from Continent to Continent. A broad distinction between the two opposite sides of the Hellespont as belonging to two different Continents, had no existence in the thought of those who lived in the Ægean lands, and regarded the sea as the path connecting the Ægean countries with each other ; and the distinction had no more existence in a political point of view, for Macedonia and Asia were merely two provinces of the Roman Empire, closely united by common language and character, and divided from the Latin-speaking provinces further west.

After an inaccurate statement that Macedonia was "the natural highroad between the East and the West" (the Ægean was the real highroad, and Corinth was "on the way of them that are being slain to God," *Church in R. E.*, p. 318 f.), Lightfoot finds in Alexander the Great the proof of the greatness of the step which Luke here records in Paul's work, and even says that "each successive station at which he halted might have reminded the Apostle of the great services rendered by Macedonia as the pioneer of the Gospel !" That is mere riot of pseudo-historical fancy ; and it is hardly possible to believe that Lightfoot ever composed it in the form and with the suggestion that it has in this essay. This is one of not a few places in his *Biblical Essays* in which the expansion of his own "briefest summary" by the aid of notes of his oral lectures taken by pupils has not been thoroughly successful. The pages of the essay amount to a practical demonstration that, on mere grounds of historical geography alone, one cannot explain the marked emphasis laid on this new departure.

In the second place, the sweep and rush of the narrative is unique in *Acts* : point after point, province after province are hurried over. The natural development of Paul's work along the great central route of the Empire was forbidden, and the next alternative that rose in his mind was forbidden : he was led across Asia from the extreme south-east to the extreme north-west corner, and yet prevented from preaching in it ; everything seemed dark and perplexing, until at last a vision in Troas explained the purpose of this strange journey. As before (p. 104), we cannot but be struck with the fact, that in this paragraph the idea seems to clothe itself in the natural words, and not to have been laboriously expressed by a foreign mind. And the origin of the words becomes clear when we look at the concluding sentence : " immediately *we* sought to go forth into Macedonia, assuredly gathering that ' God has called *us* for to preach the Gospel unto them ' ". The author was with Paul in Troas ; and the intensity of this paragraph is due to his recollection of the words in which Paul had recounted the vision, and explained the whole Divine plan that had guided him through his perplexing wanderings. The words derive their vivid and striking character from Paul, and they remained indelibly imprinted on Luke's memory.

3. THE COMING OF LUKE. The introduction of the first person at this striking point in the narrative

must be intentional. This is no general statement like
XIV 22 (though even there the first person has a marked
effect, p. 123). Every one recognises here a distinct
assertion that the author was present. Now the paragraph as a whole is carefully studied, and the sudden
change from third to first person is a telling element in
the total effect : if there is any passage in *Acts* which
can be pressed close, it is this. It is almost universally
recognised that the use of the first person in the sequel
is intentional, marking that the author remained in
Philippi when Paul went on, and that he rejoined the
Apostle some years later on his return to Philippi. We
must add that the precise point at which the first-personal
form of narrative begins is also intentional ; for, if
Luke changes here at random from third to first person,
it would be absurd to look for purpose in anything he
says. The first person, when used in the narrative of
XVI, XX, XXI, XXVII, XXVIII, marks the companionship of Luke and Paul ; and, when we carry out
this principle of interpretation consistently and minutely,
it will prove an instructive guide. This is the nearest
approach to personal reference that Luke permits himself ;
and he makes it subservient to his historical purpose by
using it as a criterion of personal witness.

Luke, therefore, entered into the drama of the *Acts*
at Troas. Now it is clear that the coming of Paul to
Troas was unforeseen and unforeseeable ; the whole point
of the paragraph is that Paul was driven on against
his own judgment and intention to that city. The meeting, therefore, was not, as has sometimes been maintained, pre-arranged. Luke entered on the stage of this
history at a point, where Paul found himself he knew

not why. On the ordinary principles of interpreting literature, we must infer that this meeting, which is so skilfully and so pointedly represented as unforeseen, was between two strangers : Luke became known to Paul here for the first time. Let us, then, scrutinise more closely the circumstances. The narrative pointedly brings together the dream and the introduction of the first-personal element, " when *he* saw the vision, straightway *we* sought to go " ; and collocation is everywhere one of the most telling points in Luke's style.

When we examine the dream, we observe that in it " a certain man of Macedonia " was seen by Paul. Paul did not infer his Macedonian origin from his words, but recognised him as a Macedonian by sight. Now, there was nothing distinctive in the appearance or dress of a Macedonian to mark him out from the rest of the world. On the contrary, the Macedonians rather made a point of their claim to be Greeks ; and undoubtedly they dressed in the customary Greek style of the Ægean cities. There was, therefore, only one way in which Paul could know the man by sight to be a Macedonian— the man in the dream was personally known to him ; and, in fact, the Greek implies that it was a certain definite person who appeared (ἀνήρ τις, Latin *quidam*, very often followed by the person's name ; V 1, VIII 9, IX 10, 33, 36, X 1, etc.).

In the vision, then, a certain Macedonian, who was personally known to Paul, appeared, and called him over into Macedonia. Now, it has been generally recognised that Luke must have had some connection with Philippi ; and we shall find reason to think that he had personal knowledge of the city. Further, Paul, whose life had been spent in the eastern countries, and who had come so far west only a few days past, was not likely to be personally acquainted with natives of Macedonia. The idea then suggests itself at once, that Luke himself was the man seen in the vision ; and, when one reads the paragraph with that idea, it acquires new meaning and increased beauty. As always, Luke seeks no effect from artifices of style. He tells nothing but the bare facts in their simplest form ; and leaves the reader to catch the causal connection between them. But we can imagine how Paul came to Troas in doubt as to what should be done. As a harbour, it formed the link between Asia and Macedonia. Here he met the Macedonian Luke ; and with his view turned onwards he slept, and beheld in a vision his Macedonian acquaintance beckoning him onward to his own country.

Beyond this we cannot penetrate through the veil in which Luke has enveloped himself. Was he already a Christian, or did he come under the influence of Christianity through meeting Paul here ? for the prohibition against preaching in Asia would not preclude Paul from using the opportunity to convert an individual who was brought in contact with him. No evidence remains ; " something sealed the lips of that evangelist," so far as he himself is concerned. But we have gathered from the drift of the passage that they met as strangers ; and in that case there can be no doubt where the probability lies. The inference that they met accidentally as strangers is confirmed by the fact that Luke was a stranger to the Levant (p. 317). In one of the many ways in which men come across one another in travelling, they were brought into contact at

Troas : Luke was attracted to Paul ; and the vision was taken by Luke, as well as by Paul, for a sign. He left all, and followed his master.

All this he suggests to us only by the same kind of delicate and subtle literary devices, consisting merely in collocation of facts, order of words, and slight changes of form, by which he suggested the development of Paul's method and the change in his relation to Barnabas (p. 82 f.). Luke always expects a great deal from his readers, but some critics give too little attention to literary effect. These will ask me for proofs ; but proofs there are none. I can only point to the facts : they that have eyes to see them know ; they that have not eyes to see them will treat this section (and others) as moonstruck fancy. All that can be said is that, if you read the book carefully, observing these devices, you recognise a great work ; if you don't, and follow your denial to its logical consequences, you will find only an assortment of scraps. Probably there will always be those who prefer the scraps.

It is quite in Luke's style to omit to mention that Paul related the vision to his companions. So also he omitted in XIII 7, 8, to mention that Paul expounded the doctrine to the proconsul. Luke always expects a great deal from his readers. But here the Bezan Reviser inserts the missing detail, as he so often does (*e.g.*, XIII 9).

While there is no authority for the circumstances of the meeting, conjecture is tempting and perhaps permissible. It will appear that Luke, though evidently acquainted with Philippi and looking to it as his city, had no home there. His meeting with Paul, then, did not take place merely on an excursion from Philippi; and he was probably one of the many Greeks in all ages who have sought their fortune away from home. His acquaintance with medicine is certain from the words of Paul himself, "Luke, the beloved physician" (*Col.* IV 14), and from the cast of his language in many places;[1] and it is quite natural and probable that the meeting might have been sought by Paul on that account, if Luke was resident in Troas and wellknown there.

4. THE ENTRANCE INTO MACEDONIA. (XVI 11) WE SET SAIL THEN FROM TROAS, AND MADE A STRAIGHT RUN TO SAMOTHRACE; AND THE DAY FOLLOWING *we came* TO *the harbour* NEAPOLIS, (12) AND THENCE TO PHILIPPI, WHICH IS THE LEADING CITY OF ITS DIVISION OF MACEDONIA, AND *having the rank of* A ROMAN COLONY: AND WE WERE IN THIS CITY TARRYING CERTAIN DAYS.

It is remarkable with what interest Luke records the incidents from harbour to harbour. He has the true Greek feeling for the sea, a feeling that must develop in every race possessing any capacity for development, and any sensitiveness to the influences of nature, when settled round the Ægean coasts; for the Ægean sea is so tempting, with its regular winds and regular sunset calm, when the water lies dead, with a surface which looks like oil, dense and glistening and dark, that it seems to invite one to walk upon it.

To a certain extent the wealth of maritime details might be accounted for by the loving interest with which Luke dwelt on his journeys in company with Paul; but

---

[1] Hobart, *The Medical Language of St. Luke,* a work which has to be used with the caution that the author recognises as needful.

this does not fully explain the facts. Every one who compares Luke's account of the journey from Cæsareja to Jerusalem (which might be expected to live in his memory beyond others), or from Puteoli to Rome, with his account of any of the voyages, must be struck by the difference between the scanty matter-of-fact details in the land journeys, and the love that notes the voyage, the winds, the runs, the appearance of the shores, Cyprus rising out of the sea, the Cretan coast close in by the ship's side, the mountains towering above it from which the blast strikes down. At the same time, it is quite clear that, though he reported nautical matters with accuracy, he was not a trained and practised sailor. His interest for the sea sprang from his natural and national character, and not from his occupation.

Philippi was an inland city, and Neapolis was its harbour. Having once mentioned the port, Luke leaves it to be understood in XX 6. As usual, Paul goes on to the great city, and does not preach in the port (cp. XIV 26, XVIII 18).

The description of the dignity and rank of Philippi is unique in *Acts ;* nor can it be explained as strictly requisite for the historian's proper purpose. Here again the explanation lies in the character of the author, who was specially interested in Philippi, and had the true Greek pride in his own city. Perhaps he even exaggerates a little the dignity of Philippi, which was still only in process of growth, to become at a later date the great city of its division. Of old Amphipolis had been the chief city of the division, to which both belonged. Afterwards Philippi quite outstripped its rival ; but it was at that time in such a position, that Amphipolis was ranked first by general consent, Philippi first by its own consent. These cases of rivalry between two or even three cities for the dignity and title of " First" are familiar to every student of the history of the Greek cities ; and though no other evidence is known to show that Philippi had as yet began to claim the title, yet this single passage is conclusive. The descriptive phrase is like a lightning flash amid the darkness of local history, revealing in startling clearness the whole situation to those whose eyes are trained to catch the character of Greek city-history and city-jealousies.

It is an interesting fact that Luke, who hides himself so completely in his history, cannot hide his local feeling ; and there every one who knows the Greek people recognises the true Greek ! There lies the strength, and also the weakness, of the Greek peoples ; and that quality beyond all others has determined their history, has given them their strength against the foreigner, and their weakness as a united country.

Nationality is more conspicuous in the foibles and weaknesses of mankind, whereas great virtues and great vices have a common character in all nations. Luke shows himself the Greek when he talks of the Maltese as "the barbarians" ; when he regards the journey to Jerusalem as a journey and nothing more ; when he misrepresents the force of a Latin word (p. 225) ; when he is blind to the true character of the Roman name (the *tria nomina*) ; when he catches with such appreciation and such ease the character of Paul's surroundings in Athens. His hatred of the Jews and his obvious inability to feel the slightest sympathy for their attitude towards Paul, are also Greek. On the other hand, his touches of quiet humour are perhaps less characteristically Greek; but he was not the old Greek of the classical period: he was the Greek of his own age, when Greece had been for centuries a power in Asia; when Macedonia had long been the leading Greek country; when Stoicism and Epicureanism were the representative philosophies (XVII 18); and when the Greek language was the recognised speech of many eastern Roman provinces, along with the Latin itself. To appreciate Luke, we must study the modern Greek, as well as the Greek of the great age of freedom.

I know that all such mundane characteristics are commonly considered to be non-existent in "the early Christian"! But an "early Christian" did not cease to be a man, and a citizen. Christianity has not taught men to retire from society and from life; and least of all did Pauline Christianity teach that lesson. It has impressed on men the duty of living their life better, of striving to mould and to influence society around them, and of doing their best in the position in which they were placed. When Luke became a Christian, he continued to be a Greek, and perhaps became even more intensely a Greek, as his whole life became more intense and more unselfish. It is a complete and ruinous error for the historical student to suppose that Luke broke with all his old thoughts, and habits, and feelings, and friends, when he was converted. He lived in externals much as before; he observed the same laws of politeness and good-breeding in society (if he followed Paul's instructions); his house, his surroundings, continued much the same; he kept up the same family names; and, when he died, his grave, his tombstone, and his epitaph, were in the ordinary style. It took centuries for Christianity to disengage itself from its surroundings, and to remake society and the rules of life. Yet one rarely finds among modern historians of Christianity in the first two centuries of its growth, any one who does not show a misconception on this point ; and the climax, perhaps, is reached in one of the arguments by which Dr. Ficker attempts to disprove the Christian character of the epitaph of the Phrygian second-century saint, Avircius Marcellus, on the ground that a Christian epitaph would not be engraved on an altar. I presume his point is that the altar-shaped form of tombstone was avoided by the Christians of that time, because it was connected with the pagan worship. But a Pauline Christian would hold that "*a gravestone* will not commend us to God ; neither, if we *use* it not, are we the worse, nor if we *use* it, are we the better " (I *Cor.* VIII 8); and Avircius Marcellus mentions Paul, and Paul alone among the Apostles, in his epitaph. In fact, almost all the early Christian epitaphs at Eumeneia are engraved on altars, because there that shape was fashionable ; whereas at Apameia they are rarely on altars, because there that shape was not in such common use.

Our view that the author of *Acts* was a Macedonian does not agree with a tradition (which was believed to occur in Eusebius, see p. 389) that Luke was an Antiochian. The modern authorities who consider this tradition to be founded on a confusion between Lucas and Lucius, an official of the Antiochian Church (XIII 1), seem to have strong probability on their side. The form Lucas may very well be a vulgarism for Lucius ; but, except the name, these two persons have nothing in common. The name

Lucas is of most obscure origin: it may be a shortened form of Lucius, or Lucilius, or Lucianus, or Lucanus, or of some Greek compound name. The Latin names, Lucius, Lucilius, etc., were spelt in earlier Greek Λεύκιος, in later Greek Λούκιος; and the change may roughly be dated about A.D. 50-75, though Λεύκιος in some rare cases occurs later, and possibly Λούκιος sometimes earlier. It is noteworthy that Λουκᾶς has the later form.

The Bezan " we " in XI 28 will satisfy those who consider the Bezan Text to be Lukan; but to us it appears to condemn the Bezan Text as of non-Lukan origin. The warmth of feeling, which breathes through all parts of *Acts* dealing with the strictly Greek world, is in striking contrast with the cold and strictly historical tone of the few brief references to Syrian Antioch. If the author of *Acts* was a native bred up in Antioch, then we should have to infer that there lay behind him an older author, whose work he adapted with little change. But our view is that the Reviser had an Antiochian connection, and betrays it in that insertion, which to him recorded a historical fact, but to us seems legend in an early stage of growth.

Note 1. τὴν Φρυγίαν καὶ Γαλατικὴν χώραν. The use of καὶ to connect two epithets of the same person or place is regular in Greek (so Σαῦλος ὁ καὶ Παῦλος, Saul *alias* Paul); *e.g.*, Strabo speaks of a mouth of the Nile as τὸ Κανωβικὸν καὶ Ἡρακλεωτικόν, the mouth which is called by both names, Canopic and Heracleotic, where we should say, " the Canopic or Heracleotic mouth ". I need not dwell on such an elementary point. Another point of Greek construction comes up in XVIII 23: when a list is given in Greek, the items of which are designated by adjectives with the same noun, the regular order is to use the noun

with the first alone. Strabo has numberless examples :
767, τῶν παρακειμένων 'Αραβίων ἐθνῶν Ναβαταίων τε καὶ
Χαυλοτοπαίων καὶ 'Αγραίων ; 751, ὁ 'Αρκεύθης ποταμὸς καὶ
ὁ 'Ορόντης καὶ ὁ Λαβώτας ; 802, τὸ Μενδήσιον στόμα καὶ τὸ
Τανιτικόν (there are some interesting and delicate examples
in Strabo, on which we cannot here dwell, of the distinction between the double epithet and the double item) ;
Herodotus, II 17, τὸ δὲ Βολβιτινὸν στόμα καὶ τὸ Βουκολικόν ;
and so Luke groups two *Regiones* as τὴν Γαλατικὴν
χώραν καὶ Φρυγίαν, XVIII 23. The North-Galatian theorists insist that Φρυγίαν in XVI 6 must be a substantive ;
but they have not quoted any case in which a noun with
its adjective is coupled anarthrously by καί to a preceding
noun with the article. Dr. Chase quoted Luke III 1, τῆς
'Ιτουραίας καὶ Τραχωνίτιδος χώρας ; but the case tells
against him, for Luke's intention to use 'Ιτουραίας here as
an adjective is proved by the following reasons :—

(1) Eusebius and Jerome repeatedly interpret *Luke* III
1 in that way (see *Expositor*, Jan. 1894, p. 52 ; April, p.
289). (2) 'Ιτουραία is never used as a noun by the
ancients, but is pointedly avoided, even where ἡ 'Ιτου-
ραίων was awkward : the reason was that 'Ιτουραία, as
a noun, would indicate a political entity, whereas the
Ituræi were a wandering nomadic race, who had not a
definite and organised country. As my other reasons
have been disputed, I do not append them here ; though
I consider them unshaken. [Mr. Arnold's attempt to
find one instance of 'Ιτουραία as a noun in Appian
seems to refute itself, *Engl. Hist. Rev.*, 1895, p. 553.]

Note 2. διῆλθον τὴν Φ. κ. Γ. χώραν κωλυθέντες. Many
are likely to rest on the authority of the great MSS.,
and prefer this reading. It may be understood, by an

ellipse common in Greek, "they made a missionary progress through the Phrygian land, *viz.*, the Galatic part of it, inasmuch as they were prevented from preaching in Asia, and could not, therefore, do missionary work in the Asian part of it". But, if this were the writing of Luke, I should prefer to hold that he meant διῆλθον καὶ ἐκωλύθησαν, using a construction which he has in (1) XXIII 35 ἔφη κελεύσας *he said*, " I will hear thee, when thy accusers arrive," *and ordered* him to be imprisoned : (2) XXV 13 κατήντησαν ἀσπασάμενοι " *they arrived* at Cæsareia *and paid* their respects to Festus": (3) XVII 26 ἐποίησεν ἐξ ἑνός, ὁρίσας " *he made* all nations of one blood, *and assigned* to them limits and bounds " (here the unity of all nations is the initial idea, and the fixing of limits and distinctions is later). Blass, who thus explains XXIII 35, gives in his preface, p. 20, many examples of the present infinitive used in the same way (XVIII 23 ἐξῆλθεν διερχόμενος he went forth and made a progress through the Galatic Region, cp. VI 9 ἀνέστησαν συνζητοῦντες they rose up and disputed with Stephen, VI 11 ὑπέβαλον ἄνδρας λέγοντας they suborned men which said [also VI 13], VIII 10 προσεῖχον λέγοντες they hearkened and said, V. 36 ἀνέστη λέγων he stood up and said, VIII 18, XIV 22, etc.); and he accepts and prints in his text the reading of inferior authority in XXVIII 14 παρεκλήθημεν παρ' αὐτοῖς, ἐπιμείναντες *we were cheered* among them, *and remained* seven days. The usage is common in Paul. The use of aorist or present participle corresponds to the tense which would be used if the sentence were constructed in the fuller fashion, ἔφη καὶ ἐκέλευσεν but ἐξῆλθεν καὶ διήρχετο (Blass differs in regard to XXI 16, which he says = συνῆλθον καὶ ἤγαγον).

CHAPTER X

THE CHURCHES OF MACEDONIA

1. PHILIPPI. (XVI 13) ON THE SABBATH DAY WE WENT FORTH WITHOUT THE GATE BY THE RIVER SIDE, WHERE THERE WAS WONT TO BE HELD A MEETING FOR PRAYER; AND WE SAT DOWN, AND SPAKE UNTO THE WOMEN THAT CAME TOGETHER. (14) AND A CERTAIN WOMAN NAMED LYDIA, A SELLER OF PURPLE, OF THE CITY OF THYATIRA, A GOD-FEARING *proselyte*, WAS A HEARER; AND THE LORD OPENED HER HEART TO GIVE HEED UNTO THE THINGS THAT WERE SPOKEN BY PAUL. (15) AND WHEN SHE WAS BAPTISED AND HER HOUSE-HOLD, SHE BESOUGHT US, SAYING, "IF YE HAVE JUDGED ME TO BE FAITHFUL TO THE LORD, COME INTO MY HOUSE AND ABIDE THERE"; AND SHE CONSTRAINED US.

The omission of the article before the word "river" (ποταμόν) is one of the touches of familiarity which show the hand of one who knew Philippi well. As we say "I'm going to town," the Greeks omitted the article with familiar and frequently mentioned places or things. In this phrase the commentators in general seem to understand that the Greek words mean "along a river," which is the form of expression that a complete stranger might use about a city and a river that he had only heard of.

(213)

The text of the next clause is uncertain ; but we hold that the Authorised Version is right, following the inferior MSS. (see note, p. 235). On the first Sabbath they went along the river-bank to the regular place where the Jews in Philippi, and those non-Jews who had been attracted to Jewish customs, were wont to meet in prayer. There seems to have been no proper synagogue, which shows that the Jewish community was very small; and in the rest of the narrative no Jew is mentioned.

Lydia, the Thyatiran woman, settled at Philippi, is an interesting person in many respects. Thyatira, like the Lydian land in general, was famous for its dyeing ; and its guild of dyers is known from the inscriptions. Lydia sold the purple dyed garments from Thyatira in Philippi ; and she had, no doubt, a regular connection with a firm in her native city, whose agent she was. In ancient time many kinds of garments were woven in their perfect shape ; and there was much less cutting and sewing of cloth than at the present day. Lydia, of course, sold also the less expensive kinds of garments ; but she takes her trade-name from the finest class of her wares, indicating that she was a first-class dealer. She must have possessed a considerable amount of capital to trade in such articles. As her husband is not mentioned, and she was a householder, she was probably a widow ; and she may be taken as an ordinary example of the freedom with which women lived and worked both in Asia Minor and in Macedonia.

Lydia had probably become addicted to Jewish religious practices in her native city. There had been a Jewish colony planted in Thyatira, which had exercised consider-

able influence on the city ; and a hybrid sort of worship
had been developed, half Jewish, half pagan, which is called
in *Revelation* II 20, " the woman Jezebel".[1]

It is not to be inferred that Lydia and her household were baptised on the first Sabbath. A certain
interval must be admitted in *v.* 14, which shows Luke's
looseness about time. Lydia was present on the first
Sabbath, and became a regular hearer ; and finally her
entire household came over with her.

2. THE VENTRILOQUIST (XVI 16) AND IT CAME
TO PASS, AS WE WERE GOING TO THE PLACE OF
PRAYER, THAT A CERTAIN SLAVE-GIRL, POSSESSED OF A
SPIRIT PYTHON, *i.e.,* *a ventriloquist,* MET US, WHICH
BROUGHT HER MASTERS MUCH GAIN BY SOOTHSAYING.
(17) THE SAME, FOLLOWING AFTER PAUL AND US,
KEPT CRYING OUT SAYING, " THESE MEN ARE THE
SLAVES OF THE GOD THE HIGHEST, WHICH ANNOUNCE
TO YOU THE WAY OF SAFETY". (18) AND THIS SHE DID
FOR MANY DAYS. BUT PAUL, BEING SORE TROUBLED,
TURNED AND SAID TO THE SPIRIT, " I CHARGE THEE
IN THE NAME OF JESUS THE ANOINTED TO GO OUT
FROM HER "; AND IT WENT OUT THAT VERY MOMENT.

The idea was universally entertained that ventriloquism
was due to superhuman influence, and implied the
power of foretelling the future. The girl herself believed
this ; and in her belief lay her power. Her words need
not be taken as a witness to Christianity. " God the
Highest " was a wide-spread pagan expression, and
" salvation " was the object of many vows and prayers
to that and other gods. We need not ask too curiously
what was her motive in thus calling out at Paul's

[1] See Schürer in *Abhandlungen Weizsäcker gewidmet*, p. 39.

company. In such a case there is no distinct motive; for it is a poor and false view, and one that shows utter incapacity to gauge human nature, that the girl was a mere impostor. That her mind became distorted and diseased by her belief in her supernatural possession, is certain; but it became thereby all the more acute in certain perceptions and intuitions. With her sensitive nature, she became at once alive to the moral influence, which the intense faith by which the strangers were possessed gave them, and she must say what she felt without any definite idea of result therefrom; for the immediate utterance of her intuitions was the secret of her power. She saw in Paul what the populace at Pisidian Antioch saw in Thekla, "a devotee, bound by some unusual conditions, an inspired servant of 'the God,' who differed from the usual type" of "God-driven" devotees.

When Paul turned on her, and ordered the spirit to come forth from her in the name of his Master, the girl, who had been assiduously declaring that Paul and his companions were God-possessed, and fully believed it, was utterly disconcerted, and lost her faith in herself and with it her power. When next she tried to speak as she had formerly done, she was unable to do so; and in a few days it became apparent that she had lost her power. Along with her power, her hold on the superstitions of the populace disappeared; and people ceased to come to her to have their fortunes read, to get help in finding things they had lost, and so on. Thus the comfortable income that she had earned for her owners was lost; and these, knowing who had done the mischief, sought revenge. This was by no means a rare motive for the outbreak of persecution against the Church in later time ; and at this stage, when Christianity was an unknown religion, it was only through its interference with the profits of any individual or any class (p. 277) that it was likely to arouse opposition among the pagans.

3. ACCUSATION AND CONDEMNATION IN PHILIPPI. (XVI 19) BUT, WHEN HER MASTERS SAW THAT THEIR HOPE OF GAIN HAD DEPARTED, THEY SEIZED PAUL AND SILAS [AND DRAGGED THEM INTO THE AGORA BEFORE THE MAGISTRATES], (20) [AND BRINGING THEM TO THE PRESENCE OF THE PRÆTORS], THEY SAID, "THESE MEN DO EXCEEDINGLY DISTURB OUR CITY, JEWS AS THEY ARE, (21) AND RECOMMEND CUSTOMS, WHICH IT IS ILLEGAL FOR US TO RECEIVE OR TO OBSERVE, AS WE ARE ROMANS ". (22) AND THE POPULACE ROSE IN A BODY AGAINST THEM ; AND THE PRÆTORS, RENDING THEIR GARMENTS *in horror*, BADE *the lictors* BEAT THEM, (23) AND WHEN THEY HAD LAID MANY STRIPES ON THEM, THEY CAST THEM INTO PRISON, CHARGING THE JAILOR TO KEEP THEM SAFELY : (24) AND HE HAVING RECEIVED SUCH A CHARGE, CAST THEM INTO THE INNER PRISON, AND MADE THEIR FEET FAST IN THE STOCKS.

It is hardly possible that *vv.* 19, 20 have the final form that the writer would have given them. The expression halts between the Greek form and the Latin, between the ordinary Greek term for the supreme board of magistrates in any city (ἄρχοντες), and the popular Latin designation (στρατηγοί, *prœtores*), as if the author had not quite made up his mind which he should employ. Either of the clauses bracketed is sufficient in itself ; and it is hardly possible that a writer, whose expression is so concise, should have intended to leave in his text two clauses which say exactly the same thing.

The title Prætors was not technically accurate, but was frequently employed as a courtesy title for the supreme magistrates of a Roman colony; and, as usual, Luke moves on the plane of educated conversation in such matters, and not on the plane of rigid technical accuracy. He writes as the scene was enacted.

It is impossible and unnecessary to determine whether the slave-girl's owners were actually Roman citizens. They speak here as representatives of the general population. The actual *coloni* planted here by Augustus when he founded the colony, were probably far outnumbered by the Greek population (*incolæ*) ; and it is clear that in the colonies of the Eastern provinces, any Italian *coloni* soon melted into the mass of the population, and lost most of their distinctive character, and probably forgot even their language. The exact legal relation of the native Greek population to the Roman *coloni* is uncertain ; but it is certain that the former occupied some kind of intermediate position between ordinary provincials and Romans or Latins (when the colony was a Latin colony like Antioch). These colonies were one of the means whereby Rome sought to introduce the Roman spirit and feeling into the provinces, to romanise them ; and the accusation lodged against Paul, with the whole scene that followed, are a proof, in this vivid photographic picture, that the population prided themselves on their Roman character and actually called themselves Romans, as they called their magistrates Prætors.

Paul on other occasions claimed his right of citizen

ship; why not here? It is evident that the Prætors made a great to-do over this case : they regarded it as a case of treason, or, as it was termed in Greek, "impiety" (ἀσέβεια), rent their clothes in loyal horror, with the fussy, consequential airs that Horace satirises in the would-be Prætor of a country town (*Sat.* I 5, 34) : the fabric of the Empire was shaken to its foundations by this disgraceful conduct of the accused persons ; but the Prætors of Philippi stood firm, and the populace rose as one man, like true Romans, to defend their country against her insidious enemies. In such a scene what chance was there that Paul's protest should be listened to ? Perhaps it was made and not listened to, since the whole proceedings were so disorderly and irregular.

The first person ceases at this point ; the author was not arrested, and therefore could not speak in the first person of what happened in the prison. He did not accompany Paul further ; but remained at Philippi as his headquarters, till Paul returned there, XX 6, when the first person is resumed. It is only natural to understand that he was left in Philippi, because of his obvious suitability for the work of evangelising that city ; and his success was so striking that his "praise in the preaching of the good news *was* through all the Churches," II *Cor.* VIII 18 (a passage which is understood by early tradition as referring to Luke). At the same time it is clear that he had not been a householder in Philippi previously, for he went with Paul to enjoy Lydia's hospitality.

4. THE PRISON AND THE EARTHQUAKE. (XVI 25) BUT ABOUT MIDNIGHT PAUL AND SILAS WERE

PRAYING AND SINGING HYMNS UNTO GOD, AND THE
PRISONERS WERE LISTENING TO THEM ; (26) AND
SUDDENLY THERE WAS A GREAT EARTHQUAKE, SO
THAT THE FOUNDATIONS OF THE PRISON-HOUSE WERE
SHAKEN ; AND IMMEDIATELY ALL THE DOORS WERE
OPENED ; AND EVERY ONE'S FETTERS WERE SHAKEN
OUT. (27) AND THE JAILOR, BEING ROUSED FROM
SLEEP, AND SEEING THE PRISON-DOORS OPEN, DREW
HIS SWORD, AND WAS ABOUT TO KILL HIMSELF, CON-
SIDERING THAT THE PRISONERS HAD ESCAPED. (28)
BUT PAUL CRIED OUT WITH A LOUD VOICE, " DO
THYSELF NO HARM, FOR WE ARE ALL HERE ". (29)
AND CALLING FOR LIGHTS, HE RAN HASTILY IN, AND
TREMBLING FOR FEAR THREW HIMSELF BEFORE PAUL
AND SILAS, (30) AND BROUGHT THEM OUT [WHEN HE
HAD MADE THE REST FAST], AND SAID, "SIRS ! WHAT
MUST I DO TO BE SAVED ? " (31) AND THEY SAID,
" BELIEVE ON THE LORD JESUS, AND THOU SHALT BE
SAVED, THOU AND THY HOUSE ". (32) AND THEY
SPAKE THE WORD OF THE LORD TO HIM, WITH ALL
THAT WERE IN HIS HOUSE. (33) AND HE TOOK THEM
AT THAT HOUR OF THE NIGHT AND WASHED THEM
OF THEIR STRIPES ; AND WAS BAPTISED, HE AND ALL
HIS IMMEDIATELY. (34) AND HE BROUGHT THEM UP
INTO HIS HOUSE, AND SET MEAT BEFORE THEM, AND
REJOICED GREATLY, WITH ALL HIS HOUSE, HAVING
CONCEIVED FAITH IN GOD.

There are several difficulties which occur to every one
on first reading this passage. (1) The opening of the
doors and the undoing of the bonds by the earthquake
seem incredible to one who thinks of doors like those
in our prisons and of handcuffed prisoners. But any one

that has seen a Turkish prison will not wonder that the doors were thrown open : each door was merely closed by a bar, and the earthquake, as it passed along the ground, forced the door posts apart from each other, so that the bar slipped from its hold, and the door swung open. The prisoners were fastened to the wall or in wooden stocks, *v.* 24 ; and the chains and stocks were detached from the wall, which was shaken so that spaces gaped between the stones. In the great earthquakes of 1880 at Smyrna, and 1881 at Scio, I had the opportunity of seeing and hearing of the strangely capricious action of an earthquake, which behaves sometimes like a playful, good-natured sprite, when it spares its full terrors.

(2) Why did not the prisoners run away when their fetters were loosed? The question is natural to those who are familiar with the northern races, and their self-centred tenacity of purpose and presence of mind. An earthquake strikes panic into the semi-oriental mob in the Ægean lands; and it seems to me quite natural that the prisoners made no dash for safety when the opportunity was afforded them. Moreover, they were still only partially free ; and they had only a moment for action. The jailor was also roused by the earthquake, and came to the outer door ; he was perhaps a soldier, or at least had something of Roman discipline, giving him presence of mind ; his call for lights brought the body of *diogmitai* or other class of police who helped to guard the prisoners ; and the opportunity was lost.

(3) It was midnight, and the jailor had to call for lights : how could Paul from the inner prison see that the jailor was going to kill himself? We must understand that the inner prison was a small cell, which had

no window and no opening, except into the outer and larger prison, and that the outer prison, also, had one larger door in the opposite wall ; then, if there were any faint starlight in the sky, still more if the moon were up, a person in the outer doorway would be distinguishable to one whose eyes were accustomed to the darkness, but the jailor would see only black darkness in the prison.

The jailor was responsible with his life for the safety of his prisoners ; and, concluding from the sight of the open door that they had managed to set themselves free, and open the door, and escape, he preferred death by his own hand, to exposure, disgrace, and a dishonourable death.

The Bezan Text preserves in *v.* 30 a little detail, which is so suggestive of the orderly well-disciplined character of the jailor, that we are prompted to accept it as genuine. The jailor first attended to his proper work, and secured all his prisoners ; and thereafter he attended to Paul and Silas, and brought them forth. It seems highly improbable that a Christian in later time would insert the gloss that the jailor looked after his prisoners before he cared for his salvation ; it is more in the spirit of a later age to be offended with the statement that the jailor did so, and to cut it out.

In his subsequent action to Paul and Silas, the jailor was not acting illegally. He was responsible for producing his prisoners when called for ; but it was left to himself to keep them as he thought best.

5. RELEASE AND DEPARTURE FROM PHILIPPI. (XVI 35) AND WHEN DAY WAS COME THE PRÆTORS SENT THE LICTORS, WITH THE MESSAGE *to the jailor :* "LET THOSE MEN GO *. (36) AND THE JAILOR

REPORTED THE MESSAGE TO PAUL THAT " THE PRÆTORS
HAVE SENT *orders* THAT YOU BE SET FREE. NOW,
THEREFORE, GO FORTH AND TAKE YOUR WAY IN
PEACE." (37) BUT PAUL SAID UNTO THEM : " THEY
FLOGGED US IN PUBLIC *without investigation*, ROMAN
CITIZENS AS WE ARE, AND CAST US INTO PRISON ;
AND NOW DO THEY TURN US OUT SECRETLY ? NOT
SO ; BUT LET THEM COME IN PERSON AND BRING US
OUT." (38) AND THE LICTORS REPORTED TO THE
PRÆTORS THESE WORDS ; AND THEY WERE TERRIFIED
ON HEARING THAT " THEY ARE ROMAN CITIZENS " ;
(39) AND THEY WENT AND BESOUGHT THEM, AND
BROUGHT THEM OUT, AND ASKED THEM TO GO AWAY
FROM THE CITY. (40) AND THEY WENT OUT FROM
THE PRISON AND ENTERED INTO LYDIA'S HOUSE ; AND
THEY SAW AND EXHORTED THE BRETHREN, AND WENT
AWAY.

The sudden change of attitude on the part of the
Prætors is remarkable. One day they sent the prisoners
for careful custody : the next morning they send to
release them. The Bezan Reviser felt the inconsequence,
and inserts an explanation : " And when day was come
the Prætors [*assembled together in the agora, and
remembering the earthquake that had taken place, they
were afraid, and*] sent the lictors ". But, though
this is modelled on Luke's language (cp. I 15, etc.),
it is hardly in his style of narrative. It is more
characteristic of him to give no explanation, but simply
to tell the facts. Perhaps the earthquake had roused
their superstitious fears on account of the irregular and
arbitrary proceedings of yesterday. Perhaps they felt
some misgivings about their action, if we are right in

thinking that Paul and Silas had appealed vainly to their rights as Romans.

Whatever be the reason, there can be no mistake as to Luke's intention to bring out the contrast (1) between the orders sent to the jailor in the morning, and the charge given to him at night; (2) between the humble apology of the Prætors in the morning, and their haughty action on the previous day; (3) between the real fact, that the Prætors had trampled on Roman order and right, and their fussy pretence of vindicating the majesty of Rome. And so the same Prætors who had ordered them to be beaten and imprisoned now begged them to go away from the city. In the Bezan Text the request of the Prætors is put at greater length, and with obvious truth: " the magistrates, being afraid lest there should be another conspiracy against Paul, and distrusting their own ability to keep order, said, ' Go forth from this city, lest they again make a riot and inveigh loudly against you to us ' ". The weakness of municipal government in the cities of the Ægean lands was always a danger to order ; and the Bezan Text hits off admirably the situation, and brings out with much skill the naïve desire of the magistrates to avoid an unpleasant case by inducing the innocent and weaker parties to submit to injustice and withdraw from the city. One would gladly think this Lukan.

In *v.* 37 the rendering (A.V. and R.V.) " uncondemned " does not fairly represent Paul's meaning, for it suggests that it would have been allowable for the Prætors to condemn Paul after fair trial to be flogged. But the Prætors could not in any circumstances order him to be flogged ; in fact, formal trial would only aggravate their crime, as making it more deliberate. The crime might be palliated by pleading that it was done in ignorance : and Paul would naturally cut away the plea by saying that they had made no attempt to investigate the facts. Yet the Greek is clear, and can only be translated "uncondemned". A parallel case occurs XXII 25, where Paul asks the centurion: " is it lawful for you to flog a man that is a Roman citizen, and him uncondemned ? " Here there is the same false implication that the act would be aggravated by being done without the proper formal condemnation.

Yet Paul, as a Roman citizen, must have known his rights ; and it seems clear that he could not have used the exact words which Luke reports. Now, when we consider the facts, we see that it must be so. No *civis Romanus* would claim his rights in Greek ; the very idea is ludicrous. Paul claimed them in the Roman tongue ; and we may fairly understand that the officials of a Roman colony were expected to understand Latin ; for the official language even of far less important colonies in Asia Minor was Latin. The phrase which Paul used was most probably *re incognita*, "without investigating our case ". Luke, however, had the true Greek inability to sympathise with the delicacies of Roman usage, and translates the Latin by a term, which would in some circumstances be a fair representative, but not here, nor in XXII 25.

The whole residence of Paul at Philippi seems to have been short : it is defined by Luke as being " for certain days," and apparently not much seems to have been accomplished before the incident of the ventriloquist and the resulting imprisonment. If the party was at Troas in October A.D. 50, they probably left Philippi before the end of the year. It seems probable from *v.* 40 that there were some other Christians besides those in Lydia's house. It is, however, remarkable that Luke makes no explicit reference to any other converts.

Doubtless, before Paul left, the question was discussed what should be his next centre ; and Thessalonica was suggested, probably on account of its Jewish settlers, whose synagogue offered a good opening for work. The directions which were given the travellers at starting were to make their way along the Roman road through Amphipolis and Apollonia to Thessalonica (XVII 1, where διοδεύσαντες is the verb, ὁδός denoting the Roman road).

6. THESSALONICA. (XVII 1) AND THEY WENT ALONG THE *Roman* ROAD THROUGH AMPHIPOLIS AND APOLLONIA, AND CAME TO THESSALONICA, WHERE WAS A SYNAGOGUE OF THE JEWS. (2) AND, AS WAS CUSTOMARY WITH PAUL, HE WENT IN TO ADDRESS THEM, AND FOR THREE SABBATHS HE REASONED WITH THEM FROM THE SCRIPTURES, (3) OPENING THEIR MEANING, AND QUOTING TO PROVE THAT IT WAS PROPER THAT THE ANOINTED ONE SHOULD SUFFER AND RISE AGAIN FROM THE DEAD, AND THAT " THE ANOINTED ONE IS THIS *man*, THE *very* JESUS WHOM I AM PROCLAIMING TO YOU ". (4) AND SOME OF THEM WERE PERSUADED ; AND THERE WERE IN ADDITION GATHERED TO PAUL AND SILAS MANY OF THE GOD-FEARING *proselytes*, AND A GREAT MULTITUDE OF THE GREEKS, AND OF THE LEADING WOMEN NOT A FEW.[1]

[1] In *v.* 4 καί τινες ἐξ αὐτῶν ἐπείσθησαν. καὶ προσεκληρώθησαν τῷ Παύλῳ καὶ Σιλᾷ πολλοὶ τῶν σεβομένων. καὶ Ἑλλήνων πλῆθος πολύ,

The curious and rare title "politarchs" was given to the supreme board of magistrates at Thessalonica, as is proved by inscriptions.

This passage is full of difficulty both in text and in interpretation. Our text, agreeing with many MSS. and Versions, recognises three classes of hearers besides the Jews ; whereas the Approved Text, resting on the great MSS., unites the "God-fearing" and "the Greeks" into the single class "God-fearing Greeks". In this case many reasons combine to show the error of the latter reading, and the falseness of the principle that has led Tischendorf, Westcott and Hort, and others to set almost boundless confidence in those MSS. (see note 2, p. 235).

In *v.* 4 Paul goes on to a wider sphere of influence than the circle of the synagogue ; and a lapse of time is implied in the extension of his work over the general population of the city (called here by the strictly correct term, Hellenes). Between the two opposite groups, the Jews and the Hellenes, there is interposed the intermediate class of God-fearing proselytes ; and there is added as a climax a group of noble ladies of the city. In Macedonia, as in Asia Minor, women occupied a much freer and more influential position than in Athens ; and it is in conformity with the known facts that such prominence is assigned to them in the three Macedonian cities.

In this journey a more pointed distinction than before between the short period of synagogue work, and the longer period of general work, may be noticed. The

γυναικῶν τε τῶν πρώτων οὐκ ὀλίγαι, approximating to the Bezan Text, and to that of the inferior MSS. followed in the Authorised Version.

three Sabbaths of *v.* 2 must be taken as the entire period of work within the circle of the synagogue; and the precise statement of time may also be taken as an indication that the usual quarrel with the Jews took place earlier at Thessalonica than in former cases.

That a considerable time was spent in the wider work is proved both by its success, and by the language of I *Thess.* I, II, which cannot reasonably refer only to work in the synagogue or to a short missionary work among the general population. Paul clearly refers to a long and very successful work in Thessalonica. His eagerness to return, and his chafing at the ingenious obstacle preventing him, are explained by his success: he was always eager to take advantage of a good opening. Further Paul mentions that the Philippians, IV 16, "sent once and again unto my need in Thessalonica". It is reasonable to think that some interval elapsed between the gifts (especially as Paul had to work to maintain himself, I *Thess.* II 9). Dec. 50—May 51 seems a probable estimate of the residence in Thessalonica.

7. THE RIOT AT THESSALONICA. (XVII 5) AND THE JEWS BECAME JEALOUS; AND WITH SOME WORTHLESS ASSOCIATES OF THE LOWER ORDERS THEY GATHERED A MOB AND MADE A RIOT; AND, ASSAULTING THE HOUSE OF JASON, THEY SOUGHT TO BRING *Paul and Silas* BEFORE A PUBLIC MEETING. (6) AND WHEN THEY FOUND THEM NOT, THEY BEGAN TO DRAG JASON AND CERTAIN BRETHREN BEFORE THE POLITARCHS, SHOUTING, "THESE THAT HAVE TURNED THE CIVILISED WORLD UPSIDE DOWN HAVE COME HITHER ALSO, (7) AND JASON HATH RECEIVED THEM; AND THE WHOLE OF THEM ARE VIOLATING THE IMPERIAL LAWS, ASSERTING THAT

THERE IS ANOTHER EMPEROR, JESUS ". (8) AND THEY
TROUBLED THE PEOPLE AND THE POLITARCHS, WHO
HEARD THIS. (9) AND THE POLITARCHS TOOK SECURI-
TIES FOR GOOD BEHAVIOUR FROM JASON AND THE
OTHERS, AND LET THEM GO.

The description of this riot is more detailed than any
of the preceding. The lower classes, the least educated,
and the most enslaved to paganism on its vulgarest and
most superstitious side, were the most fanatical opponents
of the new teaching ; while the politarchs were by no
means inclined to take active measures against it, and the
better educated people seem to have supplied most of
the converts. Men of all classes were impressed by the
preaching of Paul, but only women of the leading
families ; and the difference is obviously due to the fact
that the poorer women were most likely to be under the
sway of superstition. A similar distinction is mentioned
at Berœa (XVII 12), where not a few of the high-born
Greek ladies and of the male population in general were
attracted by the new teaching.

It would appear that this riot was more serious than
the words of Luke would at first sight suggest. The
language of Paul in his first letter to the Thessalonians,
II 14-16, shows that a powerful, dangerous, and lasting
sentiment was roused among the classes which made
the riot.

The charge brought against Paul was subtly conceived
and most dangerous. The very suggestion of treason
against the Emperors often proved fatal to the accused ;
and it compelled the politarchs to take steps, for, if they
failed to do so, they became exposed to a charge of
treason, as having taken too little care for the honour of

the Emperor. Many a man was ruined by such a charge under the earlier Emperors.

The step taken by the politarchs was the mildest that was prudent in the circumstances : they bound the accused over in security that peace should be kept. This was a penalty familiar in Roman law, from which it must have been adopted in the ordinary practice of provincial towns like Thessalonica.

Paul evidently felt very deeply his sudden and premature separation from the Church of Thessalonica : it was at once so promising and so inexperienced, that he was unusually eager to return to it ; and as he says, " we endeavoured the more exceedingly to see your face with great desire ; because we would fain have come to you, I Paul once and again ; and Satan hindered us ". What is the meaning of the strange expression, " Satan hindered us " ? How did Paul, who was so eager to go back to Thessalonica, find an insurmountable obstacle in his way ? Was it mere personal danger that prevented him, or was it some more subtle device of Satanic craft that kept him out of Thessalonica ?

It is not in keeping with Paul's language to interpret " Satan " in this case as the mob, which had brought him into danger and was still enraged against him. He alludes by a very different metaphor to the opposition which he often experienced from the vulgar, uneducated, and grossly superstitious city populace. In I *Cor.* XV 32 he describes his relations with the Ephesian mob as " fighting with beasts ". This term is an interesting mixture of Greek and Roman ideas, and corresponds well to Paul's mixed education, as a Roman citizen in a Greek philosopher's lecture-room. In the lecture-

room he became familiar with the Platonic comparison
of the mob to a dangerous beast ; and amid the surroundings of the Roman Empire he became familiar with the
death-struggle of criminals against the wild beasts of
the circus. But a person who designates the mob in
this contemptuous way, uses the term " Satan " only of
some more subtle and dangerous enemy, far harder to
overcome.

Now, security against any disturbance of the peace had
been exacted from Jason and his associates, the leading
Christians of Thessalonica ; and clearly this implied that
they were bound over to prevent the cause of disturbance,
Paul, from coming to Thessalonica. This ingenious device
put an impassable chasm between Paul and the Thessalonians (ἐνέκοψεν is the strong term used). So long
as the magistrates maintained this attitude, he could
not return : he was helpless, and Satan had power. His
only hope lay in an alteration of the magistrates' policy.
They would not be long in power ; and perhaps their
successors might act differently. But the politarchs
doubtless thought that they treated the case mildly and
yet effectually ; they got rid of the cause, without
inflicting any punishment on any person.

This interpretation of the term " Satan," as denoting
action taken by the governing power against the message
from God, is in keeping with the figurative use of the
word throughout the New Testament.

8. BERŒA. (XVII 10) AND THE BRETHREN IM-
MEDIATELY SENT AWAY PAUL AND SILAS BY NIGHT
UNTO BERŒA ; AND WHEN THEY WERE COME HITHER
THEY WENT INTO THE SYNAGOGUE OF THE JEWS.
(11) NOW THESE WERE MORE NOBLE THAN THOSE IN

THESSALONICA, IN THAT THEY RECEIVED THE WORD
WITH ALL READINESS OF MIND, EXAMINING THE SCRIP-
TURES DAILY WHETHER THESE THINGS WERE SO. (12)
MANY OF THEM THEREFORE BELIEVED ; AS DID ALSO
NOT A FEW OF THE HIGH-BORN GREEK LADIES AND
OF THE MALE POPULATION. (13) BUT WHEN THE
JEWS OF THESSALONICA LEARNED THAT IN BERŒA
ALSO THE WORD OF GOD WAS PREACHED BY PAUL,
THEY CAME THERE ALSO EXCITING AND DISTURBING
THE MULTITUDES. (14) THEN FORTHWITH PAUL WAS
SENT FORTH BY THE BRETHREN TO GO TOWARDS THE
SEA ; BUT SILAS AND TIMOTHY REMAINED THERE.
(15) AND THEY THAT CONDUCTED PAUL BROUGHT
HIM AS FAR AS ATHENS ; AND RECEIVING ΓIRECTIONS
FOR SILAS AND TIMOTHY THAT THEY SHOULD COME
TO HIM WITH ALL SPEED, THEY DEPARTED.

Here, just as at Thessalonica, a wider influence than
the circle of the synagogue is distinctly implied, *v.* 12,
so that we must understand that Paul preached also to
the Greek population. The nobler conduct of the
Berœan Jews consisted in their freedom from that
jealousy, which made the Jews in Thessalonica and
many other places enraged when the offer of salvation
was made as freely to others as to themselves.

The process that compelled Paul's departure from
Berœa was evidently quite similar to that at Thessalonica ;
and probably that is the reason why the riot and the
accusation of treason against the Emperor are not
mentioned more particularly (p. 72). As usual, we
notice how lightly Luke passes over the difficulties and
dangers which drove Paul from place to place.

In *v.* 15 we must understand that Silas and Timothy

obeyed the directions, and came on to rejoin Paul. There is no point in mentioning such an order, unless it were obeyed. It is in the style of Luke to mention an intention and leave the reader to gather that it was carried into effect (p. 181). Moreover, we learn from I *Thess.* III 1 that Timothy was sent by Paul away from Athens to Thessalonica, which implies that he rejoined him. It is undeniable that the statement in XVIII 5, " when Silas and Timothy came down from Macedonia," seems at first sight to imply that they arrived from Berœa only after Paul had left Athens, and followed him on to Corinth, and met him there for the first time since his departure from Berœa. But the calculation of time shows that that could hardly be the case : it would not take nearly so long to perform the journey, and we shall see that Silas and Timothy rejoined Paul in Corinth after a mission from Athens to Thessalonica and Philippi (p. 241). In that case the narrative is very awkward and badly constructed ; and we can hardly suppose that it has received the final touches from the author's hand. It is not unnatural that the Philippian author, writing about facts with which he and his nearest audience were specially familiar, and making his narrative as brief as possible, should have omitted to mention the mission from Athens to Macedonia. But it is probable that, if he had lived to put the finishing touch to his work, he would not have left this awkwardness.

Another possible indication of incompleteness is the omission of the harbour of Berœa, a unique omission in this history (p. 70).

The question naturally occurs, why did Paul go on

from Berœa alone, leaving Silas and Timothy behind, and yet send orders immediately on reaching Athens that they were to join him with all speed? There seems at first sight some inconsistency here. But again comparison between *Acts* and *Thess.* solves the difficulty. Paul was eager "once and again" to return to Thessalonica; and was waiting for news that the impediment placed in his way was removed. Silas and Timothy remained to receive the news (perhaps about the attitude of new magistrates); and to bring it on to Paul. But they could not bring it on to him until they received his message from Athens; Paul left Berœa with no fixed plan, "sent forth by the brethren to go to the coast," and the further journey to Athens was resolved on at the harbour.

We must allow several months for the residence at Berœa, with the preaching in the synagogue and the city, and the riot. Paul must have reached Athens some time in August 51, as is shown by the dates of his residence in Corinth (p. 264).

There is an interesting addition made to the Bezan Text of *v.* 15: "and they which conducted Paul brought him as far as Athens; [and he neglected Thessalia, for he was prevented from preaching the word unto them]". Here we meet a difficult question in provincial bounds. Where should Paul go from Berœa? The one thing clear to him was that he was called to Macedonia. If Thessaly was part of that province,[1] Larissa was the

---

[1] Ptolemy gives Thessaly to Macedonia, Strabo to Achaia (for we cannot accept Mommsen's interpretation of Strab. p. 840, making Thessaly always Macedonian; cp. Strab. p. 576): at some unknown time Thessaly was separated from Achaia (Brandis thinks by Pius, Marquardt by Vespasian, but perhaps 44 may have been the time).

natural completion of his Macedonian work; and we could readily believe that he thought of it and was prevented by a revelation. But, in that case, why is "the revelation" left out? Such an omission is unique in *Acts*. On the other hand, if Thessaly was part of Achaia, Paul could not think at that time of beginning work in a new province. In Athens he was merely waiting for the chance of returning to Thessalonica (p. 240). But, in that case, we might understand, "he was prevented (by the call restricting him to Macedonia)". Perhaps the Reviser, having eliminated παρῆλθεν from XVI 8, thought that XVII 15 was a suitable place for the idea, which he wished to preserve.

Note 1. The Place of Prayer at Philippi. We take our stand upon the fact that the Bezan Text, "where there seemed to be a prayer-place" (ἐδόκει προσευχὴ εἶναι), appears to be an explanation of our text (ἐνομίζετο προσευχὴ εἶναι): it is therefore clear that in the middle of the second century our text was read, and was found difficult, and was misunderstood to mean "there was *thought* to be a prayer-place". This misunderstanding led to other attempts at correction, one of which appears in the great MSS. (ἐνομίζομεν προσευχὴν εἶναι).

Note 2. The Synagogue at Thessalonica. The true reading of XVII 4 results from a comparison of A with D. The reading of the great MSS. is impossible for these reasons : (1) It restricts Paul's converts to Jews, proselyte Greeks, and a few ladies, taking no notice of any work outside the circle of the synagogue. I *Thess.* gives the impression that converts direct from heathenism were the mass of the Church. (2) It restricts Paul's work

to three Sabbaths, which is opposed to all rational probability, to *Thess.* and to *Phil.;* whereas our text restricts
the work within the circle of the synagogue to three
Sabbaths, but adds a second stage much more important,
when a great multitude of the general population of the
city was affected.   (3) The contrast drawn between the
Jews of Berœa and of Thessalonica, *v.* 11, is very unfair
to the latter, if, as the great MSS. put it, three Sabbaths
produced such vast effect within the circle of the synagogue.   (4) That reading speaks of "a great multitude
of God-fearing Greeks," implying that the synagogue had
exercised an astonishing · influence on the population.
Lightfoot quotes the fact that Salonica is still mainly a
Jewish city, as a proof that Judaism gained and kept a
strong hold on the city throughout Christian history ; but
a visit to Salonica would have saved him from this error.
The Jews of Salonica speak Spanish as their language,
and are descended from Spanish Jews, expelled by
Ferdinand and Isabella, who found in Turkey a refuge
denied or grudged them in most European countries.
There is no reason known to me for thinking that Judaism
was strong in the city under the Byzantine Empire ; and
the strong antipathy of the Greeks to the Jews makes it
improbable.   The Thessalonian Jews were protected by
the Roman government ; but one may doubt if they
maintained their ground under the Christian Empire.

CHAPTER XI

ATHENS AND CORINTH

I ATHENS. (XVII 16) NOW WHILE PAUL WAS WAIT-
ING FOR THEM IN ATHENS, HIS SOUL WAS PROVOKED
WITHIN HIM AS HE BEHELD THE CITY FULL OF IDOLS.
(17) SO HE REASONED IN THE SYNAGOGUE WITH THE
JEWS AND THE PROSELYTES, AND IN THE MARKET-
PLACE EVERY DAY WITH CHANCE COMERS. . . . (23)
"AS I WENT THROUGH THE CITY SURVEYING THE
MONUMENTS OF YOUR RELIGION, I FOUND ALSO AN
ALTAR WITH THIS INSCRIPTION 'TO UNKNOWN
GOD'."

The picture of Paul in Athens, which is given in the
ensuing scene, is very characteristic of Athenian life.
Luke places before us the man who became "all things
to all men," and who therefore in Athens made himself
like an Athenian and adopted the regular Socratic style
of general free discussion in the agora ; and he shows
him to us in an atmosphere and a light which are
thoroughly Attic in their clearness, delicacy, and charm.

It is evident from *v.* 23, and our conception of Paul's
character forces the same view on us, that he was not
indifferent even to the "sights" of the great university
city of the world, which united in itself so many memorials
of history and of education. The feelings which would

rise in the mind of an American scholar from Harvard, seeing Oxford for the first time, were not alien to Paul's spirit. The mere Jew could never have assumed the Attic tone as Paul did. He was in Athens the student of a great university, visiting an older but yet a kindred university, surveying it with appreciative admiration, and mixing in its society as an equal conversing with men of like education.

This extraordinary versatility in Paul's character, the unequalled freedom and ease with which he moved in every society, and addressed so many races within the Roman world, were evidently appreciated by the man who wrote this narrative, for the rest of Chapter XVII is as different in tone from XIII as Athens is different from Phrygia. Only a writer who was in perfect sympathy with his subject could adapt his tone to it so perfectly as Luke does. In Ephesus Paul taught "in the school of Tyrannus"; in the city of Socrates he discussed moral questions in the market-place. How incongruous it would seem if the methods were transposed! But the narrative never makes a false step amid all the many details, as the scene changes from city to city; and that is the conclusive proof that it is a picture of real life.

Athens in Paul's time was no longer the Athens of Socrates ; but the Socratic method had its roots in the soil of Attica and the nature of the Athenian people. In Athens Socrates can never quite die, and his spirit was in Paul's time still among the people, though the learned lecturers of the university felt already the coming spirit of Herodes Atticus more congenial to them. Among the people in the agora, then, Paul reasoned in the Socratic fashion ; but when the Professors came upon the scene, they soon demanded of him a display in the style of the rhetorician.

As Paul wandered through Athens, the interest in its monuments and its university was soon overpowered by the indignation roused by the idols with which it was crowded. In this centre of the world's education, amid the lecture-rooms where philosophers had taught for centuries that it was mere superstition to confuse the idol with the divine nature which it represented, the idols were probably in greater numbers than anywhere else in Paul's experience. Though he was only waiting for the message to go back to Thessalonica, and resume the work in Macedonia to which he had been called, yet indignation would not let him keep silence during the short stay which he anticipated in Athens. He began to discourse in the synagogue, and to hold Socratic dialogue in the agora with any one whom he met.

Here we observe the same double mission as in Berœa, Thessalonica, and elsewhere; and, as in other cases, the Jewish mission is mentioned first. There is one marked difference between this passage and the corresponding descriptions at Berœa and Thessalonica. In those cases great results were attained; but in Athens no converts are mentioned at this stage, either in the synagogue or in the agora. The lack of results at this stage is, however, fully explained by the shortness of the time. Paul's stay in Athens can hardly have been longer than six weeks, and was probably less than four; and the process described in *v.* 17 was brought to a premature close by the great event of his visit, which the historian describes very fully.

The time spent in Athens may be deduced approximately from the following considerations. Probably less than a fortnight elapsed before Silas and Timothy joined him there, according to his urgent directions. They brought with them no favourable news: it was still impossible for him to return to Thessalonica, and he "thought it good to be left in Athens alone, and sent Timothy to comfort the Thessalonians concerning their faith" (I *Thess.* III 1, 2).

Since Paul remained alone, Silas also must have been sent away from Athens; and as, some two months later, Silas with Timothy rejoined Paul from Macedonia, he was probably sent to Philippi, for frequent communication was maintained at this time between Paul and his first European Church (*Phil.* IV 15 f.).

Paul was still looking forward to a return to his proper work in Macedonia; and it is clear that he intended to remain in Athens until Silas and Timothy came back from their mission, which makes it probable that their absence was not intended to be a long one. Doubtless they travelled to Thessalonica together, and Timothy waited there while Silas went to Philippi, discharged his mission, and returned; and then they came to Athens together. They found Paul no longer there, for he had in the meantime gone to Corinth. Circumstances that happened in Athens had forced him to abandon the city and go to Corinth: "after this he departed from Athens and came to Corinth" (XVIII 1). In this sentence it might seem that the words "departed from Athens" are wasted; and that it would have been sufficient to say "after this he came to Corinth"; but our principle is that every minute fact stated in *Acts* has its own significance, and the departure from Athens (χωρισθεὶς ἐκ τῶν 'Aθηνῶν) is emphasised, because it was a violation of the intended plan under the compulsion of events.

The same word is used in XVIII 1 to describe Paul's departure from Athens, and in 2 to describe Aquila's enforced departure from Rome. On our view (p. 252) the idea of sudden, premature departure is contained in each.

Further, it is clear that Paul had been in Corinth for some time and attained a certain measure of success, before Silas and Timothy arrived ; and, if we allow seven weeks for their mission, which seems ample, he must have spent altogether about three or four weeks in Athens and five or six in Corinth.

2. IN THE UNIVERSITY AT ATHENS. (XVII 18) AND CERTAIN ALSO OF THE STOIC AND EPICUREAN PHILOSOPHERS ENGAGED IN DISCUSSIONS WITH HIM ; AND SOME SAID, "WHAT WOULD THIS SPERMOLÓGOS [*ignorant plagiarist*] SAY ? " AND OTHERS, " HE IS APPARENTLY AN EXPONENT OF FOREIGN DIVINITIES " [BECAUSE HE WAS GIVING THE GOOD NEWS OF " JESUS " AND " RESURRECTION "]. (19) AND THEY TOOK HOLD OF HIM AND BROUGHT HIM BEFORE THE *Council of* AREOPAGUS, SAYING, " MAY WE LEARN WHAT IS THIS NEW TEACHING WHICH IS SPOKEN BY THEE ? (20) FOR THOU BRINGEST SOME THINGS OF FOREIGN FASHION TO OUR EARS ; WE WISH THERE-FORE TO LEARN WHAT IS THEIR NATURE." (21) BUT THE WHOLE *crowd of* ATHENIANS AND RESIDENT STRANGERS *who formed the audience* WERE INTER-ESTED ONLY IN SAYING OR HEARING SOMETHING NEW *and smart.* (22) AND PAUL STOOD IN THE MIDST OF THE *Council of* AREOPAGUS AND SAID . . .

(33) THUS PAUL WENT FORTH FROM THE MIDST OF
THEM.

The explanatory clause in *v.* 18 is wanting in the Bezan
Text and an old Latin Version, and is foreign to Luke's
fashion of leaving the reader to form his own ideas with
regard to the scene. It is apparently a gloss, suggested
by *v.* 32, which found its way into the text of almost all
MSS.

The different opinions of the philosophers in *v.* 18
are purposely placed side by side with a touch of gentle
sarcasm on their inability, with all their acuteness, to agree
in any opinion even about Paul's meaning. The first
opinion is the most interesting. It contains a word of
characteristically Athenian slang, *Spermológos*, and is
clearly caught from the very lips of the Athenians (as
Dr. Blass happily puts it). This term was used in two
senses—(1) a small bird that picks up seeds for its food,
and (2) a worthless fellow of low class and vulgar habits,
with the insinuation that he lives at the expense of others,
like those disreputable persons who hang round the
markets and the quays in order to pick up anything
that falls from the loads that are carried about. Hence,
as a term in social slang, it connotes absolute vulgarity
and inability to rise above the most contemptible
standard of life and conduct ; it is often connected with
slave life, for the *Spermológos* was near the type of the
slave and below the level of the free man ; and there
clings to it the suggestion of picking up refuse and scraps,
and in literature of plagiarism without the capacity to use
correctly. In ancient literature plagiarism was not
disapproved when it was done with skill, and when the
idea or words taken from another were used with success :

the literary offence lay in the ignorance and incapacity displayed when stolen knowledge was improperly applied.

To appreciate fully a term of social slang requires the greatest effort to sympathise with and recreate the actual life of the people who used the term. Probably the nearest and most instructive parallel in modern English life to *Spermológos* is " Bounder," allowing for the difference between England and Athens. In both there lies the idea of one who is "out of the swim," out of the inner circle, one who lacks that thorough knowledge and practice in the rules of the game that mould the whole character and make it one's nature to act in the proper way and play the game fair. The English term might be applied to a candidate for a professorship, whose life and circumstances had lain in a different line and who wanted knowledge and familiarity with the subject ; and that is the way in which St. Paul is here called a *Spermológos*, as one who aped the ways and words of philosophers. Dean Farrar's rendering, " picker-up of learning's crumbs," is happy, but loses the touch of slang.

The general tendency of recent opinion is that Paul was taken to the Hill of Ares, in order to give an address in quiet surroundings to a crowd of Athenians on the spot where the Council that derived its name from the hill sat to hold solemn trials for murder ; and the view taken in the Authorised Version and the ancient authorities, such as Chrysostom and Theophylact, that Paul was subjected to a trial before the Council, is rejected on the ground that in the proceedings there is nothing of a judicial type, no accuser, no accusation, and no defensive character in Paul's speech, which is addressed not to a court but to a general Athenian audience. These reasons quite disprove the view that the scene described in *vv.* 19-34 was a trial. But the idea that the assembly of Athenians went up to the hill-top as a suitable place for listening to an address is even more unsatisfactory. The top of the little hill is a most unsuitable place from its small size and its exposed position ; and it is quite out of keeping with the habits of the people to go to such a place for such a purpose. Curtius has led the way to a proper view of the whole incident, which lies wholly in the agora.

Further, it is inconsistent with the patriotism and pride of the Athenians that they should conduct a foreigner for whom they expressed such contempt to the most impressive seat of Athenian religious and national history, in order that he might there talk to them. The Athenians were, in many respects, flippant ; but their flippancy was combined with an intense pride in the national dignity and the historic glory of the city, which would have revolted at such an insult as that this stranger should harangue them about his foreign deities on the spot where the Athenian elders had judged the god Ares and the hero Orestes, where the goddess Athena had presided in the highest court of her chosen people, and where still judgment on the most grave cases of homicide was solemnly pronounced.

Nor would it be a permissible interpretation that a small number of philosophic inquirers retired to this quiet spot for unimpeded discussion. The scene and the speech breathe the spirit of the agora, and the open, free, crowded life of Athens, not the quiet atmosphere of the philosophic study or class-room ; while the tone of the opinions expressed in *v.* 18 is not one of philosophic interest and careful discussion, but of contempt, dislike. and jealousy. Moreover, it would be an insult to address philosophic inquirers in the language of *vv.* 22-3. The philosophers did not dedicate altars to an Unknown God, but regarded all such proceedings as the mere superstition of the vulgar. Paul's speech is an exceedingly skilful one, if addressed to a popular audience ; but to philosophers it would be unskilful and unsuitable.

But the language shows clearly that Paul was brought *before the Council* and not simply conducted *to the Hill.* He stood "in the midst of the Areopagus," *v.* 22, and "he went forth from the midst of them ": he that went forth from the midst of them must have been standing in the midst of them. In this scene, full of the Attic spirit and containing typical words of Athenian slang like *Spermológos,* we require some distinctly Greek sense for each detail ; and "Paul stood in the middle of the Hill" is in Greek an absurdity. He stood in the middle of the Council, a great and noble, but not a friendly assembly, as in IV 7 Peter stood "in the midst" of the Sanhedrim ; and in *Acts* and the Gospels many similar expressions occur. (See note, p. 260.)

The philosophers took hold of Paul. When a man, especially an educated man, goes so far as to lay his hands on another, it is obvious that his feelings must be moved ; and the word must have some marked sense in a writer whose expression is so carefully studied as Luke's. It occurs as a sign of friendly encouragement to a person in a solitary and difficult position, IX 27, XXIII 19 ; but more frequently it denotes hostile action, as XXI 30, XVIII 17, XVI 19. There must have been some stronger feeling among the philosophers than mere contempt mingled with some slight curiosity, before they actually placed their hands on Paul. Now they certainly did not act as his friends and sponsors in taking him before the Council, therefore we must understand that they took him there from dislike and with malice.

What then was their object? Every attempt to explain the scene as a trial has failed, and must fail (p. 243). Even the idea of a preliminary inquiry is unsuitable; for, if it were so, none of the marked features of the scene are preserved in the narrative, which would be contrary to our experience in Luke's descriptions. In estimating the situation, we must remember that in *vv*. 18, 19, Paul is among the lecturers and professors of the university. Therein lies the chief interest of the scene, which is unique in *Acts*. We have seen Paul in various situations, and mixing in many phases of contemporary life. Here alone he stands amid the surroundings of a great university, disputing with its brilliant and learned teachers; and here, as in every other situation, he adapts himself with his usual versatility to the surroundings, and moves in them as to the manner born.

Two questions have to be answered in regard to the scene that follows: why was Paul taken before the Council? and what were the intentions of the philosophers in taking him there? It is clear that Paul appeared to the philosophers as one of the many ambitious teachers who came to Athens hoping to find fame and fortune at the great centre of education. Now, certain powers were vested in the Council of Areopagus to appoint or invite lecturers at Athens, and to exercise some general control over the lecturers in the interests of public order and morality. There is an almost complete lack of evidence what were the advantages and the legal rights of a lecturer thus appointed, and to what extent or in what way a strange teacher could find freedom to lecture in Athens. There existed something in the way of privileges vested in the recognised lecturers ; for the fact that Cicero induced the Areopagus to pass a decree inviting Cratippus, the Peripatetic philosopher, to become a lecturer in Athens, implies that some advantage was thereby secured to him. There certainly also existed much freedom for foreigners to become lecturers in Athens, for the great majority of the Athenian professors and lecturers were foreign. The scene described in *vv.* 18-34 seems to prove that the recognised lecturers could take a strange lecturer before the Areopagus, and require him to give an account of his teaching and pass a test as to its character.

When they took him to the court to satisfy the supreme university tribunal of his qualifications, they probably entertained some hope that he would be overawed before that august body, or that his teaching might not pass muster, as being of unsettling tendency (for no body is so conservative as a University Court).

The government in Greek cities exercised a good deal of control over the entire system of education, both for boys and for young men, who were trained in graduated classes and passed on from one to another in regular course. There is good reason for thinking that in Athens this control was exercised by the Council of Areopagus, in the case both of boys and of young men : it rises naturally out of their ancient charge of the manners and morals of the citizens, of the public hygiene and the state physicians, and of offences against religious ritual (though serious charges of impiety and of introducing foreign religion were not tried before the Areopagus but before the popular courts) ; and it is, in ancient view, related to the control of peace and order which they exercised in the Roman period.   Moreover, Quintilian mentions that the Areopagus punished a boy who used to pluck out the eyes of quails, which implies their jurisdiction over the young.

In the rhetorical displays of that period, the general audience (*corona*) was an important feature. The influence of the audience is familiar to every reader of the literature of that time ; and the younger Pliny says that even the lawyers of his time spoke more to gain the approval and applause of the audience than to influence the opinion and judgment of the court. Owing to the difficulty in multiplying copies of literary productions, public opinion could not be so well appealed to or expressed in any other way ; and the applause or disapproval of the circle of hearers came to represent to a great extent the public verdict on all intellectual achievements. Luke, therefore, could not well omit the audience, even in this brief account; and he touches it off in *v.* 21, where the force of the imperfect tense is important : Luke is not describing the general character of the Athenian people (which would require a present tense): he places another element in the scene alongside of those already described. While the philosophers insisted with some malevolent intention on having a test applied, the general crowd of Athenians and resident strangers were merely moved by curiosity.

The unmistakable tone of contempt in the description suits a Macedonian describing an Athenian crowd (for the two peoples always disliked and despised each other) ; and it is not undeserved. As Mr. Capes says in his *University Life in Ancient Athens :* " the people

commonly was nothing loath to hear : they streamed as
to a popular preacher in our own day, or to an actor
starring in provincial towns : the epicures accepted the
invitation to the feast of words, and hurried to the theatre
to judge as critics the choice of images, and refinement of
the style, and all the harmony of balanced periods ".   As
Luke says, they were as eager to make smart criticisms as
to listen.

3. THE SPEECH BEFORE THE COUNCIL OF
AREOPAGUS. (XVII 22) AND PAUL STOOD IN THE
MIDST OF THE COUNCIL AND SAID, "YE MEN OF
ATHENS, IN ALL RESPECTS I OBSERVE THAT YOU ARE
MORE *than others* RESPECTFUL OF WHAT IS DIVINE.
(23) FOR AS I WAS GOING THROUGH *your city* AND
SURVEYING THE MONUMENTS OF YOUR WORSHIP, I
FOUND ALSO AN ALTAR WITH THE INSCRIPTION TO
UNKNOWN GOD.   THAT *divine nature*, THEN,
WHICH YOU WORSHIP, NOT KNOWING *what it is*, I
AM SETTING FORTH TO YOU. (24) THE GOD THAT
MADE THE WORLD AND ALL THINGS THEREIN, HE,
LORD AS HE IS OF HEAVEN AND EARTH, DWELLETH
NOT IN SHRINES MADE WITH HANDS, (25) AND IS NOT
SERVED BY HUMAN HANDS AS THOUGH HE NEEDED
ANYTHING, SINCE HE HIMSELF GIVETH TO ALL LIFE
AND BREATH AND ALL THINGS. (26) AND HE MADE
OF ONE *nature* EVERY RACE OF MEN TO DWELL ON
ALL THE FACE OF THE EARTH ; AND FIXED DEFINED
TIMES AND BOUNDS OF THEIR HABITATION, (27) THAT
THEY SHOULD SEEK THE GOD, IF HAPLY THEY MIGHT
FEEL AFTER HIM AND FIND HIM, BEING AS INDEED
HE IS NOT FAR FROM EACH ONE OF US. (28) FOR IN
HIM WE LIVE AND MOVE AND ARE, AS CERTAIN ALSO

OF YOUR POETS HAVE SAID, FOR WE ARE ALSO HIS OFFSPRING. (29) BEING THEN THE OFFSPRING OF GOD, WE OUGHT NOT TO THINK THAT THE DIVINE NATURE IS LIKE UNTO GOLD OR SILVER OR STONE, GRAVEN BY ART AND DEVICE OF MAN. (30) NOW THE TIMES OF IGNORANCE GOD OVERLOOKED, BUT AT PRESENT HE CHARGETH ALL MEN EVERY-WHERE TO REPENT, (31) INASMUCH AS HE HATH SET A DAY ON WHICH, IN *the person of* THE MAN WHOM HE HATH ORDAINED, HE WILL JUDGE THE WORLD IN RIGHTEOUSNESS ; AND HE HATH GIVEN ALL A GUAR-ANTEE BY RAISING HIM FROM THE DEATH." (32) AND WHEN THEY HEARD OF " RAISING FROM THE DEAD," SOME MOCKED, AND OTHERS SAID, " WE WILL HEAR THEE CONCERNING THIS YET AGAIN ". (33) THUS PAUL WENT OUT FROM THE MIDST OF THEM. (34) BUT CERTAIN MEN CLAVE UNTO HIM AND BELIEVED ; AMONG WHOM ALSO WAS DIONYSIUS, A MEMBER OF THE COUNCIL, AND A WOMAN NAMED DAMARIS, AND OTHERS WITH THEM. (XVIII 1) AND THEREAFTER HE LEFT ATHENS, AND WENT TO CORINTH.

The influence of Paul's Athenian surroundings may be traced in the " philosophy of history " which he sketches briefly in his address. In the Socratic position the virtue of " knowing " was too exclusively dwelt on, and in some of the earlier Platonic dialogues the view is maintained that virtue is knowledge and vice ignorance ; and Greek philosophy was never clear about the relation of will and permanent character to " knowing ". The Greek philo-sophers could hardly admit, and could never properly understand, that a man may know without carrying his knowledge into action, that he may refuse to know when knowledge is within his grasp, and that the refusal exercises a permanent deteriorating influence on his character. Now Paul, in his estimate of the relation of the pre-Christian world to God, adopts a different position in the Athenian speech from that on which he afterwards took his stand in his letter to the Romans, I 19-32. In the latter place he recognises (to quote Lightfoot's brief analysis) that the pagan world " might have seen God through His works. They refused to see Him. They disputed, and they blinded their hearts. . . . Therefore they were delivered over to impurity. . . . They not only did those things ; but they took delight in those who did them." Here we have a full recognition of that fundamental fact in human nature and life, which Æschylus expressed in his greatest drama[1] as a conception of his own differing from the common Greek view : " the impious act breeds more, like to its own kind : it is the nature of crime to beget new crime, and along with it the depraved audacious will that settles, like an irresistible spirit of ill, on the house ". But to the Athenians Paul says, " the times of ignorance, therefore, God overlooked " ; and those times are alluded to as a period, when men were doing their best to find and to worship " God Unknown ". We must not, of course, demand that the entire theology of Paul should be compressed into this single address ; but yet there is a notable omission of an element that was unfamiliar and probably repugnant to his audience, and an

---

[1] *Agamemnon* 730 f., a passage where the text is very uncertain and is terribly maltreated by many editors : Paley turns it into an elaborate genealogical tree, while Wecklein conjectures away the depravation of the will, which is the key to the philosophic position of Æschylus.

equally notable insistence on an element that was familiar
to them.   The Stoic ring in 23 f. is marked (pp. 147, 150).

One woman was converted at Athens ; and it is not said
that she was of good birth, as was stated at Berœa and
Thessalonica and Pisidian Antioch.   The difference is true
to life.   It was impossible in Athenian society for a woman
of respectable position and family to have any opportunity of hearing Paul ; and the name Damaris (probably
a vulgarism for *damalis*, heifer) suggests a foreign woman,
perhaps one of the class of educated *Hetairai*, who might
very well be in his audience.

It would appear that Paul was disappointed and perhaps
disillusioned by his experience in Athens.   He felt that
he had gone at least as far as was right in the way of
presenting his doctrine in a form suited to the current
philosophy ;   and the result had been little more than
naught.   When he went on from Athens to Corinth, he
no longer spoke in the philosophic style.   In replying
afterwards to the unfavourable comparison between his
preaching and the more philosophical style of Apollos, he
told the Corinthians that, when he came among them, he
" determined not to know anything save Jesus Christ, and
Him crucified " (I *Cor.* II 2) ;   and nowhere throughout
his writings is he so hard on the wise, the philosophers,
and the dialecticians, as when he defends the way in
which he had presented Christianity at Corinth.   Apparently the greater concentration of purpose and
simplicity of method in his preaching at Corinth is referred
to by Luke, when he says, XVIII 5, that when Silas and
Timothy rejoined him there, they found him wholly
possessed by and engrossed in the word.   This strong
expression, so unlike anything else in *Acts*, must, on our

hypothesis, be taken to indicate some specially marked character in the Corinthian preaching.

4. CORINTH. (XVIII I) AFTER THESE EVENTS HE LEFT ATHENS AND WENT TO CORINTH. (2) AND, FINDING A CERTAIN JEW NAMED AQUILA, A MAN OF PONTUS BY BIRTH, WHO HAD LATELY COME FROM ITALY, AND PRISCILLA HIS WIFE, BECAUSE CLAUDIUS HAD COMMANDED ALL THE JEWS TO LEAVE ROME, HE ACCOSTED THEM. (3) AND BECAUSE HE WAS OF THE SAME CRAFT, HE ABODE WITH THEM, AND WROUGHT AT HIS TRADE [FOR THEY WERE TENTMAKERS BY THEIR CRAFT]. (4) AND HE USED TO DISCOURSE IN THE SYNAGOGUE EVERY SABBATH, AND TRIED TO PERSUADE JEWS AND GREEKS. (5) AND WHEN SILAS AND TIMOTHY ARRIVED FROM MACEDONIA, HE WAS WHOLLY ABSORBED IN PREACHING, ATTESTING TO THE JEWS THAT THE ANOINTED ONE IS JESUS.

Almost all MSS. add to *v.* 3 the explanation which we have given in parentheses ; but it comes in very awkwardly, for Luke, who said at the beginning of the verse, " because he was of the same craft," did not intend to say at the end, " for they were tentmakers by craft ". The Bezan Text and an old Latin Version (*Gig.*) omit this detail ; and they must here represent the original state of the text. In order to make the explanation a little less awkward, the two great MSS. read, " he abode with them and they wrought ". The explanation is a gloss, which crept from the margin into the text. It is doubtless very early, and perfectly trustworthy : its vitality lies in its truth, for that was not the kind of detail that was invented in the growth of the Pauline legend.

Aquila, a man of Pontus, settled in Rome bears a

Latin name; and must therefore have belonged to the
province and not to non-Roman Pontus. This is a good
example of Luke's principle to use the Roman provincial
divisions for purposes of classification (pp. 91, 196).

There is here a reference to Imperial history. Aquila
and Priscilla had come recently from Rome, on account of
an edict of Claudius expelling the Jews from Rome.
Suetonius says that the expulsion was caused by a series of
disturbances " due to the action of Chrestus "; and in all
probability this Chrestus must be interpreted as " the
leader of the Chrestians " (p. 47 f.), taken by a popular
error as actually living. In the earliest stages of
Christian history in Rome, such a mistake was quite
natural; and Suetonius reproduces the words which he
found in a document of the period. As Dion Cassius
mentions, it was found so difficult to keep the Jews out
of Rome on account of their numbers, that the Emperor
did not actually expel them, but made stricter regulations
about their conduct. It would therefore appear that the
edict was found unworkable in practice; but Suetonius is
a perfect authority that it was tried, and it is quite
probable that some Jews obeyed it, and among them
Aquila. Neither Suetonius nor Dion gives any clue to
the date; but Orosius says that it occurred in Claudius's
ninth year, 49. I believe that this date is a year wrong,
like that of the famine (p. 68), and for the same reason :
the edict must be placed in the end of 50, and thus Aquila
arrived in Corinth six or seven months before Paul came
in Sept. 51.

The careful record of Aquila's antecedents must, on our
hypothesis, be taken as not a mere picturesque detail;
Luke mentioned his Roman residence, because it had

some bearing on his subject. After some time (during most of which Paul had been in Aquila's company at Corinth and at Ephesus), a journey to Rome is announced as Paul's next intention, XIX 21. Aquila was able to tell him of the events that had occurred in Rome " at the action of Chrestus "; and his experience showed him how important it was to go direct to the great centres of Roman life. The connection of Luke with the Macedonian journey (p. 203) is an interesting parallel.

Paul mentions in writing to the Romans, XV 24, that he intended to go on from Rome to Spain. Such an intention implies in the plainest way an idea already existent in Paul's mind of Christianity as the religion of the Roman Empire. Spain was by far the most thoroughly romanised district of the Empire, as was marked soon after by the act of Vespasian in 75, when he made the Latin status universal in Spain. From the centre of the Roman world Paul would go on to the chief seat of Roman civilisation in the West, and would thus complete a first survey, the intervals of which should be filled up by assistants, such as Timothy, Titus, etc.

5. THE SYNAGOGUE AND THE GENTILES IN CORINTH. (XVIII 6) AND WHEN THEY BEGAN TO FORM A FACTION AGAINST HIM AND BLASPHEME, HE SHOOK OUT HIS GARMENTS AND SAID UNTO THEM, " YOUR BLOOD ON YOUR OWN HEAD! I ON MY SIDE AM CLEAN! FROM HENCEFORTH I WILL GO UNTO THE GENTILES," *i.e., in this city.* (7) AND HE CHANGED HIS PLACE *from the synagogue,* AND WENT INTO THE HOUSE OF A CERTAIN MAN NAMED TITIUS JUSTUS, A GOD-FEARING *proselyte,* WHOSE HOUSE JOINED HARD TO THE SYNAGOGUE. (8) BUT CRISPUS, THE ARCHISYNA-

GOGOS, BELIEVED IN THE LORD WITH ALL HIS HOUSE;
AND MANY OF THE PEOPLE OF CORINTH USED TO
HEAR AND BELIEVE AND RECEIVE BAPTISM. (9) AND
THE LORD SAID IN THE NIGHT BY A VISION UNTO
PAUL, "BE NOT AFRAID, BUT SPEAK ON, AND HOLD
NOT THY PEACE; (10) BECAUSE I AM WITH THEE,
AND NO MAN SHALL SET ON THEE TO HARM THEE;
BECAUSE I HAVE MUCH PEOPLE IN THIS CITY". (11)
AND HE SETTLED A YEAR AND SIX MONTHS, TEACH-
ING AMONG THEM THE WORD OF GOD.

The distinction between the period of work in the
synagogue, and that of direct preaching to the populace,
is expressed with marked emphasis at Corinth. Corinth
stood on the highroad between Rome and the East; and
was therefore one of the greatest centres of influence in
the Roman world. Macedonia was in this respect quite
secondary, though one of the routes to the East passed
across it; and hence Paul was ordered to sit down for
a prolonged stay when he reached Corinth. It is
characteristic of Luke to define the entire stay before
relating some incidents that occurred in it (pp. 153, 289).

It must be acknowledged that Paul had not a very
conciliatory way with the Jews when he became angry.
The shaking out of his garments was undoubtedly a very
exasperating gesture; and the occupying of a meeting-
house next door to the synagogue, with the former
archisynagogos as a prominent officer, was more than
human nature could stand. Probably he found unusual
opposition here, pp. 143, 287; but it is not strange that the
next stage of proceedings was in a law-court.

Titius Justus was evidently a Roman or a Latin, one
of the *coloni* of the colony Corinth. Like the centurion

Cornelius, he had been attracted to the synagogue. His citizenship would afford Paul an opening to the more educated class of the Corinthian population.

It seems to be implied by *vv.* 8, 17, that there was only one *archisynagogos* in the Corinthian synagogue; and, when Crispus became a Christian, a successor was appointed. At Pisidian Antioch there were several *archisynagogoi*. M. S. Reinach has shown from a Smyrnaean inscription that the title in Asia Minor did not indicate an office, but was a mere expression of dignity, "a leading person in the synagogue"; and the Bezan Text of XIV 2 distinguishes clearly between the *archons* of the synagogue (officials, probably two in number), and the *archisynagogoi*.

6. THE IMPERIAL POLICY IN ITS RELATION TO PAUL AND TO CHRISTIAN PREACHING. (XVIII 12) BUT WHILE GALLIO WAS PROCONSUL OF ACHAIA, THE JEWS WITH ONE ACCORD ROSE UP AGAINST PAUL, AND BROUGHT HIM BEFORE THE TRIBUNAL, SAYING, (13) "THIS MAN PERSUADETH PEOPLE TO WORSHIP GOD CONTRARY TO THE LAW". (14) BUT WHEN PAUL WAS ABOUT TO OPEN HIS MOUTH, GALLIO SAID UNTO THE JEWS, "IF A MISDEMEANOUR OR A CRIME WERE IN QUESTION, YE JEWS, REASON WOULD THAT I SHOULD BEAR WITH YOU; (15) BUT IF THEY ARE QUESTIONS OF WORD, *not deed*, AND OF NAMES, *not things*, AND OF YOUR LAW, *not Roman law*, YE YOUR-SELVES WILL LOOK TO IT: TO BE A JUDGE OF THESE MATTERS I *for my part* HAVE NO MIND". (16) AND HE DROVE THEM FROM THE TRIBUNAL. (17) AND ALL THE GREEKS SEIZED SOSTHENES, THE ARCHISYNAGOGOS, AND PROCEEDED TO BEAT HIM BEFORE THE TRIBUNAL; AND GALLIO TOOK NO NOTICE OF THIS CONDUCT.

Achaia was governed by a proconsul from B.C. 27 to A.D. 15, and from A.D. 44 onwards. It was a province of the second rank, and was administered by Roman officials, after holding the prætorship, and generally before the consulship. Corinth had now become the chief city of Achaia, and the residence of its governors (as Marquardt infers from this passage).

Here we have another point of contact with Roman history. Gallio was a brother of the famous Seneca, and shared his fortunes. Seneca was in disgrace from 41 to 49 ; but in 49 he was recalled from banishment and appointed prætor for A.D. 50. Pliny mentions that Gallio attained the consulship, which was probably after his proconsulship in Achaia. In his career of office Gallio must have been prætor not less than five years before he went to Achaia ; but no evidence survives to show in what year he held the prætorship (except that it cannot have been between 41 and 49) : as the elder brother, he probably held it before Seneca. There is no other evidence that Gallio governed Achaia ; but the statement of Luke is corroborated by the fact, which Seneca mentions, that Gallio caught fever in Achaia, and took a voyage for change of air.

Either the Jews at Corinth did not manage their accusation so well as those of Thessalonica, or Gallio elicited the true character of their complaints against Paul as being really matters of mere Jewish concern. It is clear that Gallio's short speech represents the conclusion of a series of inquiries, for the accusation, as it is quoted, does not refer to words or names, but only to the Law. But it is reasonable to suppose that the Jews put their accusation at first in a serious light, with a view to some serious penalty being inflicted; and Gallio, on probing their allegations, reduced the matter to its true dimensions as a question that concerned only the self-administering community of " the Nation of the Jews in Corinth ". It would have been interesting to know more about this case, for it seems to show that Gallio shared the broad and generous views of his brother about the policy of Rome in regard to the various religions of the provinces. The Greeks, who always hated the Jews, took advantage of the marked snub which the governor had inflicted on them, to seize and beat Sosthenes, who had been appointed to replace Crispus as *Archisynagogos*, and who doubtless was taking a prominent part in the proceedings. Gallio took no notice of this piece of " Lynch law," which probably seemed to him to be a rough sort of justice.

The fact that Sosthenes (whether the same or another) joined with Paul in writing to the Corinthians, I 1, caused an early misapprehension of the scene. It was understood that Gallio, after deciding against the Jews, allowed them to console themselves by beating a Christian; and the word " Greeks " is omitted in the great MSS. under the influence of this mistake. But such action is inconceivable in the Roman governor ; and the text of the inferior MSS. which substitutes a lifelike and characteristic scene for one that is utterly foolish, must undoubtedly be preferred. Probably two persons at Corinth named Sosthenes were brought into relations with Paul, one a Jew, the other a prominent Christian ; or perhaps the Jew was converted at a later date.

This action of the Imperial government in protecting him from the Jews, and (if we are right) declaring freedom in religious matters, seems to have been the crowning fact in determining Paul's line of conduct. According to our view, the residence at Corinth was an epoch in Paul's life. As regards his doctrine he became more clearly conscious of its character, as well as more precise and definite in his presentation of it ; and as regards practical work he became more clear as to his aim and the means of attaining the aim, namely, that Christianity should be spread through the civilised, *i.e.*, the Roman, world (not as excluding, but as preparatory to, the entire world, *Col.* III 11), using the freedom of speech which the Imperial policy as declared by Gallio seemed inclined to permit. The action of Gallio, as we understand it, seems to pave the way for Paul's appeal a few years later from the petty outlying court of the procurator of Judæa, who was always much under the influence of the ruling party in Jerusalem, to the supreme tribunal of the Empire (p. 306 f.).

The letters to the Thessalonians belong to the earlier part of his stay in Corinth, before he had definitely reached the new stage of thought and aim. To the new stage, when he had attained full consciousness and full dominion over his own plans, belong the four great letters, *Gal.*, I and II *Cor.*, *Rom.*

Note 1. ὁ Ἄρειος Πάγος was often used, in a conversational way, in place of the cumbrous technical form, ἡ ἐξ Ἀρείου Πάγου βουλή. The decisive passages are pointed out to me by two friends and old pupils, Mr. A. Souter and Rev. A. F. Findlay. Cicero says to Atticus, I 14, 5, *Senatus* Ἄρειος Πάγος, "our Senate is a veritable Areopagus". Cicero picked up the conversational usage during his six months' residence in Athens; and hence he uses *Areopagus* to denote the Court, *Nat. D.* II 29, 74, *Rep.* I 27, 43. Again in an inscription of A.D. 50-100 (Cavvadias, *Fouilles d'Epidaure*, I p. 68, No. 206) we find Ἄρειος Πάγος ἐν Ἐλευσῖνι λόγους ἐποιήσατο. (Pape quotes other cases, which are not so clear, and are denied by some authorities.) Here, as everywhere, we find Luke using the language of educated conversation.

Note 2. Gallio. One of the many difficulties in which Dr. Clemen's theory involves him is that he has to deny the identity of Luke's Gallio with Seneca's brother. Gallio's voyage from Achaia, undertaken on account of a local fever (Seneca, *Ep. Mor.* 104, 1), was not the same as his voyage from Rome to Egypt after his consulship on account of phthisis (Pliny, XXXI 33), though probably the first also was to Egypt.

CHAPTER XII

THE CHURCH IN ASIA

ι. THE SYRIAN VOYAGE AND THE RETURN TO EPHESUS. (XVIII 18) AND PAUL TOOK HIS LEAVE OF THE BRETHREN, AND SAILED [1] THENCE FOR SYRIA, AND WITH HIM PRISCILLA AND AQUILA; AND HE SHORE HIS HEAD IN CENCHREÆ, FOR HE HAD A VOW. (19) AND THEY REACHED EPHESUS, AND HE LEFT THE OTHERS THERE. AND FOR HIMSELF, HE WENT INTO THE SYNAGOGUE, AND DELIVERED A DISCOURSE UNTO THE JEWS. (20) AND WHEN THEY ASKED HIM TO ABIDE A LONGER TIME, HE CONSENTED NOT; (21) BUT HE TOOK HIS LEAVE OF THEM, AND SAID, ["I MUST BY ALL MEANS PASS THE COMING FEAST IN JERUSALEM]; IF GOD PLEASE, I WILL RETURN UNTO YOU;" AND HE SET SAIL FROM EPHESUS. (22) AND, REACHING CÆSAREIA, HE WENT UP *to Jerusalem*, SALUTED THE CHURCH, AND *then* WENT DOWN TO ANTIOCH. (23) AND, HAVING SPENT SOME TIME *there*, HE WENT FORTH, AND MADE A PROGRESS IN ORDER *from first to last* THROUGH THE GALATIC REGION AND THE PHRYGIAN *Region*, CONFIRMING ALL THE DISCIPLES. . . . (XIX 1) AND IT CAME TO PASS THAT PAUL, MAKING A MISSIONARY PROGRESS THROUGH THE

---

[1] ἐξέπλει, *lit.* " he set about the voyage " : contrast XX 6, ἐξεπλεύσαμεν *aor.*

HIGHER-LYING QUARTERS *of Asia,* CAME TO *the capital of the province* EPHESUS (*Expositor,* July, 1895, p. 39).

Just as in XX 6 the company sailed away from Philippi (Neapolis, where they really embarked, being omitted, p. 70), so here Paul sailed from Corinth, the harbour being left out of sight. Then the harbour is brought in as an afterthought : before actually embarking at Cenchreæ, the eastern port of Corinth, Paul cut his hair, marking the fulfilment of a vow which apparently was connected with safe embarkation from Corinth. Though the grammatical construction of *v.* 18 would suggest that Aquila made the vow, and one old Latin Version makes this sense explicit, yet the natural emphasis marks Paul as the subject here.

Aquila and Priscilla remained in Ephesus until the end of 55 (I *Cor.* XVI 19) ; but in 56 they returned to Rome, where they were in the early part of A.D. 57 (*Rom.* XVI 3). We may fairly suppose that Timothy came with Paul to Ephesus, and went up on a mission from thence to his native city and the other Churches of Galatia.

This is an important passage for dating the journey. If we accept the longer reading of *v.* 21 (which appears in the Bezan Text, and elsewhere), it is certain that Paul was hurrying to Jerusalem for the coming feast, which may be confidently understood as the Passover. But even with the shorter reading of the great MSS., it would be highly probable that the reason why he postponed accepting the invitation to work in Ephesus and hurried on to Cæsareia, could lie only in his desire to be present at Jerusalem on some great occasion ; and the Passover is the feast which would attract him.

Paul seems to have made a practice of beginning his journeys in the spring.

According to our view the whole journey took place thus. Paul was always eager to profit by any " open door," and an invitation from his own people to preach to them in Ephesus must have been specially tempting to him. Nothing but some pressing duty, which seemed to him to imperatively require his presence in Jerusalem at the feast, was likely to hurry him away from them. Further, the feast must have been close at hand, otherwise he could have waited some weeks before going on. Now, in A.D. 53, Passover fell on March 22 ; and navigation began as a rule only on March 5. But Paul took an early ship for Cæsareia, probably a pilgrim ship, carrying from Corinth and Ephesus many Jews for the coming Passover, and directing its course accordingly. In these circumstances he could not lose a day on the road, and could merely promise to return, " if God will ".

On reaching Cæsareia, he went up and saluted the Church. Dr. Blass considers that he went up from the harbour to the city of Cæsareia and saluted the Church there, and then " went down " to Antioch. That inter- pretation is impossible for several reasons. (1) It is impossible to use the term " went down " of a journey from the coast-town Cæsareia to the inland city Antioch. On the contrary, one regularly " goes down " to a coast-town (XIII 4, XIV 25, XVI 8, etc.). (2) The terms " going up " and " going down " are used so frequently of the journey to and from Jerusalem as to establish this usage. Usually the phrase is given in full, " they went up to Jerusalem " ; but Dr. Blass accepts as Lukan a reading in XV 6, in which " to go up to the Elders" is used in the sense of "to go up to Jerusalem to the Elders". If he admits that sense in XV 6, why not also in XVIII 22? Conversely, the phrase "to go down" is used XXIV 22, where the reader has to understand "from Jerusalem to Cæsareia". Now, the aim of Paul's journey to Jerusalem, having been put in the reader's mind by the words of *v.* 21, is readily and naturally supplied in *v.* 22.

The shipload of pilgrims to Jerusalem, with Paul among them, landed at Cæsareia, and went up to Jerusalem to the Passover in regular course. Paul exchanged greetings with the Church (this phrase implies that he made only a brief stay), and went down to Antioch. There he received serious news about the Galatian Churches (p. 190); and with all convenient speed he went by the land route through Cilicia, to Derbe, Lystra, Iconium, and Pisidian Antioch. With the shortest stay that can be supposed, when he was seeing old and loved friends after years of absence, Paul can hardly have reached Derbe before July 53. We cannot allow less than two months for confirming the wavering Churches of Galatia, especially as on this visit (I *Cor.* XVI 1) he probably planned the collection for the poor in Jerusalem, which was made universal throughout his new Churches during the following three years. Thus he would have completed his work in Galatia by the beginning of September. Then he went on to Ephesus, taking the higher-lying and more direct route, not the regular trade route on the lower level down the Lycus and Mæander valleys. As he made a missionary progress through the upper lands, he can hardly have reached Ephesus before the end of September, A.D. 53, and October is a more probable time. Such a journey must have occupied much time, even if we cut it down to the shortest possible limits. The distances are very great, and progression was very slow; and even on a rapid journey many interruptions must be allowed for (as any one who travels in these countries knows only too well).

In interpreting *v.* 22, we had to understand that the thought of Jerusalem as Paul's aim had been suggested to the reader's mind by *v.* 21. That is the case when the longer form of *v.* 21 is accepted ; but with the shorter text it becomes too harsh and difficult to supply the unexpressed thought in *v.* 22. We conclude that the longer form is the original text, and the shorter form is a corruption. But how did the corruption originate ? A curious error appears in Asterius (c. 400, A.D.), and in Euthalius (probably c. 468), and therefore was probably part of the early tradition, according to which Pisidian Antioch, not Syrian Antioch, was alluded to in *v.* 22. By that misconception the whole journey is obscured, and especially a visit to Jerusalem in *v.* 22 becomes impossible. Two ways of curing the difficulty were tried. The Bezan Text retained the allusion to Jerusalem and the feast in *v.* 22, and explained the supposed failure to pay the visit by interpolating in XIX 1 the statement, "now when Paul wished according to his own plan to go to Jerusalem, the Spirit bade him turn away into Asia". On the other hand, in the text of the great MSS., the reference to the intended visit to Jerusalem is cut out of *v.* 21. Each of these seems a deliberate and conscious effort made by some editor to eliminate a difficulty from the passage as it stood originally

2. APOLLOS, PRISCILLA AND AQUILA. During the time that Paul was absent from Ephesus, there came thither an Alexandrian Jew named Apollos, a good speaker, and well read in the Scriptures. He had learned in Alexandria the doctrine of John the Baptist and his prophecy of the immediate coming of Christ ; and this he preached in Ephesus with great fervour and detailed proof from Scripture. Priscilla and Aquila, having heard his preaching, instructed him with regard to the fulfilment of John's prophecy. Afterwards he conceived the intention of crossing over to Achaia ; and the Brethren gave him letters of recommendation to the disciples in Corinth. When he settled there he became an effective preacher, and a powerful opponent of the Jews, showing how in Jesus the prophecies with regard to the Anointed One were fulfilled.

This episode is obviously introduced, not so much for its own intrinsic importance, as for the sake of rendering the opening of Paul's first letter to the Corinthians clear and intelligible. A contrast is drawn there between the more elaborate and eloquent style of Apollos and the simple Gospel of Paul ; and it is implied that some of the Corinthian Brethren preferred the style and Gospel of Apollos. The particulars stated here about Apollos have clearly been selected to throw light on the circumstances alluded to, but not explained in the letter.

In the Bezan Text the account of Apollos appears in a different form, which has all the marks of truth, and yet is clearly not original, but a text remodelled according to a good tradition. The name is given in the fuller form Apollonius ; but Paul uses the diminutive Apollos ; and Luke, to make his explanation clearer would naturally use the same form. Moreover, Luke regularly uses the language of conversation, in which the diminutive forms were usual; and so he speaks of Priscilla, Sopatros and Silas always, though Paul speaks of Prisca, Sosipatros and Silvanus. On that principle we must prefer the form Apollos.

Again, the text of almost all MSS. mentions Priscilla first; but the Bezan Text alters the order, putting Aquila first. Elsewhere also the Bezan Reviser shows his dislike to the prominence assigned to women in *Acts*. In XVII 12 he changes "not a few of the honourable Greek women and of men" into "of the Greeks and the honourable many men and women". In XVII 34 he cuts out Damaris altogether. In XVII 4 he changes the "leading women" into "wives of the leading men". These changes show a definite and uniform purpose, and therefore spring from a deliberate Revision of the original Received Text.

The unusual order, the wife before the husband (so XVIII 18), must be accepted as original; for there is always a tendency among scribes to change the unusual into the usual. Paul twice (II *Tim.* IV 19, *Rom.* XVI 3) mentions Prisca before Aquila; that order was, therefore, a conversational custom, familiar in the company among whom they moved; though it must have seemed odd to strangers in later generations.

Probably Prisca was of higher rank than her husband, for her name is that of a good old Roman family. Now, in XVIII 2 the very harsh and strange arrangement of the sentence must strike every reader. But clearly the intention is to force on the reader's mind the fact that Aquila was a Jew, while Priscilla was not; and it is characteristic of Luke to suggest by subtle arrangement of words a distinction which would need space to explain formally (pp. 85, 204). Aquila was probably a freedman. The name does indeed occur as *cognomen* in some Roman families ; but it was also a slave name, for a freedman of Mæcenas was called (C. Cilnius) Aquila. There is probably much to discover with regard to this interesting pair, but in this place we cannot dwell on the subject.

The order in which the different threads of the narrative here succeed one another exactly recalls the method of XI 27-XII 25. There *vv.* 27-30 narrate the events in Antioch, and bring Barnabas and Saul to the gates of Jerusalem ; next, the events in Jerusalem are brought up to date ; and then the action of the envoys in Jerusalem is described. So here Paul's journey is narrated, and he is brought to the frontier of Asia ; next, the events in Ephesus are brought up to date ; and then Paul's entrance into Asia and his action at Ephesus are described.

3. EPHESUS. (XIX 1) AND IT CAME TO PASS, THAT, WHILE APOLLOS WAS AT CORINTH, PAUL, HAVING PASSED THROUGH THE UPPER DISTRICTS, CAME TO EPHESUS. (8) AND HE ENTERED INTO THE SYNAGOGUE, AND SPAKE BOLDLY FOR THE SPACE OF THREE MONTHS, REASONING AND PERSUADING AS TO WHAT CONCERNS THE KINGDOM OF GOD. (9) BUT WHEN SOME WERE HARDENED AND DISOBEDIENT, SPEAKING EVIL OF THE WAY BEFORE THE MULTITUDE, HE DEPARTED FROM THEM AND SEPARATED THE DISCIPLES, REASON-ING DAILY IN THE SCHOOL OF TYRANNUS [FROM THE FIFTH TO THE TENTH HOUR]. (10) AND THIS CON-TINUED FOR THE SPACE OF TWO YEARS.

The distinction between the period of preaching in the synagogue and the direct address to the Ephesian population is very clearly marked, and the times given in each case. In *vv.* 2-7 a strange episode is related before Paul entered the synagogue. He found twelve men who had been baptised by the baptism of John, and induced them to accept re-baptism. This episode I must confess not to understand. It interrupts the regular method of Luke's narrative ; for in all similar cases, Paul goes to the synagogue, and his regular efforts for his own people are related before any exceptional cases are recorded. The circumstances, too, are difficult. How had these twelve escaped the notice of Aquila, Priscilla, and Apollos, and yet attracted Paul's attention before he went to the synagogue? Perhaps the intention is to represent Paul as completing and perfecting the work begun by Apollos ; re-baptism was, apparently, not thought necessary for Apollos, and now Paul lays down the principle that it is required in all such cases. But that seems distinctly below the level on which Luke's conception of Paul is pitched. If there were any authority in MS. or ancient Versions to omit the episode, one would be inclined to take that course. As there is none, I must acknowledge that I cannot reconcile it with the conception of Luke's method, founded on other parts of the narrative, which is maintained in this book. Possibly better knowledge about the early history of the Ephesian Church might give this episode more significance and importance in the development of history than it seems to possess.

We should be glad to know more about the lecture-room of Tyrannus. It played the same part in Ephesus that the house of Titius Justus adjoining the synagogue did in Corinth. Here Paul regularly taught every day ; and the analogy which we have noticed in other cases (pp. 75, 243) between his position, as it would appear to the general population, and that of the rhetors and philosophers of the time, is very marked. There is one difference, according to the Bezan Text of *v.* 9 Paul taught after the usual work of the lecture-room was concluded, *i.e.,* "after business hours ". Doubtless he himself began to work (XX 34, I *Cor.* IV 12) before sunrise and continued at his trade till closing time, an hour before noon. His hours of work are defined by himself, I *Thess.* II 9, "ye remember our labour and toil, working day and night "; there, as often in ancient literature, the hours before daybreak are called "night," and his rule at Thessalonica may be extended to Ephesus. Public life in the Ionian cities ended regularly at the fifth hour ; and we may add to the facts elsewhere stated a regulation at Attaleia in Lydia that public distribution of oil should be "from the first to the fifth hour "[1]. Thus Paul himself would be free, and the lecture-room would be disengaged after the fifth hour ; and the time, which was devoted generally to home-life and rest, was applied by him to mission-work.

In the following narrative the powers of Paul are brought into competition with those of Jewish exorcists and pagan dabblers in the black art, and his superiority to them demonstrated. Ephesus was a centre of all such magical arts and practices, and it was therefore inevitable that the new teaching should be brought in

---

[1] In an inscription, *Bulletin de Corresp. Hellen.*, 1887, p. 400.

contact with them and triumph over them.   There can
be no doubt that, in the conception of Luke, the
measure of success lay in the extent to which Divine
power and inspiration was communicated to a new
Church; and perhaps the whole description may be
defended as the extremest example of that view.   But
it seems undeniable that, when we contrast this passage
with the great scene at Paphos, or the beautiful though
less powerful scene with the ventriloquist at Philippi,
there is in the Ephesian description something like
vulgarity of tone, together with a certain vagueness and
want of individuality, very different from those other
scenes.   Such details, too, as are given, are not always
consistent and satisfactory.   The seven sons in *v.* 14
change in an unintelligible way to two in *v.* 16 (except
in the Bezan Text); and the statement that the seven
were sons of a chief priest, looks more like a popular
tale than a trustworthy historical statement.   There is
no warrant in the text for the view sometimes advocated,
that Sceva was merely an impostor who pretended to
be a chief priest.   The money value of the books that
were destroyed is another touch that is thoroughly
characteristic of the oriental popular tale.   The inability
of the vulgar oriental mind to conceive any other aim,
object, or standard in the world except money, and its
utter slavery to gold, are familiar to every one who has
seen the life of the people, or studied the *Arabian
Nights*: in the West one sees nothing like the simple,
childish frankness with which the ordinary oriental
measures all things by gold, and can conceive of no
other conscious aim except gold.   So far as the oriental
peasant is natural and unconscious, he is interesting and

delightful, and his complete difference of nature at once attracts and holds at a distance the man of Western thoughts ; but so far as he consciously attempts to conceive motives and form plans, gold is his sole standard of value.

In this Ephesian description one feels the character, not of weighed and reasoned history, but of popular fancy ; and I cannot explain it on the level of most of the narrative. The writer is here rather a picker-up of current gossip, like Herodotus, than a real historian. The puzzle becomes still more difficult when we go on to *v.* 23, and find ourselves again on the same level as the finest parts of *Acts.* If there were many such contrasts in the book as between *vv.* 11-20 and 23-41, I should be a believer in the composite character of *Acts.* As it is, I confess the difficulty in this part ; but the existence of some unsolved difficulties is not a bar to the view maintained in the present treatise (p. 16).

4. THE CHURCH IN THE PROVINCE OF ASIA. (XIX 10) THIS CONTINUED FOR THE SPACE OF TWO YEARS, SO THAT ALL THEY THAT DWELT IN ASIA HEARD THE WORD. . . . (21) NOW AFTER THESE THINGS WERE ENDED, PAUL PURPOSED IN THE SPIRIT, WHEN HE HAD MADE A PROGRESS THROUGH MACEDONIA AND ACHAIA, TO GO TO JERUSALEM, SAYING, " AFTER I HAVE BEEN THERE, I MUST ALSO SEE ROME ". (22) AND, HAVING SENT INTO MACEDONIA TWO OF THEM THAT ASSISTED HIM, TIMOTHY AND ERASTUS, HE HIMSELF STAYED IN ASIA FOR A WHILE.

The work in Asia, which had been Paul's aim in A.D. 50 (p. 198), was now carried out. The long residence suits the greatness of the work, for Asia was the richest, one of the largest, and in many ways the leading province of the East.

Ephesus, as the seat of government, was the centre from which the whole province of Asia could best be affected (p. 104) ; and the effect of Paul's long work there extended far over that vast province, but chiefly, of course, along the great lines of communication. For example, Churches arose in three cities of the Lycos Valley, Laodiceia, Colossai, and Hierapolis, though Paul himself did not go there. All the seven Churches mentioned in the *Revelation* were probably founded during this period, for all were within easy reach of Ephesus, and all were great centres of trade. It is probable that they, being the first foundations in the province, retained a sort of representative character ; and thus they were addressed in the *Revelation* (perhaps as heads over districts), when there were certainly other Churches in the province.

In the ordinary communication between the capital and the other cities of the province, the influence from Ephesus would be carried to these cities ; but that was not the only way in which these other Churches grew. Paul had with him a number of subordinate helpers, such as Timothy, Erastus, Titus, etc. The analogy of many other cases in the early history of the Church would leave no room to doubt that helpers were often employed in missions to the new Churches ; and, as Timothy joined with Paul in the letter to the Colossians, it may be inferred that he had been working in that city.

The clear conception of a far-reaching plan revealed in *v.* 21 is confirmed by *Rom.* XV 24 (see p. 255).

It has been argued by some (and notably by Light

foot) that Paul made a short visit to Corinth, during his Ephesian mission. But this conjectural visit (II *Cor.* XII 14, XIII 1) is more likely to have been made from Philippi (p. 283), for clearly (*Acts* XIX 9, 10) Paul resided in Ephesus throughout the period Oct. 53 to Jan. 56. In the latter part of autumn 55 he sent to Corinth the First Epistle ; and at that time his intention was to remain in Ephesus till Pentecost 56 (XVI 8), and then to go through Macedonia to Corinth. But this was an alteration of a previous plan to sail direct from Ephesus to Corinth, thence going to Macedonia, and returning to Corinth, from whence he should sail for Jerusalem (II *Cor.* I 16). That intention was abandoned, and a letter, I *Cor.*, was sent instead : the full knowledge of the state of things in Corinth, which is revealed in that letter, was gained by the report of some envoys (XVI 17, compare p. 284). The abandonment of the plan was doubtless due to the conviction that the success of the work in Asia demanded a longer residence. He, therefore, cut out of his programme the first of these two proposed visits to Corinth, and restricted himself to one, which he should pay after a progress through Macedonia (I *Cor.* XVI 5). He sent Timothy and Erastus to Macedonia, instructing the former to go on to Corinth, and he told the Corinthians, IV 17, that Timothy was coming, "who shall put you in remembrance of my ways which be in Christ". Finally, when his Asian work was cut short, he went from Philippi to Corinth, April 56 (see *Preface*).

The analogy of this case strengthens our interpretation of the Galatian letter (p. 190). In each case

Paul had to encounter a serious and dangerous situation in a distant Church. In the case of Corinth, he could not go, but sent a substitute and a letter explaining that the substitute was on the way, and the bearer would give the reason why Paul could not go then ; but he adds in the letter a promise to go later, though " some of them fancied that he was not coming ". In the case of Galatia he was able to go immediately, and sent off a hasty letter in front, the bearer of which would announce that he was following. But on the usual theory, Paul, in that serious emergency in Galatia, neither thought of going there, nor of explaining that he could not go.

No allusion to Timothy occurs between XVIII 5 (where he rejoined Paul at Corinth) and XIX 22. According to the analogy of Luke's method (p. 46 f.), this shows that he was understood by the author to have been attached to Paul's service during the intervening period, ready for any mission, such as that to Galatia, or this to Macedonia. According to I *Cor.* IV 17, Timothy was to go on to Corinth : Luke speaks only of Macedonia. Both are correct ; it becomes clear from II *Cor.* that Timothy did not go on to Corinth, and that Paul found him in Macedonia : probably he met Titus on his way back to report to Paul the result of the first letter, and waited instructions before going on. See p. 285.

The plan of staying in Ephesus till Pentecost was interrupted by a popular riot. Already in the autumn of 55 Paul spoke of the difficulties in Ephesus caused by the opposition of the vulgar populace (p. 230, I *Cor.* XV 32) ; and the character of the city shows how inevitable that was.   The superstition of all Asia was concentrated in Ephesus.   Throughout the early centuries the city mob, superstitious, uneducated, frivolous, swayed by the most commonplace motives, was everywhere the most dangerous and unfailing enemy of Christianity, and often carried the imperial officials further than they wished in the way of persecution.   Moreover, round the great Ephesian temple, to which worshippers came from far, many tradesmen got their living from the pilgrims, supplying them with victims and dedicatory offerings of various kinds, as well as food and shelter.   During the year 55, the tension in Ephesus grew more severe : on the one hand, the teaching spread so fast that Paul was tempted to remain longer than he had intended (p. 275) : on the other hand, his success only enraged and alarmed the opposing forces.   " A great door and effectual is opened unto me, and there are many adversaries " (I *Cor.* XVI 9) : " after the manner of men I fought with beasts in Ephesus " (*ib.* XV 32, p. 230).

The most sensitive part of " civilised " man is his pocket ; and it was there that opposition to Christian changes, or " reforms," began.   Those " reforms " threatened to extinguish some ancient and respectable trades, and promised no compensation ; and thus all the large class that lived off the pilgrims and the temple service was marshalled against the new party, which threatened the livelihood of all.

5. DEMETRIUS THE SILVERSMITH.   The scene which follows is the most instructive picture of society in an Asian city at this period that has come down to us. It is impossible here to treat it so fully as it deserves ; and we can only enumerate the more striking points, and refer to previous discussions.   A certain Demetrius was a

leading man in the associated trades, which made in various
materials, terra-cotta, marble and silver, small shrines (*naoi*)
for votaries to dedicate in the temple, representing the
Goddess Artemis sitting in a niche or *naiskos*, with her
lions beside her. Vast numbers of these shrines were
offered to the goddess by her innumerable votaries. The
rich bought and offered them in more expensive materials
and more artistic form, the poor in simple rude terra-cotta.
The temple and the sacred precinct were crowded with
dedications; and the priests often cleared away the old
and especially the worthless offerings to make room for
new gifts. The richer tradesmen made shrines in the
more expensive material, and silver was evidently a
favourite material among the wealthy. Demetrius, then,
must have had a good deal of capital sunk in his business.
He called a meeting of the trades, doubtless in a guild-
house where they regularly met, and pointed out that Paul,
by teaching the worthlessness of images, was seriously
affecting public opinion and practice over almost the
whole province Asia,[1] and endangering their business as
well as the worship of the goddess. The tradesmen were
roused; they rushed forth into the street;[2] a general scene
of confusion arose, and a common impulse carried the
excited crowd into the great theatre. The majority of the
crowd were ignorant what was the matter; they only
knew from the shouts of the first rioters that the worship
of Artemis was concerned; and for about two hours the

[1] I formerly erred as to the sense of Asia in XIX 26, 27, *Church
in R. E.*, p. 166.

[2] We adopt this and some other touches from *Cod. Bez.*, as either
original or added from a trustworthy tradition: our reasons have
been stated elsewhere.

vast assembly, like a crowd of devotees or howling dervishes, shouted their invocation of "Great Artemis". In
this scene we cannot mistake the tone of sarcasm and
contempt, as Luke tells of this howling mob; they themselves thought they were performing their devotions, as
they repeated the sacred name; but to Luke they were
merely howling, not praying.

A certain Alexander was put forward by the Jews to
address the mob; but this merely increased the clamour
and confusion. There was no clear idea among the
rioters what they wanted: an anti-Jewish and an anti-
Christian demonstration were mixed up, and probably
Alexander's intention was to turn the general feeling away
from the Jews. It is possible that he was the worker in
bronze, who afterwards did Paul much harm (II *Tim.* IV 14).

Our conception of the scene assumes that the Bezan
reading in 28, 34 (μεγάλη "Αρτεμις) is original. The
accepted text, "Great is Artemis," gives a different tone to
the scene : that is the quiet expression in which a worshipper
recognises and accepts a sign of the goddess's power,
drawing an inference and expressing his respect and
gratitude. "Great Artemis" was a common formula of
devotion and prayer, as is attested by several inscriptions;
and it gives a more natural and a far more effective tone to
the scene.

Two of Paul's companions in travel, Gaius and Aristarchus, had been carried into the theatre with the crowd;
and he himself was on the point of going there, but the
disciples would not allow him, and his friends among the
Asiarchs sent urging him not to risk himself among the
mob. It is noteworthy that Luke, as usual, adds no
comments or reflections of his own as to the danger in

which Paul was placed. But the slightest consideration suffices to show that he must have been at this period in the most imminent danger, with the mob of a great Ionian coast-city raging against him. In the speech of Demetrius are concentrated most of the feelings and motives that, from the beginning to the end, made the mob so hostile to the Christians in the great oriental cities. Paul himself says, "concerning our affliction which befell in Asia, that we were weighed down exceedingly, beyond our power, insomuch that we despaired even of life" (II *Cor.* I 8). His immediate withdrawal from Ephesus, in the midst of his promising work, was forced on him.

It is a question whether the reading of some few MSS., "Gaius and Aristarchus a Macedonian," should not be followed. Gaius, in that case, would be the native of Derbe mentioned in XX 4. Luke, himself a Macedonian, does not omit the little touch of national pride in Aristarchus ; but he was not so interested in the nationality of Gaius. The peculiar phraseology, with the ethnic in singular (Μακεδόνα) following two names, and preceding συνεκδήμους, led naturally to the change (Μακεδόνας), which appears in most MSS. The epithet, "travelling companions," seems to point forward to XX 4, as we have no reason to think that either Gaius or Aristarchus had hitherto been companions of Paul on a journey. Prof. Blass, recognising the probability that Gaius is the travelling companion of XX 4, accepts Valckenaer's alteration of the text in that place, making Gaius a Thessalonian, and Timothy a man of Derbe ; and that alteration would be very tempting, were it not for the insurmountable statement, XVI 1, that Timothy was a Lystran.

The reference to the Asiarchs is very important, both

in respect of the nature of that office (on which it throws great light, though that opens up a wide and disputed field), and as a fact of Pauline history. The Asiarchs, or High Priests of Asia, were the heads of the imperial, political-religious organisation of the province in the worship of " Rome and the Emperors " (p. 134) ; and their friendly attitude is a proof both that the spirit of the imperial policy was not as yet hostile to the new teaching, and that the educated classes did not share the hostility of the superstitious vulgar to Paul. Doubtless, some of the Asiarchs had, in the ordinary course of dignity, previously held priesthoods of Artemis or other city deities ; and it is quite probable that up to the present time even the Ephesian priests were not at all hostile to Paul. The eclectic religion, which was fashionable at the time, regarded new forms of cult with equanimity, almost with friendliness ; and the growth of each new superstition only added to the influence of Artemis and her priests. My friend, Mr. J. N. Farquhar, Principal of the L.M.S. College, Calcutta, writes that he is struck with similar facts in the situation of mission work in India, and its relation to the priests and people.

Luke, having stated the accusation against Paul, does not fail to show up its utter groundlessness in the eyes of responsible officials. The speech of the Town-clerk, which is given at length, is a very skilful and important document, in its bearing on the whole situation, and on Luke's plan (p. 304 f.). The Clerk was probably the most important official in Ephesus, and therefore in close contact with the court of the proconsul, who generally resided in that city ; and his speech is a direct negation of the charges commonly brought against Christianity, as flagrantly disrespectful in action and in language to the established institutions of the State. He points out that the only permissible method of procedure for those who have complaints against a Christian is action before the courts of the province, or the assembly of the municipality ; and he warns the rioters that they are bringing themselves into danger by their disorderly action.

This address is so entirely an *apologia* of the Christians that we might almost take it as an example of the Thucydidean type of speech, put into the mouth of one of the actors, not as being precisely his words, but as embodying a statesmanlike conception of the real situation. At any rate, it is included by Luke in his work, not for its mere Ephesian connection, but as bearing on the universal question of the relations in which the Church stood to the Empire (p. 306). The well-known rescripts of Hadrian to Fundanus, and of Antoninus Pius to the Greek cities, take their stand on the same permanent and obvious ground, which at all times formed the one statesmanlike principle of action, and the basis for the Church's claim to freedom and toleration.

CHAPTER XIII

THE VOYAGE TO JERUSALEM

1. THE SECOND EUROPEAN JOURNEY. (XX 1)
AND AFTER THE RIOT CEASED, PAUL, HAVING SENT
FOR THE DISCIPLES AND EXHORTED THEM, BADE
THEM FAREWELL, AND DEPARTED TO MAKE HIS WAY
INTO MACEDONIA. (2) AND HAVING MADE A PROGRESS
THROUGH THOSE QUARTERS, AND EXHORTED THEM
WITH MUCH PREACHING, HE WENT INTO GREECE. (3)
AND HE SPENT THREE MONTHS *there*.

Paul took a coasting vessel from Ephesus, we may be
sure ; and, as was often the case, he had to transship in
Troas. Here "a door was opened to him" (II *Cor.*
II 12). Doubtless he had to wait some time for a
passage to Macedonia ; for, though in January a passage
could be easily obtained along the safe Asian coast, it
was more difficult to find opportunity for the longer
voyage over the open sea to Macedonia ; perhaps none
was found till general navigation began, March 5. It
is probable that already in the voyages between Ephesus
and Macedonia, the new teaching had effected a lodging
in Troas (XIX 10) ; and in the delay there, Paul had a
good opening. In Troas Paul had expected to meet
Titus ; and was much disappointed that he was not
there. At the same time he was greatly dispirited by
the strong opposition which had driven him prematurely

from Ephesus (II *Cor.* I 8 f.) ; and was in a depressed frame of mind owing to ill-health (*ib.* IV 7 f.).

Titus is the most enigmatic figure in early Christian history. His omission from *Acts* has been alluded to (p. 59). He enters on the stage of history for a short time in A.D. 45-6, and then we hear nothing of him, until we learn that Paul expected to find him in Troas in January or February 56. He was now on his way from Corinth to Macedonia ; and he joined Paul after he had arrived at Philippi in February or March, bringing a detailed report of the state of the Corinthian Church. Now in II *Cor.* Titus is prominent to a degree unique in Paul's letters ; he is named nine times, and always with marked affection and distinction. Why, then, is he never mentioned in I *Cor.?* There is one satisfactory reason, and only one, so far as I can judge : he was the bearer of the first letter.[1] His special interest in Corinth is mentioned, VII 13, VIII 16. He was eager to return on a second mission to Corinth, VIII 17, and along with him Paul sent the Brother whose praise in the delivery of the good tidings was spread over all the Churches (Luke, according to an early tradition), and another, who was selected on account of the confidence that he felt in the Corinthians. It may be safely assumed that the Titus of II *Cor.* is the same Titus that is mentioned in *Gal.* II 1.

Titus, then, had been sent on his first mission to Corinth in autumn 55, probably by direct ship. He could not come back across the open sea during the winter (Nov. 10 to March 5), and must take a coasting

[1] Suggested as possible by Dr. Plumptre in *Introd. to II Cor.*, p. 350.

voyage by Macedonia. Paul expected to find him in Troas; but he was detained too long, and met Paul in Philippi in February or early March 56; and he returned thence on a second mission to Corinth.

As Titus was at hand in Ephesus about October 55, it is hardly open to doubt that he had been in Paul's company on the whole of the third journey. It is equally clear that he had not been with Paul on the first or the second journey, for he is mentioned in *Gal.* II 1 as a stranger to the Galatians, whose Greek birth had to be explained to them. Probably it was his Greek origin that had prevented Paul from taking him as a companion on earlier journeys. We have seen how careful Paul was to conciliate the Jews on his second journey; and we may fairly consider that the grumbling of the Jews in Jerusalem in 46 (even when Titus was bringing food to them) had warned Paul that it was not expedient to have Titus with him when he entered the synagogues of strange cities. For his companions on the second journey he selected Silas, a Jewish Roman, and Timothy, half-Greek, half-Jew. Finally, on his third journey, when he was putting down the Judaising tendency in Galatia, he took Titus with him by a carefully-planned stroke of policy: one of the arguments by which the Judaisers proved that Judaic Christianity was the higher stage was that Paul had circumcised Timothy before promoting him to an office of trust. He replied by taking Titus with him to Galatia; and from II *Cor.* we gather that Titus proved one of the most congenial and useful of his assistants. The space which he fills in II *Cor.*[1] is a unique fact in Paul's letters; and in the

[1] II 13, VII 6 f., 13 f., VIII 6 f., 16-24, XII 18.

loving and tender sympathy of Paul's language about
him we may read a wish to compensate for the neglect
that had during many years sacrificed him to the
thankless policy of conciliating the Jews.

The importance of Titus in subsequent years confirms
the impression derived from II *Cor.* He seems to have
remained in Europe when Paul went to Jerusalem in
March 57. At a later time he was sent to Dalmatia,
II *Tim.* IV 10; and near the end of Paul's career he
was entrusted with the general oversight of the Churches
in Crete, *Tit.* I 5.

Paul spent the summer and autumn of 56 in Macedonia.
He found Timothy waiting him either in Thessalonica
or in Berœa; and they joined in addressing the second
letter to the Corinthians, enforcing in a more personal
way the instructions already sent through the three
envoys who had come from Philippi. The common view
(which is as old as the subscription added in some MSS.
to the letter), that the envoys carried with them II *Cor.*,
seems improbable. In winter Paul went on to Hellas
(the Greek term for the country forming the main part
of the Roman province), and spent December, January,
and February in Corinth.

2. THE CONTRIBUTION OF THE FOUR PRO
VINCES. (3) AND WHEN HE HAD SPENT THREE
MONTHS, AND A PLOT WAS LAID AGAINST HIM BY THE
JEWS WHILE HE WAS ON THE POINT OF SETTING SAIL
FOR SYRIA, HE ADOPTED THE PLAN OF MAKING HIS
RETURN JOURNEY *to Jerusalem* THROUGH MACEDONIA.
(4) AND THERE ACCOMPANIED HIM *on the journey to
Jerusalem* SOPATER, SON OF PYRRHUS OF BERŒA, AND
on the part OF THE THESSALONIANS ARISTARCHUS AND

SECUNDUS, AND GAIUS OF DERBE AND TIMOTHY, AND THE ASIANS TYCHICUS AND TROPHIMUS (NOW THESE *Asian delegates,* COMING TO MEET US, AWAITED US IN TROAS). (5) AND WE SAILED AWAY FROM PHILIPPI AFTER THE DAYS OF UNLEAVENED BREAD, AND CAME UNTO THEM TO TROAS.

At the opening of navigation, Paul had arranged to sail from Corinth to Jerusalem, obviously with the intention of celebrating the Passover there; but the discovery of a Jewish plot to kill him altered his plans. The style of this plot can be easily imagined. Paul's intention must have been to take a pilgrim ship carrying Achaian and Asian Jews to the Passover (p. 264). With a shipload of hostile Jews, it would be easy to find opportunity to murder Paul. He therefore abandoned the proposed voyage and sailed for Macedonia, where he easily arrived in time to celebrate the Passover in Philippi.

It is clear that the plot was discovered at the last moment, when delegates from the Churches had already assembled. The European delegates were to sail from Corinth, the Asian from Ephesus, where doubtless the pilgrim ship would call (as in 53, p. 264). When the plan was changed, word was sent to the Asian delegates; and they went as far as Troas to meet the others, for in ancient voyages it could be calculated with certainty that Paul's company would put in at that harbour.

The purpose of this numerous company is not stated in this part of the text; but in XXIV 17, Paul says : " I came to bring alms to my nation, and offerings," and the reason is often alluded to in the Epistles to

Corinth and Rome. In *Rom.* XV 25, written from Corinth about Jan. 57, Paul says: "Now I go unto Jerusalem, acting as an administrator of relief to the saints". The scheme of a general contribution collected week by week for a long time in all the Pauline Churches of Galatia, Asia, Macedonia, and Achaia, has been well described by Mr. Rendall (*Expositor*, Nov. 1893, p. 321). The great importance which Paul attached to this contribution, and to the personal distribution of the fund (διακονία), is attested, not merely by the long and careful planning of the scheme, and by the numerous body of delegates who carried it to Jerusalem, but also by his determination to conduct the delegates personally, in spite of all the dangers which, as he knew, awaited him there: "I go constrained by the Spirit unto Jerusalem, not knowing what shall befall me there, save that the Holy Spirit testifieth unto me in every city, saying that bonds and afflictions await me". It is evident that he thought this scheme the crowning act of his work in these four provinces; and as soon as it was over, his purpose was to go to Rome and the West (p. 255), and cease for the time his work in the Eastern provinces (XX 25).

The scheme is not alluded to in the letter to the Galatian Churches: but it seems to have been inaugurated there by oral instructions during the third visit (I *Cor.* XVI 1). The mission of Timothy and of Titus in 56 doubtless helped to carry it out in Europe. Luke evidently took it up with special zeal, and he was from an early date selected as one of the administrators who were to carry it to Jerusalem (II *Cor.*

VIII 19). In the list, *v.* 4, Luke omits his own name, but suggests his presence by his familiar device. No representative from Achaia is on the list ; but perhaps we may understand that the Corinthians had asked Paul himself to bear their contribution, the amount of which he praises (II *Cor.* IX 2).

In *v.* 4 we have probably a case like XVI 19 f., in which the authority hesitated between two constructions, and left an unfinished sentence containing elements of two forms. The facts were probably as stated in our rendering ; and it would lead too far to discuss the sentence, which perhaps never received the author's final revision.

3. THE VOYAGE TO TROAS. (XX 6) WE SAILED AWAY FROM PHILIPPI AFTER THE DAYS OF UN-LEAVENED BREAD, AND CAME UNTO THEM TO TROAS IN FIVE DAYS ; AND THERE WE TARRIED SEVEN DAYS. (7) AND ON THE FIRST DAY OF THE WEEK WHEN WE WERE GATHERED TOGETHER TO BREAK BREAD, PAUL DISCOURSED WITH THEM, BEING ABOUT TO DE-PART ON THE MORROW ; AND HE PROLONGED HIS SPEECH UNTIL MIDNIGHT. . . . (13) AND WE, GOING BEFORE TO THE SHIP, SET SAIL FOR ASSOS.

In A.D. 57 Passover fell on Thursday, April 7. The company left Philippi on the morning of Friday, April 15, and the journey to Troas lasted till the fifth day, Tuesday, April 19. In Troas they stayed seven days, the first of which was April 19, and the last, Monday, April 25. Luke's rule is to state first the whole period of residence, and then some details of the residence (see pp. 153, 256, and XIX 10). On the Sunday evening just before the start, the whole congregation

at Troas met for the Agape; religious services were
conducted late into the night; and in the early morning of Monday the party went on board and set sail.
In A.D. 56, 58, 59, the incidence of Passover is not
reconcilable with Luke's statistics; as is apparent from
the attempts that have been made to torture his words
into agreement. (Luke now rejoins Paul, p. 201.)

4. EUTYCHUS. (XX 7) AND UPON THE FIRST DAY
OF THE WEEK, WHEN WE WERE GATHERED TOGETHER
TO BREAK BREAD, PAUL DISCOURSED TO THEM, IN-
TENDING TO GO AWAY ON THE MORROW; AND HE
PROLONGED HIS SPEECH UNTIL MIDNIGHT. (8) AND
THERE WERE MANY LIGHTS IN THE UPPER CHAMBER,
WHERE WE WERE GATHERED TOGETHER. (9) AND
THERE SAT IN THE WINDOW A CERTAIN YOUNG MAN
NAMED EUTYCHUS, WHO WAS GRADUALLY OPPRESSED
BY SLEEP AS PAUL EXTENDED HIS DISCOURSE FURTHER,
AND BEING BORNE DOWN BY HIS SLEEP HE FELL
FROM THE THIRD STORY TO THE GROUND, AND WAS
LIFTED UP DEAD. (10) AND PAUL WENT DOWN AND
FELL ON HIM, AND EMBRACING HIM SAID, "MAKE YE
NO ADO; FOR HIS LIFE IS IN HIM". (11) AND HE
WENT UP, AND BROKE BREAD AND ATE, AND TALKED
WITH THEM A LONG WHILE, EVEN TILL BREAK OF
DAY; AND THUS HE DEPARTED. (12) AND THEY
BROUGHT THE LAD ALIVE, AND WERE NOT A LITTLE
COMFORTED. (13) BUT WE, GOING BEFORE TO THE
SHIP, SET SAIL FOR ASSOS, INTENDING TO TAKE PAUL
ON BOARD FROM THENCE; FOR SO HE HAD ARRANGED,
INTENDING HIMSELF TO GO BY LAND.

In this case the author vouches that Eutychus was dead,
implying apparently that, as a physician, he had satis-

fied himself on the point. In XIV 19 he had no authority for asserting that Paul *was* dead, but only that his enemies considered him dead.

The sequence of the narrative is remarkable : the young man fell : Paul declared he was not dead : Paul went upstairs again, partook of the common meal (conceived here as a sacrament), and conversed till break of day : they brought the young man living. But the interruption of the story of Eutychus's fate is intentional. The narrator was present in the upper chamber, and saw Eutychus fall, and heard Paul declare that he was not dead ; but he does not claim to have been a witness of the man's recovery, and he marks the difference by a break in the narrative. The ship, having to round the projecting cape Lectum, would take longer time to reach Assos than the land journey required ; and Paul stayed on to the last moment, perhaps to be assured of Eutychus's recovery, while the other delegates went on ahead in the ship. Thus the fact that Eutychus recovered is in a sense the final incident of the stay at Troas. The Bezan reading makes the sequence clearer : " and while they were bidding farewell, they brought the young man living ; and they were comforted ".

There is a very harsh change of subject in *v.* 12 ; the persons who brought the youth are not those who were comforted (as Dr. Blass points out). A similar change of subject, but not quite so harsh, occurs in XIII 2-3. The word "brought," not "carried," implies that Eutychus was able to come with some help.

5. THE VOYAGE TO CÆSAREIA. (14) AND WHEN HE MET US AT ASSOS, WE TOOK HIM ON

BOARD, AND CAME TO MITYLENE; (15) AND SAILING
FROM THENCE ON THE FOLLOWING DAY, WE REACHED
a point on the mainland OPPOSITE CHIOS; AND ON
THE MORROW WE STRUCK ACROSS TO SAMOS, AND
[AFTER MAKING A STAY AT TROGYLLIA] ON THE NEXT
DAY WE CAME TO MILETUS. (16) FOR PAUL HAD
DECIDED TO SAIL PAST EPHESUS, TO AVOID SPENDING
TIME IN ASIA;[1] FOR HE WAS HASTENING, IF IT WERE
POSSIBLE FOR HIM, TO BE AT JERUSALEM THE DAY OF
PENTECOST. (17) AND FROM MILETUS HE SENT TO
EPHESUS, AND SUMMONED THE ELDERS OF THE
CHURCH. (18) AND WHEN THEY WERE COME TO HIM,
HE SAID UNTO THEM. . . . (36) AND WHEN HE HAD
THUS SPOKEN, HE KNEELED DOWN WITH THEM ALL, AND
PRAYED. (37) AND THEY ALL WEPT SORE, AND FELL
ON PAUL'S NECK, AND KISSED HIM, SORROWING MOST
OF ALL FOR THE WORD WHICH HE HAD SPOKEN, THAT
THEY WILL BEHOLD HIS FACE NO MORE. (38) AND
THEY BROUGHT HIM ON HIS WAY UNTO THE SHIP.
(XXI 1) AND WHEN IT CAME TO PASS THAT WE,
TEARING OURSELVES FROM THEM, SET SAIL, WE MADE
A STRAIGHT RUN TO COS, AND THE NEXT DAY TO
RHODES, AND FROM THENCE TO PATARA [*and Myra*].
(2) AND, FINDING A SHIP GOING OVER SEA TO PHŒNICE,
WE WENT ON BOARD AND SET SAIL. (3) AND, HAVING
SIGHTED CYPRUS, LEAVING IT ON OUR LEFT, WE SAILED
UNTO SYRIA, AND LANDED AT TYRE ; FOR THERE THE
SHIP WAS TO UNLADE. (4) AND HAVING FOUND THE
DISCIPLES, WE TARRIED THERE SEVEN DAYS ; AND
THESE SAID THROUGH THE SPIRIT TO PAUL NOT

[1] Literally, " that it might not come to pass that he spent time
in Asia ".

TO SET FOOT IN JERUSALEM. (5) AND WHEN IT CAME
TO PASS THAT WE HAD FINISHED OUR TIME, WE
DEPARTED AND WENT ON OUR JOURNEY ; AND THEY
ALL, WITH WIVES AND CHILDREN, BROUGHT US ON
OUR WAY TILL WE WERE OUT OF THE CITY. AND
KNEELING DOWN ON THE BEACH, WE PRAYED, (6)
AND BADE EACH OTHER FAREWELL ; AND WE WENT
ON BOARD SHIP, BUT THEY RETURNED HOME AGAIN.
(7) AND FINISHING THE *short* RUN FROM TYRE,
WE REACHED PTOLEMAIS ; AND WE SALUTED THE
BRETHREN AND ABODE WITH THEM ONE DAY.

The ship evidently stopped every evening. The
reason lies in the wind, which in the Ægean during
the summer generally blows from the north, beginning
at a very early hour in the morning ; in the late afternoon
it dies away ; at sunset there is a dead calm, and thereafter a gentle south wind arises and blows during the
night. The start would be made before sunrise ; and
it would be necessary for all passengers to go on board
soon after midnight in order to be ready to sail with
the first breath from the north.

In *v.* 14 our translation (agreeing with Blass) assumes
that the reading συνέβαλεν is correct ; but the great
MSS. read συνέβαλλεν, and perhaps the imperfect may
be used, implying that Paul did not actually enter
Assos, but was descried and taken in by boat as he
was nearing the city. On Monday, April 25, they
reached Mitylene before the wind fell ; and on Tuesday
afternoon they stopped at a point opposite Chios
(probably near Cape Argennum). Hence on Wednesday
morning they ran straight across to the west point
of Samos, and thence kept in towards Miletus ; but

when the wind fell, they had not got beyond the promontory Trogyllia at the entrance to the gulf, and there, as the Bezan Text mentions, they spent the evening. Early on Thursday, April 28, they stood across the gulf (which is now in great part filled up by the silt of the river Mæander) to Miletus. Here they found that they could reckon on a stay of some days, and Paul sent a messenger to Ephesus. The messenger could not reach Ephesus that day, for the land road round the gulf made a vast circuit, and the wind would prevent him from sailing across to Priene in the forenoon. Moreover, it would take some time to land, and to engage a messenger. In the early afternoon there would arise a sea-breeze blowing up the gulf (called in modern times *Imbat*, ἐμβάτης), which would permit the messenger to sail to the north side of the gulf. He would probably land at Priene, cross the hills, and thereafter take the coast road to Ephesus, which he might reach during the night. Some time would be required to summon the presbyters ; and they could not travel so fast as a single chosen messenger. They would show good speed if they reached Priene in the evening and were ready to sail to Miletus with the morning wind. The third day of Paul's stay at Miletus, then, was devoted to the presbyters ; and we cannot suppose that the ship left Miletus before Sunday morning, May 1, while it is possible that the start took place a day later.

On that day they reached Cos, on May 2 Rhodes, May 3 Patara, May 4 Myra, and, probably, May 7 Tyre.

In Tyre they stayed seven days, and sailed on May

13 for Ptolemais, where they spent the day, and on May 14 they reached Cæsareia. As Pentecost was on May 28, they had still a considerable time before them. If Paul remained several days in Cæsareia, then, the reason must be that there was still plenty of time to do so without endangering his purpose.

We reach the same conclusion from observing the author's concise style. After stating the object of the journey in *v.* 16, he leaves the reader to gather from his silence that the object was attained. The fact was clear in his own mind, and he was content with one single incidental allusion to it, not for its own sake (he as a Greek felt little interest in Jewish festivals), but to explain a point in which he was interested, *viz.*, the sailing past Ephesus without touching there.

The statement in *v.* 16 has led to a common misconception that Paul was sailing in a vessel chartered by himself, whose stoppages he could control as he pleased. But if Paul had been able to fix where the vessel should stop, it was obviously a serious waste of time to go to Miletus and summon the Ephesian elders thither ; the shorter way would have been to stop at Ephesus and there make his farewell address. Clearly the delay of three days at Miletus was forced on him by the ship's course, and the facts of the journey were these. From Neapolis they sailed in a ship bound for Troas. Here they had to transship ; and some delay was experienced in finding a suitable passage. Paul would not voluntarily have spent seven days at Troas : the length of a coasting voyage was too uncertain for him to waste so many days at the beginning, when he was hastening to Jerusalem. After a week, two chances presented themselves : one ship intended to make no break on its voyage, except at Miletus, the other to stop at Ephesus. The latter ship was, for some reason, the slower ; either it was not to sail further south than Ephesus (in which case time might be lost there in finding a passage) ; or it was a slow ship, that intended to stop in several other harbours. The shortness of the time determined Paul to choose the ship that went straight to Miletus, and " to sail past Ephesus " ; and the pointed statement proves that the question had been discussed, and doubtless the Ephesian delegates begged a visit to their city.

To Luke the interest of Pentecost lay not in itself, but in its furnishing the reason why Paul did not go to Ephesus.   There, as in so many other touches, we see the Greek, to whom the Jews were little more than " Barbaroi ".

We notice that Paul, having been disappointed in his first intention of spending Passover at Jerusalam, was eager at any rate to celebrate Pentecost there.   For the purpose which he had at heart, the formation of a perfect unity between the Jewish and the non-Jewish sections of the Church, it was important to be in Jerusalem to show his respect for one of the great feasts.

Modern discussion of the voyage to Cæsareia illus- trates the unnecessary obscurity in which a remarkably accurate narrative has been involved by over-subtlety, want of experience of rough-and-ready travel, and in- attention to the peculiar method of Luke as a narrator. As we have seen, only two numbers are at all doubtful : the length of the stay at Miletus, and the duration of the over-sea voyage to Tyre ; but in each case a day more or less is the utmost permissible variation. We find that Paul had fully thirteen days to spare when he reached Cæsareia. Yet many excellent scholars have got so far astray in this simple reckoning of days as to maintain that Paul was too late. Even Weiss, in his edition (in many respects excellent), so lately as 1893, concludes that already in Tyre Paul found that it was impossible to reach Jerusalem in time. Yet, at a pinch, the journey from Tyre to Jerusalem could have been performed in four days.

The farewell speech to the Ephesians, simple, pathetic, and characteristic of Paul as it is, contains little that concerns our special purpose. Paul intimates clearly that this is his farewell before entering on his enterprise in the West : " Ye all shall no longer see my face ". With a characteristic gesture he shows his hands : " *these* hands ministered unto my necessities ".

Incidentally we notice the ancient custom of reckoning time : the residence in Asia, which can hardly have been more than two years six months at the most, is estimated loosely as " three years ".

The clinging affection which is expressed in the farewell scene, and in the " tearing ourselves away " of XXI 1, makes a very pathetic picture.

Myra is mentioned on this voyage in the Bezan Text, and there can be no doubt that the ship on which the company was embarked either entered the harbour of Myra, or, at least, went close to it before striking across the open sea west of Cyprus to the Syrian coast. The voyage may be taken as typical of the course which hundreds of ships took every year, along a route familiar from time immemorial. It had been a specially frequented route since the age of the earlier Seleucid and Ptolemaic kings, when, as Canon Hicks remarks, "there must have been daily communication between Cos and Alexandria".[1]

The harbour of Myra seems to have been the great port for the direct cross-sea traffic to the coasts of Syria and Egypt. It was the seat of the sailors' god, to whom they offered their prayers before starting on the direct long course, and paid their vows on their safe arrival ; this god survived in the Christianised form, St. Nicholas of Myra, the patron-saint of sailors, who held the same position in the maritime world of the Levant as St. Phokas of Sinope did in that of the Black Sea (where he was the Christianised form of Achilles Pontarches, the Ruler of the Pontos).

Myra is termed by the pilgrim Sæwulf (as I learn from Dr. Tomaschek) "the harbour of the Adriatic Sea, as Constantinople is of the Ægean Sea"; and this importance is hardly intelligible till we recognise its relation to the Syrian and Egyptian traffic. The prevailing winds in the Levant throughout the season are westerly ; and these westerly breezes blow almost with the steadiness of trade-winds. Hence the ancient ships, even though they rarely made what sailors call " a long leg " across the sea, were in the habit of running direct from Myra to the Syrian, or to the Egyptian coast. On the return voyage an Alexandrian ship could run north to Myra, if the wind was nearly due west ; but, if it shifted towards north-west (from

[1] Paton and Hicks' *Inscriptions of Cos*, p. xxxiii. I should hardly venture to speak so strongly ; but Mr. Hicks is an excellent authority on that period.

which quarter the Etesian winds blew steadily for forty days from July 20), the ships of Alexandria ran for the Syrian coast. The same steady winds, which favoured the run from Myra to Tyre, made the return voyage direct from Tyre to Myra an impossibility. Hence the regular course for ships from Syria was to keep northwards past the east end of Cyprus till they reached the coast of Asia Minor ; and then, by using the land winds which blow off the coast for some part of almost every day, and aided also to some extent by the current which sets steadily westward along the Karamanian coast (as it is now called), these traders from Syria worked their way along past Myra to Cnidos at the extreme south-western corner of Asia Minor.

It may, then, be safely assumed that Myra was visited by Paul's ship, as the Bezan Text asserts. But the addition of " and Myra " is a mere gloss (though recording a true fact), for it implies that the transshipment took place at Myra. We need not hesitate to accept the authority of the great MSS. that Paul and his company found at Patara a ship about to start on the direct Syrian course, and went on board of it (probably because their ship did not intend to make the direct voyage, or was a slower vessel). Luke then hurries over the direct voyage, mentioning only the fact which specially interested him, that they sighted the western point of Cyprus. He did not mention Myra ; he was giving only a brief summary of the voyage, and for some reason the visit to Myra did not interest him.

Many circumstances might occur to deprive the visit of interest and to make Luke omit it (as he omits many other sights) from his brief summary of the voyage. Formerly I illustrated this by my own experience. I was in the port of Myra in the course of a voyage; yet I never saw either the town or the harbour, and would probably omit Myra, if I were giving a summary description of my experiences on that voyage.

At Tyre the vessel stayed seven days unloading; it must therefore have been one of the larger class of merchant vessels; and probably only that class ventured to make the direct sea voyage from Lycia by the west side of Cyprus. Small vessels clung to the coast. As the same ship[1] was going on as far as Ptolemais, and as there was still abundant time for the rest of the journey, Paul remained until the allotted time of its stay was over, *v*. 5. None of the party seems to have known Tyre, for they had to seek out the Brethren there. The hearty welcome which they received from strangers, whose sole bond of union lay in their common religion, makes Luke dwell on this scene as showing the solidarity of feeling in the Church. There took place a kindly farewell on the shore at Tyre, as at Miletus; but the longing and sorrow of long personal friendship and love could not here be present to the same extent as there. The scenes are similar, and yet how different! Such touches of diversity amid resemblance could be given only by the eye-witness.

The ship completed the short voyage to Ptolemais early; and the party spent the day with the Brethren; and went on to Cæsareia next day. Probably they went in the same ship. The emphasis laid on "finishing the voyage" from Tyre to Ptolemais is due to the fact that it was probably over about 10 A.M.

---

[1] In *v*. 2 "a ship," in *v*. 6 "the ship".

6. C Æ S A R E I A   A N D   J E R U S A L E M.   (XXI 8) ON
THE MORROW WE DEPARTED, AND CAME INTO CÆS-
AREIA. AND, ENTERING INTO THE HOUSE OF PHILIP
THE EVANGELIST, WHO WAS ONE OF THE SEVEN, WE
ABODE WITH HIM. (9) NOW THIS MAN HAD FOUR
DAUGHTERS, VIRGINS, WHICH DID PROPHESY. (10)
AND, AS WE TARRIED THERE SOME[1] DAYS, THERE
CAME DOWN FROM JUDÆA A CERTAIN PROPHET NAMED
AGABUS. (11) AND COMING TO US AND TAKING PAUL'S
GIRDLE, HE BOUND HIS OWN FEET AND HANDS AND
SAID: "THUS SAITH THE HOLY SPIRIT, 'SO SHALL THE
JEWS BIND AT JERUSALEM THE MAN THAT OWNETH
THIS GIRDLE, AND DELIVER HIM INTO THE HANDS OF
THE GENTILES' ' . . . . (15) AND AFTER THESE
DAYS, WE, HAVING EQUIPPED *horses*, PROCEEDED ON
OUR WAY TO JERUSALEM. (16) AND THERE WENT
WITH US ALSO *some* OF THE DISCIPLES FROM CÆSAREIA,

CONDUCTING US TO *the house* OF ONE MNASON, AN EARLY DISCIPLE, WHERE WE SHOULD FIND ENTERTAINMENT. (17) AND WHEN WE ARRIVED AT JERUSALEM, THE BRETHREN RECEIVED US GLADLY.

and these conducted us where we should find entertainment; and, reaching a certain village, we were in the house of Mnason, an early disciple; and going out thence we came to Jerusalem, and the Brethren received us gladly.

The length of the stay at Cæsareia is concealed, with
Luke's usual defective sense of time, by the vague
phrase, *v.* 10, ἡμέρας πλείους. The sense of this expression varies greatly according to the situation (cp.
XXIV 17, with XIII 31, XXVII 20); but here it is
not likely to be less than nine or ten.

---

[1] Literally, "more days," a considerable number of days.

The party was therefore cutting down the time for the journey to the utmost. Evidently they desired to remain as long as possible with the Brethren ; and the plan for the journey was arranged for them, so that with Cæsareian guidance and help it could be done with comfort and certainty when time necessitated departure. Now, it is an elementary principle of prudent living in Southern countries that one should avoid those great exertions and strains which in Northern countries we often take as an amusement. The customs of the modern peoples (whom we on superficial knowledge are apt to think lazy, but who are not so) show that this principle guides their whole life ; and it may be taken as certain that in ancient time the same principle was followed. Moreover, Paul was accompanied by his physician, who fully understood the importance of this rule, and knew that Paul, subject as he was to attacks of illness, and constantly exposed to great mental and emotional strains, *must* not begin his work in Jerusalem by a hurried walk of sixty-four miles from Cæsareia, more especially as it is clear from a comparison of the Bezan with the Accepted Text that the journey was performed in two days. We conclude, then, that the journey was not performed on foot ; and when we look at the words with this thought in our minds we find there the verb which means in classical Greek, "to equip or saddle a horse". Chrysostom took the word in that sense ;[1] but the modern commentators have scorned or misunderstood him.

Some of the Brethren from Cæsareia accompanied them as far as a village on the road, where they stayed

---

[1] He says λαβόντες τὰ πρὸς τὴν ὁδοιπορίαν (*i.e.*, ὑποζύγια).

for a night with Mnason of Cyprus, one of the earliest Christian converts. The next day the Brethren returned with the conveyances to Cæsareia, while Paul and his company performed the rest of the journey (which was probably not far) on foot. Time had passed rapidly, when a convert of A.D 30 or 31 was "ancient" in 57 ; but the immense changes that had occurred made the Church of 30 seem divided by a great gulf from these Macedonian and Asian delegates as they approached Jerusalem.

7. THE CRISIS IN THE FATE OF PAUL AND OF THE CHURCH. From the moment when Paul was arrested onwards, the narrative becomes much fuller than before. It still continues true to the old method of concentrating the reader's attention on certain selected scenes, which are described in considerable detail, while the intervening periods are dismissed very briefly. Thus XXI 17-XXIV 23 describes the events of twelve days, XXIV 24-27 of two years, XXV 1-XXVIII 7 of about five months, XXVIII 8-11 of three months. But the scenes selected for special treatment lie closer together than formerly ; and it is beyond doubt that, on our hypothesis, the amount of space assigned to Paul's imprisonment and successive examinations marks this as the most important part of the book in the author's estimation. If that is not the case—if the large space devoted to this period is not deliberately intended by the author as proportionate to its importance— then the work lacks one of the prime qualities of a great history. It is essential to our purpose to establish that we are now approaching the real climax, and that what has hitherto been narrated leads up to the great

event of the whole work. If we fail in that, we fail in the main object for which we are contending ; and we should have to allow that *Acts* is a collection of episodic jottings, and not a real history in the true sense of the word.

It must strike every careful reader that Luke devotes special attention throughout his work to the occasions on which Paul was brought in contact with Roman officials. Generally on these occasions, the relations between the parties end in a friendly way : the scene with the proconsul of Cyprus is the most marked case ; but Gallio, too, dismissed the case against him, and the formal decision of a proconsul had such weight as a precedent that the trial practically resulted in a declaration of religious liberty for the province.

To come to subordinate Roman officials, the " Prætors " of the colony Philippi, though treating him severely at first, ended by formally apologising and acknowledging his rights, and only begged of him as a favour to move on—a request which he instantly granted. In the colonies Antioch and Lystra he was treated severely, but the blame is laid entirely on the Jews, and the magistrates are not directly mentioned ; while in both cases it is brought out in the narrative that condemnation was not pronounced on fair charges duly proved. But though the reader's attention is not drawn to the magistrates, there can be no doubt that, at least in Antioch, the magistrates took action against Paul ; and there is some probability that in each place he was scourged by lictors (p. 107), though these and many other sufferings are passed over. In the first stages of his work in Asia Minor, he was in collision with Roman colonial officials ;

but these events are treated lightly, explained as due to error and extraneous influence, and the Roman character of the cities is not brought out. While the picture is not discoloured, yet the selection of details is distinctly guided by a plan.

The clerk (*Grammateus*) of the city of Ephesus was not a Roman official, but, as the most important officer of the capital of the province, he was in closer relations with the Roman policy than ordinary city magistrates : and he pointedly acquitted Paul of any treasonable design against the State or against the established order of the city, and challenged the rioters to bring any charge against Paul before the Roman Courts. The Asiarchs, who were officials of the province, and therefore part of the Roman political system, were his friends, and showed special care to secure his safety at that time. Even the jailor at Philippi was an officer of Rome, though a very humble one ; and he found Paul a friend in need, and became a friend in turn.

The magistrates of ordinary Greek cities were not so favourable to Paul as the Roman officials are represented. At Iconium they took active part against him ; and the silence about the magistrates of the colonies Antioch and Lystra is made more marked by the mention of those of Iconium. At Thessalonica the magistrates excluded him from the city as a cause of disorder. At Athens the Areopagus was contemptuous and undecided. The favourable disposition of Roman officials towards Paul is made more prominent by the different disposition of the ordinary municipal authorities.

These facts acquire more meaning and more definite relation to the historian's purpose when we come to the last scenes of the book. We cannot but recognise how pointedly the Imperial officials are represented as Paul's only safeguard from the Jews, and how their friendly disposition to him is emphasised. Even Felix, one of the worst of Roman officials, is affected by Paul's teaching, and on the whole protects Paul, though his sordid motives are not concealed, and he finally left Paul bound, as " desiring to gain favour with the Jews," XXIV 27 ; but at least there was no official action on the part of Felix against him. Festus, his successor, is described as just and fair towards Paul; he found in him "nothing worthy of death," and had difficulty in discovering any definite charge against him that he could report when sending him for trial before the supreme court of the Empire. The inferior officials, from the tribune Claudius Lysias, to the centurion Julius, are represented as very friendly. This is all the more marked, because nothing is said at any stage of the proceedings of kindness shown to Paul by any others ; yet no one can doubt that the household of Philip and the general body of Christians in Cæsareia tried to do everything possible for him. We see then that the historian, out of much that might be recorded, selects for emphasis the friendliness of the Roman officials : in the climax of his subject he concentrates the reader's attention on the conduct of Romans to Paul,[1] and on their repeated statements that Paul was innocent in the eyes of Roman Imperial law and policy.

Throughout the whole book, from the time when the centurion Cornelius is introduced, great art is shown in

---

[1] Luke says nothing about kindness shown to Paul by James and others in Jerusalem; but we do not (like Dean Farrar) gather that they were unfriendly

bringing out without any formal statement the friendly relations between the Romans and the new teaching, even before Paul became the leading spirit in its development. To a certain extent, of course, that lies in the subject matter, and the historian simply relates the facts as they occurred, without colouring them for his purpose ; but he is responsible for the selection of details, and while he has omitted an enormous mass of details (some of which we can gather from other informants), he has included so many bearing on this point, as to show beyond all question his keen interest in it.

Further, when we compare Luke with other authorities in their treatment of the same subject, we see how much more careful he is than they in bringing out the relations in which Christianity stood to the Imperial government. In the Third Gospel, Luke alone among the four historians records formally the attempt made by the Jews to implicate Jesus in criminal practices against the Roman Empire, [1] and the emphatic, thrice [2] repeated statement of Pilate acquitting Him of all fault (XXIII 2, 4, 14, 22) before the law.

We must conclude, then, that the large space devoted to the trial of Paul in its various stages before the Roman Imperial tribunals is connected with a strongly marked interest and a clear purpose running through the two books of this history ; and it follows that Luke conceived the trial to be a critical and supremely important stage in the development of the Church.

The next question that faces us is whether Luke is justified as a historian in attaching such importance to this stage in the development of Christianity. Perhaps

[1] Less formally, *John* XVIII 30.   [2] *John* XVIII 38 ; *Matth.* XXVII 24.

the question may be best answered by quoting some words used in a different connection and for a different purpose. "It is both justifiable and necessary to lay great stress on the trial of Paul. With the legal constructiveness and obedience to precedent that characterised the Romans, this case tried before the supreme court must have been regarded as a test case and a binding precedent, until some act of the supreme Imperial authority occurred to override it. If such a case came for trial before the highest tribunal in Rome, there must have been given an authoritative and, for the time, final judgment on the issues involved."

But, further, it is obvious that the importance of the trial for Luke is intelligible only if Paul was acquitted. That he was acquitted follows from the Pastoral Epistles with certainty for all who admit their genuineness ; while even they who deny their Pauline origin must allow that they imply an early belief in historical details which are not consistent with Paul's journeys before his trial, and must either be pure inventions or events that occurred on later journeys. I have elsewhere argued that the subsequent policy of Nero towards the Church is far more readily intelligible if Paul was acquitted. But, if he was acquitted, the issue of the trial was a formal decision by the supreme court of the Empire that it was permissible to preach Christianity : the trial, therefore, was really a charter of religious liberty, and therein lies its immense importance. It was, indeed, overturned by later decisions of the supreme court ; but its existence was a highly important fact for the Christians.

The importance of the preliminary stages of the

trial lies in its issue ; and it is obviously absurd to relate these at great length, and wholly omit the final result which gives them intelligibility and purpose. It therefore follows that a sequel was contemplated by the author, in which should be related the final stages of the trial, the acquittal of Paul, the active use which he made of his permission to preach, the organisation of the Church in new provinces, and the second trial occurring at the worst and most detested period of Nero's rule. That sequel demands a book to itself; and we have seen that the natural implication of Luke's expression in *Acts* I 1, *if he wrote as correct Greek as Paul wrote*, is that his work was planned to contain, a least, three books.

This view of Luke's historical plan suits well the period at which he wrote. It is argued in Ch. XVII § 2 that he was engaged in composing this book under Domitian, a period of persecution, when Christians had come to be treated as outlaws or brigands, and the mere confession of the name was recognised as a capital offence. The book was not an apology for Christianity : it was an appeal to the truth of history against the immoral and ruinous policy of the reigning Emperor ; a temperate and solemn record, by one who had played a great part in them, of the real facts regarding the formation of the Church, its steady and unswerving loyalty in the past, its firm resolve to accept the facts of Imperial government, its friendly reception by many Romans, and its triumphant vindication in the first great trial at Rome. It was the work of one who had been trained by Paul to look forward to Christianity becoming the religion of the Empire and of the world

who regarded Christianity as destined not to destroy
but to save the Empire.

8. FINANCES OF THE TRIAL. It has been asked
where Paul got the money which he required to pay
the expenses of four poor men (XXI 23), purifying
themselves in the temple ; and the suggestion has been
made that the elders who advised him to undertake
this expense, followed up their advice by giving him
back some of the money which the delegates from the
four provinces had just paid over to them. Without
laying any stress on the silence of Luke as to any
such action, we cannot believe that Paul would accept that
money for his own needs, or that James would offer it.
They were trustees of contributions destined for a
special purpose ; and to turn it to any other purpose
would have been fraudulent. It is incredible that Paul,
after laying such stress on the purpose of that contribution, and planning it for years (p. 288), should divert
part of it to his own use the day after he reached
Jerusalem.

But several other facts show clearly that, during the
following four years, Paul had considerable command
of money. Imprisonment and a long lawsuit are
expensive. Now, it is clear that Paul during the following four years did not appear before the world as a
penniless wanderer, living by the work of his hands.
A person in that position will not either at the present
day or in the first century be treated with such marked
respect as was certainly paid to Paul, at Cæsareia, on
the voyage, and in Rome. The governor Felix and
his wife, the Princess Drusilla, accorded him an interview and private conversation. King Agrippa and his

Queen Berenice also desired to see him. A poor man never receives such attentions, or rouses such interest. Moreover, Felix hoped for a bribe from him ; and a rich Roman official did not look for a small gift. Paul, therefore, wore the outward appearance of a man of means, like one in a position to bribe a Roman procurator. The minimum in the way of personal attendants that was allowable for a man of respectable position was two slaves ; and, as we shall see, Paul was believed to be attended by two slaves to serve him. At Cæsareia he was confined in the palace of Herod ; but he had to live, to maintain two attendants, and to keep up a respectable appearance. Many comforts, which are almost necessities, would be given by the guards, so long as they were kept in good humour, and it is expensive to keep guards in good humour. In Rome he was able to hire a lodging for himself and to live there, maintaining, of course, the soldier who guarded him.

An appeal to the supreme court could not be made by everybody that chose. Such an appeal had to be permitted and sent forward by the provincial governor ; and only a serious case would be entertained. But the case of a very poor man is never esteemed as serious ; and there is little doubt that the citizen's right of appeal to the Emperor was hedged in by fees and pledges. There is always one law for the rich man and another for the poor : at least, to this extent, that many claims can be successfully pushed by a rich man in which a poor man would have no chance of success. In appealing to the Emperor, Paul was choosing undoubtedly an expensive line of trial. All this had certainly been estimated before the decisive step was

taken. Paul had weighed the cost; he had reckoned
the gain which would accrue to the Church if the
supreme court pronounced in his favour; and his past
experience gave him every reason to hope for a
favourable issue before a purely Roman tribunal, where
Jewish influence would have little or no power. The
importance of the case, as described in the preceding
section, makes the appeal more intelligible.

Where, then, was the money procured? Was it from
new contributions collected in the Churches? That
seems most improbable, both from their general poverty,
from Paul's personal character, and from the silence of
Luke on the point. Luke himself was probably a man
dependent on his profession for his livelihood. His
name is not that of a man of high position. There
seems no alternative except that Paul's hereditary
property was used in those four years. As to the exact
facts, we must remain in ignorance. If Paul hitherto
voluntarily abstained from using his fortune, he now
found himself justified by the importance of the case
in acting differently. If, on the other hand, he had for
the time been disowned by his family, then either a
reconciliation had been brought about during his danger
(perhaps originating in the bold kindness of his young
nephew), or through death property had come to him as
legal heir (whose right could not be interfered with by
any will). But, whatever be the precise facts, we must
regard Paul as a man of some wealth during these years.

He appeared to Felix and to Festus, then, as a
Roman of Jewish origin of high rank and great learning,
engaged in a rather foolish controversy against the whole
united power of his nation (which showed his high

standing, as well as his want of good judgment). That is the spirit of Festus's words, " Paul ! Paul ! you are a great philosopher, but you have no common sense ".

On the details given of the incidents in Jerusalem and Cæsareia, I shall not enter. I am not at home on the soil of Palestine ; and it seems better not to mix up second-hand studies with a discussion of incidents where I stand on familiar ground.

Note. Procuratorship of Felix. The remarkable contradiction between Josephus (who makes Cumanus governor of Palestine 48-52, Felix being his successor in 52), and Tacitus (who makes Felix governor of Samaria [and probably of Judæa], contemporary with Cumanus as governor of Galilee, the latter being disgraced in 52, and the former acquitted and honoured at the same trial), is resolved by Mommsen in favour of Tacitus as the better authority on such a point ; and most students of Roman history will agree with him.

CHAPTER XIV

THE VOYAGE TO ROME

IN describing the voyage from Cæsareia to Malta, we are guided by the excellent work of James Smith, *Voyage and Shipwreck of St. Paul* (third edition, 1866); but as there are some points of interest which he has not explained satisfactorily, we shall briefly describe the voyage, and treat more elaborately such points as need to be added to Smith's results.

1. C Æ S A R E I A   T O   M Y R A. A convoy of prisoners was starting for Rome under charge of a centurion of the Augustan cohort, and a detachment of soldiers ; and Paul was sent along with it. He, of course, occupied a very different position from the other prisoners. He was a man of distinction, a Roman citizen who had appealed for trial to the supreme court in Rome. The others had been in all probability already condemned to death, and were going to supply the perpetual demand which Rome made on the provinces for human victims to amuse the populace by their death in the arena.

The cohorts of the Roman legions never bore surnames, and it would therefore seem that this "Augustan cohort" was one of the auxiliary cohorts, which had regularly one or more surnames. But the duty which is here performed by the centurion was never performed

(314)

by an auxiliary officer, but only by an officer of a legion. It would therefore appear that an auxiliary officer is here represented in a position which he could not hold.

But, when we recollect (1) that Luke regularly uses the terms of educated conversation, not the strict technical names, and (2) that he was a Greek who was careless of Roman forms or names, we shall not seek in this case to treat the Greek term ($\sigma\pi\epsilon\hat{\iota}\rho\alpha$ $\Sigma\epsilon\beta\alpha\sigma\tau\acute{\eta}$) as a translation of a correct Roman name; but we shall look for a body in the Roman service which was likely to be called "the troop of the Emperor" by the persons in whose society Luke moved at the time. We give the answer to which Mommsen seems to incline *Berlin Akad. Sitzungsber*, 1895, p. 501, adding the evidence of Luke's style, but otherwise quoting Mommsen. First we ask what officer would be likely to perform the duty here assigned to Julius. It would naturally be a legionary centurion on detached service for communication between the Emperor and his armies in the provinces (as described on p. 348). That the centurion whom Luke alludes to was one of this body is confirmed by the fact that, when he reached Rome, he handed Paul over to his chief. We conclude, then, that the "troop of the Emperor" was a popular colloquial way of describing the corps of officer-couriers; and we thus gather from *Acts* an interesting fact, elsewhere unattested but in perfect conformity with the known facts.

Luke uses the first person throughout the following narrative; and he was therefore in Paul's company. But how was this permitted? It is hardly possible to suppose that the prisoner's friends were allowed to accompany him. Pliny mentions a case in point (*Epist.* III 16). Paetus was brought a prisoner from Illyricum to Rome, and his wife Arria vainly begged leave to accompany him ; several slaves were permitted to go with him as waiters, valets, etc., and Arria offered herself alone to perform all their duties ; but her prayer was refused. The analogy shows how Luke and Aristarchus accompanied Paul : they must have gone as his slaves, not merely performing the duties of slaves (as Arria offered to do), but actually passing as slaves. In this way not merely had Paul faithful friends always beside him ; his importance in the eyes of the centurion was much enhanced, and that was of great importance. The narrative clearly implies that Paul enjoyed much respect during this voyage, such as a penniless traveller without a servant to attend on him would never receive either in the first century or the nineteenth.

In the harbour of Cæsareia there was no convenient ship about to sail for Rome ; and the convoy was put on board of an Adramyttian ship which was going to make a voyage along the coast towns of the province Asia. Communication direct with Rome might be found in some of the great Asian harbours, or, failing any suitable ship in the late season, the prisoners might be taken (like Ignatius half a century later) by Troas and Philippi and the land road to Dyrrachium, and thence to Brundisium and Rome.

The direct run from Lycia to the Syrian coast was often made, but it is hardly possible that a direct run from Syria back to Myra was ever attempted by ancient ships. They never ventured on such a run except when a steady wind was blowing which could be trusted to

last. But westerly breezes blow with great steadiness
through the summer months in the Levant; and it is
certain that ancient ships westward bound sailed east
of Cyprus, as the Adramyttian ship now did. Luke
explains why they sailed on this side of Cyprus; and
he must, therefore, have expected to take the other
side. Now, a sailor or a person accustomed to these
seas would not have thought of making any explanation, for the course of the ship was the normal one.
But Luke had come to Sidon from Myra by the west
side of Cyprus, and he, therefore, was impressed with
the difference, and (contrary to his usual custom) he
gives a formal explanation; and his explanation stamps
him as a stranger to these seas.

The ship worked slowly along the Cilician and Pamphylian coast, as the sailors availed themselves of
temporary local land breezes and of the steady westward current that runs along the coast. The description
given in the *Periodoi of Barnabas* of a voyage from
Seleuceia in Syria to Cyprus in the face of a prevailing
steady westerly wind, the work of a person familiar with
the circumstances, illustrates perfectly the voyage on this
occasion. The Adramyttian ship crept on from point to
point up the coast, taking advantage of every opportunity to make a few miles, and lying at anchor in the
shelter of the winding coast, when the westerly wind
made progress impossible.

Smith in his masterly work collects several other
examples of the same course which was adopted by
the Adramyttian ship. Modern sailing ships, even with
their superior rig, have several times been forced by
the steady westerly wind towards the north, keeping

east of Cyprus, and using the breezes which blow at intervals from the Caramanian coast.

In this description there is an addition made in the Later Syriac version and some other authorities, which Westcott and Hort put in the margin as one " which appears to have a reasonable probability of being the true reading ". The ship, in this addition, is said to have spent fifteen days in beating along the Cyprio-Pamphylian coast. This addition obviously suits the situation, and may be unhesitatingly accepted as true, whether as written by Luke or as a well-informed gloss. Most probably it is Lukan, for Luke gives rough statements of the time throughout this voyage ; and an exact estimate at this point is quite in his style. It perhaps dropped out of most MSS., as wanting interest for later generations.

If we may judge from the *Periodoi Barnabæ*, the coasting voyage was accomplished comparatively rapidly as far as Myra (see also p. 320).

In the harbour of Myra, the centurion found an Alexandrian ship on a voyage towards Italy. He embarked his convoy on board of this ship. It is characteristic of the style of Luke that he does not mention the class of ship or the reason of its voyage from Alexandria to Italy ; but simply tells facts as they occur. Now, Egypt was one of the granaries of Rome ; and the corn trade between Egypt and Rome was of the first importance and of great magnitude. There is, therefore, a reasonable probability that this ship was carrying corn to Rome ; and this inference is confirmed by Luke himself, who mentions in *v.* 38 that the cargo was grain.

A ship-captain familiar with the Levant informed me that he had known ships going west from Egypt keep well to the north, in order to avail themselves of the shelter of the Cretan coast. No ancient ship would have ventured to keep so much out to sea as to run intentionally from Egypt to Crete direct, and moreover the winds would rarely have permitted it; but it is probable that this Alexandrian ship had sailed direct to Myra across the Levant. The steady westerly breezes which prevented ships from making the direct run from Sidon, were favourable for the direct run from Alexandria. Probably this course was a customary one during a certain season of the year from Alexandria to Italy. Any one who has the slightest knowledge of " the way of a ship in the sea," will recognise that, with a steady wind near west, this was the ideally best course; while if the breeze shifted a little towards the north, it would be forced into a Syrian port; and, as we know from other sources, that was often the case.

As we saw (p. 298), Myra was one of the great harbours of the Egyptian service. It is, therefore, unnecessary and incorrect to say, as is often done, that the Alexandrian ship had been blown out of its course. The ship was on its regular and ordinary course, and had quite probably been making a specially good run, for in the autumn there was always risk of the wind shifting round towards the north, and with the wind N.W. the Alexandrian ships could only fetch the Syrian coast.

A voyage which Lucian, in his dialogue *The Ship*, describes as made by a large Egyptian corn-ship, may be accepted as a fair description of what might occur in the first or second century; and it illustrates well the course

of both the Alexandrian and the Adramyttian ship.
Lucian's *Ship* attempted to run direct from Alexandria
to Myra. It was off the west point of Cyprus (Cape
Akamas) on the seventh day of its voyage, but was thence
blown to Sidon by a west wind so strong that the ship had
to run before it. On the tenth day from Sidon it was
caught in a storm at the Chelidonian islands and nearly
wrecked ; ten days from Sidon to the islands would
correspond to fully thirteen from Cæsareia to Myra.
Thereafter its course was very slow ; it failed to keep
the proper course to the south of Crete ; and at last it
reached Piræus on the seventieth day from Alexandria.

2. FROM MYRA TO FAIR HAVENS. (XXVII 7)
AND WHEN WE HAD SAILED SLOWLY MANY DAYS, AND
WERE COME WITH DIFFICULTY OFF CNIDOS, AS THE
WIND DID NOT PERMIT *our straight course* ONWARDS,
WE SAILED UNDER THE LEE OF CRETE, OFF *Cape*
SALMONE ; (8) AND COASTING ALONG IT WITH DIFFI-
CULTY, WE CAME UNTO A CERTAIN PLACE CALLED FAIR
HAVENS, NIGH TO WHICH WAS A CITY LASEA.

From Myra the course of both the Adramyttian
and the Alexandrian ship would coincide as far as
Cnidos. But they found great difficulty in making
the course, which implies that strong westerly winds
blew most of the time. After a very slow voyage
they came opposite Cnidos ; but they were not able
to run across to Cythera (a course that was sometimes attempted, if we can accept Lucian's dialogue
The Ship, as founded on possible facts) on account of
strong northerly winds blowing steadily in the Ægean,
and threatening to force any ship on the north coast of
Crete, which was dangerous from its paucity of harbours

Accordingly, the choice was open either to put in to Cnidos, and wait a fair wind, or to run for the east and south coast of Crete. The latter alternative was preferred in the advanced season ; and they rounded the eastern promontory, Salmone (protected by it from a north-westerly wind), and began anew to work slowly to the west under the shelter of the land. They kept their course along the shore with difficulty until they reached a place named Fair Havens, near the city Lasea, which, as Smith has shown conclusively, is the small bay, two leagues east of Cape Matala, still bearing the same name (in the modern Greek dialect $\Lambda\iota\mu\epsilon\hat{\omega}\nu\alpha\varsigma$ $K\alpha\lambda o\acute{v}\varsigma$) ; and there they lay for a considerable time. It is not stated in the narrative why they stayed so long at this point, but the reason is clear to a sailor or a yachtsman : as Smith points out, Fair Havens is the nearest shelter on the east of Cape Matala, whilst west of that cape the coast trends away to the north, and no longer affords any protection from the north or north-west winds, and therefore they could go no farther so long as the wind was in that quarter.

The voyage to Cnidos had been slow and hard, and the course along Crete was made with difficulty. At the best that part of the voyage must always have been troublesome, and as the difficulty was unusually great in this case, we cannot allow less time between Myra and Fair Havens than from September 1 to 25. The arrival at Fair Havens is fixed by the narrative ; and thus we get the approximate date, August 17, for the beginning of the voyage from Cæsareia.

3. THE COUNCIL. (XXVII 9) AND WHEN A LONG TIME ELAPSED, AND SAILING WAS NOW DANGEROUS (AS

THE FAST ALSO WAS ALREADY OVER), PAUL OFFERED HIS ADVICE (10) IN THESE WORDS: "SIRS, I PERCEIVE THAT THE VOYAGE IS LIKELY TO BE ACCOMPANIED WITH HARDSHIP AND MUCH LOSS, NOT MERELY TO SHIP AND CARGO, BUT ALSO TO OUR LIVES". (11) BUT THE CENTURION WAS INFLUENCED MORE BY THE SAILING-MASTER AND THE CAPTAIN THAN BY WHAT PAUL SAID. (12) AND, AS THE HAVEN WAS BADLY SITUATED FOR WINTERING IN, THE MAJORITY *of the council* APPROVED THE PLAN TO GET UNDER WEIGH FROM THENCE, AND ENDEAVOUR TO MAKE PHŒNIX AS A STATION TO WINTER IN—A HARBOUR THAT FACES SOUTH-WEST AND NORTH-WEST.

The groat Fast fell in 59 on Oct. 5, and, as Paul and Aristarchus observed the Fast, Luke uses it as an indication of date. The dangerous season for navigation lasted from Sept. 14 to Nov. 11, when all navigation on the open sea was discontinued. The ship reached Fair Havens in the latter part of September, and was detained there by a continuance of unfavourable winds until after Oct. 5. We might be disposed to infer that the Feast of Tabernacles, Oct. 10, fell after they left Fair Havens, otherwise Luke would have mentioned it rather than the Fast, as making the danger more apparent. The picturesque ceremonies of the Tabernacles would have remained in Luke's mind; but at sea they were not possible; and the Fast was therefore the fact that impressed him, as it was observed by Paul and Aristarchus.

In these circumstances a meeting was held to consider the situation, at which Paul was present, as a person of rank whose convenience was to some extent consulted, and whose experience as a traveller was known to be.

great. It is characteristic of Luke's style not to mention formally that a council was held. He goes straight to what was the important point in his estimation, *viz.*, Paul's advice ; then he explains why Paul's advice was not taken ; and in the explanation it comes out in what circumstances the advice was given. The whole scene forms, in point of narrative method, an exact parallel to the interview at Paphos (p. 75). We notice also that Luke as a mere servant could not have been present at the council, and depended on Paul's report ; and his account follows the order in which Paul would describe the proceedings. We can imagine that Paul on coming forth, did not formally relate to his two friends that the council met, that the chairman laid the business before it, and so on, but burst forth with his apprehension that " they had made a mistake in not taking the prudent course ".

At the council it is implied that the centurion was president, while the captain and sailing-master were merely advisers. To our modern ideas the captain is supreme on the deck of his ship ; and, even if he held a meeting to decide on such a point as the best harbour to lay up in, or consulted the wishes of a distinguished officer in the military service, yet the ultimate decision would lie with himself. Here the ultimate decision lies with the centurion, and he takes the advice of the captain. The centurion, therefore, is represented as the commanding officer, which implies that the ship was a Government ship, and the centurion ranked as the highest officer on board. That, doubtless, is true to the facts of the Roman service. The provisioning of the vast city of Rome, situated in a country where farming had ceased to pay owing to the ruinous foreign competition in grain, was the most serious and pressing department of the Imperial administration. Whatever else the Emperor might neglect, this he could not neglect and live. In the urban populace he was holding a wild beast by the ear ; and, if he did not feed it, the beast would tear him to pieces. With ancient means of transport, the task was a hundred times harder than it would be now ; and the service of ships on which Rome was entirely dependent was not left to private enterprise, but was a State department. It is, therefore, an error of the Authorised and Revised Versions to speak of the owner (ναύκληρος) of this Alexandrian ship :[1] the ship belonged to the Alexandrian fleet in the Imperial service. The captains of the fleet [2] made dedications on account of safe passage at Ostia, and Seneca sat in his house at Puteoli and watched the advance ships sail in announcing the approach of the Alexandrian fleet (*Ep. Mor.* 77). Passengers were landed at Puteoli ; but cargo was carried on to Ostia. As a general rule the ships sailed in fleets ; but, of course, incidental reasons often kept one ship apart (as we see in XXVIII 11, and in the opening of Lucian's dialogue *The Ship*).

Now, there was not in Rome that strict separation between the naval and the military services which now exists. There was only one service ; the same person

---

[1] The owners of private merchant ships are distinguished as ἔμποροι from the captains, in a Delian inscription, οἱ καταπλέοντες εἰς Βιθυνίαν ἔμποροι καὶ ναύκληροι, *Bulletin de Corresp. Hellen.* 1880, p. 222.

[2] οἱ ναύκληροι τοῦ πορευτικοῦ ᾽Αλεξανδρείνου στόλου, Kaibel, *Inscript. Græc. in Italia*, No. 918.

was at one moment admiral of a fleet, at another general of a land army and an officer might pass from one branch to the other. The land-service, however, ranked higher, and a legionary centurion was certainly of superior rank to the captain of a vessel of the Alexandrian fleet. In this case, then, the centurion sat as president of the council. Naturally, he would not interfere in navigation, for his life might pay the forfeit of any error, but the selection of a port for wintering in was more in his line. Now, it was the regular practice for all Roman officials, who often had to take responsibility in cases in which they were not competent alone to estimate all the facts, to summon a council (*consilium*) of experienced and competent advisers before coming to a decision. Such was the nature of the meeting here described.

The centurion, very properly, was guided in this matter, against the advice of Paul, by the opinion of his professional advisers, who were anxious to get on as far as possible before navigation ceased on November 11, and it was resolved to take any fair opportunity of reaching the harbour of Phœnix, which was not only further on, but also better protected.

In the council-scene, then, when we put events in their sequence in time, and add those facts of the situation which Luke assumes as familiar to his readers, we have a vivid and striking incident, agreeing with the general type of Roman procedure, and yet giving us information about life on board a Government transport such as we could not find in any other part of ancient literature.

There has been a good deal of discussion as to the

description of the harbour Phœnix, the modern Lutro, "the only secure harbour in all winds on the south coast of Crete". This, however, faces the east, not the west. Smith tries to interpret the Greek words in that sense; but it must be observed that Luke never saw the harbour, and merely speaks on Paul's report of the professional opinion. It is possible that the sailors described the entrance as one in which inward-bound ships looked towards N.W. and S.W., and that in transmission from mouth to mouth, the wrong impression was given that the harbour looked N.W. and S.W.

4. THE STORM. (XXVII 13) AND WHEN A MODERATE SOUTHERLY BREEZE AROSE, SUPPOSING THAT THEY HAD GOT THEIR OPPORTUNITY,[1] THEY WEIGHED ANCHOR AND SAILED ALONG THE CRETAN COAST CLOSE IN. (14) BUT AFTER NO LONG TIME THERE STRUCK DOWN FROM THE ISLAND A TYPHONIC WIND, WHICH GOES BY THE NAME EURAQUILO. (15) AND WHEN THE SHIP WAS CAUGHT BY IT, AND COULD NOT FACE THE WIND, WE GAVE WAY AND LET THE SHIP DRIVE. (16) AND, WHEN WE RAN UNDER THE LEE OF A SMALL ISLAND, CAUDA BY NAME, WE WERE ABLE WITH DIFFICULTY TO HAUL IN THE BOAT. (17) AND HAVING SECURED IT, THEY ATTEMPTED TO EASE THE SHIP BY UNDERGIRDING IT; AND BEING IN TERROR LEST THEY BE CAST ON "THE GREAT QUICKSANDS," THEY REDUCED SAIL, AND LET THE SHIP DRIFT IN THAT POSITION (*viz., laid-to under storm-sails*).

One morning, after the council, their chance came with a moderate south wind, which favoured their westerly voyage. At this point the writer says that they

---

[1] *Literally*, had got their purpose.

went close inshore ; and this emphatic statement, after they had been on a coasting voyage for weeks, must in a careful writer have some special force. Cape Matala projected well out to the south about six miles west of Fair Havens, and it needed all their sailing power to clear it on a straight course. From Luke's emphasis we gather that it was for some time doubtful whether they could weather the point ; and in the bright late autumn morning we can imagine every one gathered on the deck, watching the wind, the coast and the cape ahead. If the wind went round a point towards the west, they would fail ; and the anxious hour has left its record in the single word of *v.* 13 (ᾶσσον), while the inability of some scribes or editors to imagine the scene has left its record in the alteration (θᾶσσον).

After passing Cape Matala, they had before them a fair course with a favouring breeze across the broad opening of the Gulf of Messara. But before they had got halfway across the open bay,[1] there came a sudden change, such as is characteristic of that sea, where "southerly winds almost invariably shift to a violent northerly wind". There struck down from the Cretan mountains, which towered above them to the height of over 7000 feet, a sudden eddying squall from about east-north-east. Every one who has any experience of sailing on lakes or bays overhung by mountains will appreciate the epithet "typhonic," which Luke uses. As a ship-captain recently said to me in relating an anecdote of his own experience in the Cretan waters, "the wind comes down from those mountains fit to blow the ship out of the water ".

[1] Seventeen miles from shore to shore on their course, according to Smith.

An ancient ship with one huge sail was exposed to extreme danger from such a blast; the straining of the great sail on the single mast was more than the hull could bear; and the ship was exposed to a risk which modern vessels do not fear, foundering in the open sea. It appears that they were not able to slacken sail quickly; and, had the ship been kept up towards the wind, the strain would have shaken her to pieces. Even when they let the ship go, the leverage on her hull must have been tremendous, and would in a short time have sent her to the bottom. Paul, who had once already narrowly escaped from such a wreck, drifting on a spar or swimming for a night and a day (II *Cor.* XI 25), was justified in his advice at Fair Havens not to run the risk of coasting further in the dangerous season on a coast where such sudden squalls are a common feature. In this case the ship was saved by getting into calmer water under the shelter of an island, Cauda (now Gozzo), about twenty-three miles to leeward.

At this point Smith notices the precision of Luke's terminology. In *v.* 4 they *sailed under* the lee of Cyprus, keeping northwards with a westerly wind on the beam (ὑπεπλεύσαμεν); here they *ran before a wind under* the lee of Cauda (ὑποδραμόντες).

The sailors knew that their only hope was in the smoother water behind Cauda, and kept her up accordingly with her head to the wind, so that she would make no headway, but merely drifted with her right side towards the wind (" on the starboard tack ").

Here three distinct operations were performed; and it is noteworthy that Luke mentions first among them, not the one which was the most important or necessary, but the one in which he himself took part, *viz.*, hauling in the boat. In the light breeze it had been left to tow behind, and the squall had come down too suddenly to haul it in. While the other operations required skill, any one could haul on a rope, and Luke was pressed into the service. The boat was waterlogged by this time; and the historian notes feelingly what hard work it was to get it in, *v.* 16.

While this was going on, ropes were got out, and the ship undergirded to strengthen her against the storm and the straining of her timbers. The scholars who discuss nautical subjects seem all agreed that undergirders were put longitudinally round the ship (*i.e.*, horizontal girders passed round stem and stern). If any of them will show how it was possible to perform this operation during a storm, I shall be ready to accept their opinion; but meantime (without entering on the question what "undergirders," ὑποζώματα, were in Athenian triremes) I must with Smith believe that cables were passed underneath round the ship transversely to hold the timbers together. This is a possible operation in the circumstances, and a useful one.

Luke mentions last what a sailor would mention first, the most delicate and indispensable operation, *viz.*, leaving up just enough of sail to keep the ship's head to the wind, and bringing down everything else that could be got down. It is not certain that he fully understood this operation, but perhaps the Greek (χαλάσαντες τὸ σκεῦος) might be taken as a technical term denoting the entire series of operations, slackening sail, but leaving some spread for a special purpose.

This operation was intended to guard against the danger of being driven on the great quicksands of the African coast, the Syrtes. These were still far distant; but the sailors knew that at this late season the wind might last many days. The wind was blowing straight on the sands; and it was absolutely necessary, not merely to delay the ship's motion towards them, but to turn it in a different direction. In the Gulf of Messara, the wind had been an eddying blast under the mountains; but further out it was a steady, strong east-north-easterly gale.

Dragging stones or weights at the end of ropes from the stern, which is the meaning elicited by some German commentators and writers on nautical matters, might be useful in other circumstances; but how that meaning can be got from the Greek words (χαλάσαντες τὸ σκεῦος), I confess that I cannot see. Moreover, as we have said, what the sailors wished was not merely to delay their course towards the Syrtes, but to turn their course in another direction.

Accordingly, the ship drifted, with her head to the north, steadied by a low sail, making lee-way proportionate to the power of the wind and waves on her broadside. As Smith shows in detail, the resultant rate of motion would vary, according to the size of the ship and the force of the wind, between ¾ and 2 miles per hour; and the probable mean rate in this case would be about 1½ miles per hour; while the direction would approximate to 8° north of west. The ship would continue to drift in the same way as long as the wind blew the same, and the timbers and sails held; and at the calculated rates, if it was under Cauda towards evening, it would on the fourteenth night be near Malta.

5. DRIFTING. (XXVII 18) AND, AS WE LABOURED

EXCEEDINGLY WITH THE STORM, THE NEXT DAY THEY
BEGAN TO THROW THE FREIGHT OVERBOARD, (19) AND
ON THE THIRD DAY WE CAST OUT, WITH OUR OWN
HANDS ACTUALLY, THE SHIP'S FURNITURE. (20) AND AS
NEITHER SUN NOR STARS WERE VISIBLE FOR MANY DAYS,
AND A SEVERE STORM WAS PRESSING HARD ON US, ALL
HOPE THAT WE SHOULD BE SAVED WAS GRADUALLY
TAKEN AWAY. (21) AND WHEN THERE HAD BEEN LONG
ABSTINENCE FROM FOOD, THEN PAUL STOOD FORTH IN
THE MIDST OF THEM, AND SAID : " THE RIGHT COURSE,
GENTLEMEN, WAS TO HEARKEN TO ME, AND NOT TO SET
SAIL FROM CRETE AND INCUR THIS TROUBLE AND LOSS.
(22) AND MY ADVICE TO YOU IN THE PRESENT IS TO
TAKE HEART ; FOR LOSS OF LIFE THERE SHALL BE NONE
AMONG YOU, BUT OF THE SHIP. (23) FOR THERE STOOD
BY ME THIS NIGHT AN ANGEL OF THE GOD WHOSE I AM,
WHOM ALSO I SERVE, (24) SAYING : ' FEAR NOT, PAUL ;
THOU MUST STAND BEFORE CÆSAR ; AND, LO ! THERE
HAVE BEEN GRANTED THEE BY GOD ALL THEY THAT
SAIL WITH THEE '. (25) WHEREFORE TAKE HEART, GEN-
TLEMEN ; FOR I BELIEVE GOD, THAT IT SHALL BE SO AS
IT HATH BEEN SPOKEN UNTO ME. (26) HOWBEIT WE
MUST BE CAST ON SOME ISLAND."

In their situation the great danger was of foundering
through leakage caused by the constant straining due to
the sail and the force of the waves on the broadside, which
ancient vessels were not strong enough to stand. To
lessen the danger, the sailors began to lighten the ship, by
throwing away the cargo. On the day after, the whole
company, Luke among them, sacrificed the ship's equipment. *V.* 19 is a climax ; " with our own hands we threw
away all the ship's fittings and equipment," the extreme

act of sacrifice. The first person, used in the Authorised Version, occurs only in some less authoritative MSS., but greatly increases the effect. The sailors threw overboard part of the cargo ; and the passengers and supernumeraries, in eager anxiety to do something, threw overboard whatever movables they found, which was of little or no practical use, but they were eager to do something. This makes a striking picture of growing panic ; but the third person, which appears in the great MSS., is ineffective, and makes no climax.

One of the miserable accompaniments of a storm at sea is the difficulty of obtaining food ; and, if that is so in a modern vessel, it must have been much worse in an ancient merchant ship, inconveniently crowded with sailors and passengers. Moreover, the sacrifice of the ship's furniture must have greatly increased the difficulty of preparing food.

Worse than all, the leakage was steadily growing from the straining of the mast, and yet they dared not cut the mast away, as it alone helped them to work off the dreaded African sands. Day after day the crew sat doing nothing, eating nothing, waiting till the ship should sink. In such a situation the experience of many cases shows that some individual, often one not hitherto prominent, and not rarely a woman, comes forward to cheer the company to the hope of escape and the courage of work ; and many a desperate situation has been overcome by the energy thus imparted. In this case Paul stood forth in the midst of the helpless, panic-struck crowd. When caution was suitable (*v.* 10), he had been the prudent, cautious adviser, warning the council of prospective danger. But now, amidst panic and despair, he appears cool, confident, assured of safety ; and he speaks in the only tone that could cheer such an audience as his, the tone of an inspired messenger. In a vision he has learned that all are to escape ; and he adds that an island is to be the means of safety.

6. LAND. (XXVII 27) BUT WHEN THE FOURTEENTH NIGHT WAS COME, AS WE WERE DRIVEN TO AND FRO IN THE ADRIA, TOWARDS MIDNIGHT THE SAILORS SURMISED THAT SOME LAND WAS NEARING THEM ; (28) AND THEY SOUNDED, AND FOUND TWENTY FATHOMS ; AND AFTER A LITTLE SPACE THEY SOUNDED AGAIN, AND FOUND FIFTEEN FATHOMS. (29) AND FEARING LEST HAPLY WE SHOULD BE CAST ON ROCKY GROUND THEY LET GO FOUR ANCHORS FROM THE STERN, AND PRAYED THAT DAY COME ON. (30) AND AS THE SAILORS WERE SEEKING TO MAKE THEIR ESCAPE FROM THE SHIP, AND HAD LOWERED THE BOAT INTO THE SEA, UNDER PRETENCE OF LAYING OUT ANCHORS FROM THE BOW, (31) PAUL SAID TO THE CENTURION AND THE SOLDIERS, " UNLESS THESE ABIDE IN THE SHIP, YOU CANNOT BE SAVED ". (32) THEN THE SOLDIERS CUT AWAY THE ROPES OF THE BOAT AND LET HER FALL AWAY. (33) AND WHILE THE DAY WAS COMING ON, PAUL BESOUGHT THEM ALL TO TAKE SOME FOOD, SAYING : " THIS DAY IS THE FOURTEENTH DAY THAT YOU WATCH AND CONTINUE FASTING, AND HAVE TAKEN NOTHING. (34) WHEREFORE, I BESEECH YOU TO TAKE SOME FOOD, FOR THIS IS FOR YOUR SAFETY ; FOR THERE SHALL NOT A HAIR PERISH FROM THE HEAD OF ANY OF YOU." (35) AND WHEN HE HAD SAID THIS HE TOOK BREAD AND GAVE THANKS

TO GOD IN THE PRESENCE OF ALL ; AND HE BRAKE
IT, AND BEGAN TO EAT. (36) THEN WERE THEY ALL
OF GOOD CHEER, AND THEMSELVES ALSO TOOK SOME
FOOD. (37) AND WE WERE IN ALL ON THE SHIP 276
SOULS. (38) AND WHEN THEY HAD EATEN ENOUGH,
THEY PROCEEDED TO LIGHTEN THE SHIP, THROWING
OUT THE WHEAT INTO THE SEA.

Luke seems to have had the landsman's idea that they
drifted to and fro in the Mediterranean. A sailor would
have known that they drifted in a uniform direction ; but
it seems hardly possible to accept Smith's idea that the
Greek word ($\delta\iota\alpha\phi\epsilon\rho o\mu\acute\epsilon\nu\omega\nu$) can denote a straight drifting
course.

The name Adria has caused some difficulty. It was
originally narrower in application ; but in the usage of
sailors it grew wider as time passed, and Luke uses the
term that he heard on shipboard, where the sailors called
the sea that lay between Malta, Italy, Greece, and Crete
"the Adria ". As usual, Luke's terminology is that of life
and conversation, not of literature. Strabo the geographer,
who wrote about A.D. 19, says that the Ionian sea on the
west of Greece was " a part of what is now called Adria,"
implying that contemporary popular usage was wider than
ancient usage. In later usage the name was still more
widely applied : in the fifth century " the Adria " extended
to the coast of Cyrene ; and mediæval sailors distinguished
the Adriatic, as the whole Eastern half of the Mediterranean, from the Ægean sea (see p. 298).

On the fourteenth midnight, the practised senses of the
sailors detected that land was nearing : probably, as Smith
suggests, they heard the breakers, and, as an interesting
confirmation of his suggestion, one old Latin version reads

"that land was resounding".[1] It was now necessary to choose where they should beach the vessel ; for the sound of the breakers warned them that the coast was dangerous. In the dark no choice was possible ; and they therefore were forced to anchor. With a strong wind blowing it was doubtful whether the cables and anchors would hold ; therefore, to give themselves every chance, they let go four anchors. Smith quotes from the sailing directions that in St. Paul's Bay (the traditional scene of the wreck), "while the cables hold there is no danger, as the anchors will never start". He also points out that a ship drifting from Cauda could not get into the bay without passing near the low rocky point of Koura, which bounds it on the east. The breakers here warned the sailors ; and the charts show that after passing the point the ship would pass over 20 fathoms and then over 15 fathoms depth on her course, W. by N.

Anchoring by the stern was unusual ; but in their situation it had great advantages. Had they anchored by the bow, the ship would have swung round from the wind ; and, when afterwards they wished to run her ashore, it would have been far harder to manage her when lying with her prow pointing to the wind and away from the shore. But, as they were, they had merely to cut the cables, unlash the rudders, and put up a little foresail (*v.* 40) ; and they had the ship at once under command to beach her at any spot they might select.

As the ship was now lying at anchor near some land, the sailors were about to save themselves by the boat and abandon the ship to its fate without enough skilled

---

[1] 1. Resonare *Gig.* Compared with προσαχεῖν B, as Prof. Rendel Harris suggests to me, this implies an early Greek reading προσηχεῖν.

hands to work it ; but Paul, vigilant ever, detected their design, and prevented it. Then, in order that the company might have strength for the hard work that awaited them at daybreak, he encouraged them once more with the assurance of safety, urged them to eat with a view thereto, and himself set the example. There is perhaps an intention in *v.* 35 to represent Paul as acting like Jesus at the last Passover ; and the resemblance is more pointed if the words added in one MS. and some versions are original, "giving also to us". But it would be necessary to understand "us" to mean only Luke and Aristarchus (as Dr. Blass agrees) ; and this is harsh after the word has been so often used in a much wider sense. It is characteristic of Christianity in all periods to seek after resemblances between the Founder and any great hero of the faith at some crisis of history ; and this addition seems a later touch to bring out the resemblance.

7. PAUL'S ACTION ON THE SHIP. The account of the voyage as a whole is commonly accepted by critics as the most trustworthy part of *Acts* and as "one of the most instructive documents for the knowledge of ancient seamanship," (Holtzmann on XXVII 4, p. 421). But in it many critics detect the style of the later hand, the supposed second-century writer that made the work out of good and early documents, and addressed his compilation to Theophilus. Many hold that this writer inserted *vv.* 21-26, and some assign to him also *vv.* 33-35, because the character there attributed to Paul is quite different from his character in the genuine old document, especially *vv.* 10 and 31 ; in the original parts Paul is represented as a simple passenger, cautious to a

degree, suffering from hunger, apprehensive of the future, keenly alive to prospective danger, and anxious to provide against it : on the other hand, in *vv.* 21-26 he knows that their safety is assured ; he speaks as the prophet, not the anxious passenger ; he occupies a position apart from, and on a higher plane than human.

This is a fair hypothesis, and deserves fair and dispassionate consideration ; no one whose mind is not already definitely made up on all questions can pass it by ; and only those who feel that they understand the entire narrative in every turn and phrase and allusion would willingly pass it by, for every real student knows how frequently his knowledge is increased by changing his point of view.

We may at once grant that the narrative would go on without any obvious awkwardness if 21-26 were omitted, which is of course true of many a paragraph describing some special incident in a historical work.

But it is half-hearted and useless to cut out 21-26 as an interpolation without cutting out 33-38 ; there, too, Paul is represented as the prophet and the consoler on a higher plane, though he is also the mere passenger suffering from hunger, and alive to the fact that the safety of all depends on their taking food and being fit for active exertion in the morning. Some critics go so far as to cut out *vv.* 33-35. But it is not possible to cut these out alone ; there is an obvious want of sequence between 32 and 36, and Holtzmann therefore seems to accept 33-35. But if they are accepted I fail to see any reason for rejecting 21-26 ; these two passages are so closely akin in purport and bearing on the context that they must go together ; and all the mischief attri-

buted to 21-26 as placing Paul on a higher plane is done
in 33-35.

Further, the excision of 21-26 would cut away a vital
part of the narrative. (1) These verses contain the additional fact, natural in itself and assumed in *v.* 34 as
already known, that the crew and passengers were starving and weak. (2) They fit well into the context, for
they follow naturally after the spiritlessness described in
v. 20, and Paul begins by claiming attention on the
ground of his former advice (advice that is accepted by
the critics as genuine because it is different in tone from
the supposed interpolation). " In former circumstances,"
says he, " I gave you different, but salutary advice,
which to your cost you disregarded ; listen to me now
when I tell you that you shall escape." The method of
escape, the only method that a sailor could believe to
be probable, is added as a concluding encouragement.

But let us cut out every verse that puts Paul on a
higher plane, and observe the narrative that would
result : Paul twice comes forward with advice that is
cautiously prudent, and shows keen regard to the chance
of safety. If that is all the character he displayed
throughout the voyage, why do we study the man
and his fate ? All experience shows that in such a
situation there is often found some one to encourage
the rest ; and, if Paul had not been the man to comfort
and cheer his despairing shipmates, he would never
have impressed himself on history or made himself an
interest to all succeeding time. The world's history
stamps the interpolation-theory here as false.

Moreover, the letters of Paul put before us a totally
different character from this prudent calculator of

chances. The Paul of *Acts* XXVII is the Paul of the
Epistles: the Paul who remains on the interpolation-
theory could never have written the Epistles.

Finally, the reason why the historian dwells at such
length on the voyage lies mainly in *vv.* 21-26 and
33-38. In the voyage he pictures Paul on a higher
plane than common men, advising more skilfully than
the skilled mariners, maintaining hope and courage
when all were in despair, and breathing his hope and
courage into others, playing the part of a true Roman
in a Roman ship, looked up to even by the centurion, and
in his single self the saviour of the lives of all. But the
interpolation-theory would cut out the centre of the
picture.

There remains no reason to reject *vv.* 21-26 which I
can discover, except that it introduces the superhuman
element. That is an argument to which I have no reply.
It is quite a tenable position in the present stage of
science and knowledge to maintain that every narrative
which contains elements of the marvellous must be an
unhistorical and untrustworthy narrative. But let us
have the plain and honest reasons; those who defend
that perfectly fair position should not try to throw in
front of it as outworks flimsy and uncritical reasons,
which cannot satisfy for a moment any one that has not
his mind made up beforehand on that fundamental
premise. But the superhuman element is inextricably
involved in this book: you cannot cut it out by any
critical process that will bear scrutiny. You must accept
all or leave all.

8. ON SHORE. (XXVII 39) AND WHEN IT WAS DAY
THEY DID NOT RECOGNISE THE LAND; BUT THEY WERE

AWARE OF A SORT OF BAY OR CREEK WITH A SANDY
BEACH, AND THEY TOOK COUNSEL, IF POSSIBLE, TO
DRIVE THE SHIP UP ON IT.   (40) AND CASTING OFF
THE ANCHORS, THEY LEFT THEM IN THE SEA, WHILST
LOOSING THE FASTENINGS OF THE RUDDERS, AND
SETTING THE FORESAIL TO THE BREEZE, THEY HELD
FOR THE OPEN BEACH.   (41) AND CHANCING ON A
BANK BETWEEN TWO SEAS, THEY DROVE THE SHIP
ON IT ; AND THE PROW STRUCK AND REMAINED
IMMOVABLE, BUT THE AFTER PART BEGAN TO BREAK
UP FROM THE VIOLENCE.   (42) AND THE SOLDIERS'
COUNSEL WAS TO KILL THE PRISONERS, LEST ANY
SHOULD SWIM AWAY AND ESCAPE ; (43) BUT THE CEN-
TURION, WISHING TO SAVE PAUL, STAYED THEM
FROM THEIR PURPOSE, AND BADE THEM THAT COULD
SWIM TO LEAP OVERBOARD AND GET FIRST TO LAND,
(44) AND THE REST, SOME ON PLANKS, AND SOME ON
PIECES FROM THE SHIP.   AND SO IT CAME TO PASS
THAT ALL ESCAPED SAFE TO THE LAND.

No description could be more clear and precise,
selecting the essential points and omitting all others.
Smith quotes some interesting parallels from modern
narratives of shipwreck.

Some doubt has arisen whether "the bank between
two seas" was a shoal separated from the shore by deep
water, or, as Smith says, a neck of land projecting
towards the island of Salmonetta, which shelters St.
Paul's Bay on the north-west.   But the active term
"drove the ship on it" (ἐπέκειλαν) implies purpose, and
decides in Smith's favour.   The fact that they "chanced
on a ridge between two seas" might at the first glance
seem to imply want of purpose ; but, as Smith points

out, they could not, while lying at anchor, see the exact
character of the spot. They selected a promising point,
and as they approached they found that luck had led
them to the isthmus between the island and the mainland. In their situation the main object was to get the
ship close up to the shore, and safe from being rapidly
and utterly smashed up by the waves. No place could
have better favoured their purpose. The ship (which
probably drew eighteen feet of water) "struck a bottom of
mud, graduating into tenacious clay, into which the fore
part would fix itself, and be held fast, while the stern
was exposed to the force of the waves". Thus the
foreship was held together, until every passenger got
safe to dry land. Only the rarest conjunction of favourable circumstances could have brought about such a
fortunate ending to their apparently hopeless situation ;
and one of the completest services that has ever been
rendered to New Testament scholarship is James Smith's
proof that all these circumstances are united in St. Paul's
Bay. The only difficulty to which he has applied a
rather violent solution is the sandy beach: at the traditional point where the ship was run ashore there is no
sandy beach; but he considers that it is "now worn
away by the wasting action of the sea". On this detail
only local knowledge would justify an opinion.

In *v.* 41 "the violence" is the expression used by a
person standing on the shore and watching the waves
smash up the ship: he does not need to specify the
kind of violence. This expression takes us on to the
beach, and makes us gaze on the scene. The humblest
scribe can supply κυμάτων here, and most of them have
done so.

In *v.* 43 Luke mentions that the directions were given, and leaves the reader to understand that they were carried into effect (compare pp. 181, 233, 295).

9. MALTA. (XXVIII 1) AND WHEN WE WERE ESCAPED, THEN WE LEARNT THAT THE ISLAND IS CALLED MELITA. (2) AND THE BARBARIANS SHOWED US NO COMMON KINDNESS; FOR THEY KINDLED A FIRE, AND WELCOMED US ALL, BECAUSE OF THE PRESENT RAIN AND BECAUSE OF THE COLD. (3) BUT WHEN PAUL HAD GATHERED A BUNDLE OF STICKS AND LAID THEM ON THE FIRE, A VIPER CAME OUT BY REASON OF THE HEAT AND FASTENED ON HIS HAND. (4) AND WHEN THE BARBARIANS SAW THE BEAST HANGING FROM HIS HAND, THEY SAID TO ONE AN-OTHER, " NO DOUBT THIS MAN IS A MURDERER, WHOM, THOUGH HE HATH ESCAPED FROM THE SEA, YET JUSTICE WILL NOT SUFFER TO LIVE ". (5) HOWBEIT HE SHOOK OFF THE BEAST INTO THE FIRE, AND TOOK NO HARM. (6) BUT THEY EXPECTED THAT HE WOULD HAVE SWOLLEN OR FALLEN DOWN DEAD SUDDENLY; BUT WHEN THEY WERE LONG IN EXPECTATION AND BEHELD NOTHING AMISS COME TO HIM, THEY CHANGED THEIR MINDS, AND SAID THAT HE WAS A GOD. (7) NOW IN THE NEIGHBOURHOOD OF THAT PLACE WERE LANDS BELONGING TO THE FIRST *man* OF THE ISLAND, NAMED POPLIUS, WHO RECEIVED US AND ENTERTAINED US THREE DAYS COURTEOUSLY. (8) AND IT WAS SO THAT THE FATHER OF POPLIUS LAY SICK OF A FEVER AND DYSENTERY; AND PAUL ENTERED IN UNTO HIM, AND PRAYED, AND LAYING HIS HANDS ON HIM HEALED HIM. (9) AND WHEN THIS WAS DONE THE REST ALSO WHICH HAD DISEASES IN THE ISLAND CAME AND WERE

CURED ; (10) WHO ALSO HONOURED US WITH MANY
HONOURS, AND WHEN WE SAILED PUT ON BOARD SUCH
THINGS AS WE NEEDED.

The name Poplius is the Greek form of the *prænomen*
Publius ; but it is not probable that this official would
be called by a simple *prænomen.* Poplius might perhaps
be the Greek rendering of the *nomen* Popilius. Yet possibly the peasantry around spoke familiarly of " Publius"
by his *prænomen* simply ; and Luke (who has no sympathy
for Roman nomenclature) took the name that he heard in
common use. The title " first " is technically correct in
Melita : it has inscriptional authority.

Doubtless many of the sailors had been at Malta
before, for eastern ships bound for Rome must have
often touched at the island, *v.* 11. " But St. Paul's
Bay is remote from the great harbour, and possesses
no marked features by which it could be recognised "
from the anchorage in the bay.

The objections which have been advanced, that there
are now no vipers in the island, and only one place
where any wood grows, are too trivial to deserve notice.
Such changes are natural and probable in a small
island, populous and long civilised.

The term " barbarians," *v.* 2, is characteristic of the
nationality of the writer. It does not indicate rudeness
or uncivilised habits, but merely non-Greek birth ; and
it is difficult to imagine that a Syrian or a Jew or any
one but a Greek would have applied the name to the
people of Malta, who had been in contact with
Phœnicians and Romans for many centuries.

CHAPTER XV

ST. PAUL IN ROME

ɪ. THE COMING TO ROME. (XXVIII II) AND AFTER THREE MONTHS WE SET SAIL IN A SHIP OF ALEXANDRIA, WHICH HAD WINTERED IN THE ISLAND, WHOSE SIGN WAS "THE TWIN BROTHERS". (12) AND TOUCHING AT SYRACUSE, WE TARRIED THERE THREE DAYS. (13) AND FROM THENCE, BY TACKING, WE ARRIVED AT RHEGIUM. AND AFTER ONE DAY A SOUTH WIND SPRANG UP, AND ON THE SECOND DAY WE CAME TO PUTEOLI: (14) WHERE, FINDING BRETHREN, WE WERE CONSOLED AMONG THEM, REMAINING SEVEN DAYS ;[1] AND THEREUPON WE CAME TO ROME. (15) AND FROM THENCE THE BRETHREN, HEARING THE NEWS ABOUT US, CAME TO MEET US AS FAR AS "APPIUS' MARKET" AND "THREE TAVERNS": WHOM, WHEN PAUL SAW, HE THANKED GOD AND TOOK COURAGE. (16) AND WHEN WE ENTERED INTO ROME [*the centurion delivered the prisoners to the stratopedarch,*

---

[1] The text of most MSS., "we were entreated to tarry with them seven days," seems irreconcilable with Paul's situation as a prisoner. However friendly Julius was to Paul, he was a Roman officer, with whom discipline and obedience to rule were natural. With Blass, we follow the text of the inferior MSS. (see p. 212).

and] PAUL WAS SUFFERED TO ABIDE BY HIMSELF WITH THE SOLDIER THAT GUARDED HIM [*outside of the camp*]. . . . (30) AND HE ABODE TWO YEARS IN HIS OWN HIRED DWELLING, AND RECEIVED ALL THAT WENT IN UNTO HIM, (31) AND PREACHED THE KINGDOM OF GOD, AND TAUGHT WHAT CONCERNED THE LORD JESUS CHRIST WITH ALL BOLDNESS, NONE FORBIDDING HIM (see note, p. 362).

The wreck took place before the middle of November (p. 322) ; therefore they sailed from Malta in February. That is earlier than the usual beginning of over-sea navigation ; but we may understand that favourable weather tempted them to an early start ; and as the autumn was unusually tempestuous, it is probable that fine weather began early. Luke does not tell what sort of wind blew, leaving the reader to understand that it was from a southerly quarter (as otherwise no ancient ship would attempt the over-sea voyage). The wind fell and they had to wait three days in Syracuse. Then, though the breeze was not from the south, they were able by good seamanship to work up to Rhegium.[1] Here, after one day, a south wind arose ; and they sailed across to Puteoli, arriving there on the second day.

The passage probably took not much over twenty-four hours, beginning one day and ending the following morning : with a following wind, these large merchant vessels sailed fast. The passengers landed in Puteoli ; but the cargo, doubtless, was carried to Ostia, where it

---

[1] Westcott and Hort prefer the text of the great MSS. περιελόντες, which could hardly mean more than "casting off," an unnecessary piece of information here, though important in XXVII.

had to be transshipped to smaller vessels which could
go up the Tiber to Rome.

Luke mentions the name of the last vessel, but not
of any of the others. The reason lies in the circumstances. He heard the news about the last vessel
before he saw it ; but he became acquainted with the
others by seeing them. Probably the news that the
Dioscuri, of the Alexandrian Imperial fleet, was lying
in the great harbour, reached the shipwrecked party
during the three days when they were in Poplius's house ;
and was so noted in Luke's memoranda. But he had
not the sailor's mind, who thicks of his ship as a living
friend, and always speaks of her by her name ; hence
the other ships were to him only means of conveyance,
whereas the name of the *Dioscuri* was the first fact
which he learned about her.

Puteoli, as a great harbour, was a central point and a
crossing of intercourse ; and thus Christianity had
already established itself there. All movements of
thought throughout the Empire acted with marvellous
rapidity on Rome, the heart of the vast and complicated
organism ; and the crossing-places or knots[1] on the
main highways of intercourse with the East—Puteoli,
Corinth, Ephesus, Syrian Antioch—became centres from
which Christianity radiated. At Pompeii, which is not
far from Puteoli, the Christians were a subject of gossip
among loungers in the street before it was destroyed
by the eruption of Vesuvius in 79.

The double expression of arrival at Rome in *vv.* 14
and 16 is remarkable ; and has caused much speculation

---

[1] Each of them may be called πάροδος, the epithet applied to
Bphesus by Ignatius, *Rom.* 12, *Church in R. E.*, p. 318 f.

among commentators. Blass is inclined to seek a change of text, giving the sense "we proceeded on our way (*imperfect*) to Rome, then we came to Appii Forum, etc., and finally we entered Rome". Others prefer other interpretations. But the double expression seems due to the double sense that every name of a city-state bears in Greek : the word Rome might either include the entire territory of the city, the XXXV tribes as they were completed in B.C. 241, *i.e.*, the whole *ager Romanus*, or be restricted to the walls and buildings. Thus *v.* 13, " we reached the state Rome," the bounds of which were probably pointed out as the party reached them ; in 14, " we passed through two points in the *ager Romanus* "; and in 15, " we entered the (walls of) Rome " (see p. 111).

It is evident that Paul, when he reached this crisis of his fate, was feeling dispirited ; for the tendency to low spirits is always one of the most trying concomitants of his chronic disorder, as described in Ch. V § 2. The allusions to the consolation that he received from meeting Brethren at Puteoli, Appius's Forum, and the Three Taverns, must be taken as indications of some marked frame of mind. We have already observed him in a similar state of depression when he was in Troas and Philippi (p. 283 f.).

When the party reached Rome, the centurion delivered his charge to his superior officer, who bears the title *Chief of the Camp* (*Stratopedarch*) in the Greek text. This title has always hitherto been interpreted as denoting the Prefect of the Prætorian Guard, stationed in a large camp adjoining the walls of Rome. But that interpretation is not well suited either to the natural character of language or to the facts of the Roman service. The title could not properly designate an officer of such high rank ; and the Prætorian Prefect would hardly be concerned with a comparatively humble duty like the reception of and responsibility for prisoners. The Greek title *Stratopedarch* very rarely occurs ; and it remained for Mommsen, aided by the form given in an old Latin version, *Princeps Peregrinorum*, to explain who the officer really was, and to place the whole episode of Paul's Roman residence in a new light (see p. 315).

Augustus had reduced to a regular system the maintenance of communications between the centre of control in Rome and the armies stationed in the great frontier provinces. Legionary centurions, called commonly *frumentarii*, went to and fro between Rome and the armies ; and were employed for numerous purposes that demanded communication between the Emperor and his armies and provinces. They acted not only for commissariat purposes (whence the name), but as couriers, and for police purposes, and for conducting prisoners ; and in time they became detested as agents and spies of Government. They all belonged to legions stationed in the provinces, and were considered to be on detached duty when they went to Rome ; and hence in Rome they were " soldiers from abroad," *peregrini*. While in Rome they resided in a camp on the Cælian Hill, called *Castra Peregrinorum ;* in this camp there were always a number of them present, changing from day to day, as some came and others went away. This camp was under command of the *Princeps Peregrinorum ;* and it is clear that *Stratopedarch* in *Acts* is the Greek name for that officer (see p. 315).

This whole branch of the service is very obscure. Marquardt considers that it was first organised by Hadrian ; but Mommsen believes that it must have been instituted by Augustus.

2. THE RESIDENCE IN ROME. Paul was treated in Rome with the utmost leniency. He was allowed to hire a house or a lodging in the city, and live there at his own convenience under the surveillance of a soldier who was responsible for his presence when required. A light chain fastened Paul's wrist to that of the soldier. No hindrance was offered to his inviting friends into his house, or to his preaching to all who came in to him ; but he was not allowed to go out freely.

After the depression of spirit in which Paul entered Rome, *Acts* concludes with a distinct implication of easier and more hopeful circumstances. His work went on unimpeded, while the rest after the fatigue and hardships of the voyage would be beneficial to his physical health (even though September might afterwards prove unhealthy) ; and thus the two chief reasons for his gloomy frame of mind on landing in Italy were removed. He regarded himself as " an ambassador in a chain " (*Eph.* VI 20) ; he asked for the prayers of the Colossians and the Asian Churches generally for his success in preaching ; his tone is hopeful and full of energy and spirit for the work (*l. c., Col.* IV 3, 4) ; and he looked forward to acquittal and a visit to Colossai (*Philem.* 22). We may date these letters to Philemon, to Colossai, and to the Asian Churches generally (*Eph.*) near the middle of the long imprisonment ; an accurate date is impossible, but for brevity's sake we may speak of their date as early in 61.

The presence of many friends in Rome also cheered Paul. He had been permitted to take two personal attendants with him from Cæsareia ; but though his other companions in Jerusalem were prevented from accompanying him in his voyage, some of them followed him to Rome. Timothy was with him during great part of his imprisonment, was sent on a mission to Philippi about the end of 61 (*Phil.* II 19), and thereafter seems to have had his headquarters in Asia, whence he was summoned by Paul to join him during his second imprisonment. Tychicus also joined Paul in Rome in 60, and was sent on a mission to Asia, and especially to the Churches of the Lycos valley, early in 61. They probably left Cæsareia when Paul sailed for Rome, visited on the way their own homes, and arrived in Rome not long after Paul himself.

Moreover, Mark, who had become reconciled with Paul (probably during his residence at Jerusalem, or his imprisonment in Cæsareia), came also to Rome. He left Rome in 61, contemplating an extended tour in the province Asia, in the course of which he would probably visit Colossai. Oral instructions had been already sent to the Colossians, and, doubtless, other Pauline Churches (probably by Onesimus and Tychicus), to welcome him as Paul's deputy ; and Paul writes to the Colossians a formal recommendation of him (IV 10). The terms in which Paul speaks suggest that he had not taken any active interest in the new Pauline Churches since the unfortunate quarrel in Pamphylia, and that there was likely to be some coldness towards him among the Pauline Christians. From this year, apparently, began a new era in Mark's life. His work seems to have lain in Asia during the next few years, for about the close of his life Paul bids Timothy (IV 11) bring Mark with him to Rome, implying that they were near each other ; and Timothy was in Ephesus at the time. Probably Paul had been informed of Mark's desire to rejoin him in his troubles. At a later date Mark is associated with the greeting of I *Peter* V 13 to the Churches of the provinces of Asia Minor, in such a way as to imply personal acquaintance with them ; and this wide range of work, though not easily reconcilable with the earlier dates assigned to that Epistle, suits naturally and well the date about 80 (*Church in R. E.*, p. 280 f.). On this view Mark after Paul's death must have devoted himself to work in the more easterly provinces of Asia Minor ; and returned to Rome ten or twelve years later.

It is remarkable that Luke has not a word to say about the process by which Christianity spread to Rome ; but, according to the plan which we have already seen to be shadowed forth for the sequel of this history, the process would form part of the contemplated Third Book. That Book would naturally open with a brief statement of the western dispersion and the planting of Christianity in Italy, going back for the moment to an earlier date, just as in XI 27 the historian, when he has to include Antioch in the stage of his drama, turns back to the movement originating in Stephen's work. So here he brings Paul to Rome; and thereafter he would probably have made a new start with the Churches of the West and the new impulse imparted to them by Paul's acquittal. We are compelled to make some conjecture on this point ; for no one can accept the ending of *Acts* as the conclusion of a rationally conceived history. Such an ending might exist in a diary, which has no determining idea, but not in a history; and we, who work on the hypothesis that *Acts* is a history, must strive to understand the guiding idea of an unfinished work.

According to modern ideas, the rapidity with which every movement in the provinces influenced Rome is a sign of strong vitality and intimate union of the parts of that vast Empire. The Imperial policy fostered inter-communication and unity to the utmost; and it is not too much to say that travelling was more highly developed, and the dividing power of distance was weaker, under the Empire than at any time before or since, until we come down to the present century. But that fact, which we estimate as probably the best measure of material civilisation, was regarded with horror by the party of old Roman thought and manners, which was stubbornly opposed in mind to the Imperial rule, though it was powerless against it. They saw that the old Roman character was changed, and the old Roman ideals of life and government were destroyed, by the influx of provincial thoughts and manners. The Orontes was pouring its waters into the Tiber; Syrian and Greek vices were substituted for Roman virtues; and prominent among these vices were Judaism, Christianity, and other "debasing superstitions".

The new movement made marked progress in the vast Imperial household; and Paul, in sending to the Philippian Church the greetings of the Roman Christians, says, "All the saints salute you, especially they that are of Cæsar's household". This is quite to be expected

The Imperial household was at the centre of affairs and in most intimate relations with all parts of the Empire; and in it influences from the provinces were most certain to be felt early. There can be no doubt that Lightfoot is right in considering that Christianity effected an entrance into Cæsar's household before Paul entered Rome; in all probability he is right also in thinking that all the slaves of Aristobulus (son of Herod the Great) and of Narcissus (Claudius's favourite freedman) had passed into the Imperial household, and that members of these two *familiæ* are saluted as Christians by Paul (*Rom.* XVI 10 f.).

3. SENECA AND PAUL. The question has been much discussed what relation, if any, existed between Seneca and Paul at this time. A tradition existed in the fourth century that they had been brought into close relation. It is, however, exceedingly doubtful whether this tradition had any other foundation than the remarkable likeness that many of Seneca's phrases and sentiments show to passages in the New Testament. But, however striking these extracts seem when collected and looked at apart from their context, I think that a careful consideration of them as they occur in the books, must bring every one to the conclusion advocated by Lightfoot, by Aubé, and by many others, that the likeness affords no proof that Seneca came into such relations with Paul as to be influenced in his sentiments by him : resemblances quite as striking occur in works written before Paul came to Rome (according to the received, although not always absolutely certain, chronology of Seneca's works), as in those written after. Nor was it among the professed

philosophers that Paul was likely to be listened to : they considered that they knew all he had to say, and could quote from their own lectures a good moral precept to set alongside of anything he could tell them.

Yet there can be no doubt that some very striking parallels between Senecan and Pauline sayings occur ; and this is true of Seneca to a greater extent than of any other non-Christian writer. It is possible that the philosophical school of Tarsus had exercised more influence on Paul than is commonly allowed ; and it is certain that Seneca was influenced by Athenodorus of Tarsus. Lightfoot refers especially to the fact that both Paul and Seneca "compare life to a warfare, and describe the struggle after good as a contest with the flesh ". Seneca makes one long quotation from Athenodorus *(de Clem.,* 4), and in it the idea that life is a warfare is worked out elaborately ; and the saying *(Ep.* X), "So live with men, as if God saw you ; so speak with God, as if men heard you," occurs immediately after a quotation from Athenodorus,[1] and seems to be a reflection in Seneca's words of Athenodorus's intention. Athenodorus lived much in Rome, and died there in Cato's house, 60-50 B.C. ; but it is probable both that his system exercised great influence in the university of his own city, and that Paul's expression and language may contain traces of his university training in Tarsus.

But though there is no reason to think that Seneca was influenced by Paul's language or thoughts, yet there

---

[1] " Know that you are set free from passions only when you have reached such a stage that you ask God for nothing which you cannot ask openly."

is every reason to think that the liberal policy of the Empire at this period in religion was due to Seneca's broad views. It is certain that he had exercised very great influence on the Imperial policy, since his pupil Nero became Emperor in 54 ; and it is highly probable that the energy with which that policy was carried out in the East, and the generous freedom with which all religious questions were treated during that period, are due to Seneca's spirit. He is perhaps the only distinguished politician of the first century who shows some of the wide views of Hadrian; and it is remarkable that both Seneca and Hadrian were sprung from Spain, being thus thoroughly Roman and yet absolutely free from the old narrow Roman spirit. It is clear that, in the later years of Nero's reign, the Empire began to fall into dangerous disorganisation, while in his early years the government at home and abroad seems to have been remarkably successful ; and it is not easy to account for the contrast, except by connecting the success with Seneca's guiding spirit. Now, the tone which marks the relations of the State to Paul throughout the period described in *Acts*, is quite different from that which began in A.D. 64 and subsequently became intensified. Surely we can best account for the change by the disgrace and retirement of Seneca in 62 : his spirit departed from the administration by rapid steps after that date. Circumstances had given him for a few years such influence as perhaps never again was exercised by a private citizen in the Empire. As a rule, the Emperors held the reins of government tight in their own hands, and allowed no subordinate to exert any influence on the general conduct of affairs ; and there are many great

Emperors, but only one great Minister under the Empire, Seneca.

The household of Seneca during his ascendancy was likely to be brought into close relations with the great movements that were agitating the Empire. It is therefore natural to expect that the new religion should affect it in some degree, as it did the Imperial household. Nor are we left to mere conjecture on this point. A remarkable inscription of somewhat later date has been found at Ostia, " M. Annaeus Paulus to M. Annaeus Paulus Petrus, his very dear son : " the name " Paul Peter " must be taken as an indubitable proof of religion. These persons possibly belong to a family of freedmen connected with the household of Seneca ; but, assuming that, it is no more admissible to quote this inscription as corroborating Seneca's traditional subjection to Christianity, than it would be to quote the strong leaven of Christianity in Cæsar's household in proof of Cæsar's amenability to the same influence.

4. THE TRIAL. It is doubtful why Paul's trial was so long delayed. Perhaps his opponents, despairing of obtaining his condemnation, preferred to put off the trial as long as possible ; and there were then, as there are now, many devices in law for causing delay. Perhaps the case was being inquired into by the Imperial Office: the trial had to take place before the Emperor or one of his representatives (probably one of the two Prefects of the Prætorian Guard). The whole question of free teaching of an oriental religion by a Roman citizen must have been opened up by the case ; and it is quite possible that Paul's previous proceedings were inquired into.

The trial seems to have occurred towards the end of A.D. 61. Its earliest stages were over before Paul wrote to the Philippians, for he says, I 12, " the things *which happened* unto me have fallen out rather unto the progress of the Good News ; so that my bonds became manifest in Christ in the whole *Prætorium,* and to all the rest ; and that most of the Brethren in the Lord, being confident in my bonds, are more abundantly bold to speak the word of God without fear ". This passage has been generally misconceived and connected with the period of imprisonment ; and here again we are indebted to Mommsen for the proper interpretation. The *Prætorium* is the whole body of persons connected with the sitting in judgment, the supreme Imperial Court, doubt-less in this case the Prefect or both Prefects of the Prætorian Guard, representing the Emperor in his capacity as the fountain of justice, together with the assessors and high officers of the court. The expression of the chapter as a whole shows that the trial is partly finished, and the issue as yet is so favourable that the Brethren are emboldened by the success of Paul's courageous and free-spoken defence and the strong impression which he evidently produced on the court ; but he himself, being entirely occupied with the trial, is for the moment prevented from preaching as he had been doing when he wrote to the Colossians and the Asian Churches generally.

That *Philippians* was written near the end of the imprisonment has been widely recognised, though the powerful opposition of Lightfoot has carried away the general current of opinion in England. When Paul was writing to the Church at Philippi, his custom of sending his subordinates on missions had stripped him of companions; and so he says, " I have no man like-minded (*with Timothy*) who will show genuine care for your state, for they all seek their own, not the things of Jesus Christ, but ye recognise his proved character " (*Phil.* II 20 f.). It seems impossible to believe that Paul could have written like this, if he had had with him Tychicus, "faithful minister and fellow-servant in the Lord," Aristarchus, Mark, and above all Luke. Yet, if anything is sure about that period, it is that Aristarchus and Luke had been with Paul from his arrival in Rome till after *Coloss., Philem.* and *Eph.* were written, while Tychicus probably joined him with Timothy in 60. On our supposition, Mark and Tychicus had already been sent on missions to Asia; Luke is either the "true yoke-fellow" addressed in *Phil.* IV 3, or was actually the bearer of the letter to Philippi; Aristarchus also had been sent on a mission during the summer of 61; and Epaphras naturally had returned to the Lycos valley. There remained some friends with Paul (IV 21), probably Demas among them (*Col.* IV 14, *Philem.* 24); but he did not feel sure of their thorough trustworthiness, and his doubt about Demas was after-wards justified (II *Tim.* IV 10). Hence his eagerness to get back to the company of real and trusty friends (II 24 ff.).

Amid the general tone of hopefulness and confidence in *Philippians*, there are some touches of depression, which may be attributed to the absence of so many intimate friends, to the increased strain that the trial now proceeding must have put on his powers (p. 94 f.), and to the probable closer confinement necessitated by the trial, that he might always be accessible in case of need. There is more eagerness for the issue of the long proceedings manifest in *Phil.* than in the other letters from Rome; but it is part of human nature to be more patient when the end is still far off, and more excited and eager as the end approaches.

The letter to Philippi was not called forth by any dangerous crisis there, as were the letters to Colossai and to the Asian Churches generally (*Eph.*). Hence *Col.* and *Eph.* "exhibit a more advanced stage in the development of the Church" than *Phil.* Lightfoot and others are indubitably right in that point; but their inference that *Phil.* was written earlier than the others does not follow. The tone of *Col.* and *Eph.* is determined by the circumstances of the Churches addressed. The great cities of Asia were on the highway of the world, which traversed the Lycos valley, and in them development took place with great rapidity. But the Macedonians were a simple-minded people in comparison with Ephesus and Laodiceia and Colossai, living further away from the great movements of thought. It was not in Paul's way to send to Philippi an elaborate treatise against a subtle speculative heresy, which had never affected that Church. His letter was called forth by the gifts which had been sent by the Philippians; it is a recognition of their thoughtful kindness; and hence it has a marked character, being "the noblest reflection of St. Paul's personal character and spiritual illumination, his large sympathies, his womanly tenderness, his delicate courtesy" (to use once more the words of Lightfoot). It is plain that he did not actually need the help that they now sent; but his gratitude is as warm and

genuine as if he had been in deep need, and he recurs
to the former occasions when his real poverty had been
aided by them. The freedom from anxiety about the
development at Philippi, and the hearty affection for
kind friends, make this in many respects the most
pleasing of all Paul's letters.

Though prepared to face death if need be, Paul was
comparatively confident of the issue when he wrote to
Philippi : " I have the confident conviction that I shall
remain and abide for you all to your progress and joy of
believing," and " I trust that I shall come *to you* shortly ".
That he was acquitted is demanded both by the plan evident
in *Acts* (p. 308) and by other reasons well stated by others.

5. LAST TRIAL AND DEATH OF PAUL. His later
career is concealed from us, for the hints contained in the
Pastoral Epistles hardly furnish even an outline of his
travels, which must have lasted three or four years, 62-65
A.D. At his second trial the veil that hides his fate is
raised for the moment. On that occasion the circumstances were very different from his first trial. His confinement was more rigorous, for Onesiphorus had to
take much trouble before obtaining an interview with
the prisoner (II *Tim.* I 17) : " he fared ill as far as
bonds, like a criminal " (II 9). He had no hope of
acquittal : he recognised that he was " already being
poured forth as an offering, and the time of his departure was come ". The gloom and hopelessness of the
situation damped and dismayed all his friends : at his
first hearing " all forsook " him ; yet for the time he
" was delivered out of the mouth of the lion ". In every
respect the situation thus indicated is the opposite of the
circumstances described on the first trial. *Phil.* occupies

the same place in the first as II *Tim.* in the second trial; but *Phil.* looks forward to a fresh career among the Churches, while II *Tim.* is the testament of a dying man. In one respect, however, the second trial was like the first. Paul again defended himself in the same bold and outspoken way as before, expounding the principles of his life to a great audience, "that all the Gentiles might hear".

Yet the circumstances of this second trial are totally different from that "short way with the dissenters" which was customary under Domitian and Trajan and later Emperors. After his first examination Paul could still write to Asia bidding Timothy and Mark come to him, which shows that he looked forward to a considerable interval before the next stage of his trial. He was charged as a malefactor, crimes had to be proved against him, and evidence brought; and the simple acknowledgment that he was a Christian was still far from sufficient to condemn him, as it was under Domitian. It is a plausible conjecture of Conybeare and Howson that the first hearing, on which he was acquitted and "delivered out of the lion's mouth," was on the charge of complicity and sympathy with the incendiaries, who had burned Rome in 64; and that charge was triumphantly disproved. The trial in that case did not occur until the first frenzy of terror and rage against the supposed incendiaries was over; and some other species of crime had to be laid to the account of the Christians charged before the courts. The second and fatal charge, heard later, was doubtless that of treason, shown by hostility to the established customs of society, and by weakening the Imperial authority.

If our conception of the trial is correct, the precedent of

the first great trial still guided the courts of the empire (as we have elsewhere sought to prove). It had then been decided that the preaching of the new religion was not in itself a crime; and that legal offences must be proved against Christians as against any other subjects of the empire. That was the charter of freedom (p. 282) which was abrogated shortly after; and part of Luke's design was, as we have seen (p. 307), to record the circumstances in which the charter had been obtained, as a protest against the Flavian policy, which had overturned a well-weighed decision of the supreme court.

Note. Text of XXVIII 16. The failure in the great MSS. of the delivery of Paul to the Stratopedarch is a very clear case of omitting a Lukan detail, which had only a mundane interest; and the failure of similar details in XXVII 5, XVI 30, etc., may be estimated by the analogy of this case.

CHAPTER XVI

CHRONOLOGY OF EARLY CHURCH HISTORY—30-40 A.D.

1. THE STATE OF THE CHURCH IN A.D. 30. The chronological difficulty has probably weighed with many, as it has with Lightfoot (*Ed. Gal.* p. 124), in rejecting the identification which we advocate of the visit in *Acts* XI with that in *Gal.* II 1-10. It is therefore necessary to glance briefly at the chronology of the early chapters of *Acts*, in order to show that there is no real difficulty for those who (like Lightfoot) date the Crucifixion in A.D. 30. Our identification, if proved, would make it certain that the Death of Christ cannot be dated so late as 33.

Luke's historical method required him in the opening of his Second Book to give a full account of the first condition of the Church in Jerusalem, and then to concentrate attention on the critical steps and persons by whom the Universal Church was moulded to the form it had in his time.

In I, after a short preamble, connecting the narrative with the preceding book, he describes how the number of the Apostles was filled up. The organisation of the Church was always a subject of keen interest to Luke; he " evidently had the impression that the guidance of affairs rested with the Apostles in Jerusalem " (p. 53); and the appointment of this important official was in his estimation a matter of great moment. Peter took the lead ; two were selected by common agreement and vote ; and out of these the lot showed which was preferred by the Divine will.

In II 1-42 the events of Pentecost (May 26, A.D. 30), and the effect produced on the character of the converts, are described ; and the general state and conduct of this primitive Church is summed up in II 43-47.

The second part of II 47, "the Lord added to them day by day those that were being saved," is one of those phrases in which Luke often hits off a long, steady, uniform process. It is to be taken as a general description of subsequent progress in Jerusalem, during the course of which occurred the events next related.

The space devoted by Luke to Pentecost shows that he considered the events of that day to be of the highest importance. On that day the Divine grace was given to the Apostles, qualifying them (p. 45) for the work which they were now required to perform since their Master had left them.

Luke shows true historical insight in fixing the reader's attention on Pentecost. For the permanence of a movement of this kind, much depends on the successors of the first leader ; and the issue is determined in the period following the leader's removal. Has the leader shown that electrical creative power that remoulds men and communicates his own spirit to his disciples, or will the movement be found leaderless and spiritless, when the originator is taken away ? While the leader is with his disciples, they have little or no opportunity of showing independence and originality and capacity for command. When he is removed from them, the first effect must be discouragement and a sense of emptiness, proportionate to the influence exerted by the leader. Then comes the real test, which determines the vitality and permanence of the movement. Has the spirit of the founder descended on his followers? With Luke, and with all the great leaders of the first century, that was the test of every new man and every new congregation : had the Spirit been granted to them?

In the second month after their leader was taken away, on the day of Pentecost, the test was fulfilled in the primitive Church ; and the capacity of his disciples to carry on his work was shown. They became conscious of the power that had been given them, and their new power was recognised by the multitude in their words and in their looks. The same impression of a transformed and re-created nature was made on the elders and scribes, when they examined Peter and John (IV 13 f., see § 2).

By virtue of that Divine grace, "many wonders and signs were done by the Apostles," *v.* 43, during the following time. But it is vital to Luke's method not to rest contented with that general statement, but to give one special, clear example of the power communicated to the Apostles and to the Church of which they were the leaders. It would be waste of time to regret that he passes over so much that we should like to know, and devotes so much space to a marvel that is to us a difficulty : our present aim is to understand the purpose of what he does say, not to long after what he omits.

The example is given in III ; the subsequent events of the same day are narrated IV 1-4 ; and the following day is described IV 5-31, when Peter and John, in whom the proof of Divine grace had been shown forth, were examined before a meeting of "the rulers and elders and scribes ". These are represented as realising now for the first time, *v.* 13, the change that had come over Peter and John, who from "unlearned and ignorant men" had been transformed into bold and eloquent preachers. Evidently the historian conceives that this transformation, wrought at Pentecost, was now beginning to be generally felt ; and therefore he is still (as we have said) describing the immediate issue of Pentecost. Thereafter comes a second general statement of the state and character of the primitive Church, startlingly similar to II 43-47.

Thus the whole passage II 43-IV 35 hangs very closely together, and describes the Church in the period immediately succeeding May 26, A.D. 30. Two episodes of this period, exemplifying the conduct of the true and the false convert, are described IV 36-V 11 ; and then comes a third general description of the state of the Church in this period V 12-16, followed by a statement of the attempt made by the Jewish leaders to coerce the Apostles into silence V 17-41.

That at least two accounts by two different authorities underlie Luke's narrative, and have been worked up by him with little change, seems clear. It is, of course, obvious that he was entirely dependent for this period of his history on the authority of other persons ; and we see in the Third Gospel how much he was influenced by the very language of his authorities, and how little change he made on their words.[1]

---

[1] Thus the particle μὲν οὖν, so common in *Acts*, occurs only once in the Third Gospel, in a passage peculiar to Luke, III 18. In XXII 56 he added the little touch ἀτενίσασα to the narrative as used by Matthew and Mark, see p. 39.

2. TRUSTWORTHINESS OF THE NARRATIVE, *Acts* I-V. It is obvious that the trustworthiness of this part of *Acts* stands on quite a different footing from that of the Pauline narrative, which we have hitherto discussed. The author had means of knowing the later events with perfect accuracy (so far as perfection can be attained in history); but the means which helped him there fail in I-V, and the scene and surroundings were to him strange and remote (p. 19 f.). He was here dependent entirely on others, and it was more difficult for him to control and make himself master of the evolution of events. We discern the same guiding hand and mind, the same clear historical insight seizing the great and critical steps, in the early chapters, as in the later; but the description of the primitive Church wants precision in the outline and colour in the details. It seems clear that the authorities on which Luke depended were not equally good; and here second-rate incidents are admitted along with first-rate in a way that has done his reputation serious injury in the estimation of those who begin to study *Acts* from this, its necessarily weakest part. One or two examples will bring out our meaning. First we take an incident related also by Matthew.

Matthew XXVII 5-8.	*Acts I 18-19.*
AND HE WENT AWAY AND HANGED HIMSELF. AND THE CHIEF PRIESTS TOOK THE PIECES OF SILVER, AND SAID, " IT IS NOT LAWFUL TO PUT THEM INTO THE TREASURY, SINCE IT IS THE PRICE OF	NOW THIS MAN OB-TAINED A FIELD WITH THE REWARD OF HIS INIQUITY ; AND FALLING HEADLONG, HE BURST ASUNDER IN THE MIDST, AND ALL HIS BOWELS GUSHED OUT. AND IT BE-

BLOOD ". AND THEY TOOK COUNSEL, AND BOUGHT WITH THEM THE POTTER'S FIELD, TO BURY STRANGERS IN. WHEREFORE THAT FIELD WAS CALLED THE FIELD OF BLOOD, UNTO THIS DAY. CAME KNOWN TO ALL THE DWELLERS AT JERUSALEM ; INSOMUCH THAT IN THEIR LANGUAGE THAT FIELD WAS CALLED AKELDAMA, THAT IS, THE FIELD OF BLOOD.

There can be no hesitation in accepting the vivid and detailed description which Matthew gives of this incident. But, if so, the account given in *Acts* cannot be accepted as having any claim to trustworthiness in any point of discrepancy. The character of this account is marked, and its origin obvious. It is a growth of popular fancy and tradition, which preserved the main facts, *viz.*, the connection between the name, *Field of Blood*, and the price paid to the betrayer. But it is characteristic of popular tradition, while it preserves some central fact, to overlay it with fanciful accretions, which often conceal completely the historical kernel. In this case, we have the tale arrested at an early point in its growth, when its elements are still separable. The name *Field of Blood* had to be explained suitably to the remembered fact that it was bought with the betrayer's reward ; but its meaning was mistaken. Popular fancy always craves for justice ; it connected the name with the betrayer's punishment, took the Blood, which formed one element of the name, as the betrayer's blood, and evolved a myth which united fact and retributory justice in a moral apologue.

It is a remarkable thing that popular tradition should so soon distort a tale so simple and so impressive. But oriental tradition never clings to fact with anything like the same tenacity as Greek tradition; and we know how much even the latter distorts and covers over the facts that it preserves. The oriental mind has little or nothing of the proper historical tone. It remembers facts, not for their own value, but for the lesson they can convey. It substitutes the moral apologue for history in the strict sense of the term, craving for the former, and possessing little regard for the latter. It acts with great rapidity, transforming the memory of the past within the lapse of a few years; and probably those who know the East best will find least difficulty in believing that the story which Luke here gives might have been told him, when the Field of Blood was pointed out to him at Jerusalem in 57 A.D.

But in this rapid transformation of fact in Eastern popular tradition lies the best safeguard of the historical student against it. He rarely needs to doubt, as he often must in Greece, whether any narrative is history or mere popular tradition. Greek tradition often has such a natural appearance that it is hard to say where fact ends and fancy begins. But oriental tradition is so free in its creation, so unfettered by any thought of suitability in the accessories, that it is marked off from history by a broad and deep gap. By history we mean narrative founded on documents that are nearly contemporary with the actual facts, or on the accounts of eye-witnesses, not implying that "history" must be absolutely true. To give a true account even of a single incident that one has actually participated in is not within the power of all, for it needs education, skill in selection, and an eye to distinguish the relative importance of different points. To give a true account of a long series of incidents is, of course, much more difficult. No history is absolutely true; all give accounts that are more or less distorted pictures of fact. But the conception of history as an attempt to represent facts in correct perspective, even when it is poorly and feebly carried out, is a great and sacred possession, which we owe to the Greeks ; and is a generically different thing from popular tradition, which aims either at the moral apologue, or the glory of an individual or a family, and regards faithfulness to actual facts as quite a secondary thing.

The episode of Ananias and Sapphira V 1 f. excites reasonable suspicion. That Ananias should be carried forth and buried unknown to his family, unmourned by his kindred and friends, is not merely contrary to right conduct, but violates the deepest feelings of oriental life. That a man should be properly lamented and wept for by his family is and has always been a sacred right, which even crime does not forfeit. But the desire to bring into strong relief the unselfishness of the primitive Church has worked itself out in a moral apologue, which has found here an entrance alongside of real history.

Again in II 5-11 another popular tale seems to obtrude itself. In these verses the power of speaking with tongues, which is clearly described by Paul as a species of prophesying (I *Cor.* XII 10 f., XIV 1 f.), is taken in the sense of speaking in many languages. Here again we observe the distorting influence of popular fancy.

Yet alongside of these suspicious stories we find passages which show strongly the characteristic method of Luke ; and the entire plan of the narrative, concentrating attention on the successive critical steps, is thoroughly Lukan. We take one example of a Lukan passage.

The incident in IV 13 f. is especially characteristic of

Luke's style; and it has been widely misunderstood. Zeller, Holtzmann, Meyer-Wendt and others, understand these verses to mean that the members of the Sanhedrim became aware only during the trial that Peter and John had been disciples of Jesus : which, as they justly point out, is most unnatural and unsuitable. But the force of the passage seems to be very different : the Jewish leaders perceived the bold and fluent speech of Peter and John , and yet they observed from their dress and style of utterance that they were not trained scholars ; and they marvelled (for there was then probably an even more marked distinction than at the present day between the speech and thought of a fisherman or shepherd and of an educated person) ; and they further took cognisance of the fact that they were disciples of Jesus ; and they gazed on the man that had been cured standing along with his pre-servers. These were the facts of the case : all were un-deniable ; and all were vividly brought before them. What conclusion could be drawn from them ? The historian's point is that there was only one possible inference ; and, as the Jewish leaders were unwilling to draw that inference, they perforce kept silence, not having wherewithal to dis-pute the obvious conclusion.

Here, as usual, the historian does not himself draw the inference; but merely states the main facts, and leaves them to tell their own tale. But in no passage does he state the facts in more dramatic form. The conclusion lies close at hand, *viz.*, that these illiterate fishermen had acquired the art and power of effective oratory through their having been the disciples of Jesus, and through the Divine grace and power communicated to them.

We notice also that John's speech has not previously

been mentioned, yet now it is assumed that he had spoken. This is characteristic of the writer's style, as we have seen it in the second part of the work. It is evident that Peter's single speech did not exhaust the proceedings at the trial; but Luke assumes that the reader conceives the general situation and the style of procedure in such trials; and he quotes the most telling utterance, and leaves the rest to the reader's imagination.

We are struck with the marked difference of *Acts* I-V, not merely from the later chapters, but also from Luke's First Book, the *Gospel.* In composing his Book I, he had formal works of a historical kind to use for his authorities (*Luke* I 1); and he followed them very closely, not giving scope to his own method of narration or of grouping. But these formal works seem all to have ended either with the death or the ascension of the Saviour; and the most obscure and difficult period for a historian writing about 80-85 A.D. was the time that immediately succeeded the death of Jesus. Luke was dependent here on informal narratives, and on oral tradition; and, if we be right in our view that he did not live to put the last touches to his work, we may fairly suppose that the most difficult period was left the least perfect part of the whole. But we must content ourselves here with this slight indication of a view that would require much minute argument to state properly. There is a marked resemblance between I-V and XIX. In both, episodes that savour of popular fancy stand side by side with Lukan work of the best kind.

3. APPOINTMENT OF STEPHEN AND THE SEVEN. The first distinct step in development from the primitive condition of the Church, when it was a mere small and

almost unorganised community, was due to the pressure of poverty. In Jerusalem very poor Jews were numerous, and many of them had become Christian. Hence from the beginning the Church had to contend against a chronic state of want among its adherents. Probably we are apt to find a more communistic sense than Luke intended in II 44, IV 32; for II 4, IV 35 indicate judicious charity, and even the action of Barnabas in IV 37 looks more like charity than communism:[1] he and others sold their possessions and gave the money in trust to the Apostles for the good of the Church. In later years, as the Church spread, the pressure of need in Jerusalem acted as a bond to unite the scattered congregations in active ministration (pp. 49 f., 288); and at the beginning it stimulated the primitive Church to originate a better organisation.

The difficulties in which the Church was placed, which would have killed a weakly life, only stimulated its vigour and its creative energy. This creative vitality is to the historian the most interesting side of the early Church; it was free from dead conservatism; it combined the most perfect reverence for its earliest form with the most perfect freedom to adapt that form to new exigencies; it did not stifle growth on the plea that it must remain exactly as it was. It was growing so rapidly that it burst through its earliest forms, before they could acquire any binding force, or fix themselves in the prejudices of its members. This free untrammelled expansion was the law of its life, and the Divine reality of its being. In later times, on the contrary, many of its adherents have maintained that its

---

[1] The story of Ananias points more to communism. Yet even here Peter's speech regards the act of Ananias as a purely voluntary one, though V 2 seems to represent it almost as a duty.

Divine life lies in its preserving unchanged from the beginning the form that was prescribed for it. Thus the view taken in *Acts* is that the Church's Divine character lies in the free unceasing growth of its form and institutions; but the common view of later times has been that its Divine character lies in the permanence and unchangeability of its form from the beginning onwards.

At first Luke represents the superintendence and distribution of these charities as undertaken solely by the Apostles, who soon found that " it was not meet that they should forsake preaching and perform the ministration at tables" (VI 2). Moreover, in the pressure of claims and accumulation of duties, complaint was made that the widows among the Hellenist Jews were neglected in favour of the native Hebrews. It was therefore arranged that a new class of officers should be instituted,—for whom no name is here given, but who were the origin out of which the " Deacons " of the developed Church arose.

It is a remarkable fact that the Elders are not mentioned here; and this is one of the points which show Luke's want of proper authorities about the primitive Church. When we come to a period, where his information was good, we find the Elders prominent, and specially in practical business matters (pp. 52, 166, 171); and there can be no doubt that this characteristic Jewish institution existed as a matter of course in the primitive Church. The superintendence of relief measures was recognised as peculiarly their province (XI 30). It seems clear that in the memory of tradition the Apostles had survived alone as being the far more prominent figures, while the first Elders had been almost forgotten.

The new officers are here termed simply " Seven Men

in charge of this duty " (*i.e.*, *septem viri mensis ordinandis*). It would be easy to find Jewish analogies that would explain the original idea ; but it would not be easy to find any Jewish analogy to explain the vitality and adaptability of the institution. We must turn to Roman organising methods to find anything that will explain the importance and lasting effect of this step. Roman ideas were in the air ; and the vigorous life of the Church was shown in its power of seizing and adapting to its own purposes all that was strong and serviceable in the world. It suited itself to its surroundings, and used the existing political facts and ideas, "learning from the surrounding world everything that was valuable in it" (p. 149).

The Seven who were appointed bear purely Greek names ; and one was not a Jew, but a proselyte of Antioch. There can, therefore, be no doubt that a distinct step towards the Universalised Church was here made ; it was already recognised that the Church was wider than the pure Jewish race ; and the non-Jewish element was raised to official rank. Nikolaos was a proselyte of the higher and completer type (p. 43) ; and his case was therefore quite different in character from that of Cornelius (p. 42 f.), who was only *God-fearing*. In the conferring of office on Nikolaos a distinct step was made ; but it was quite in accordance with the principle of the extreme Judaistic party in the Church (p. 157). The case of Cornelius was a second and more serious step.

The consequences of this first step in advance were soon apparent. The wider sympathies and wider outlook of Hellenistic Jews quickened the life of the young community ; and Stephen, especially, was con-

spicuous for the boldness with which he advocated the
faith and opposed the narrowness of Judaism, saying, as
his accusers alleged, "that this Jesus of Nazareth shall
destroy this place, and shall change the customs which
Moses delivered unto us". Even though this is a per-
version of Stephen's meaning, yet the form implies that
Stephen had advanced beyond the previous position of
the Apostles as regards their relation to Judaism.

The critical point in chronology is to determine the date
of Stephen's accusation and martyrdom. Luke gives us
no clear evidence as to the length of the two periods that
he describes, *viz.*, (1) between Pentecost and the election of
the Seven, (2) between the election and the death of
Stephen. The latest date which our view leaves open is
A.D. 33, for Paul's conversion followed shortly after
Stephen's death, and in the fourteenth year after his
conversion he visited Jerusalem for the second time, probably in 46 (though 45 is not absolutely excluded, pp. 51,
68). Can we suppose that the necessity for the admission
of the Hellenistic Jews to official rank was felt already in
A.D. 32, and that Stephen's brief career ended in 33 ? The
space of two years has seemed sufficient to many scholars ;
some have been content with one. The difficulties which
the primitive Church had to meet by appointing the Seven
faced it from the first ; and that step was probably forced
on it very soon. The wider spirit shown in the selection
of the Seven was likely to cause an early collision with
Jewish jealousy ; and the party which had cut off Jesus
was not likely to suffer His followers to increase so rapidly
without an effort to stop the movement. Now the persecution that caused and followed Stephen's death was the
first attempt at coercion ; the actions described in IV 5 f.

and V 17 f. were mere warnings and threats, which naturally resulted soon in active measures. We cannot easily believe that repressive measures were delayed more than two or three years at the utmost ; we should rather have expected them even sooner.

It is therefore quite fair to date Stephen's death about two and a half or three years after the great Pentecost.

4. PHILIP THE EVANGELIST AND PETER. After the death of Stephen, the history widens, and several threads appear in it. The foundation of a series of Churches over Judæa and Samaria is first described ; and the author's attention is directed chiefly on three steps in the progress towards the Universalised Church, the foundation of an extra-Judæan Church in the city of Samaria, and the admission of an Ethiopian[1] and of a Roman centurion as Christians. These steps are connected with the names of Philip and Peter. The institution of a series of Churches in Palestine, a process which must have occupied a long time, is briefly but clearly indicated in VIII 40, IX 31-35, 42 f. ; but Luke's personal interest in the expansion of a still purely Judaic Church was not great. Yet the episodes of Æneas and Dorcas, IX 33-42, show that, though the details seemed to Luke not required for his purpose, the spread of the Church over Palestine was conceived by him as an important step in history. These episodes are introduced, because they proved that the Divine power worked in the process whereby the Church of Jerusalem expanded into the Church of all Palestine. In the utter absence of statement as to Luke's authority for the two episodes, they cannot be placed by the historian on a higher level than general

[1] He was evidently a proselyte (VIII 27), like Nikolaos.

belief. It is remarkable that we have no knowledge whether Luke ever met Peter. The want of any reference to Peter in XXI 18 must, in our view, be taken as a proof that he was not in Jerusalem at the time.

In the midst of the narrative describing this expansion is interposed an account of Saul's life during the three years 33-5 ;[1] and this arrangement is obviously intended to bring out the long period over which that process of expansion was spread. According to our theory it continued from A.D. 33 until it was checked to some extent by the development of the Pauline idea and the jealousy roused thereby among almost all Jews except the great and leading minds, which were able to rise more or less completely above it. Then came the supreme catastrophe of the great war, the destruction of Jerusalem, and the suppression of "the Nation" of the Jews.

The expansion of the Church beyond Palestine is first alluded to in XI 19, where the dispersion of missionaries over Phœnice, Cyprus, and Syria is mentioned (Ch. III, § 1). It is remarkable that Luke never alludes to the developmeut of the Church towards the south or east. Yet the dispersion that followed Stephen's death must have radiated in all directions ; and II 7-11, and VIII 27 f., lead naturally to some general spread of the new teaching in all directions. It is obvious that Luke has not made it his object to write the history of the whole expansion of the Church ; but selected the facts that bore on a narrower theme, *viz.*, the steps by which the Church of Jerusalem grew into the Church of the Empire,

---

[1] We shall speak of 33 as the date of Stephen's death and Paul's conversion, acknowledging, however, that perhaps 32 is the proper year.

and the position of the Church in the Empire. Egypt,
Ethiopia, and the East and South are therefore excluded
from his narrative.

5. PAUL IN JUDÆA AND ARABIA. The introduction of Paul is connected with the death of Stephen : he
was then a young man, and probably was entering for the
first time on public life.   At this point the subjective
touch in VIII 1, "Saul was consenting unto his death," is
a clear indication that Luke's authority was Paul himself.
The phrase is a confession of inward feeling, not a
historian's account of action ; and the words are Paul's
own (XXII 20). A dramatic touch like this is, on our
theory, deliberately calculated.   Luke intends to set before
his readers the scene at Cæsareia, where Philip narrated
the story of Stephen and of his own early work, and Paul
interposed the agonised confession of VIII 1.   The
narrative from VI 9 to VIII 39 probably reproduces
Philip's words very closely; while Luke has inserted
touches, as VII 58, VIII 1, and adapted the whole to his
plan.[1]

The slight variations in the three accounts of Paul's
conversion do not seem to be of any consequence.   Luke
did not seek to modify Paul's speeches in order to produce
verbal conformity with the account which seemed to him
to represent the facts fairly ; but the spirit and tone and
the essential facts are the same, IX 3·18, XXII 6-16,
XXVI 12-18.

Two difficulties, however, deserve notice in the account
of Paul's conduct during the first years after his conver-

---

[1] The enumeration of synagogues in VI 9, which does not agree
with Luke's manner, was perhaps noted down verbatim (*Expositor*,
July 1895, p. 35).

sion. In the first place, why does Luke say nothing about Paul's journey into Arabia? But we have no authority for believing that the journey was of such importance as to require a place in this history, for Luke does not enumerate all the influences that moulded Paul's development. Paul's reference to the incident (*Gal.* I 17) is clear and complete in itself, if it was not a serious journey, but a small episode in his private life. " When it pleased God to call me to the work of my life, so far was I from needing counsel or instruction from Jerusalem, that I retired into Arabia, and came back again to Damascus." Damascus was at the time subject to the King of Arabia Petræa ; and the natural interpretation is that a person describing incidents of his experience in Damascus means by Arabia the adjacent country on the east. Had this excursion been an important step in the development of Paul's thought (as Lightfoot inclines to think, when he sees in it a sojourn on Mount Sinai after the style of Moses), Luke might be expected to mention it and show how much underlies Paul's words ; but, as he does not mention it, the fair inference is that there was no more in it than Paul says explicitly.

Moreover, Luke divides Paul's stay in Damascus into two periods, a few days' residence with the disciples IX 19, and a long period of preaching 20-23. The quiet residence in the country for a time, recovering from the serious and prostrating effect of his conversion (for a man's life is not suddenly reversed without serious claim on his physical power), is the dividing fact between the two periods. The division is certainly very awkwardly and insufficiently indicated ; but Luke everywhere shows similar weakness in indicating the temporal relations of events.

In the second place, the accounts of Paul's first visit
to Jerusalem, in the third year after his conversion, are
obscure. In *Gal.* I 18 f. Paul says he went up to see
Peter (evidently regarding him as the leading spirit in
the development of the Church), and saw no other
Apostle, except James the Lord's brother. But in *Acts*
IX 28 f. "he was with the Apostles going in and going
out at Jerusalem, preaching boldly in the name of the
Lord. And he spake and disputed against the Grecian
Jews; but they went about to kill him." In weighing
this account we must bear in mind Luke's intention:
he conceived the Apostles as the permanent governing
body in Jerusalem (p. 53), and they dwarfed in his
estimation any other administrative body in the primitive
Church (p. 374). Here, therefore, he speaks loosely of
"the Apostles," meaning the governing body of the
Church, without implying that they were all present in
Jerusalem. It was one of his objects to insist on the
agreement between Paul and the leaders of the Church;
and he distinctly had, and communicates, the impression
that the opposition of the extreme Judaistic party to
Paul was factious, and was condemned by the leaders.
It therefore seemed important to him to emphasise the
harmony between Paul and the Jewish leaders at this
first visit; and, though most of the Apostles were absent,
yet the two real leaders were present. We certainly
should not naturally infer from Luke's words that the
visit lasted only fifteen days; but there is no real difficulty in supposing that Paul's life was at this time in
danger from the first. He had deserted his former friends,
and they would feel towards him the hatred that always
pursues a deserter.

On the other hand, XXVI 20 is distinctly in contradiction with all other authorities; but, as Dr. Blass points out, the Greek is solecistic, and his altered reading, "in every land to both Jews and Gentiles," seems to me to carry conviction with it.[1]

The difficulty with regard to the interval between Paul's first and second visit to Jerusalem (which we consider to have been only eleven years, whereas many take it as fourteen, *Gal.* II 1) disappears when we take the Greek in its real sense. Paul says to the Galatians, "Then, in the third year,[2] I went up to Jerusalem . . . then, when the fourteenth year was ending ". The two reckonings go together, and are estimated from the same starting-point.

[1] πᾶσάν τε τὴν χώραν τῆς Ἰουδαίας is not Lukan, and hardly Greek read εἰς πᾶσαν χώραν Ἰουδαίοις τε.

[2] "After three years" misrepresents the meaning.

CHAPTER XVII

COMPOSITION AND DATE OF *ACTS*

1. HYPOTHESIS OF "THE TRAVEL-DOCUMENT". We have seen that Luke represents himself as having been an eye witness of some of the incidents which he describes; and we have inferred, from the pointed way in which he does this, that he was not an eye-witness of the rest. In the parts where he had no personal knowledge his trustworthiness depends on his authority in each case. In a former work I have tried to show that there lies behind the narrative of Paul's journeys a document originating "from a person acquainted with the actual circumstances," and therefore "composed under St. Paul's own influence". I was careful "to express his influence in the most general terms, and to avoid any theorising about the way in which it was exercised"; and I purposely left the question untouched whether the "Travel-Document" was composed by the author of *Acts* or by a different person; for my object then was to show that the document was a trustworthy record of facts, to avoid constructing a system, to investigate each fact independently on its own evidence, and to give no opening to the criticism that I was twisting the evidence at any point in order to suit an idea derived from elsewhere.

In the present work the reasons on which the supposition of a " Travel-Document " was founded are much strengthened; and we must now put the question in a more precise form. What is the relation between the " Travel-Document " and the completed text of *Acts?* To this the answer must be that the " Travel-Document " was Luke's own written notes (supplemented by memory, and the education of further experience and reading and research). His diary, where he was an eye-witness, and his notes of conversation with Paul, and doubtless others also, were worked into the book of *Acts* suitably to the carefully arranged plan on which it is constructed. We have found traces of deep and strong emotion which must be understood as Paul's own feeling : the technical term for making a missionary progress through a district[1] is used only by Paul (I *Cor.* XVI 5) and by Luke in describing Paul's work;[2] while in describing the precisely similar work of other missionaries, he uses a different and a more usual Greek construction.[3] This line of investigation might be carried much further so as to show that Luke everywhere follows with minute care the best authority accessible to him ; and in *Acts* especially Paul and Philip. As we have seen, Ch. XVI, § 2, the period in which he found greatest difficulty was that which intervened between the conclusion of his formal historical authorities for the life of the Saviour, and the beginning of the careful narratives which he had noted down from Paul and Philip about their own personal experiences.

[1] *Itinerating* is the modern equivalent, I am told.
[2] XIII 6, XIV 24, XV 3, 41, XVI 6, XVIII 23, XIX 1, 21, XX 2.   [3] VIII 4, 40, XI 19, IX 32, *Luke* IX 6.

One episode, which bears all the marks of vivid personal witness, comes under neither of these categories, *viz.*, the story of Peter's imprisonment and escape, XII. Here some other authority was used ; and the narrative suggests distinctly that the authority was not Peter himself, but one of those in the house of Mary. John Mark, who is pointedly mentioned as being in Jerusalem, XII 25, and who was afterwards with Luke and Paul in Rome, was almost certainly (*v.* 12) the ultimate authority here.

Luke added to these authorities an obvious acquaintance with Paul's own letters   He rarely states anything that is recorded in them ; he assumes them as known ; and he makes it one of his objects to set them in a clearer light.

The whole of his materials he used with the true historical sense for the comparative importance of events and for the critical steps in a great movement, and also with a wide and careful study of the general history of the contemporary world (*i.e.*, the Roman Empire). The research which Luke applied in the execution of his work is shown with especial clearness in the chronological calculations which he introduced in Book I (similar to those which he would probably have added in Book II, see p. 23). These calculations deserve fresh study with a view to estimate the work which the author has compressed into them. The accuracy of one of them (*viz.*, the statement about Philip in *Luke* III 1) I have defended elsewhere, and, as I believe, on grounds which would carry conviction to every one, were it not that they are inconsistent with the dominant North-Galatian theory. Again the census (*Luke* II 1) under Quirinius is pointedly called *the first*, implying that it was the first of a series of *census*. A census is known to have been made in

Syria by Quirinius in his second government, about 6 A.D., which suggests that they were perhaps decennial. We have no other evidence as to a census in 5-4 B.C.; but when we consider how purely accidental is the evidence [1] for the second census, the want of evidence for the first seems to constitute no argument against the trustworthiness of Luke's statement. It is certain that the dependent kingdoms paid tribute to Rome exactly as if they had been part of the Empire; and it is in perfect accord with the methodical character of Augustus's administration that he should order such *census* to be made regularly throughout "the whole world". Incidentally we observe in this phrase that Luke's view is absolutely confined to the Roman Empire, which to him is "the world". Luke investigated the history of this series of *census*.

2. DATE OF THE COMPOSITION OF *ACTS*. The elaborate series of synchronisms by which Luke dates the coming of John the Baptist are especially remarkable; and it is to them we turn for evidence as to the date of composition. On our view the Crucifixion took place at the Passover of A.D. 30, the fourth Passover in the public career of Jesus. Now John was six months older than Jesus; and his career began in his thirtieth year, a little before the coming of Jesus. Thus we reach the conclusion that the synchronisms of *Luke* III 1, 2, are calculated for the summer (say July) of A.D. 26; and he calls this year the fifteenth of the reign of Tiberius, implying that he

---

[1] An inscription found in Venice is the sole authority. As the stone was lost, the inscription was pronounced a forgery, apparently for no reason except that it mentioned Quirinius's census. Even Mommsen refused to admit it as genuine, until, fortunately, part of the stone was rediscovered

reckoned his reign to begin A.D. 12, when Tiberius was associated by Augustus in the Empire. But such a method of reckoning the reign of Tiberius was unknown. According to Roman reckoning, Tiberius, in July A.D. 26, was either in his twelfth year (reckoning from the death of his predecessor) or in his twenty-eighth year (reckoning his tenure of the tribunician power). No other way of reckoning his reign was ever employed by Romans. How then could Luke speak of his fifteenth year? There can hardly be any other reason than that the calculation was made under an Emperor whose years were reckoned from his association as colleague; so that Luke, being familiar with that method, applied it to the case of Tiberius. Now that was the case with Titus. His reign began from his association with his father on 1st July A.D. 71.

We thus get a clue, though in itself an uncertain one, to suggest the date when Luke was at work. His chronological calculations were probably inserted as the finishing touches of Book I (p. 23), while Titus was reigning as sole Emperor, 79-81 A.D. ; and the com-position of that book belongs to the years immediately preceding, while the composition of Book II belongs to the years immediately following. This argument, taken by itself, would be insufficient ; but it is confirmed by the impression which the book as a whole makes. *Acts* could not have been written so late as Trajan, when long persecution had altered the tone and feeling of the Church towards the State. It is the work of a man whose mind has been moulded in a more peaceful time, and who has not passed through a time like the reign of Domitian (p. 22). On the other hand, its tone is not that of assured conviction about the relation to the State,

such as we observe in Paul's Epistles.   It is the tone of
one who seeks to prove a position that is doubtful and
assailed, but still of one who believes that it may be
proved.   As we have seen, there runs through the entire
work a purpose which could hardly have been conceived
before the State had begun to persecute on political
grounds.   So long as Christians were proceeded against
merely on the ground of crimes, which the accuser sought
to prove by evidence (as was the case with Paul, p. 360),
there was no necessity to establish that Christianity was
legal.   Defence then consisted in disproving the specific
crimes charged against the individual Christian; but,
after the Flavian policy had declared Christianity illegal
and proscribed the Name, the first necessity for defence
was to claim legal right.

3. T H E O P H I L U S.   It has an important bearing on
Luke's attitude towards the Roman State that his work
is addressed to a Roman officer,[1] who had become a
Christian.   We may safely say that in the first century a
Roman official would hardly bear the name Theophilus ; and
therefore it must be a name given to him at baptism, and
used or known only among the Christians.   The fact that
his public name is avoided, and only the baptismal name
used, favours the supposition (though not absolutely
demanding it) that it was dangerous for a Roman of rank
to be recognised as a Christian.   In the narrative of *Acts*
there is not the slightest trace of private or baptismal

---

[1] The epithet κράτιστος is technical and distinctive, and not a mere
usitata appellatio hominum dignitate præstantium, as even Blass takes
it, on *Acts* XXIII 26.   Luke uses it strictly there and in XXIV 3,
XXVI 25, implying equestrian rank.   Some Greeks were not so
accurate as Luke.

names. These seem to have been adopted under the pressure of necessity and from the desire for concealment. Thus the very dedication of the work points to a developed state of the relations between Church and State, and carries us down to the time of Domitian.

4. THE FAMILY OF LUKE. We have made it an object to collect the scanty traces of Luke's personality that remain in *Acts;* and we may therefore conclude our task by referring to the tradition about his birthplace. The later tradition, as it appears in Jerome, Euthalius, etc., declares that Luke was an Antiochian,[1] but it is practically certain that the authority for all the later statements is Eusebius. Eusebius, however, does not say that Luke was an Antiochian ; he merely speaks of him as " being according to birth of those from Antioch ".[2] This curious and awkward expression is obviously chosen in order to avoid the statement that Luke was an Antiochian ; and it amounts to an assertion that Luke was not an Antiochian, but belonged to a family that had a connection with Antioch. Eusebius therefore had access to a more detailed and distinct tradition, which he reproduces in this brief form. The older tradition must have told that Luke had a family connection with Antioch ; and Eusebius carefully restricts himself to that statement ; but the tradition probably set forth the exact connection, and it is perhaps allowable to conclude our study with a conjecture.

Antioch, as a Seleucid foundation, had almost certainly a Macedonian element in its population. It is now well-established that the military strength of the Seleucid

[1] Ἀντιοχεὺς γὰρ οὗτος ὑπάρχων τὸ γένος, Euthalius in Migne, *Patr Gr.* vol. 85, p. 633. *Lucas medicus Antiochensis,* Jerome, *Vir. Ill.*

[2] Λουκᾶς δὲ τὸ μὲν γένος ὢν τῶν ἀπ' Ἀντιοχείας, *Hist. Eccles.* III 4.

colonies lay usually in a contingent of Macedonians; and a considerable number of Seleucid cities style themselves *Macedones* on coins or inscriptions. It is quite probable that intercourse and connection may have been maintained between the Macedonian element in Antioch and their original home; and migrations to and fro are likely to have occurred between Macedonia and Antioch in the constant and easy intercourse of the centuries following the foundation. Thus it may very well have happened that Luke was a relative of one of the early Antiochian Christians; and this relationship was perhaps the authority for Eusebius's carefully guarded statement. Further, it is possible that this relationship gives the explanation of the omission of Titus from *Acts*, an omission which every one finds it so difficult[1] to understand. Perhaps Titus was the relative of Luke; and Eusebius found this statement in an old tradition, attached to II *Cor.* VIII 18, XII 18, where Titus and Luke (the latter not named by Paul, but identified by an early tradition) are associated as envoys to Corinth. Luke, as we may suppose, thought it right to omit his relative's name, as he did his own name, from his history. There is not sufficient evidence to justify an opinion; but this conjecture brings together an enigmatic expression in Eusebius and a serious difficulty in *Acts*, and finds in each a satisfactory solution of the other.

[1] We cannot agree with Lightfoot, who solves the difficulty by denying that Titus was important enough to deserve mention in *Acts* (*Biblical Essays*, p. 281).

INDEX I

PASSAGES QUOTED FROM THE NEW TESTAMENT

(391)

Index

II.—CHRONOLOGICAL INDEX TO THE LIFE

OF ST. PAUL

* References are given in parentheses to discussion of some dates in the *Church in the Roman Empire before 170.*

(395)

INDEX III

THE (CHRISTIAN) CIRCLE OF ST. PAUL.*

* Roman officials in Index IV.

(397)

IV.—GENERAL INDEX

SIR WILLIAM M. RAMSAY

ARCHAEOLOGIST AND
NEW TESTAMENT SCHOLAR

by
W. Ward Gasque

LIST OF ABBREVIATIONS[1]

1 Excepting *HDB*, all works are by Ramsay. Complete bibliographical data is given in the bibliography.

BRD *The Bearing of Recent Discovery on the Trustworthiness of the New Testament*, 1915.

CB *The Cities and Bishoprics of Phrygia*, 1895 and 1897.

CRE *The Church in the Roman Empire before A.D. 170*, 1893.

CSP *The Cities of St. Paul: Their Influence on His Life and Thought*, 1907.

EC *The Education of Christ: Hill-Side Reveries*, 1902.

FCC *The First Christian Century: Notes on Dr. Moffatt's Introduction to the Literature of the New Testament*, 1911.

HCG *A Historical Commentary on St. Paul's Epistle to the Galatians*, 1899.

HDB James Hastings (ed.), *Dictionary of the Bible*, 1898-1904.

HG *The Historical Geography of Asia Minor*, 1890.

LP *Luke the Physician and Other Studies in the History of Religion*, 1908.

LSC *The Letters to the Seven Churches of Asia*, 1904.

PAC *Pictures of the Apostolic Church: Studies in the Book of Acts*, 1910.

POS *Pauline and Other Studies in Early Christian History*, 1906.

SPT *St. Paul the Traveller and the Roman Citizen*, 1895.

TP *The Teachings of Paul in Terms of the Present Day*, 1913.

WCB *Was Christ Born at Bethlehem?* 1898.

I

AN INTRODUCTION TO THE MAN
AND HIS WORK

In the person of Sir William Ramsay (1851-1939) one finds a rare combination. He was, on the one hand, a classical scholar and archaeologist, "the foremost authority of his day on the topography, antiquities, and history of Asia Minor in ancient times"[1]; at the same time he was one of the foremost authorities in the study of the New Testament, especially the Book of Acts and the letters of Paul. Few men are able to become masters in one field of study; Ramsay was master in two.

William Mitchell Ramsay was born the youngest son of a third-generation lawyer in Glasgow, Scotland, on March 15, 1851. His father passed away when he was six years old. Shortly thereafter the family moved from the city of Glasgow to the family home in the country district near Alloa.

His older brother and maternal uncle, Andrew Mitchell, made it possible for him to have the best education attainable. He received excellent preparation for university at the Aberdeen Gymnasium and from there went on to study at the University of Aberdeen, where he achieved high distinction.

In March, 1868, at the end of his second year at the university, he was enjoying his college work immensely and finding every moment spent in classwork or in preparation a delight. Of this time he later wrote, "The idea was simmering unconsciously in my mind that scholarship was the life for me: not the life of teaching, which was repellent, but the life of discovery."[2] When

---

1 J. G. C. Anderson, "Sir William Mitchell Ramsay," *Dictionary of National Biography 1931-1940*, p. 727.
2 *BRD*, p. 7.

the final day of the school term arrived, the members of the second-year class were all gathered in the Latin classroom. Ramsay later remarked that he had the feeling that something significant was going to happen that morning. Both the Professor of Greek and the Professor of Latin announced to the class that he was the number one student in each subject. Then and there his life was determined; he formed the resolve to be a scholar and to make everything else in his life subservient to that purpose and career.[3] Forty-five years later, he looked back on that day:

> In the class-room, also, one other matter settled itself. The border-land between Greece and the East, the relation of Greek literature to Asia, had already a vague fascination for me; and this was to be the direction of the life that I imagined in the future. As it turned out that thought of the relation between Greece and the East was an anticipation of my life; but the form developed in a way that I did not imagine until many years passed. I thought of work in a room or a library, but it has lain largely in the open air and on the geographical frontier where Greek-speaking people touched the East. I thought of Greek literature in its relation to Asia; but the subject widened into the relation between the spirit of Europe and of Asia through the centuries.[4]

How was he to achieve his goal to be a scholar? He knew the only path lay in an Oxford Fellowship, so before the meeting ended he had made his plans in that direction. However, he was careful to tell no one but his closest friends, for his family had intended that he compete for an appointment in the Indian Civil Service. When he finally did tell them three years after that memorable day in March, there was strong disapproval on the part of some; they thought it was foolish to turn to a life of scholarship with its vague uncertainties. But in 1872, the year following his graduation, he began what turned out to be five years of study at Oxford University with the aid of an Aberdeen graduate scholarship and another scholarship from St. John's College, Oxford. Here he received further academic honors.

During the course of his second year at Oxford, he was enabled by his uncle to spend a time studying Sanskrit at the University of Göttingen, Germany, under the great scholar, Theodor Benfey. This experience was, in his own words, a critical event in his life.

> Then for the first time, under the tuition of Professor Theodor Benfey, I came into close relations with a great scholar of the modern type, and gained some insights into modern methods of literary investigation; and my thoughts have ever since turned towards the border lands between European and Asiatic civilization.[5]

He later wrote of this experience:

---

3 *BRD*, pp. 9-10.
4 *BRD*, p. 10.
5 Letter of dedication to Andrew Mitchell, Esq., appended to first edition of *SPT*.

> The way of scholarship had been hitherto arid in my education, the
> sense of discovery was never quickened, and the power of perceiving
> truth was becoming atrophied. Scholarship had been a learning of
> opinions, and not a process of gaining real knowledge. One learned what
> others had thought, but not what truth was. Benfey was a vivifying
> wind, to breathe life into dry bones, for he showed scholarship as dis-
> covery and not as a rehearsing of wise opinions.[6]

Further inspiration was received from Henry Jardine Bidder,
of St. John's College, Oxford, "who first opened his eyes to the
true spirit of Hellenism and so helped to fit him for the work
which he had in view."[7]

In July, 1879, while vacationing in Scotland with his recently
acquired wife, he received a letter from Mr. Stuart Poole, Keeper
of the Coins in the British Museum, telling of a travelling
studentship offered by Exeter College, Oxford, for three years'
"travel and research in the Greek lands"; Mr. Poole advised
Ramsay that he should come to the museum and study in preparation for it. The letter mentioned one other outstanding candidate for the award, a recent graduate of Trinity College, Dublin.
That candidate turned out to be the later famous scholar, critic,
dramatist, and poet, Oscar Wilde. Ramsay won the scholarship;
and, being advised by Sir Charles Newton of the British Museum
to go to the west coast of Asia Minor rather than to Athens, he
and his young wife set off for Smyrna (now Izmir). There they
landed early in May of 1880.

At Smyrna he met Sir Charles Wilson, who was then British
consul-general in Anatolia and an experienced explorer. Wilson
gave him helpful advice concerning the exploration of the unknown inland regions of the country, and he invited him to
accompany him on two long journeys into the interior. This
gave him his first opportunity to study the geography and
archaeology of Roman proconsular Asia, Phrygia, Lycaonia, Cappadocia, and Galatia at firsthand and to begin an exploration
that was continued, except for one break (1891-1899),[8] until
1914, and to embark on a long life of devotion to Anatolian
studies.

We are given two interesting portraits of Ramsay the archae-
ologist at work by two of his fellow workers. The first is from
The Accidents of an Antiquary's Life, the autobiography of D.
G. Hogarth, another great archaeologist.

---

6 BRD, p. 13.
7 Anderson, *op. cit.*, p. 727.
8 An attack of cholera, contracted on a ship coming from Alexandretta, Turkey, in-
capacitated him for these years; during this time he aimed at finding and financing a successor rather than continuing his field work himself. He found a successor in a pupil of his
earliest years at Aberdeen, J. G. C. Anderson, later Professor of Classical Art and Archaeology at Oxford. BRD, p. 29.

The apparatus of travel, which we gathered in Smyrna, was of the simplest — a single tent and a few pots and pans, but no canned stores; and two simple villagers were hired to serve us. The qualifications of the one chosen to cook became manifest on the second night in camp. We had left railhead at Seraikeuy, and ridden up the Lycus valley to the foot of the white cliffs of Hierapolis. Mehmet bought a turkey of the peasants of Pambuk Kalessi, and was bidden to have it ready for the next night's supper. Early on the morrow we went up to the site, and all that day, under a broiling sun and among some of the best-preserved Roman tombs in Asia Minor, I entered on an arduous apprenticeship to the best epigraphist in Europe. Sharpset at nightfall we hurried down, expectant of our turkey. Mehmet sat placid, the bird at his feet. It was a corpse, indeed, but no more, not even a plucked one. "What am I to do with this?" said Mehmet. He learned better as time went on; but throughout that journey we had little except sodden messes to eat, faring worse than any traveller need fare. It was partly because our leader cared little for what he ate, but more because, like his followers, he journeyed on a slender purse. Ramsay had made to himself a European reputation as an explorer of Asia Minor at a cost which another man would think scarcely sufficient for the tour of Germany; and it had become his principle, as, for similar reasons, it has become Petrie's, to suffer none but the barest means to his end. If both have pushed their practice to exceeding discomfort, both have taught several young Britons how little is necessity and how much superfluity; and it is not the least of my many debts to Ramsay that I gained in my first tour of exploration the will and the capacity to go farther at less cost than perhaps anyone but my master.9

The second picture is a description of Ramsay at work from two letters of Miss Gertrude Bell, who shared some of his travels and researches.

Madan Shehar
May 25, 1907

The Ramsays arrived yesterday. I was in the middle of digging up a Church, when suddenly two carts hove into sight and there they were. It was about three in the afternoon. They instantly got out, refused to think of going to the tents, Lady R. made tea (for they were starving) in the open, and R. oblivious of all other considerations was at once lost in the problems the Church presented. It was too delightful to have someone as much excited about it as I was. . . .

Daile
June 8, 1907

We are getting so much material that it will certainly make a book. Our plan is that Sir W. shall write the historic and epigraphic part and I the architectural. It will be worth doing, for this is the first time that an accurate study has been made of any one district in these parts; hitherto people have only travelled through and seen what they could see and gone on. . . . I should have been helpless without Sir W., and the more I work with him the more I like him and respect his knowledge. In fact, it is being a magnificent success, quite everything I hoped it would be.10

---

9 Quoted in W. F. Howard, *The Romance of New Testament Scholarship* (London: Epworth Press, 1949), pp. 143-144.
    10 Quoted in Stephen Neill, *The Interpretation of the New Testament 1861-1961* (London: Oxford University Press, 1964), p. 141.

In 1885 Ramsay became the first Professor of Classical Art and Archaeology at Oxford. The following year he was appointed Regius Professor of Humanity, as the Latin professorship is called, at his alma mater, the University of Aberdeen. There he remained until his retirement in 1911.[11]

Ramsay was knighted in 1906 on the occasion of the four hundredth anniversary of the founding of the University of Aberdeen for his distinguished service to the scholarly world. In addition to this honor he received many other academic distinctions in his lifetime. He was recipient of three honorary fellowships from Oxford colleges (Exeter in 1898, Lincoln in 1899, and St. John's in 1912), and he was honored by doctorates from nine universities: Oxford, St. Andrews, Glasgow, Aberdeen, Cambridge, Edinburgh, New York, Bordeaux, and Marburg. He was one of the original members of the British Academy and an honorary member of just about every scholarly association devoted to archaeological and historical research. In 1893 he was awarded the Gold Medal of Pope Leo XIII and in 1906 the Victoria Medal of the Royal Geographical Society. His travels took him not only to Turkey, but also to the great universities of the world for lectures; he visited America on three occasions (1894, 1910, and 1913) for special lectures at leading universities and seminaries.[12]

According to his obituary notice in *The Times* (London),

> Ramsay's abiding fame will rest first on his comprehensive exploration of Asia Minor; ... and secondly, on the new method which he developed and taught to students of ancient geography. On account of both he received worldwide recognition.[13]

In his work in Asia Minor he was concerned primarily with the problem of geographical identification. When he first began, very few historical places could be identified with any certainty, especially in the interior.

> Taking into his purview sites of all periods down to the Byzantine, he sought the help of evidence neglected or little used before, notably that of local coin types, and that of Christian authors and legends, and set out to interpret the ancient geography of Asia Minor by noting the relative positions of points on roads and by applying the method of exclusion to administrative groups of towns, of which some members were already fixed with fair certainty in the map.[14]

---

11 Howard, *Romance*, p. 139, suggests that Ramsay retired due to ill health. If this is correct, he certainly recovered quickly, for he was active as a writer and lecturer until the end of his life. In a personal letter to the author, Professor F. F. Bruce suggests that he was able to retire at the rather early age of sixty due to the steady income derived from the publication of his books — which went through many editions — by Hodder and Stoughton. "In those days there was no fixed retirement age for Scottish professors, who were appointed *ad vitam aut culpam*, and some went on into their eighties!"
12 Anderson, *op. cit.*, pp. 727-728.
13 April 22, 1939, p. 14.
14 *Ibid.*

This was combined with extensive exploration and excavation throughout the south-central part of the sub-continent.

In the year of his first visit to Asia Minor (1879), Ramsay contributed about one hundred articles on classical subjects to the ninth edition of the *Encyclopaedia Britannica;* most of these were too short to have a signature. At the very beginning of his exploration Ramsay made a name for himself by publishing the results of his discoveries in various European scholarly journals, most notably the *Journal of Hellenic Studies.* Because his articles were scattered throughout so ˏmany different periodicals, the French archaeologist Perrot was moved to sigh, "What trouble Ramsay would have spared us all by writing one book!"[15] That book came at last when his monumental work on *The Historical Geography of Asia Minor*[16] was published by the Royal Geographical Society in 1890.

This work did not appear, however, without a great deal of labor and discouragement. Ramsay explains in his preface:

> In May, 1886, the first sketch of it was read before the Society. The difficulty of the subject, and the distraction caused by other work both as a Professor (first in Oxford and afterwards in Aberdeen), and as a traveller (I left London for Smyrna the day after reading the paper, and spent considerable part of the summer of 1886, 1887, and 1888 in Asia Minor), delayed the completion and publication of the sketch. In the beginning of April, 1888, I brought the complete MS. with me to London to hand over to the printer. I discovered, thirty-six hours after starting from Aberdeen, that the manscript was no longer in the bag where I had placed it, and which had been for the most of the time close to my hand, and I have never found the slightest clue to the time or manner of its loss.... All notes for it had been destroyed....[17]

This would have crushed a lesser man. Ten years of research gone! Yet Ramsay did his best to rewrite the book and even added a second part, which included a collection of new material for the history and antiquities of the area. Even though the rewritten book — on the author's confession — was a less finished work than the original had been, it marked an epoch in the study of ancient geography and established Ramsay's prominence in the field. *The Historical Geography* is foundational for all later study in the history and geography of Asia Minor.

The presupposition of all Ramsay's work is this:

> Topography is the foundation of history. No one who has familiarized himself with Attic history in books and has afterwards ascended Pentelicus and seen that history spread forth before him in the valleys and mountains and sea that have moulded it will ever disbelieve in the value

15 *The Times* (London), April 22, 1939, p. 14.
16 Royal Geographical Society, Supplementary Papers, Vol. 4 (London: John Murray, 1890; repr. Amsterdam: Adolph M. Hakkert, 1962).
17 *HG*, p 3.

of topography as an aid to history. . . . If we want to understand the Ancients, especially the Greeks, we must breathe the same air as they did and saturate ourselves with the same scenery and the same nature that wrought upon them. For this end correct topography is a necessary though humble servant.[18]

And this is exactly what Sir William Ramsay did: he saturated himself with the geography and history of the Graeco-Roman world. He always insisted upon originality in research and first-hand acquaintance with the facts. Throughout his life he had little time for those who would assume the position of authorities on the history and geography of Asia Minor or the missionary travels of the Apostle Paul without having a firsthand acquaintance with the facts of the matter.

Two things characterize Ramsay above all else. He was original and he was thorough. He writes this in the introduction to his *Historical Geography:*

My scheme has been (after several experiences of the difficulties caused by accepting wrong conjectures of modern writers) to make an absolutely fresh work founded on the ancient authorities alone, in which the geographical situation, the natural surroundings and the commercial advantages of each city should be set forth in an account of its history.[19]

Ninety-five per cent of the references made to ancient writers in his work, the reader is assured, were found by the author in his own perusal of the original authorities, most of whom were read several times in the original.[20] This is quite a feat, for he quotes from ninety different ancient writers, from classical historians to early church fathers, in both Greek and Latin.

Ramsay's *Historical Geography* is divided into two parts. The first is entitled, "General Principles," and the second, "A Sketch of the Historical Geography of the Various Provinces." Part one begins with a discussion of the conflict between Orientalism and Hellenism in Asia Minor. His observations here laid the foundation for much further thought on the matter culminating in his Gifford Lectures in the University of Edinburgh for 1915-1916.[21] The very character of the plateau as a borderland between the East and the West has, according to Ramsay, marked it out as a battleground between the Oriental and European spirit.

The idea of this great struggle was a formative principle which moulded the gradual development of the Iliad, and gave the tone to Herodotus's epic history. We can trace its main features from that time onwards. Greece and Persia were the representative antagonists for two centuries. Then the conquests of Alexander, organized and consolidated later by the genius of Rome, made the European spirit apparently victorious for many centuries.

18 *HG.* pp. 51-52.
19 *HG*, p. 6.
20 *HG*, pp. 6-7.
21 *Asianic Elements in Greek Civilization* (London: John Murray, 1927).

But the conquest was not real. Romans governed Asia Minor because, with their marvellous governing talent, they knew how to adapt their administration to the people of the plateau. It is true that the great cities put on a western appearance, and took Latin or Greek names; Latin and Greek were the languages of government, of the educated classes, and of polite society. Only this superficial aspect is attested in literature and in ordinary history, and when I began to travel the thought never occurred to me that there was any other. The conviction has gradually forced itself on me that the real state of the country was very different. Greek was not the popular language of the plateau even in the third century after Christ: the mass of people spoke Lycaonian, and Galatian, and Phrygian, although those who wrote books wrote Greek, and those who governed spoke Latin. The people continued to believe in their own religion, their gods were identified by educated persons with the gods of Greece and Rome, and called by Greek names; but they had none of the Greek or Roman character, they were Asiatic deities. Christianity conquered the land, and succeeded in doing what Greece and Rome had never done: it imposed its language on the people. But the Christianity of Phrygia was never like the Christianity of Europe....
The foundation of Constantinople was a sign that the West had not really conquered Asia Minor.[22]

He carries on with an important discussion of the great roads and trade routes of ancient Anatolia, from the so-called "Royal Road" of the Persian period to the Byzantine roads, which were the basis of the modern Turkish road system. He discusses the value of the various ancient geographical authorities for Asia Minor and concludes with an important note on the change of site of ancient cities. In part two, after a brief general introduction to the area as a whole, he goes through the various provinces, city by city, listing all of the available geographical and historical information that he has been able to uncover in the study of historical sources and in his extensive explorations. The order is to a great extent the order of discovery. This, together with the limits of Professor Ramsay's travels (principally in Asia, Phrygia, Galatia, Lycaonia, and Cappadocia), prevents the book from being a full-fledged and systematic discussion of the historical geography of Asia Minor as a whole — as the title might indicate.

The second great work Ramsay produced in the area of archaeology was the monumental volume, *The Cities and Bishoprics of Phrygia*.[23] This is described in the sub-title as "an essay of the local history of Phrygia from the earliest times to the Turkish conquest." The work was intended to be a multi-volumed work, but only one volume (in two parts) was completed due to lack of evidence. The first part, published in 1895, surveys those

---

22 HG, pp. 24-25.
23 (Oxford: Clarendon Press, 1895, Vol. 1, pt. 1; 1897, Vol. 1, pt. 2).

cities in the area of the Lycus (Lycos) River valley; Laodicea, Hierapolis, Colossae, and other less important cities. The second part, published in 1897, covers the cities of west and west-central Phrygia, the most important of which are Eumereia and Apameia. This latter section includes two important chapters on early Christian inscriptions and one on the Jews in Phrygia. Basing his argument on a tradition of the Talmud, he argues that the Jews of this region were generally absorbed into the Christian church at an early date.[24]

Perhaps the least known of Sir William Ramsay's contributions to the study of ancient history and geography are the articles he wrote for the five volumes of Hastings' *Dictionary of the Bible* between 1898 and 1904. These are sixty-three in number and deal primarily with cities and geographical terms of Greece and Asia Minor.[25] The two most important in this series are the extensive essays in the extra volume on the "Religion of Greece and Asia Minor."[26] and "Roads and Travel in the New Testament."[27] The first of these begins with the primitive Anatolian and pre-Hellenic religion and carries the story down to the Christian era; it includes valuable sections on the cult of the Great Mother, the mysteries, and the attitude of St. Paul to Greek philosophy. The second answers just about any questions one would have about travel in the time of the New Testament and includes two excellent maps, the first tracing the most important routes by land and sea in the Roman Empire and the second covering Asia Minor in detail.

Under the general category of archaeology one should mention the three articles contributed to the volume written by Ramsay and six of his early students for the quatercentenary of the University of Aberdeen,[28] the publication of the results of

---

24 *CB*, *part* 1, pp. 674-676. However, according to Jastrow's *Dictionary of the Talmud*, the reference is not to Phrygia, but to Prugitha, a district in Northern Palestine known for its wine.
25 Cf. Appendix I.
26 *HDB*, extra vol., pp. 109-156.
27 *HDB*, extra vol., pp. 375-402.
28 "Preliminary Report to the Wilson Trustees on Exploration in Phrygia and Lycaonia," "The War of Moslem and Christian for the Possession of Asia Minor," "The Tekmoreian Guest-Friend: An Anti-Christian Society on the Imperial Estates at Pisidian Antioch," in William M. Ramsay (ed.), *Studies in the History and Art of the Eastern Provinces of the Roman Empire* (Aberdeen: Aberdeen University Press, 1906), pp. 231-377. The influence of Ramsay in inspiring research in Asia Minor can be seen from this quotation from the preface: "We venture to lay before the University and the distinguished guests, both strangers and graduates, who come to greet its entrance on the fifth century of work, a sample of the research that has been performed in one line alone of classical study by its students. It was the writer's wish to compile a bibliography of Asia Minor exploration during the last twenty-seven years . . . but this volume could not have appeared in time if the compilation had been included. The bibliography would show in statistics that, notable as have been the writings in that department of a series of excellent scholars, many of whose names are now household words in the world of learning, *the bulk at any rate of the work of Aberdeen graduates in the department equals the bulk of all the rest*, even taking into account the stately German folios on Pergamon, Lycia, etc., and the beautiful French volumes on Myrina" (pp. ix-x, italics mine).

his and Miss Gertrude Bell's excavation of the "Thousand and
One Churches" (actually only about 28 — a typical example of
Oriental exaggeration!) in the region of Kara Dagh (Black
Mountain),[29] and his Gifford Lectures on the *Asianic Elements
in Greek Civilization.* The end of his life found him laboring on
an extensive work on *The Social Basis of Roman Power in Asia
Minor,* edited and published posthumously by his former stu-
dent, Professor J. G. C. Anderson of Oxford.[30]

This survey of the work of Sir William Ramsay, the historian
and archaeologist, could not be concluded without focusing
attention upon what is probably the best popular essay on the
historical geography of Asia Minor ever written. This appeared
in *The National Geographic Magazine* in 1922 under the title,
"A Sketch of the Geographical History of Asia Minor."[31] It
began with this excellent description of Asia Minor:

> In shape the peninsula of Asia Minor may be compared by a rough
> analogy to the right hand laid palm upward, with the fingers pointing
> to the west. The palm is the central plateau, which is surrounded with a
> rim of mountains. Like fingers, five chains of mountains extend from
> the plateau, most of them stretching far out into the Aegean Sea, as if
> they were trying to force their way to Europe.
> These mountain chains are continued by chains of islands, which form,
> as it were, stepping-stones for the march of a giant from Asia to Europe.[32]

29 Sir William M. Ramsay and Miss Gertrude L. Bell, *The Thousand and One Churches*
(London: Hodder and Stoughton, 1909).
30 (Aberdeen: Aberdeen University Press, 1941). Ramsay had evidently made an
agreement with Professor J. R. S. Sterrett (d. 1914), of Cornell University, to make use
of some of his discoveries and to publish the results in this work.
31 42 (Nov. 1922): 553-570.
32 *Ibid.,* p. 553.

II

LUKE THE HISTORIAN

Although it was as an archaeologist and a geographer that
Ramsay did his most substantial work, this is regarded merely as
foundational for the purpose of this book. His firsthand investigation into the antiquities of Asia Minor provides the background for his study of the New Testament. The immense
amount of knowledge that he had accumulated in the study of
the historical and geographical condition of the Roman provinces in Asia Minor was later brought to bear on the interpretation of the New Testament. And it is as a New Testament
scholar that we now want to look at him.

Any discussion of Sir William Ramsay and the New Testament
must begin with the Book of Acts, because it is here that he first
became interested in the study of the New Testament, and it is
here that he made his most significant contribution.

During Ramsay's days as a university student, the study of
apostolic history was dominated by Ferdinand Christian Baur
(1792-1860) and his so-called Tübingen School. Reading Acts
and the letters of Paul in the light of the Hegelian dialectic
interpretation of history and the assumption that only four
Pauline epistles were undoubtedly genuine (Galatians, Romans,
1 and 2 Corinthians), they radically altered the traditional
understanding of New Testament history. They saw in the early
church two opposing elements (thesis and antithesis) represented by Peter and Paul; in Acts they found the reconciliation
(synthesis) of these two parties in the Catholic Church of the

second century. Their conclusions demanded a very late date for most of the New Testament writings, especially Acts.[1]

When he first began his work in Asia Minor, Ramsay's views concerning the Book of Acts were under the influence of this school of thought. "I had read a good deal of modern criticism about the book," he wrote,

> and dutifully accepted the current opinion that it was written during the second half of the second century by an author who wished to influence the minds of people in his own time by a highly wrought and imaginative description of the early Church. His object was not to present a trustworthy picture of facts in the period of about A.D. 50, but to produce a certain effect on his own time by setting forth a carefully coloured account of events and persons of that older period. He wrote for his contemporaries, not for truth. He cared nought for geographical or historical surroundings of the period A.D. 30 to 60. He thought only of the period A.D. 160-180, and how he might paint the heroes of old times in situations that should touch the conscience of his contemporaries. Antiquarian or geographical truth was less than valueless in a design like this: one who thought of such things was distracting his attention from the things that really mattered, the things that would move the minds of men in the second century.[2]

In his search for information bearing on the geography and history of Asia Minor he at first paid slight attention to the early Christian authorities. He had gained the impression in his studies that these were quite unworthy of consideration for a historian; anything having to do with religion belonged to the realm of the theologians, not that of the historians. When he spent time copying Christian inscriptions in his earliest years of travel, he felt the time to be wasted — even though a sense of duty compelled him to make copies of them. Finally, in a desperate search for any information of a geographical and antiquarian nature, he began to study the journeys of Paul in this region of the world as described in the Book of Acts. He hardly expected to find any information of value regarding the condition of Asia Minor in the time of Paul; rather, he thought he would find material bearing upon the second half of the second century of the Christian era, i.e. the age (he thought) in which the author of Acts lived.

In his book, *The Bearing of Recent Discovery on the Trustworthiness of the New Testament,* Ramsay tells how he came to

---

1 On the Tübingen School, see Horton Harris, The Tübingen School (Oxford: Clarenden Press, 1975). Cf. also W. W. Gasque, A History of the Criticism of the Acts of the Apostles (Grand Rapids: Eerdmans, 1975), pp. 21-54.
2 BRD, pp. 37-38.

change his mind on the subject.[3] The first thing that caused him to begin to doubt the conclusion which he had assumed was a careful study of Acts 14:5-12. Here it is said that Paul and Barnabas, on account of an angry mob, fled from Iconium "to Lystra and Derbe, cities of Lycaonia, and the surrounding region" (v. 6). In these words it is implied that the apostles crossed over a frontier into Lycaonia; that is, that the border of Lycaonia lay between the cities of Iconium and Lystra, and that Iconium did not belong to the country called Lycaonia.

Now, it was formerly assumed in modern treatises on ancient geography that Iconium was a city of Lycaonia. This passage in the fourteenth chapter of Acts was thought of as a typical example of the lack of local exactitude by the author of Acts, who was writing at a much later date than the events he was narrating. Assuming that Iconium was a city of Lycaonia, then to speak of going from Iconium into Lycaonia would be the same as if someone today were to speak of going from Chicago into Illinois, or from London to England. The impression left upon the mind is that "this detail of the journey of Paul and Barnabas was deliberately invented by the writer (who was under the false impression about the situation of Iconium and the frontier) ...."[4]

However, as Ramsay went on to demonstrate conclusively,[5] this is not, in point of fact, the case. Iconium was not a part of Lycaonia; rather, it belonged to Phrygia, an entirely different district of Asia Minor. The people were of a different stock, and they spoke a different language from that of the Lycaonians. Once this fact is realized, the narrative of Acts 14 comes to life with local color and detailed accuracy as to the actual situation. Rather than the narrative bearing the stamp of a historical fiction, it becomes plausible that the account is based upon personal experience and that Paul himself could be the source behind the account. Facts incidental to the story, such as crossing the border between Phrygia and Lycaonia (v. 6) and the speech of the people of Lystra being in the Lycaonian tongue (v. 11), point in this direction. The fact that, once inside the border of Lycaonia, Paul and Barnabas were safe from the Iconium mob and the contrast between the Phrygian language and that which they heard upon their arrival at Lystra would have impressed these incidents upon their minds. Futhermore, Ramsay goes on to note the connection between Zeus and Hermes as associated gods

---

3 pp. 39-52. Full bibliographical data for Ramsay's books of a biblical nature will be found in the bibliography at the end of the book.
4 BRD, p. 41.
5 Cf. BRD, pp. 53-78.

in this region as a further demonstration of the authenticity of the narrative.

This may sound like a small point to the uninitiated, but it is a very important one in the thought of Ramsay. The inference of these facts led him to conclude that this passage in Acts is meticulously accurate in regard to its professed historical setting.

> The boundaries mentioned are true to the period in which the action lies: they are not placed through the mistaken application by a later author of ancient statements to a time when they ceased to be pertinent: they are based on information given by an eye-witness, a person who had been engaged in the action described. The reader, if he reads the narrative rightly, can see with the eyes and hear with the ears of a man who was there and witnessed all that happened.[6]

The conclusion that slowly forced itself upon Ramsay was the exact opposite of the one he had hitherto assumed in regard to Acts. And if the theory to which he had committed himself could not be relied upon in respect to this one detail, he surmised that it evidently could not be relied upon in other details without being thoroughly tested. To state it more positively, if the author proves to be carefully accurate in a matter of one detail, would it not be likely that he would prove to be the same in regard to others?

> There is a certain presumption that a writer who proves to be exact and correct in one point will show the same qualities in other matters. No writer is correct by mere chance, or accurate sporadically. He is accurate by virtue of a certain habit of mind. Some men are accurate by nature; some are by nature loose and inaccurate.[7]

His attitude towards the Book of Acts was now radically changed. Instead of assuming the book to be untrustworthy in regard to its avowed historical situation, he now began to approach Acts with an open mind that it might after all prove to be accurate in any given detail. He now realized, as F. F. Bruce has stated, that if an author's trustworthiness "is vindicated in points where he can be checked, we should not assume that he is less trustworthy where we cannot test his accuracy."[8] Ramsay would at least give the writer of Acts the benefit of the doubt.

He writes of his new outlook in *The Bearing of Recent Discovery*:

> In the special work on which I was engaged at the time, some fresh investigation of the case was indispensable. Good and safe evidence about Asia Minor in the Imperial time or earlier was urgently required by an explorer and discoverer. If I could find such evidence, and test it in the country, a long vista of profitable work opened itself before me. . . . If

---

6 BRD, p. 79.
7 BRD, p. 80.
8 *Acts*, p. 17.

> Luke's narrative was trustworthy, it was for me exceptionally valuable, as giving evidence on a larger scale. There was nothing else like it. No other ancient traveller has left an account of the journeys which he made across Asia Minor [Xenophon gives little more than names and distances]; and if the narrative of Paul's travels rests on first-class authority, it placed in my hands a document of unique and exceptional value to guide my investigations. To determine the value of this narrative was a fundamental condition for my future work.[9]

Over the years the opinion gradually forced itself upon him that Luke's history of early Christian origins was unsurpassed for its accuracy.

> Further study of Acts XIII.-XXI. showed that the book could bear the most minute scrutiny of an authority for the facts of the Aegean world, and that it was written with such judgement, skill, art, and perception of the truth as to be a model of historical statement.[10]

After more than thirty years of close study of the milieu of first-century Christianity, he penned these words:

> The more I have studied the narrative of the Acts, and the more I have learned year after year about Graeco-Roman society and thoughts and fashions, and organization in those provinces, the more I admire and the better I understand. I set out to look for truth on the borderland where Greece and Asia meet, and found it here. You may press the words of Luke in a degree beyond any other historian's, and they stand the keenest scrutiny and the hardest treatment, provided always that the critic knows the subject and does not go beyond the limits of science and of justice.[11]

In the spring of 1892, Ramsay was invited to give six lectures at Mansfield College, Oxford. This gave him his first opportunity to set forth some of the views he had been developing concerning early Christian history. In the course of these lectures he dealt with the history of the church from A.D. 64 to 170, especially as regards the problem of persecution. When he published these lectures as *The Church in the Roman Empire before A.D. 170,* he added an introductory part covering the earliest stage of development. Here he first sought to articulate the development in his thoughts regarding the account of Paul's missionary journeys in Acts. From a comparison with his later works, one can observe that he was only beginning at this time to appreciate the great historical value of Acts. All he ventured to argue for was "that the narrative in Acts of Paul's journeys is founded on, actually incorporates, an account written under the immediate influence of Paul himself."[12]

The ideas found in seminal form in *The Church in the Roman Empire* are found fully developed in his *magnum opus, St. Paul*

---

9 BRD, pp. 81-82.
10 BRD, p. 85.
11 BRD, p. 89.
12 CRE, pp. 6-7.

the Traveller and the Roman Citizen, published first in 1895. This work established Ramsay's reputation as a Biblical scholar, as The Historical Geography of Asia Minor established him in the field of archaeology. It is in this work that Ramsay has undoubtedly made his greatest contribution to New Testament scholarship.

When he wrote the introductory chapters to The Church in the Roman Empire, he had no theory as to the date and composition of the Book of Acts. He was only concerned with one small part of the book — the travel narratives relating to Paul's missionary journeys. However, when he was invited to visit the United States two years later for lectures at Auburn Seminary (and incidentally at Harvard, Johns Hopkins, and Union Seminary, New York), he had thoroughly worked through the whole of Acts and had come to a definite conclusion. He stated the view at which he had arrived in St. Paul the Traveller (the publication of his American lectures):

> Our hypothesis is that *Acts* was written by a great historian, a writer who set himself to record the facts as they occurred, a strong partisan indeed, but raised above partiality by his perfect confidence that he had only to describe the facts as they occurred, in order to make the truth of Christianity and the honour of Paul apparent.... I shall argue that the book was composed by a personal friend and disciple of Paul, and if this be once established there will be no hesitation in accepting the primitive tradition that Luke was the author.[13]

The author of Acts is not to be regarded as the author of historical romance, legend, or third- or second-rate history. Rather he is the writer of an historical work of the highest order, a work to be compared with that of Thucydides, the greatest of the Greek historians.[14]

It is of greatest significance that Ramsay came to the study of Acts — and the rest of the New Testament — as a Roman historian rather than as a theologian. This is one factor that makes his books so fresh and so noteworthy. He did not come to prove a certain point of view; he simply aimed at an examination of the facts. Throughout the whole of his life he never held any theory as to the inerrancy of the Bible as a result of its special inspiration. His position in this regard is expressed in the following statement:

> In maintaining our hypothesis it is not necessary either to show that the author made no mistake, or to solve every difficulty.... We are making a historical and literary investigation. The greatest historians of

---

13 P. 14.
14 *SPT*, pp. 2-3.

other periods are not above error; and we may admit the possibility that a first-century historian has made errors.[15]

He notes, further, that there remain many unsolved problems in every ancient writer of value and that this is no less true of the author of Acts. However, these problems do not detract from his ability as a historian. One reason for our difficulty with Luke is that his

> style is compressed to the highest degree; and he expects a great deal from the reader. He does not attempt to sketch the surroundings and set the whole scene like a picture before the reader; he states the bare facts that seem to him important, and leaves the reader to imagine the situation.[16]

A second problem was closely related in the thought of Ramsay to the problem of the reliability of Acts. Who are the churches of Galatia to whom Paul writes and whom he addresses as Galatians (Gal. 1:2; 3:1) ? Is the reference to ethnic or political Galatia? That is, does it signify the central mountainous region of Asia Minor occupied by the descendants of the Gauls who emigrated from Europe in the third century B.C.? Or does it refer to the Roman province of this name, which was a much larger district (including "South Galatia") ?

The question is involved with many problems and is still vigorously debated today. The classic defender of the North Galatian theory in Ramsay's day was J. B. Lightfoot (1828-1888), the dean of Pauline scholars.[17] He argued that the natural meaning of the term would refer to the district which the Gauls inhabited. Furthermore, the main characteristics of the Gauls as a people stand out in Paul's letter — especially their fickleness and instability of character (Gal. 1:6, 3:1), and their concern for a more external and ritualistic religion (Gal. 3:3).[18]

But the question may be asked, how does this fit in with Acts? Acts speaks of Paul's extensive missionary activity in the South Galatian region, i.e. in the cities of Pisidian Antioch, Iconium, Lystra, and Derbe (Acts 13:14-14:23; 16:1-5), but we do not read of any missionary work in North Galatia. Those who hold the North Galatian theory point to two verses which refer (according to this view) to Paul's evangelistic work in this region: Acts 16:6 and 18:23. The first of these reads:

---

15 *SPT*, p. 16.
16 *SPT*, p. 17.
17 *The Epistle of St. Paul to the Galatians* (Repr. Grand Rapids, Michigan: Zondervan Publishing House, 1962), pp. 1-35.
18 *Ibid.*, pp. 13-17.

And they went through the region of Phrygia and Galatia, having been forbidden by the Holy Spirit to speak the word in Asia (RSV).

Διῆλθον δὲ τὴν Φρυγίαν καὶ Γαλατικὴν χώραν, κωλυθέντες ὑπὸ τοῦ Ἁγίου Πνεύματος λαλῆσαι τὸν λόγον ἐν τῇ Ἀσίᾳ.

And the second:

After spending some time there [in Syrian Antioch] he departed and went from place to place through the region of Galatia and Phrygia, strengthening all the disciples (RSV).

Καὶ ποιήσας χρόνον τινὰ ἐξῆλθεν, διερχόμενος καθεξῆς τὴν Γαλατικὴν χώραν καὶ Φρυγίαν, στηρίζων πάντας τοὺς μαθητάς.

The first of these references is taken by the exponents of the North Galatian hypothesis to refer to evangelistic activity conducted by Paul in the regions of (ethnic) Galatia and Phrygia. Great stress is laid upon the fact that τὴν Φρυγίαν καὶ Γαλατικὴν χώραν must refer to two distinct regions. Further, it is characteristic of Luke to use regional rather than political terms.

> Mysia, Phrygia, Pisidia, are all "geographical expressions" destitute of any political significance; and as they occur in the same parts of the narrative with Galatia, it seems fair to infer that the latter is similarly used.[19]

Moreover, Luke distinctly calls Lystra and Derbe cities of Lycaonia (13:6) and designates Antioch by the words "of Pisidia" (13:14) – all by geographical terms rather than by the provincial title of Galatia. James Moffatt argued that the word, διῆλθον, ("went through") meant not merely "transit across" but "transit with preaching activity"[20]; hence there is evidence that Paul may have established churches in this region.

Ramsay, however, was not satisfied with the traditional view. When he first began his study of the New Testament, he was guided by Lightfoot;[21] but the more he studied the facts as a Roman historian the more he became convinced that this theory just did not fit the facts. He confesses,

> To maintain this idea I had to reject the plain and natural interpretation of some passages; but when at last I found myself compelled to abandon it, and to understand Galatians as inhabitants of Roman Galatia, much that had been dark became clear, and some things that had seemed loose and vague became precise and definite.[22]

19 Lightfoot, *Galatians*, p. 19.
20 *Introduction to the Literature of the New Testament* (3rd ed. rev.; New York; Charles Scribner's Sons, 1922), p. 95.
21 CRE, pp. 8-9.
22 CRE, p. 9.

His views on the matter were first stated in *The Church in the Roman Empire*[23] and further developed in *St. Paul the Traveller*.[24] In 1899 he published his *Historical Commentary on St. Paul's Epistle to the Galatians;* here he gave this view its most cogent expression.[25] The result has been that most British scholars (with the notable exception of Ramsay's faithful antagonist, James Moffatt) have been impressed with the force of Ramsay's arguments and have tended to accept the South Galatian theory. German scholarship, with a few exceptions,[26] has maintained the defense of the older view.

Several factors worked together to compel Ramsay to abandon the North Galatian view. First, there was the marked difference between the rustic Gaulish population of North Galatia, who were probably little affected by Greek manners and language, and the population of the cities, who were for the most part not Gauls.[27] If Paul followed his custom and worked in the cities (rather than the country district) of this area (assuming, for the sake of argument, that he did do missionary work in North Galatia) , then his converts would have not for the most part been Galatians in the ethnic sense; and to refer to them as Galatians would be no more appropriate than in reference to the people of the South Galatian area. Again, it was Paul's general practice to work in cities that were generally Hellenized and where there was a Jewish population; this would not have been the case, according to Ramsay's researches, in North Galatia in the first century. Furthermore, there is little evidence for the existence of Christianity in North Galatia until a quite late date. On the other hand, a close study of the antiquities of the South Galatian region convinced him that the simple name of Galatians would be the ideal name to use in referring to the people of the cities of Pisidian Antioch, Iconium, Lystra, and Derbe. In fact, it is the *only* name that would be apropos to the situation.[28] They could not be addressed as "the churches of Lycaonia" or "Lycaonians," because Antioch and Iconium were in the region of Phrygia. Again, many of the inhabitants of these cities were not natives to the region; therefore, the description of them as Lycaonian or Phrygian would be quite inappropriate — especially since some of the people would be Roman citizens (Antioch and Lystra were

---

23 Pp. 8-11, 16-111.
24 Pp. 89-151, 178-193.
25 Pp. 1-234.
26 For example, Theodore Zahn, *Introduction to the New Testament*, trans. from the third German edition by J. M. Trout *et al.* (Repr. Grand Rapids, Mich.: Kregel Publications, 1953), 1:164-202.
27 Ramsay, "Galatia," *HDB*, 2:84.
28 Ramsay, "Galations," *HDB*, 2:91-92.

Roman colonies) . Besides, the term Phrygian was a term with a very bad connotation and would not in good taste be used in referring to the people of that region. The only all-inclusive term available to use in speaking of the members of the churches that Paul founded in the region of South Galatia would be "Galatians," and he would naturally, as a Roman, follow the Roman provincial divisions and ignore those national distinctions which were opposed to the organized Roman unity.[29] It was Paul's practice to use the titles of the Roman provinces in his letters, e.g., Achaia, Asia, and Macedonia. And it is significant that Paul refers to both Thessalonians and Philippians as "Macedonian" (2 Cor. 9:2, 4), when they actually belong to a geographical district whose indigenous people were called "Thracian."

One of the important factors leading Ramsay to the acceptance of the South Galatian Theory was a growing conviction concerning the nature of Luke as a historian. Now, one of the determining factors in the character of a historian is his selection of topics. "Does he show the true historian's power of seizing the great facts, and marking clearly the development of his subject?"[30] Ramsay was impressed more and more that one finds a remarkable sense of proportion in Acts, contrary to the prevailing view of his day. The plan of the author is to concentrate on important events; those events he lays stress on are the ones that are important in the life and ministry of Paul. On the other hand,

> Where the author passes rapidly over a period or journey, we shall find reason to believe that it was marked by no striking feature and no new foundation.... Our hypothesis is that Luke's silence about an incident or person should always be investigated as a piece of evidence, on the principle that he had some reason for his silence....[31]

If this be admitted, then he would certainly not have omitted (or made only slight reference to) the account of the foundation of the Galatian churches which are so important to Paul. If the author of Acts has failed to include such an important aspect of the ministry of Paul, Ramsay argued, then we must change our opinion of him as a first-rate historian and admit that Acts and the letters of Paul cannot be harmonized and that the latter are to be preferred over the former.[32] However, if the churches in the regions of Lycaonia and Phrygia (Lystra, Derbe, Inconium, and Pisidian Antioch) be equated with the churches addressed

---

29 The author of Acts, on the other hand, follows the common Greek usage and uses regional terms.
30 *SPT*, p. 18.
31 *SPT*, p. 19.
32 This is exactly the approach John Knox has taken in his *Chapters in a Life of Paul* (New York and Nashville: Abingdon Press, 1950).

in Paul's Epistle to the Galatians, then the two books fit together perfectly in this regard.

According to Ramsay, τὴν Φρυγίαν καὶ Γαλατικὴν χώραν (Acts 16:6) refers to "the Phrygio-Galatic region," i.e. that part of the Roman province of Galatia known as Phrygia. The similar expression in Acts 18:23 (τὴν Γαλατικὴν χώραν καὶ Φρυγίαν) was taken to mean the Galatic region of Lycaonia (as distinct from that part of Lycaonia which did not lie within the province of Galatia) and the Phrygian region; the first term would refer to the cities of Derbe and Lystra, and the second, to Iconium and Pisidian Antioch.[33]

Other incidental factors contribute to the acceptance of the South Galatian view. According to Paul's letter his first visit to the Galatians was occasioned by a physical illness (Gal. 4:13), the implication being that he had come there to convalesce. It would be extremely unlikely that he would have gone to the North Galatian district, an area far off the beaten track and necessitating a very difficult journey. On the other hand, Ramsay knew from personal experience that it would be quite natural for a person who had contracted malarial fever in the hot lowlands of Pamphylia to journey to the higher ground of the interior to obtain relief.[34] This would go hand in hand with his arrival at Pisidian Antioch in Acts 13. Again, it is unlikely that the Judaizers, who dogged Paul's steps, would have been active in the out-of-the-way district of North Galatia; the more accessible southern region is a better setting for their activity. Moreover, Paul makes reference in 1 Corinthians 16:1 to the fact that the churches of Galatia are to share in the collection for the Jerusalem church, and we find two members of the South Galatian churches — Gaius of Derbe[35] and Timothy of Lystra (Acts 20:4) — and no representative from North Galatia accompanying Paul to Jerusalem, presumably with the collection.[36] Incidental details in the epistle such as the reception of the apostle by the Galatians as "a messenger [angel] of God" (Gal. 4:14; cf. incident at Lystra in Acts 14:12) and the reference to "the marks of the Lord Jesus" (Gal. 4:17; cf. the stoning in Acts 14:19) could also be taken as pointing in the direction of South Galatian recipients of the

---

33 Ramsay, "Galatia (Region of)," *HDB*, 2:90-91. Cf. Bruce, *Acts* pp. 309-310, 350.
34 *SPT*, pp. 92-93. Ramsay goes on to argue for the novel idea that Paul's "thorn in the flesh" (2 Cor. 12:7) was a species of chronic malarial fever. *SPT*, pp. 94-97.
35 The Western Text reads Doberus, which would be in Macedonia.
36 It might be suggested that there is no mention made of delegates from Corinth or Philippi. However, a good case can be made that Titus although not mentioned in Acts, represented the Corinthian church (1 Cor. 16:3; 2 Cor. 8:16-24) and that Luke was a delegate from Philippi. Cf. Donald Guthrie, *New Testament Introduction: The Pauline Epistles* (London: Tyndale Press, 1961), p. 78. Ramsay suggested that the reason Titus is not mentioned in Acts lies in the fact that he was a relative of Luke. *SPT*, p. 390.

letter. Finally, there is the fact that Barnabas is mentioned in Galatians 2:1 as a person well known to the readers; yet he was only on Paul's first missionary journey (i.e. to the Southern Galatian cities) and could not have visited the North Galatian area. None of these factors in and of itself demonstrates the South Galatian hypothesis. Yet the cumulative force of the evidence seems to demand the probability of this view. At least, it convinced Ramsay, and his arguments have impressed a surprising number of scholars; e.g. E. D. Burton,[37] G. S. Duncan,[38] E. J. Goodspeed,[39] W. Michaelis,[40] F. F. Bruce,[41] C. S. C. Williams,[42] H. N. Ridderbos,[43] Jack Finegan,[44] E. M. Blaiklock,[45] and Donald Guthrie.[46] Ramsay's later conclusion that an early date for Galatians provides a more satisfactory exegesis of the letter gives even more weight to the theory.[47]

But, we may ask, why was this interpretation lost for so many centuries and recovered only in the nineteenth century? The answer is clear.

> It was lost because, during the second century, the term Galatia ceased to bear the sense which it had to a Roman in the first century. The whole of central and southern Lycaonia was, before the middle of the second century, separated from Galatia, and formed into a province Lycaonia, which was united with Isauria and Cilicia under the title of "the three Eparchies," and put under the command of a governor of the highest rank. From this time onwards the true sense of the term Galatia in St. Paul's time was lost....[48]

Thus the South Galatian theory becomes a helpful ally in the defense of the trustworthiness of Acts and its setting in the first century.

Ramsay never submitted the Gospel of Luke to the same thorough study that he did Acts. However, he cannot be criticized too harshly for this because this was really outside the realm of

---

37 *A Critical and Exegetical Commentary on the Epistle to the Galatians* (Edinburgh: T. and T. Clark, 1921), pp. xvii-xliv.
38 *The Epistle of Paul to the Galatians* (London: Hodder and Stoughton, 1934), pp. xviii-xxi.
39 *An Introduction to the New Testament* (Chicago: University of Chicago Press, 1937), pp. 34-38.
40 *Einleitung in das Neue Testament* (Bern: Beg-Verlag, 1946), pp. 181-187.
41 *Acts,* p. 38.
42 *A Commentary on the Acts of the Apostles* (London: Adam and Charles Black, 1957), pp. 175-177.
43 *The Epistle of Paul to the Churches of Galatia,* trans. by Henry Zylstra (Grand Rapids, Mich.: Wm. B. Eerdmans Publishing Co., 1953), pp. 22-31.
44 *Light from the Ancient Past* (Princeton, N. J.: Princeton University Press, 2nd edition, 1959), pp. 340-345.
45 *The Acts of the Apostles* (London: Tyndale Press, 1959), pp. 104-111.
46 *NTI: Pauline Epistles,* pp. 72-79.
47 In his early writings (*CRE, SPT, HCG*) Ramsay dated the Epistle to the Galatians in the year 53, after Paul's second missionary journey. However, by the time he wrote *The Teaching of Paul in Terms of the Present Day* (1913) he had decided that an earlier date of 49, just prior to the Jerusalem Council, was preferable. Cf. "The Chronology of the Life of St. Paul as It Appears in 1920," introductory chapter added to the 14th edition of *SPT* (1920), p. xxxi.
48 *CRE,* p. 111.

his qualifications. He was an expert in Graeco-Roman studies and had little acquaintance with Palestinian and Semitic studies. In fact, there are times when one can observe that he has a definite lack of appreciation of things Semitic.[49] Nevertheless, he did make an attempt to study the Gospel.

In a review of *St. Paul the Traveller* a distinguished foreign scholar (Schürer?) challenged Ramsay's view of Luke's rank as a historian. "If Luke is a great historian, what would the author of this book make of Luke 2:1-3?"[50] The reviewer need say no more. This was all the encouragement Ramsay needed to write another book.

According to his custom, Ramsay first published his ideas in *The Expositor* (April and June 1897) and expanded them into a book a year later. And so the book *Was Christ Born at Bethlehem?* came into being. This has remained one of the important studies on the historical problems involved in the second chapter of the Gospel according to Luke, although some of his conclusions would need to be modified today.[51]

Luke 2:1-5 reads,

> In those days a decree went out from Caesar Augustus that all the world should be enrolled. This was the first enrollment, when Quirinius was governor of Syria. And all went to be enrolled, each to his own city. And Joseph also went up from Galilee, from the city of Nazareth, to Judea, to the city of David, which is called Bethlehem, because he was of the house and lineage of David, to be enrolled with Mary, his betrothed, who was with child.

Against the historicity of this statement, the following points had been advanced: (1) There is no evidence for a general census of the whole Roman world in the time of Caesar Augustus. (2) Even if there were such a census, it would not have been held in Palestine during the reign of Herod the Great. (3) Even if there had been a census made in Palestine, there would have been no necessity for Joseph and Mary to travel to Bethlehem. (4) No such census was ever held in Judea until A.D. 6-7; Josephus regards the census at that time as an innovation which caused a Jewish rebellion on that account. (5) A census held under Quirinius could not be held while Herod was king, for he was not the governor of Syria until a decade after Herod's death.[52]

Taking his cue from the newly discovered papyri that indicated there was a regular census in Egypt every fourteen years,

49 Cf. *SPT*, pp. 368-370; *LSC*, p. 72.
50 *BRD*, p. 223.
51 For a discussion of the problems involved, see Jack Finegan, *Handbook of Biblical Chronology* (Princeton, N. J.: Princeton University Press, 1964), pp. 234-238; Lily Ross Taylor, "Quirinius and the Census of Judea," *American Journal of Philology*, 54 (1933): 120-133; A. N. Sherwin-White, *Roman Society and Roman Law in the New Testament* (London: Oxford University Press, 1963), pp. 162-171.
52 *WCB*, pp. 102-110.

Ramsay demonstrated that there could well have been a census in Judea previous to the one mentioned in Acts 5:27. Evidence that Ramsay included in his study and more recent evidence has led many scholars to conclude — contrary to the opposition — that an earlier enrollment, as described by Luke,

> (a) may have taken place in the reign of Herod the Great, (b) may have involved the return of everyone to his family home, (c) may have formed part of an empire-wide census, and (d) may have been held during a previous governorship of Quirinius over Syria.[53]

The problem of Quirinius is a thorny one, and there is still no definite proof that he served as governor during the time of the census mentioned in Luke 2. However, we cannot assume that Luke is in error in regard to this detail when he has been demonstrated to be so carefully accurate elsewhere. A recent scholar who has devoted a great deal of study to the problem of New Testament chronology concludes his discussion of this problem with a suggestion:

> The question remains whether, at some time in the latter years of Herod, Quirinius might have been connected with such a census in Palestine. Since Quirinius was a high Roman official with important assignments in the East, and since at least by 6 B.C. the Homanadensian War was probably under control, this does not appear unlikely. Tertullian says in fact that the census at the time of the birth of Jesus was "taken in Judea by Sentius Saturninus." According to the list of governors of Syria this would mean sometime in the years 9-6 B.C. No reason is evident why Quirinius could not have been associated with Saturninus in such a project. In view of the sequence of known events in his career a likely time might have been in 6 or 5 B.C. That Quirinius actually took this census is still only concretely affirmed by Lk. 2:2; under the circumstances as we have reconstructed them the affirmation is not unlikely.[54]

Several other interesting aspects of Luke's Gospel are discussed in *Was Christ Born at Bethlehem?* Ramsay's study begins with an exegesis of Luke's statement of the purpose in the first four verses of his first book. He concludes (1) that Luke claims to have access to authorities of the first rank, (2) that he had made a careful and thorough personal investigation of the origin and developments of the events he is about to narrate, (3) that his intention is to give a comprehensive narrative of the events from the first to the last, and (4) that he makes an emphatic claim that his account is trustworthy and certain.[55] Ramsay goes on to observe a number of details which point to the conclusion that the author's point of view is that of a Greek provincial and that

---

53 Bruce, *The New Testament Documents: Are They Reliable?* (Fifth edition, London: Inter-Varsity Fellowship, 1961), p. 86.
54 Finegan, *Chronology*, pp. 237-238.
55 WCB, pp. 3-22.

he is writing with a single Roman or a Roman circle of readers in view.[56] Ramsay's discussion of the story with the birth of Christ may lack depth, but his theory that the narrative bears the mark of a private family tradition which would likely have been gained from a personal conversation with Mary, or someone close to her, is an attractive one.[57]

---

56 *WCB*, pp. 49-72.
57 *WCB*, pp. 73-91.

III

PAUL THE MISSIONARY STATESMAN

It is as an interpreter of the New Testament, rather than as an apologist, that Sir William Ramsay is at his best. When he turns the searchlight of his vast knowledge concerning the life of the first-century Roman Empire upon the Book of Acts, the epistles of Paul, or some other part of the early Christian literature, the New Testament at once comes to life for the student. When all is said and done, Ramsay's major contribution to New Testament scholarship probably lies in this area.

When he begins to study the life of the Apostle Paul, the student must first determine the value and the relationship between his basic sources. The sources that present themselves to the student are two: the Acts of the Apostles and the group of letters identified as having been written by Paul himself. How, then, are these two sources related? And what contribution do they make to the reconstruction of the life and work of Paul? Are both to be accepted as equal authorities? Furthermore, are all the letters purported to have been written by Paul really his? The answers given to these questions will determine one's approach to the study of the life of Paul; they will also to some degree determine the resulting picture of the man Paul.

The approach of John Knox in his *Chapters in a Life of Paul* is typical of a certain group of New Testament scholars.[1] In breaking ground for the construction of an outline of the life of Paul, Knox maintains, first of all, that Acts must be regarded as secondary and that Paul's letters are to be regarded as the pri-

---

1 Cf. Martin Dibelius, *Paul*, edited and completed by Werner Georg Kümmel, trans. by Frank Clarke (London: Longmans, Green, and Co., 1953), pp. 1-14.

mary source materials. Now everyone would agree with this statement in its abstract form. However, in the hands of Knox and other critics this thesis becomes a tool to demonstrate the necessary contradiction between the two sources; it almost seems as though the author of Acts is pre-judged in the matter. The result is that the biographical data contained in the letters of Paul are pitted over against the material contained in the Acts. In addition, Knox and other scholars assume that the letters of Paul to Timothy and Titus, known as the Pastorals, and the so-called Epistle to the Ephesians (perhaps 2 Thessalonians and Colossians as well) are pseudonymous and, therefore, cannot be considered as source materials.

The view expressed here is not a new one; it was current in the time of Ramsay, although it may have been stated in a slightly different form. Through a thorough comparison of the Acts with the letters of Paul, Ramsay became convinced that the opposite of this was true. If Luke was the first-rate historian that Ramsay had judged him to be, and if he was the personal friend and disciple of Paul, then there must be a basic agreement between the biographical data concerning Paul in Acts and the autobiographical material of his letters. Otherwise, we would have to change our opinion concerning his character as a historian. Ramsay argues forcefully:

> We must face the facts boldly. If Luke wrote Acts, his narrative *must* agree in a striking and convincing way with Paul's: they *must* confirm, explain and complete one another. This is not a case of two commonplace, imperfectly educated, and not very observant witnesses who give divergent accounts of certain incidents which they saw without paying much attention to them. We have here two men of high education, one writing a formal history, the other speaking under every obligation of honour and conscience to be careful in his words: the subjects they speak of were of the most overpowering interest to both: their points of view must be very similar, for they are personal friends, and one was the teacher of the other, and naturally had moulded to some extent his mind during long companionship. If ever there was a case in which striking agreement was demanded by historical criticism between two classes of documents, it is between the writings of Paul and Luke.[2]

The Paul portrayed by Luke the historian was

> the centre of interest wherever he went, dominating all by his personality, heralded before he came, alike in Thessalonica and in Rome, the man that has "turned the world upside down," the storm-centre of society, from whom originates revolution wherever he goes, educated in his thoughts and polished in his tone of courtesy, yet fiery and vehement in his temper, versatile and adaptable so that he moves at his ease in every class of society, the Socratic dialectician in the Athenian marketplace, the philosophic rhetorician in the Ephesian School of Tyrannus,

---

2 *SPT*, pp. 14-15; cf. Bruce, *Acts*, pp. 34-40.

conversing in a tone of courteous respect with Kings and great Roman
officials, "standing" before an Emperor, giving wise advice at a hasty
council on a ship in the season of danger, cheering a dejected crew to
make one more effort for life, reminding Roman soldiers of their duty
and Roman colonial magistrates of their error in trampling on Roman
law, making a great trade corporation anxious about the future of its
business and a small firm of slave-owners despondent about its income,
the friend of the leading men in the province of Asia, to whom a wealthy
Roman procurator with a queen as his mistress looked expecting to
receive bribes: where Paul is, all eyes and many hearts are attracted,
while the vulgar and the mob and the Jews, the magians [sic] and the
soothsayers, hate and fear him.[3]

That this picture painted by Luke of the great apostle is a true
one is the presupposition of all but Ramsay's earliest discussions
of the life and work of Paul. Ramsay argued that Acts and the
letters of Paul can be demonstrated to complement — rather
than contradict — each other. If either of them is neglected, the
portrait of Paul is only partial; if they are put side by side, the
information contained in both fits together, and the result is
Paul in the round. In short, both Acts and the Pauline corpus
are found to illuminate each other. And what about the disputed
letters of Paul? Ramsay answered that the versatile man presented to us by Luke was certainly capable of writing in many
veins; he, therefore, concluded that all thirteen of Paul's letters
are genuine and can be treated as primary sources for a life of
Paul.

In the writings of Ramsay it is Paul the man who is brought to
life before the eyes of the student. The character of Paul takes
on flesh and blood as the world in which he moved and the
forces that molded his thoughts are unveiled for the reader, and
when small — almost overlooked — details from the text of Acts
or from one of his letters are breathed upon by Ramsay. W. F.
Howard gives this testimony concerning St. Paul the Traveller
and the Roman Citizen:

> Many who have devoted their lives to New Testament studies would
> say that their first eager interest in the Pauline writings was aroused by
> Lightfoot's Galatians, but their enthusiasm for Paul the man was kindled
> by this never-to-be-forgotten book of Ramsay's.[4]

Not only does Paul come to life, but also his missionary associ-
ates, Christian friends, enemies, and people met along the way —
Barnabas, John Mark, Silas, Luke, Apollos, Priscilla and Aquila,
Timothy, Elymas the magician, Demetrius the silversmith,
Sergius Paulus, Gallio, Felix, Festus, and a whole host of others.
The cities visited by the Apostles also become to the student

---

3 TP, pp. vi-vii.
4 Romance, pp. 147-148.

more than mere names on a map or on a page in his notebook; each one — Tarsus, Syrian Antioch, Paphos, Pisidian Antioch, Iconium, Lystra, Derbe, Philippi, Thessalonica, Beroea, Athens, Corinth, Ephesus — has its own distinctive personality and makes its own contribution toward a better understanding of Paul's world and work.

As has already been indicated, Ramsay brings Paul and his companions to life by expertly filling in the background of the Acts and the Pauline letters by describing the world in which he moved. This is accomplished mainly by two works: *St. Paul the Traveller and the Roman Citizen* and *The Cities of St. Paul.* The first of these is a study of the text of the Book of Acts, especially the latter part of the book which deals with the life and missionary travels of Paul, from the viewpoint of its setting in the history and culture of the Roman Empire. The second, published twelve years later, surveys the history of five Pauline cities[5] — Tarsus, Pisidian Antioch, Iconium, Derbe, and Lystra — and seeks to determine what special aspects of the life of each of these cities has a bearing on Paul's life and thought. In both of these books he brings many interesting facts gained from a study of the cultural history of the eastern Roman provinces to bear upon the interpretation of the New Testament.

Some of the suggestions he makes regarding the background or the interpretation of a given passage of Scripture seem to be the product of a fantastic imagination. However, before one is quick to criticize Ramsay in this regard, he should be careful to ponder his method. His method in biblical study was the same as his geographical method. It was his custom to make an educated guess regarding the location of a certain city after he had thoroughly studied all the data available; then he proceeded to test his hypothesis. In this work a vivid imagination was a great asset. He was quite often wrong in his hypothesis, but he was more often correct. At any rate, his hypothesis concerning any given situation was something solid to work with, something he could put to the test to see whether it was after all true. So it is in his study of the New Testament. Many of his suggestions regarding the interpretation of a given passage of Scripture are merely educated guesses concerning what might possibly be the

---

5 The essay on Tarsus (CSP, pp. 85-244) is still the most substantial survey of the history of Tarsus. All of these articles are still valuable, for very little work has been done in regard to these cities since the days of Ramsay. Ramsay's suggestion for the location of Derbe must be altered, however, in view of its location in 1956 by M. Ballance; it was found to be more than thirty miles distant from the mound suggested by Ramsay. Cf. H. Ballance, *Anatolian Studies*, 7 (1957): 147-151.

background of the passage or what might possibly be the answer to some thorny problem that had been eluding interpreters for years. If his hypothesis did not turn out to fit all the facts of the case, Ramsay himself would be the first to reject it upon the basis of further consideration. In addition to his change of mind regarding the date of Galatians, which was mentioned in chapter two, an apt illustration is his interpretation of 1 Corinthians 2. In *St. Paul the Traveller* he regarded Paul's determination "to know nothing except Jesus Christ and him crucified" (1 Cor. 2:2) at Corinth as a new departure in his approach arising out of the disappointment and disillusionment experienced at Athens, where he attempted to present his doctrine in a form suited to Greek philosophy.[6] Later in *The Teaching of Paul in Terms of the Present Day*, Ramsay acknowledged that he had failed to take into consideration Paul's adaptation of the gospel message to different classes of hearers — tradesmen at Corinth and philosophers at Athens — and that his address before the Areopagus should be considered as typical of his method of speaking to educated Hellenic audiences.[7] However, the student should be careful before he rejects any of Ramsay's suggestions as too fantastic. The present writer can testify that he has more than once at first glance judged some interpretation of Ramsay's as fanciful only to come back to it after further reflection!

The Paul of the New Testament is a citizen of three worlds: the Roman, the Greek, and the Hebrew. Each of these worlds molded him; each influenced his personality and left its mark upon his thought. Paul wrote in Galatians 1:15-16 that God had set him apart before his birth and had called him to preach the gospel among the Gentiles. Here Paul expresses, according to Ramsay, a consciousness that his conversion and calling were the consummation of a process of selection and preparation that began a long time before his birth. This means that

> the family, the surroundings, and the education of Paul had been selected with the perfection of a Divine purpose to make him fit to be what he was designed to be, the Apostle of the Gentiles. There was one nation, one family and one city, out of which the Apostle must arise. The nation was the Jewish; but the family was not Palestinian, it was Tarsian. Only "a Hebrew sprung from Hebrews" could be the Apostle of the perfected Judaic faith; but he must be born and brought up in childhood among the Gentiles, a citizen of a Gentile city, and a member of that conquering aristocracy of Romans which ruled all the cities of the Mediterranean world. The Apostle to the Gentiles must be a Jew, a Tarsian citizen, and at the same time a Roman.[8]

---

6 Pp. 145, 252-253.
7 Pp. 109-112.
8 CSP, p. 87.

Each one of these aspects of Paul's background must be taken into consideration by the student of Paul. To neglect one of them is to fail to understand him fully.

Paul was, in the first place, a Jew — "A Hebrew born of Hebrews," as he wrote to the Philippian church (Phil. 3:5). This aspect of his personality was of greatest significance in shaping the man Paul and must be carefully noted in any discussion of his life and work.[9] This heritage as a Jew produced in him his basic religious convictions and gave him an open door for his message throughout the Roman world in the synagogues of the Dispersion.

However, Paul was not a narrow Jew ignorant of and hostile to Hellenic education. He was, indeed, a good Jew, but he was far more than a Jew. He was also a patriotic citizen of Tarsus and a loyal Roman. When he speaks of himself as a Pharisee (Acts 23:6; Phil. 3:5), he identifies himself with the highest ideals of Pharisaism, not with their extreme separatism and their anti-Greek and anti-Roman feelings. Paul was educated by his parents to appreciate the best of each of the worlds in which he found himself; he assimilated the good and rejected the rest.

In the second place, Paul was from Tarsus and "a citizen of no mean city" (Acts 21:39). He was not merely born there, but he had the rights of a citizen there. It is probable that his family was planted in Tarsus about 171 B.C. by Antiochus IV along with other Jews and that they were given full rights as citizens of the city.[10] According to Ramsay, Tarsus was the ideal city to produce a man like Paul, for it was the one city that was more successful than any other in uniting the oriental and the occidental elements in its society.[11]

> It was the one city which was suited by its equipoise between the Asiatic and the Western spirit to mold the character of the great Hellenist Jew; and . . . it nourished in him a strong sense of loyalty and patriotism as the "citizen of no mean city."[12]

In the uniting of the two spirits in Tarsus, the oriental seemed to dominate. Ramsay brings this fact to bear upon the interpretation of Paul's prescription concerning the veiling of women in 1 Corinthians 11:3-16. His remarks are worth quoting in detail.

We may notice in passing how strong an effect was produced on the

---

9 It must be admitted that Ramsay, because of his reaction against those scholars who tended to interpret Paul too narrowly within the confines of Palestinian Judaism and because of his lack of equipment in things Judaic, tended to over-emphasize the Graeco-Roman background of Paul. His discussion of Paul ought to be balanced by the insights of W. D. Davies, *Paul and Rabbinic Judaism* (London: S. P. C. K., 1948) and W. C. Van Unnik, *Tarsus or Jerusalem, the City of Paul's Youth?*, trans. by G. Ogg (London: Epworth Press, 1962).
10 *CSP*, pp. 174-180.
11 *CSP*, pp. 88-89.
12 *CSP*, p. 235.

mind of St. Paul by his Tarsian experience.... The Apostle prescribes
to the Corinthians a very strict rule about the veiling of women (I Cor.
xi 3-16). Whereas men are to have their heads uncovered in Church, it is
disgraceful for women to be unveiled there. Now it would be quite possible that a Greek or a Roman should reach this opinion about women's
dress and conduct in Church. So far as this command goes, it was quite
in accordance with the ideas of the most orderly and thoughtful among
those peoples and quite in keeping with the customs of good society.
But there is one little touch in St. Paul's sermon about women that reveals the man brought up amid Oriental custom. He says that "the
woman ought to have authority (ἐξουσία) upon her head." This seems
so strange to the Western mind that the words have been generally reckoned among the most obscure in the whole of the Pauline writings....
Most of the ancient and modern commentators say that the "authority"
which the woman wears on her head is the authority to which she is
subject — a preposterous idea which a Greek scholar would laugh at
anywhere except in the New Testament, where (as they seem to think)
Greek words may mean anything that commentators choose. Authority
or power that belongs to the wearer, such power as the magistrate possesses in virtue of his office, was meant by the Greek word ἐξουσία. . . .
The woman who has a veil on her head wears authority on her head:
that is what the Greek text says. To the European the words are unintelligible; but that is because he is a European. He must cease for a
moment to be a European and pass into the realm of life and thought
in which the words apply. Then he will understand them. To the Oriental the words are simple and clear: they describe the ordinary fact of
life....
In Oriental lands the veil is the power and the honour and dignity of
the woman. With the veil on her head, she can go anywhere in security
and profound respect. She is not seen; it is the mark of thoroughly bad
manners to observe a veiled woman in the street. She is alone. The rest
of the people around are non-existent to her, as she is to them. She
is supreme in the crowd. She passes at her own free choice, and a space
must be left for her....
But without the veil the woman is a thing of nought, whom any one
may insult. The true Oriental, if uneducated in Western ways, seems to
be inclined naturally to treat with rudeness, to push and ill-treat, a
European lady in the street. A woman's authority and dignity vanish
along with the all-covering veil that she discards. That is the Oriental
view, which Paul learned in Tarsus.[13]

In the third place, Paul was a Roman citizen.[14]

That character superseded all others before the law and the general
opinion of society; and placed him amid the aristocracy of any provincial town. In the first century, when the citizenship was still jealously
guarded, the *civitas* may be taken as a proof that his family was one of
distinction and at least moderate wealth. It also implies that there was
in the surroundings amid which he grew up, a certain attitude of
friendliness to the Imperial government....[15]

---

13 CSP, pp. 202-205. But cf. F. W. Grosheide, *Commentary on the First Epistle to the
Corinthians* (Grand Rapids, Mich.: Wm. B. Eerdmans, 1953), and Leon Morris, *The First
Epistle of Paul to the Corinthians* (London: Tyndale Press, 1958), *loc. cit.*
14 For an excellent recent discussion of Paul's citizenship, see Sherwin-White, *Roman
Society*, pp. 144-162.
15 SPT, pp. 30-31.

Paul's Roman citizenship influenced his thought and ministry in a number of ways. Besides the obvious fact that it got him out of jams on a number of occasions, it influenced his plan of making centers of Roman administration and Greek culture centers for his evangelistic activity and his vision of a world-wide church after the order of the Empire. Paul, the Roman, was a missionary statesman "animated with the instinct of administration"; he developed the conception of the church as consisting of many parts, widely separated by geography and self-governing units, yet each part the perfect ideal of the whole after the analogy of the Roman view that "every group of Roman citizens meeting together in a body *(conventus Civium Romanorum)* in any part of the vast Empire formed a part of the great conception 'Rome,' and that such a group was not an intelligible idea, except as a piece of the great unity.[16]

In a remarkable essay published in *The Contemporary Review* in 1901 and republished five years later as a chapter in *Pauline and Other Studies*,[17] Ramsay discussed in detail Paul's Roman point of view and his imperial ideals. He pointed out that the Roman policy of the first century of our era aimed at the amalgamation of the various races and nations into a unity, with Rome at the center. Old national lines of separation were deliberately obliterated. This imperial ideal was the great fact of the age in which Paul lived and had a profound influence on his life and thought.

As Paul the young, devout Jew grew up he would have been impressed with two facts: "the lofty, stern purity of the true Judaism among the pagan world, and the danger that the Jews might slip back towards the pagan level."[18] Only one remedy for the situation presented itself to him: "Judaism in the midst of Roman society must assimilate that society and raise it to a higher level, or it must perish."[19] Either Judaism must conquer the Empire, or it must be conquered by it; it must be a power to raise Graeco-Roman society to its own level, or it must sink to the level of that society. There were no other alternatives open to him. His goal from his youth must have been to see the religion of his race become the religion of the Empire. However, it was not until after his conversion to Jesus as the Messiah that he saw the possibility of making this goal a reality.

As a Christian Paul slowly came to realize that God no longer

16 *SPT*, p. 125; cf. pp. 135-140.
17 Pp. 49-100.
18 *POS*, pp. 65-66.
19 *POS*, p. 66.

confined His work primarily to the Jewish people, but that Christ had made both Jew and Gentile one and that the Word of God was to go out to all men. This he came to realize early in his ministry as an apostle, but it was not until his second missionary journey, when he fixed his eyes on Ephesus, that we begin to see his deliberate strategy for the conquest of the Empire. From this moment forward it becomes obvious to all that his aim is co-extensive with the Empire: he thinks in terms of Roman provinces; he organizes his scattered congregations in the East into a unity as extensive as the Imperial organization; and he begins to make plans to visit Rome on his way to Spain, the extreme limit of the Western Roman Empire.

It is strange that Ramsay only made incidental reference to Paul's scheme of a general contribution to be collected among the churches of Galatia, Asia, Macedonia, and Achaia for the poor of the Jerusalem church, although this plan fits in perfectly with his observations concerning the Apostle's imperialistic ideals. In his discussion of Paul's background and relation to the Roman, Greek, and Hebrew worlds, he also failed to dilate upon the Pauline principle of becoming "all things to all men" as stated in 1 Corinthians 9.

In addition to his discussion of the life and work of Paul in the two books mentioned above and in his commentary on Galatians, which was noted in chapter two, Ramsay produced several other works that are concerned primarily with Paul. Two more historical commentaries were written for *The Expositor*, but they were never published separately. These were "A Historical Commentary on the Epistles to the Corinthians," published during the first eleven months of 1900, and "A Historical Commentary on the Epistles of Timothy," published over the period 1909-1911. In 1909 he wrote a series of fifty-two articles for *The Sunday School Times* (Philadelphia) on the Acts of the Apostles; these were published a year later under the title, *Pictures of the Apostolic Church*. Another work on Paul, *The Teaching of Paul in Terms of the Present Day*, was published in 1913; although it contains some significant remarks regarding the relationship of Paul to the mystery religions,[20] it falls far below the general standard of his other work. In fact, the general observation may be made that his later work in the biblical area — especially when he is concerned with exegesis and theology, rather than historical backgrounds — is much below the high quality of his earlier work. Ramsay had gained a reputation as a writer, and there was

20 TP, pp. 283-305.

a market for his books. Possibly due to the urging of his publisher, every year or so a group of his essays were gathered together without much rhyme or reason — and without an index! — and were thrust into the hands of an eager reading public. *Luke the Physician and Other Studies in the History of Religion* and *Pauline and Other Studies* are the most notable examples of this sort of action.

Ramsay commented on so many incidents in the life of Paul and so many different passages of the New Testament that it would be impossible even to list his most significant comments. The reader's best introduction to Ramsay as an expositor would be to read his comments on various subjects and biblical passages of special interest to him. As an aid in this connection, the reader is referred to the indexes of select subjects and biblical references appended to this book.

IV

THE SEVEN CHURCHES OF ASIA

A basic principle in the interpretation of the Bible is that one must first ask what a given Scripture was intended to mean to the people for whom it was originally written; only then is the interpreter free to ask what meaning it has for Christians today.

Failure to ask this primary question and to investigate the historical setting of Scripture have prevented many Christians from coming to a correct understanding of some parts of the Bible. Nowhere is this more true than in respect to the last book in the Bible. Here there has been a singular lack of appreciation for the historical background of the book; the book has been interpreted as if it were primarily written for the day in which the expositor lives (which is usually thought to be the end time), rather than in terms of what it meant to the first-century Christians of the Roman province of Asia for whom it was originally written. This has resulted in all sorts of grotesque and fantastic conclusions of which the author of the Revelation and its early recipients never would have dreamed.

In all his writings Ramsay has underlined the importance of the historical setting of the various books of the New Testament for their interpretation. He has done this in regard to the Revelation in his work on *The Letters to the Seven Churches of Asia and Their Place in the Plan of the Apocalypse*. As with so many of his works, this one was also first published as a series of essays in *The Expositor* and later in book form (1904). *The Letters to the Seven Churches* is not generally so well known as Ramsay's other books, but it is most certainly one of his more important ones. It is still the only work of a scholarly nature that has been devoted to a historical survey of the life of these seven Asian cities as a background to the understanding of the Apocalypse.[1]

Ramsay begins his work with a series of general essays portraying the world in which these early Christian communities grew up. The second part of the book is devoted to a detailed interpretation of each of the seven letters in light of the principles laid down and the features of the historical background discussed in the earlier part of the book. The author's point of view is strongly preterist; that is, he argues that the Book of Revelation as a whole must be interpreted in terms of its historical setting in the first century of the Christian era, true to the cultural and political situation in the Roman province of Asia at that time, and as it would have been understood by the members of those seven churches who were undergoing a period of intense persecution during the reign of the Emperor Domitian (A.D. 81-96). It must be understood as having only the most general reference to the future. He boldly rejects the futuristic interpretation: "The most dangerous kind of error that can be made about the Apocalypse is to regard it as a literal statement and prediction of events."[2]

The introductory chapters of the book on letter writing and travel in the first century, especially among the early Christian communities, combine to make an important contribution to the discussion of the origin and nature of the early Christian literature.[3] A good deal has been written on the subject by men who are technical theologians and biblical scholars, but here is a survey of the matter by a scholar who is intimately acquainted with the customs and culture of the Roman Empire in this regard.

Ramsay observes that it was easier and safer to send letters and to travel widely during the first century than ever before; in fact, it was much easier and safer in that part of the world in the first century A.D. than it was in Ramsay's day. This constant communication by letter, supplemented by travelling, was the greatest factor in binding together all the individual and independent churches into one universal church.[4] Ramsay argued that the Christian church developed a new type of letter that does not

---

1 Ethelbert Stauffer, *Christ and the Caesars* (London: SCM Press, 1955) contains much valuable background information concerning the imperial cult and the life of the Roman Empire, but it is not devoted primarily to Asia. David Magie, *Roman Rule in Asia Minor* (2 vols.; Princeton: Princeton University Press, 1950) and A. H. M. Jones, *The Cities of the Eastern Roman Provinces* (London: Oxford University Press, 1937), pp. 28-95, also contain a great deal of information, but there is no reference in its place in the interpretation of the New Testament. There is much material related to the life of the seven cities mentioned in the Apocalypse contained in these works, but it must be extracted and applied by the biblical interpreter.

2 *LSC*, p. 112.

3 *LSC*, pp. 1-34. Much of this material is also contained in Ramsay's essay on "Roads and Travel in the New Testament" in the extra volume of *HDB*.

4 *LSC*, p. 21.

really fall into the two categories identified by Adolf Deissmann.[5] The early Christian letters are not really true letters, and they are not stricty literary epistles. That is, they are not merely personal and occasional letters, intended only for the eye of the person or persons addressed; and they are not written primarily for public display. Some aspects of both categories are combined in these early Christian letters.

> These are true letters, in the sense that they spring from the heart of the writers; that they were often written in answer to a question, or called forth by some special crisis in the history of the persons addressed, so that they rise out of the actual situation in which the writer conceives the readers to be placed; that they express the writer's keen and living sympathy with the participation in the fortunes of the whole class addressed; that they are not affected by any thought of a wider public than the persons whom he directly addresses; in short, he empties out his heart in them. On the other hand, the letters of this class express general principles of life and conduct, religion and ethics, applicable to a wider range of circumstances than those which have called forth the special letter; and they appeal as emphatically and intimately to all Christians in all times as they did to those addressed in the first instance.[6]

Paul's letter to the Colossian church illustrates this double character. In bidding the Colossian Christians to share the letter with their Laodicean brethren, he recognized that what he had written had a wider application than just to the Colossian situation. But the letter was not composed primarily with that wider circle in view, but the critical situation at Colossae in mind. "The wider application arises out of the essential similarity of human nature in both congregations and in all mankind."[7] The situation that has arisen here is likely to arise elsewhere some other time. In this lies the newness of the early Christian letters:

> In the individual case they discover the universal principle, and state it in such a way as to reach the heart of every man similarly situated; and yet they state this, not in the way of formal exposition, but in the way of direct personal converse, written in place of spoken.[8]

Such letters are somewhat analogous to the imperial rescripts, which were strictly only replies to requests of guidance in special cases, but which were regarded as setting forth the general principles of policy that applied to the special case. Some of the letters of Paul take on the most personal quality, and the so-called Catholic Epistles tend to be more literary; yet neither group falls easily into either of Deissmann's two categories. Even though the letters to the seven churches of Asia in chapters two and three of

---

5 *Light from the Ancient East*, trans. by Lionel R. M. Strachan (3rd edition: New York and London: Harper and Brothers, 1927), pp. 228-230.
6 *LSC*, pp. 24-25.
7 *LSC*, p. 25.
8 *LSC*, p. 25.

the Revelation are part of a larger literary work and were never intended to be circulated separately, they also partake of the same dual character as the other early Christian letters. They are intensely personal, with the unique situation of each individual church in mind; yet they have a message for the whole church in the province of Asia, the church of God scattered throughout the Empire, and the Christian church of any age.

Although Ramsay recognizes that much of the symbolism of the Apocalypse is Jewish (especially in the latter part), he argues that there is a much greater influence of the Graeco-Roman world on the symbolism of the book than is generally recognized by commentators.[9] This is especially true of the letters contained in the second and third chapters, which are filled with allusions to the life and character of each individual city and the social, religious, and political situation of the province of Asia in the first century. The natural scenery, the geographical surroundings, the history, the traditions, the political life — all bear upon the imagery of the letters, and therefore, must not be neglected in the attempt to interpret any given symbol.[10]

Ramsay considers the Apostle John to be the author of the book. The book was written during his banishment to the island of Patmos during the persecution of the church under Domitian. One mark of its apostolic origin is its tone of "unhesitating and unlimited authority" which is so different from the other examples of early Christian literature written by non-apostolic authors (e.g., Clement of Rome and Ignatius).[11] Following a brief discussion of the problem of authorship, Ramsay goes on to describe various aspects of the general historical background of the book: the Flavian persecution in the province of Asia, the organization and character of the imperial religion, the character of cities of Asia as meeting places of the Greek and Asiatic spirit, the Jews in the province of Asia, and the place and influence of pagan converts to Christianity in the life of the early church. All of these discussions provide excellent materials for understanding the historical situation of these early churches; the chapters on the imperial religion[12] are important not only as background to the Apocalypse, but also as a part of the background of the life of the New Testament church in general.

---

9 Ramsay's general lack of sympathy for the Jewish aspect of the New Testament must be noted once again. *The Letters to the Seven Churches* is marred by a singular lack of appreciation of the apocalyptic form of literature. According to Ramsay, John's work achieves spiritual and literary greatness only to the degree he is able to free himself from the apocalyptic form, "which seriously fettered and impeded him by its fanciful and unreal character"! LSC, p. 35; cf. p. 72.
10 LSC, pp. 50-56.
11 LSC, pp. 74-81.
12 LSC, pp. 114-117.

The question has often been asked as to why these seven churches are the only churches of the province of Asia mentioned in the Revelation. It is certain that there were many other churches in the province, some of which were located in even more important cities than several of those included in the list. It is obvious that the number seven has symbolic importance for the author, but the question still remains as to why these particular seven churches were   selected. James Moffatt confesses, "Why these particular churches were selected remains a mystery."[13] Martin Kiddle suggests that John's choice of this group of seven churches, rather than any other group of seven churches, was determined by "the representative nature of their problem, their varying degrees of success in meeting those problems, and their aptness as illustrative details in a symbolical design."[14] Ramsay views these seven churches as representative of seven groups of churches in the province of Asia.

> There are seven groups of Churches in Asia; each group is represented by one outstanding and conspicuous member: these representatives are the Seven Churches. These Seven representative Churches stand for the Church of the Province: and the Church of the Province, in its turn, stands for the entire Church of Christ.[15]

The question naturally follows, was this singling out of these seven churches made for the first time by John in the Apocalypse? Or was there already present in Asia the recognition of seven groups of churches? Ramsay argues for the latter view. Several factors point in this direction. First, there is the grouping of the three churches of the Lycus River valley together already when the Epistle to the Colossians was written. It seems that Laodicea gradually grew in prominence and became the administrative center of the group. This can be regarded as typical of the situation in other areas of the province. Secondly, there is the fact that all seven cities mentioned lie on the great circular road that bound together the most important region of the province of Asia. Ramsay took his cue from the observation of Hort in his notes on the First Epistle of Peter that the reason for the peculiar order in which the provinces are enumerated at the beginning of this letter lies in the route along which the messenger had to travel when he delivered the letter to the central cities of the various provinces;[16] he concluded that the circular route had an importance in determining the selection of the representative

---

13 "The Revelation of St. John the Divine," *The Expositor's Greek Testament*, W. Robertson Nicoll (ed.) Repr. Grand Rapids: Wm. B. Eerdmans, 1961), pp. 285-286, n.l.
14 *The Revelation of St. John* (London: Hodder and Stoughton, 1940), p. 7.
15 *LSC*, p. 177.
16 F. J. A. Hort, *The First Epistle of St. Peter, I. 1-II. 17* (London: Macmillan and Co., 1898), pp. 17, 157-184.

cities. This leads him to the suggestion that this was the normal order for circulating letters between the churches of the area; necessity had forced the churches to develop their own private postal system for communication with the various independent churches. The seven churches, then, would represent seven "postal districts." Copies of the book (or any occasional letter) would be delivered to each of the seven churches, from which messengers would in turn deliver copies to the various churches in their district. The result was a fast and efficient system of communication among all the churches of the province.

Ramsay contends that there is a repeated emphasis in the letters upon the continuity of history between the city and the local church; there is a strong identification of the life of the Christian community with that of the city in which it was located.[17] He goes on to find numerous allusions of the various aspects of city life and history in the letters. For example, the "crown of life" of Revelation 2:10 contains the implicit allusion to the garland of magnificent buildings with the Street of Gold, which encircled Mount Pagos, and which was poetically referred to as "the crown of Smyrna."[18] There is no doubt that Ramsay went to an extreme in finding allusions to the history and geographical setting of the cities where there were none intended; yet the basic emphasis upon the actual historical situation is sound. And his detailed studies of the individual cities are extremely illuminating to the student of the Apocalypse.

The best way to illustrate Ramsay's method is to take one of the seven cities as an example. His treatment of the letter to the church at Pergamum is representative.[19]

Pergamum is the royal city, the city of authority. Both its history and natural setting impress this picture upon the mind of the student. It is the one city of Asia that was set on a huge, rocky hill from which it dominates the whole surrounding area. (Other cities had splendid hills, but as a rule the hill was only the acropolis; the city lay beneath or around the hill.) The visitor to Pergamum cannot but be moved by the awesomeness of its location.[20] It was the seat of the ruling power of the kingdom of the Attalids before the Roman period, and it was the center of Roman rule in the province after its bequest to the Romans by Attalus III in 133 B.C. The first temple of Rome and Augustus to be built in Asia Minor was built in Pergamum *ca.* 29 B.C., and

---

17 *LSC*, p. 204.
18 *LSC*, pp. 256-259, 275.
19 *LSC*, pp. 281-315.
20 The present writer can confirm this impression by his own experience.

the city continued to be the center of the imperial cult in the province. In addition, it was the seat of the worship of Zeus, Athena, Dionysus, and Asklepios. Besides the imperial worship, the two outstanding religious features of the city in the first century A.D. were the famous altar of Zeus, high up the mountain and visible for miles around, and the Asklepieion, the center of the healing cult of the God-Serpent.

John conveys this message of the exalted Lord to the church in Pergamum:

> And to the angel of the church in Pergamum write: The words of him who has the sharp two-edged sword.
> I know where you dwell, where Satan's throne is; you hold fast my name and you did not deny my faith even in the days of Antipas my witness, my faithful one, who was killed among you, where Satan dwells. But I have a few things against you: you have some there who hold the teaching of Balaam, who taught Balak to put a stumbling block before the sons of Israel, that they might eat food sacrificed to idols and practice immorality. So you also have some who hold the teaching of the Nicolaitans. Repent then. If not, I will come to you soon and war against them with the sword of my mouth. He who has an ear, let him hear what the Spirit says to the churches. To him who conquers I will give some of the hidden manna, and I will give him a white stone, with a new name written on the stone which no one knows except him who receives it. (Rev. 2:12-17)

According to Ramsay a number of features stand out as significant in this letter in view of the character of the city. First, Christ identifies himself as the One who "has the sharp two-edged sword" (v. 12) ; that is, He is the One who "wears the symbol of authority, and is invested with the power of life and death,"[21] the two-edged sword being the symbol of the highest order of Roman official authority with which the proconsul of Asia was invested *(jus gladii)*. The readers are reminded that Jesus Christ, rather than the Emperor and his representative, is in the final analysis the One with absolute authority.

Second, the church of Pergamum is portrayed as dwelling "where Satan's throne is" (v. 13) . The reference here is primarily to the fact that Pergamum is the center of the state religion and the worship of the divine Emperor as well as the administrative capital of the province.[22] From the rest of the book it is obvious that the Christians of Asia were undergoing an intense time of persecution at the hand of the state religion. However, the reference to Satan's throne need not be limited to the Emperor cult, but may also include an allusion to the pagan activities asso-

---

21 *LSC*, p. 291.
22 Cf. 2 Thess. 2:3-4, 9-10.

ciated around the great altar of Zeus and Asklepios, all of which is abhorrent to God and to His people.

A third item illumined by the historical background is the reference to the Nicolaitans (v. 15). We do not know all the historical details we would like to know regarding this group that is mentioned in two of the seven letters, but it evidently represents an attempt at a reasonable compromise with the pagan world surrounding the church. Perhaps they argued that a pinch of incense on the altar to the Emperor was really unimportant.

The mention of the "hidden manna" (v. 17) is a touch of Judaism and possibly alludes to the tradition that the manna laid up in the Ark of the Covenant was to be revealed when Messiah comes. Here the symbol is used to indicate the heavenly food the Savior gives to sustain the believer. Finally, the reference to the "white stone" with a new name known only to the bearer written on it (v. 17) could be taken as alluding to a number of customs of the day: possibly a sort of "ticket" of admission to some special event. In contrast to a ticket or coupon for some temporary purpose, this white tessera given by the Lord is lasting and imperishable.

Whether or not one is able to follow Ramsay in all of his suggestions (and here the fact that many of these are merely suggestions must again be underlined), it must be admitted that he has set the importance of the *Sitz im Leben* of the Apocalypse in bold relief. And until someone writes a better and more up-to-date book on the subject, *The Letters to the Seven Churches* will remain a basic tool for the student in his study of the Book of Revelation.

V

POTPOURRI

Ramsay had a flair for denouncing scholars with whom he disagreed and who he felt were absolutely at odds with the facts. In this aspect of his life he belonged more to a bygone age than to the modern. When he wishes to emphasize the absurdity of his opponent's position, he heaps up sarcasm to a degree surpassed only by some of the Protestant Reformers. He confesses on more than one occasion his debt to German scholarship and his great admiration for men of the stature of Theodor Mommsen; at the same time he finds himself constantly at odds with the radical conclusions of many of the German critics. To say that he was not always unemotional in his criticism of some of the tendencies of German scholarship is an understatement. However, his judgment upon his fellow Britishers who failed to do original work and tended merely to mimic the most recent (and sometimes the not-so-recent) opinions of Continental scholarship was even more severe. In one place he apologizes for making such frequent reference to German works, but he then goes on to defend himself with the observation that some scholars will not believe anything unless it is written in German. Elsewhere he muses that some scholars seem to have imputed that same quality of inerrancy to a certain group of German critics which our grandparents reserved for the Bible!

In 1910, James Moffatt published *An Introduction to the Literature of the New Testament*[1] as the successor of his earlier work, *The Historical New Testament*.[2] His new *Introduction*

---

1 (New York: Charles Scribner's Sons, 1911).
2 (Edinburgh: T. and T. Clark, 1901).

was warmly received by the scholarly world in Britain, as were most of Moffatt's multifarious writings, even though he was much less traditional in his views than the typical British scholar. There was one notable exception to this generally friendly reception: Sir William Mitchell Ramsay! Ramsay, who was in Asia Minor at the time, exploded in a series of articles in *The Expositor* which should never have been written — certainly not in the tone in which they were written. These essays were published in book form in 1911 as *The First Christian Century: Notes on Dr. Moffatt's Introduction to the Literature of the New Testament,* and so the greatest blemish to Ramsay's reputation as a scholar was immortalized.

Ramsay said that he could at least pardon the viewpoint of the earlier work as the attempt of a brilliant — but inexperienced — "young scholar," but to be guilty of putting the same general ideas into print ten years later was unforgivable. He had hoped that Moffatt's later work would have shown a greater maturity, but he was keenly disappointed. Several quotations illustrate the tone of his review. "I can detect no broadening of the outlook, no deepening of the sympathy, little sign of growing independence of thought. The book is antiquated, as if it belonged to the nineteenth century."[3] "To put my opinion in a sentence, I should say that the author never reaches the historical point of view; he never shows any comprehension of the way in which great events work themselves out."[4] The work "savours too much of flippant journalism"[5]; it is "indicative of the literary rather than the historical temperament."[6] And so on.

Rather than give a detailed and thoroughly scholarly critique of Moffatt's work, Ramsay was content to make a few general criticisms and a few more incidental criticisms. The result was inconclusive, and Ramsay was the injured one rather than Moffatt. Even the conservative scholar, James Denney, felt compelled to comment:

> I find Sir W. M. Ramsay on Moffatt too discursive and irrelevant, and even in the ordinary sense too impertinent to be very pleasant or profitable reading. What right has he to lecture Moffatt as he does? I agree with him that Moffatt is wrong about the Papias tradition, but if one may say so, he has a right to be wrong; he is a master in this business, and Ramsay has no right to talk to him as he does.[7]

Why did Ramsay vent his wrath so unmercifully upon the

---

3 FCC, pp. 3-4.
4 FCC, p. 9.
5 FCC, p. 11.
6 FCC, p. 15.
7 *Letters of Principal James Denney to His Family and Friends,* edited by James Moffatt (London: Hodder and Stoughton, n.d.), p. 161.

head of James Moffatt rather than others? There were many others who held similar opinions and who wrote similar works, but he did not take time out to castigate them. Perhaps it was because Moffatt was a fellow Scot, and Ramsay felt under obligation to set him straight on this account. Or perhaps it was due to Moffatt's steadfast refusal to admit the force of Ramsay's arguments for the South Galatian hypothesis. Furthermore, Moffatt's method of balancing the opinions of the critics one against the other in determining the answer to a given problem was directly contrary to Ramsay's temperament and method. In the preface to the first edition of his *Introduction,* Moffatt lists the two great commandments of research that underlie his work. First, "Thou shalt work at the sources"; and secondly, "Thou shalt acquaint thyself with work done before thee and beside thee."[8] Now, Ramsay would not quibble with these "commandments" in their abstract form, for he certainly followed them in all of his work. But it seemed to him that Moffatt had inverted the proper order and had, in reality, given very little consideration to original research. According to Ramsay, Moffatt's work was characterized by the

> perfectly confident assumption that the right way of study lies in sifting and weighing these theories [of most recent scholarship] and thus discovering in them "here a little and there a little" which is correct and valuable....[9]

The result, argues Ramsay, is that Moffatt is wrong in his initial principle, and this in turn affects the whole of his work. What does the great archaeologist suggest as a prescription for Moffatt's problem?

> Dr. Moffatt must change his method radically, before he can succeed in doing what he was born to do. He ought to give up reading modern authorities for ten years, and devote that time to thinking and studying the original authorities.[10]

If he does this, he will cease to be dominated by the thought of bad historical critics and will learn to distinguish good from bad criticism!

There is no doubt that Moffatt needed some criticism and that Ramsay's basic contention regarding Moffatt's heavy reliance upon the bulk of "modern scholarship" rather than original sources was correct. Yet *The First Christian Century* remains primarily a negative example of the would-be scholar; it is an illustration of the type of book a scholar should *not* write, or

8 *Introduction,* p. viii.
9 FCC, p. 4.
10 FCC, p. 199.

how *not* to win supporters for one's opinions and influence the world of New Testament scholarship.

Some may accuse Ramsay of being too independent, but no one is able to say that he lacked originality. This was his great strength, as it was sometimes, alas, his weakness. Few have followed him in his suggestions regarding the First Epistle of Peter[11] and the Epistle to the Hebrews,[12] but his views concerning both illustrate his freedom to depart from tradition and to follow truth wherever it may lead.

The First Epistle of Peter was the one book in the New Testament that he felt did not fit the traditionally assigned authorship and date. He agreed with many other scholars that the picture of the persecution of the church in Asia Minor points to a date after the death of the Apostle Peter, which was thought to have occurred in the seventh decade of the first century. Stimulated by a conversation with Professor Hort, he began to consider the possibility that the tradition concerning Peter's martyrdom was wrong and that he did not die until a later period. He then concluded that 1 Peter was written about A.D. 75 or later by the Apostle, whose ministry was longer than traditionally thought.[13]

His views concerning the date and authorship of the Epistle to the Hebrews were (1) that it was written in April or May, A.D. 59, towards the end of the governorship of Felix; (2) that it treats topics that had been frequently discussed between Paul and the leading brethren of the church at Caesarea during his imprisonment there; (3) that it was really a letter from the church in Caesarea to the Jewish party of the church in Jerusalem, represented in the writing by Philip the evangelist (Acts 21:8); and (4) that the plan of writing such a letter was discussed beforehand with Paul, the letter was submitted to him for approval, and the last few verses were actually appended by him.[14] This ingenious hypothesis would solve a number of the problems regarding the nature of the letter, but it would leave others unsolved and even add a few of its own. It is only mentioned as an example of the freedom Ramsay had in his approach to the various problems that confront New Testament scholars.

Ramsay wrote widely and at great length. His published books contain more than eight thousand pages (rivaling F. C. Baur in volume!). This does not include the great mass of essays Ramsay published in various scholarly journals and in the more popular

---

11 CRE, pp. 279-295.
12 LP, pp. 301-328.
13 POS, pp. 268-270.
14 LP, p. 304.

magazines, and the extensive articles in Hastings' *Dictionary of the Bible*. His range of interests included subjects outside the realms of Graeco-Roman studies, New Testament criticism, and the history of the early church, although the greater part of his life was devoted to these. The breadth of his concern is marked by the fact that his writings include two fair-sized volumes on modern Turkey,[15] and an essay on the idealism and dedication of the founders of an American college,[16] and a published lecture in the area of modern political science.[17] In addition, he wrote a plethora of articles over the years on the place of Turkey in international politics.

But the real heart of Sir William Ramsay is laid bare in a small book on Jesus and in a sermon preached before the students of the Moody Bible Institute in Chicago. *The Education of Christ: Hill-side Reveries,* published in 1902, is a delight to read. It is by no means a technical discussion of the life and teachings of Jesus; it is rather "the dream of a student's life,"[18] meditations of a mystical scholar (or a scholarly mystic) on the identity of the real Jesus and His significance for the history of the world. His comments on the importance of geography, especially mountains (the Temptation, the choosing of the Twelve, the Sermon on the Mount, the Transfiguration, the Mount of Olives, etc.), in the education of Jesus are extremely provocative.

This little book of less than one hundred fifty pages and his sermon on "The Cross of Christ the Center of History"[19] portray a man who is as devoted to his Master as he is to the cause of truth. Not only had the greatest of the Apostles cast his spell over Sir William, but also the great Apostle's Lord.

---

15 *Impressions of Turkey during Twelve Years' Wanderings* (London: 1897); Hodder and Stoughton, *The Revolution in Constantinople and Turkey: A Diary* (London: Hodder and Stoughton, 1909).
16 *The Making of a University: What We Have to Learn from Educational Ideals in America* (London: Hodder and Stoughton, 1915). An estimate of the educational work of Dr. Isaac Conrad Ketler.
17 *The Imperial Peace: An Ideal in European History* (Oxford, Clarendon Press, 1913).
18 *EC,* p. vii.
19 *The Christian Worker's Magazine,* 14 (Nov. 1913), pp. 140-148. Reprinted in Wilbur M. Smith, *Great Sermons on the Death of Christ* (Natick, Mass.: W. A. Wilde Co., 1965), pp. 235-241.

VI

CONCLUSION

What contributions has Sir William M. Ramsay made to the study of the New Testament? This is the question implied by the sub-title of this study. In conclusion, several of the assured results of the life and labor of the great archaeologist and scholar may be reiterated.

In his admirable study on *The Interpretation of the New Testament 1861-1961*, Bishop Stephen Neill mentions two conclusions of Ramsay which abide and should be guidelines to New Testament scholars in our day.[1] The first of these is the establishment of the accuracy and reliability of the Lukan writings. That the author of Luke-Acts is, as Ramsay discovered for himself, a first-rate historian should be the presupposition of twentieth-century New Testament scholarship. There is a growing awareness of this fact by both conservative and liberal critics, but the view is not accepted by all.[2] There is still a group of scholars — especially in Germany — who persist in ignoring the strong evidence in favor of the value of the book of Acts as a piece of historical writing. Some few even continue to hold the

---

1 Pp. 142-146.
2 Some of the scholars who have been strongly impressed in recent years by the evidence for the reliability of the Book of Acts are A. M. Hunter, *Interpreting the New Testament* (Philadelphia: Westminster Press, 1961), pp. 111-112; F. F. Bruce, *Acts*, pp. 15-18; C. S. C. Williams, *Acts*, pp. 30-31; Alfred Wikenhauser, *New Testament Introduction* (New York: Herder and Herder, 1958), pp. 329-340; E. M. Blaiklock, *Acts*, p. 89; C. F. D. Moule, *The Birth of the New Testament* (London: Adam and Charles Black, 1962), pp. 3, 109; J. A. Thompson, *The Bible and Archaeology* (Grand Rapids: Wm. B. Eerdmans, 1962), pp. 373-403; Floyd V. Filson, *Three Crucial Decades: Studies in the Book of Acts* (London: Epworth Press, 1964), pp. 5, 115; E. F. Harrison, *Introduction to the New Testament* (Grand Rapids: Wm. B. Eerdmans, 1964), pp. 229-231; and A. A. T. Ehrhardt, *The Framework of the New Testament Stories* (Manchester: Manchester University Press, 1964), pp. 64-102. To this can be added the testimony of the Roman historian, Sherwin-White, *Roman Society*, pp. 48-186.

untenable position that it was actually written in the second century.[3] Why is this?

One cannot but feel that many scholars have not taken the time and the trouble to examine the evidence. Many New Testament scholars are not aware of what has been done in the area of archaeological studies; fewer still have had first-hand experience in archaeological work. Neill observes that this is especially true of German scholars, few of whom "have any personal acquaintance with the archaeological evidence, and it is possible that they tend to underestimate its significance."[4] A. A. T. Ehrhardt makes an interesting observation. He notes that historians have generally maintained a much higher estimate of Luke as an historian than many theologians.[5] (Ramsay himself made the same observation on more than one occasion.) And it may be significant that almost every New Testament critic who has had a background in classical studies and a familiarity with archaeological work takes a very high view of Acts.

Connected with this failure to examine the archaeological evidence is the abiding influence of the ghost of F. C. Baur in Pauline and Lukan research, as both Neill[6] and Johannes Munck[7] have pointed out. Although the literary conjectures of the Tübingen school have ceased (for the most part) to be taken into account, the historical conjectures continue to be assumed as true: conclusions of which demand years of development in order to be true have been transferred to a period of merely three decades.[8] So we find Martin Dibelius penning these words in 1930:

> Both Strauss and Baur made many mistakes. But in their work they made use of principles which even today give guidance in the historical investigation of the New Testament. And through the new conclusions at which they arrive, they provided the scientific study of primitive Christianity with the decisive motives for further development.[9]

One may be moved to wonder whether Dibelius has ever stopped to examine the work done by Lightfoot, Zahn, and Ramsay.[10]

There is no doubt that Ramsay's influence was harmed by the nature of some of his later work and that this has been partially the cause of his neglect. However, it is unscientific for New Testament scholars on this account to ignore the high quality and

---

3   E.g., J. C. O'Neill, *The Theology of Acts in Its Historical Setting* (London: S.P.C.K., 1961). C. K. Barrett, *Luke the Historian in Recent Study* (London: Epworth Press, 1961), pp. 62, 75, suggests a date as late as A.D. 95-115.
4   *Interpretation*, p. 145.
5   *Framework*, p. 100.
6   Pp. 58-60, 222.
7   *Paul and the Salvation of Mankind* (London: SCM Press, 1959), pp. 69-86.
8   Munck, *Paul*, p. 70.
9   "National Contributions to Biblical Science: V. The Contribution of Germany to New Testament Science," *Expository Times*, 41:536.
10   One may also be moved to wonder why, if Baur and his colleagues made use of the correct method, they came up with almost totally wrong answers.

thoroughness of his earlier work. F. F. Bruce makes this comment:

> Although in his later years Ramsay was persuaded to don the mantle of a popular apologist for the trustworthiness of the New Testament records, the judgements which he publicized in this way were judgements which he had previously formed as a scientific archaeologist and student of ancient classical history and literature.[11]

Therefore, the student of the New Testament who ignores what Ramsay had to say does so to his own peril.

A second assured result of Ramsay's work mentioned by Neill is the answer he gave to the question: Who are the Galatians? His conclusion that they were members of the churches established by Paul in the area of Derbe, Lystra, Iconium, and Pisidian Antioch (i.e., South Galatia) has been judged as correct by the majority of British and American scholars, and even by a few of the Germans.[12] J. A. Findlay claimed that "all those who know the geography of Asia Minor well are South Galatians to a man."[13] The case cannot be proved to the satisfaction of all scholars, but the strength of the evidence seems to favor the South Galatian view.

A third contribution of Ramsay comes from his repeated emphasis upon the importance of thorough historical study as foundational to the study of the New Testament. Contrary to the opinion that the attitude and actions of some conservative Christians seem to convey, the Bible did not come down from heaven bound in morocco leather and translated into Jacobean English. The message of the Bible may be an eternal one, but each of its component parts has its roots deeply imbedded in the age in which it was written and must be interpreted in terms of that age. Whatever message it has for us today should be in harmony with its original message to those who first received it as a word from God. On the other hand, contrary to the thinking of some radical critics and their disciples, it is a fact that the writers of the New Testament were not merely concerned with theology, but also with history. They all write from a certain theological point of view, but this is not to say that they are not interested in history or that what they write is historically suspect. This is especially true of the writings of Luke, as Ramsay and others have demonstrated so clearly.

Finally, we must look to the future. Ramsay was the pioneer in a great work. Who will continue what he began?

There has been no one since Ramsay who has done extensive

---

11 *The New Testament Documents*, p. 90.
12 But see Harrison, *NT Introduction*, pp. 255-266, who suggests the possibility that the North Galatian theory deserves a second look.
13 Quoted in Hunter, *Interpreting the NT*, p. 67.

work in Asia Minor and then brought the knowledge gained in this experience to the study of the New Testament. A few men have brought a profound knowledge of classical studies to the study of the book of Acts,[14] but no one who has had a first-hand acquaintance with archaeological research has yet brought this to an extensive study of the early Christian writings.

Many cities of Palestine have been excavated during the past fifty years, and the knowledge gained here and through a close study of the geography of that area of the world has greatly enhanced our understanding of the Bible. Archaeological work in Greece has been quite extensive as well, although there has not been the same diligence in the correlation of the discoveries with the data of the New Testament. However, very little work, by comparison, has been done in Asia Minor. On more than one occasion Ramsay mentions the need for thorough excavation in connection with the cities of South Galatia. This need remains to this day; only Pisidian Antioch has been studied to any great extent. Although Iconium is the site of the modern city of Konya and cannot on this account be excavated to any great degree, Lystra and the newly located site of Derbe lie waiting to be excavated by someone who has the time and the money.[15] In the area of Turkey that was formerly the Roman province of Asia, only Pergamum and Ephesus have been excavated on a large scale. Some work has been done at Smyrna over the years, and Sardis is in the process of being excavated by teams from Cornell and Harvard Universities.[16] Other cities of Asia — more than twenty-five in a hundred kilometer radius of Izmir (Smyrna) — lie exposed to the elements, ready to yield detailed knowledge concerning the life and times of the early church. The results of the work in Asia Minor and Greece that already have been obtained have yet to be closely studied by New Testament scholars and to be applied to the study of the New Testament. If and when this work is done, we may rest assured that our knowledge concerning the environment of the early church and our appreciation for the writings of the New Testament will be greatly increased. This work awaits the dedicated lives of some younger scholars who are willing to give themselves to this task.

Some years before the end of his life, Ramsay wrote a letter to

---

14 Bruce in his two commentaries that have already been mentioned; and Henry J. Cadbury, *The Book of Acts in History* (London: Adam and Charles Black, 1955).
15 During conversation in his office in the summer of 1962, the Director of Antiquities in Konya expressed a strong desire to the author for scholars to come to excavate Lystra and Derbe (and any other cities of interest in that part of Turkey).
16 Work which was set to begin at Colossae during the summer of 1965 was reportedly delayed due to lack of financial assistance.

Mr. William Ridgeway, a wealthy retired manufacturer who was an avid reader and a great admirer of his. In this letter he remarked that if he were free from other obligations, there is nothing he would rather do than to go back and rework the material concerning the book of Acts.[17] Students of the New Testament will forever regret that he was unable to do this. But even with this neglect, Sir William Mitchell Ramsay has left a great legacy to the cause of New Testament scholarship for which we can be profoundly grateful.

---

17 This information was furnished by Wilbur M. Smith, who was Mr. Ridgeway's pastor at the time.

BIBLIOGRAPHY[1]

BOOKS BY RAMSAY

RAMSAY, SIR WILLIAM MITCHELL. *Asianic Elements in Greek Civilization.* (The Gifford Lectures in the University of Edinburgh, 1915-1916.) London: John Murray, 1927. xi, 303 pp.

——. *The Bearing of Recent Discovery on the Trustworthiness of the New Testament.* (The James Sprunt Lectures at Union Seminary, Virginia, for 1913.) London: Hodder and Stroughton, 1915. Repr. Grand Rapids, Mich.: Baker Book House, 1953. xiv, 427 pp.

——. *The Church in the Roman Empire before A.D. 170.* (Mansfield College Lectures, 1892.) 5th ed. London: Hodder and Stoughton, 1897. xxiii, 510 pp.

——. *The Cities and Bishoprics of Phrygia.* Oxford: Clarendon Press, 1895 and 1897. Vol. 1, pt. 1, xxii, 352 pp. Vol. 1, pt. 2, 353-791 pp.

——. *The Cities of St. Paul: Their Influence on His Life and Thought.* London: Hodder and Stoughton, 1907. Repr. Grand Rapids, Mich.: Baker Book House, 1960. xvi, 452 pp.

——. *The Education of Christ: Hill-Side Reveries.* London: Hodder and Stoughton, 1902. ix, 159 pp.

——. *The First Christian Century: Notes on Dr. Moffatt's Introduction to the Literature of the New Testament.* London: Hodder and Stoughton, 1911. viii, 195 pp.

——. *A Historical Commentary on St. Paul's Epistles to the Galatians.* London: Hodder and Stoughton, 1899. Repr. Grand Rapids, Mich.: Baker Book House, 1965. xi, 478 pp.

---

1 For an almost complete bibliography of all of Ramsay's writings up to 1923, see *Anatolian Studies Presented to Sir William Mitchell Ramsay,* edited by W. H. Buckler and W. M. Calder (Manchester: Manchester University Press, 1923).

——. *The Historical Geography of Asia Minor.* (Royal Geographical Society, Supplementary Paper, Vol. IV.) London: John Murray, 1890. Repr. Amsterdam: Adolph M. Hakkert, 1962. 495 pp.

——. *The Imperial Peace: An Ideal in European History.* Oxford: Clarendon Press, 1913. 28 pp.

——. *Impressions of Turkey during Twelve Years' Wanderings.* London: Hodder and Stoughton, 1897. xvi, 296 pp.

——. *The Letters to the Seven Churches of Asia and Their Place in the Plan of the Apocalypse.* London: Hodder and Stoughton, 1904. Repr. Grand Rapids, Mich.: Baker Book House, 1963. xx, 446 pp.

——. *Luke the Physician and Other Studies in the History of Religion.* London: Hodder and Stoughton, 1908. Repr. Grand Rapids, Mich.: Baker Book House, 1956. xiv, 418 pp.

——. *The Making of a University: What We Have to Learn from Educational Ideals in America.* (An Estimate of the Educational Work of Dr. Isaac Conrad Ketler.) London: Hodder and Stoughton, 1915. 46 pp.

——. *Pauline and Other Studies in Early Christian History.* London: Hodder and Stoughton, 1906. xi, 415 pp.

——. *Pictures of the Apostolic Church: Studies in the Book of Acts.* London: Hodder and Stoughton, 1910. Repr. Grand Rapids, Mich.: Baker Book House, 1959. xv 367 pp.

——. *The Revolution in Constantinople and Turkey: A Diary.* London: Hodder and Stoughton, 1909. xv, 323 pp.

——. *St. Paul the Traveller and the Roman Citizen.* London: Hodder and Stoughton, 1897. Repr. Grand Rapids, Mich.: Baker Book House, 1960. xxvii, 402 pp.

——. *St. Paul the Traveller and the Roman Citizen.* 15th ed. London: Hodder and Stoughton, 1925. xl, 402 pp.

——. *The Social Basis of Roman Power in Asia Minor.* Prepared for the press by J. G. C. Anderson. Aberdeen: Aberdeen University Press, 1941. xii, 305 pp.

——. *The Teaching of Paul in Terms of the Present Day.* London: Hodder and Stoughton, 1913. xiii, 457 pp.

——. and Miss Gertrude L. Bell. *The Thousand and One Churches.* London: Hodder and Stoughton, 1909. xiv, 580 pp.

——. *Was Christ Born at Bethlehem? A Study on the Credibility of St. Luke.* London: Hodder and Stoughton, 1898. xii, 280 pp.

ARTICLES BY RAMSAY

RAMSAY, SIR WILLIAM MITCHELL. "Achaia," *HDB*. 1:23.

——. "Adramyttium," *HDB*. 1:43.

——. "Antioch in Pisidia," *HDB*. 1:104.

——. "Asia," *HDB*. 1:171-172

——. "Asiarch," *HDB*. 1:172.

——. "Bithynia," *HDB*. 1:303.

——. "Cappadocia," *HDB*. 1:352.

——. "Caria," *HDB*. 1:354.

——. "The Census of Quirinius," *The Sunday School Times*. 64 (1922) : 764-765, 776-777.

——. "Chios," *HDB*. 1:383.

——. "Churches (Robbers of)," *HDB*. 1:441.

——. "Cilicia," *HDB*. 1:442.

——. "Cnidus," *HDB*. 1:451.

——. "Colonia Caesarea (Pisidian Antioch) in the Augustan Age," *Journal of Roman Studies*. 6 (1916) : 83-134.

——. "Colossae," *HDB*. 1:454.

——. "Corinth," *HDB*. 1:479-483.

——. "Cos," *HDB*. 1:500-501.

——. "The Cross of Christ the Center of History," *The Christian Worker's Magazine*. 14 (Nov. 1913) : 140-143. Repr. in Smith, Wilbur M. *Great Sermons on the Death of Christ*. Natick, Mass.: W. A. Wilde Co., 1965, pp. 235-241.

——. "Cutting Luke's Shipwreck Story to Pieces," *The Sunday School Times*. 28 (1916) : 355.

——. "The Date of the Apocalypse," *The Expository Times*. 16 (1905) : 171-174.

——. "Delos," *HDB*. 1:588.

——. "Derbe," *HDB*. 1:595.

——. "Diana of the Ephesians," *HDB*. 1:605-606.

——. "Ephesian," *HDB*. 1:713-714.

——. "Ephesus," *HDB*. 1:720-725.

——. "Excavating the Synagogue Church at Pisidian Antioch," *The Sunday School Times*. 73 (1931) : 575-576.

——. "Exploration of Asia Minor, as Bearing on the Historical Trustworthiness of the New Testament," *The Victoria Institute's Transactions*. 1907. pp. 201-217.

——. "Galatia," *HDB*. 2:81-89.

——. "Galatia," *The International Standard Bible Encyclopaedia*. Edited by James Orr *et al.* Grand Rapids, Mich.: William B. Eerdmans, 1939, 2:1154-1155. (Originally published in 1915.)

——. "Galatia (Region of)," *HDB*. 2:89-91.

——. "Galatians," *HDB*. 2:91-93.

——. "The Geographical Conditions Determining History and Religion in Asia Minor," *The Geographical Journal*. 20 (July-Dec. 1902) : 257-275.

——. "Halicarnassus," *HDB*. 2:286-287.

——. "Hierapolis," *HDB*. 2:379-380.

——. "A Historical Commentary on the Epistles to the Corinthians," *The Expositor*. Sixth Series, 1 (1900) : 19-31, 91-111, 203-217, 273-289, 380-387; 2 (1900) : 287-302, 368-381, 429-444; 3 (1901) : 93-110, 220-240, 343-360.

——. "A Historical Commentary on the First Epistle to Timothy," *The Expositor*. Seventh Series, 7 (1909) : 481-494; 8 (1909) : 1-21, 167-185, 264-282, 339-357, 399-416; 9 (1910) : 172-187, 319-333, 433-440; Eighth Series, 1 (1911) : 262-273, 356-375.

——. "How the Book of Acts Routed Its Higher Critics," *The Sunday School Times*. 58 (1916) : 291-292.

——. "Iconium," *Encyclopaedia Britannica*. 11th ed., 1910. 14: 271-272.

——. "Iconium," *HDB*. 2:443-445.

——. "Illyricum," *HDB*. 2:450-451.

——. "If You Had Been Traveling with Paul," *The Sunday School Times*. 63 (1921) : 540-541.

——. "The Image of the Beast in the New Testament," *The Sunday School Times*. 65 (1923) : 507.

——. "The Jews and the Graeco-Asiatic Cities," *The Expositor*. Sixth Series, 5 (1902) : 19-33, 92-109.

——. "Laodicea," *HDB*. 3:44-45.

——. "Lasea," *HDB*. 3:46.

——. "Luke's Narrative of the Birth of Christ," *The Expositor*. Eighth Series, 4 (1912) : 385-407, 481-507.

——. "Lycaonia," *Encyclopaedia Britannica*. 11th ed., 1910. 18: 151.

——. "Lycaonia," *HDB*. 3:174-175.

——. "Lycia," *HDB*. 3:176.

——. "Lydia (Place)," *HDB*. 3:177-178.

——. "Lystra," *HDB*. 3:178-180.

——. "Mallus," *HDB*. 3:223-224.

——. "Method of Research in History," *Contemporary Review*. 27 (1912) : 337-347.

——. "Miletus," *HDB*. 3:368-369.

——. "Myndus," *HDB*. 3:463-464.

——. "Myra," *HDB*. 3:464.

——. "A New Theory as to the Date of the Epistle to the Galatians," *The Expository Times*. 12 (1901) : 157-160.

——. "Nicopolis," *HDB*. 3:548-549.
——. "Numbers, Hours, Years, and Dates," *HDB*. 5:473-484.
——. "Pamphylia," *HDB*. 3:658-659.
——. "The Pastoral Epistles and Tacitus," *The Expositor*. Fourth Series, 8 (1893) : 110-119.
——. "Patara," *HDB*. 3:692.
——. "Perga," *HDB*. 3.747-749.
——. "Pergamus, Pergamum," *HDB*. 3:749-752.
——. "Phaselis," *HDB*. 3:829.
——. "Philadelphia," *HDB*. 3:830-832.
——. "Phoenix," *HDB*. 3:862-863.
——. "Phrygia," *HDB*. 3:863-869.
——. "Phrygians," *Encyclopaedia of Religion and Ethics*. Edited by James Hastings. Edinburgh: T. and T. Clark, 1917. 9:900-911.
——. "Pisidia," *HDB*. 3:884-885.
——. "Pisidian Antioch in Paul's Day and Today," *The Sunday School Times*. 67 (1925) : 415.
——. "Pontus," *HDB*. 4:15-18.
——. "Preliminary Report to the Wilson Trustees on Exploration in Phrygia and Lycaonia," *Studies in the History and Art of the Eastern Provinces of the Roman Empire*. Edited by W. M. Ramsay. (Written for the Quatercentenary of the University of Aberdeen by Seven of Its Graduates.) Aberdeen: Aberdeen University Press, 1906, pp. 231-277.
——. "Religion of Greece and Asia Minor," *HDB*. 5:109-156.
——. "Rhegium," *HDB*. 4:267-268.
——. "Rhodes," *HDB*. 4:268-269.
——. Roads and Travel in the New Testament," *HDB*. 5:375-402.
——. "Rome's Treatment of State Offenders," *The Sunday School Times*. 63 (1921) : 597-598.
——. "St. Paul at Ephesus," *The Expositor*. Fourth Series, 2 (1890) : 1-22.
——. "St. Paul's First Journey to Asia Minor," *The Expositor*. Fourth Series, 5 (1892) : 29-39.
——. "Samothrace," *HDB*. 4:377.
——. "Sardis," *HDB*. 4:404-405.
——. "A Sketch of the Geographical History of Asia Minor," *The National Geographic Magazine*. 42 (Nov. 1922) : 553-570.
——. "Sketches in the Religious Antiquities of Asia Minor," *The Annual of the British School at Athens*. 18 (1911-1912) : 37-79.
——. "Smyrna," *Encyclopaedia Britannica*. 11th ed., 1910. 25:281-282.

——. "Smyrna," *HDB*. 4:553-556.
——. "Studies in the Roman Province Galatia," *Journal of Roman Studies*. 7 (1917) :229-288, 8 (1918) : 107-145.
——. "A Summer Journey in Asia Minor," *The British Weekly*. July 27, 1905, pp. 377-378.
——. "Tarsus," *Encyclopaedia Britannica*. 11th ed., 1910. 26:433-434.
——. "Tarsus," *HDB*. 4:685.
——. "The Tekmoreian Guest-Friends: An Anti-Christian Society on the Imperial Estates at Pisidian Antioch," *Studies in the History and Art of the Eastern Provinces of the Roman Empire*. Aberdeen: Aberdeen University Press, 1906, pp. 305-377.
——. "Thracia," *HDB*. 4:754.
——. "Thyatira," *HDB*. 4:757-759.
——. "Town Clerk," *HDB*. 4:800-801.
——. "Troas," *HDB*. 4:813-814.
——. "Tyrannus," *HDB*. 4:821-823.
——. "The War of Moslem and Christian for the Possession of Asia Minor," *Studies in the History and Art of the Eastern Provinces of the Roman Empire*. Edited by W. M. Ramsay. Aberdeen: Aberdeen University Press, 1906, pp. 281-301.
——. "What Did Paul's Roman Citizenship Mean?" *The Sunday School Times*. 58 (1916) : 547, 549.
——. "Where Time Has No Value," *The Sunday School Times*. 57 (1915) : 525.
——. "When Quirinius Was Governor of Syria," *The Sunday School Times*. 64 (1922) : 559, 564.
——. "The White Stone and the 'Gladiatorial' Tessera," *The Expository Times*. 16 (1905) : 558-561.
——. "The Words in Acts Denoting Missionary Travel," *The Expositor*. Fifth Series, 1 (1895) : 385-399.